# THE PREDICTIVE MIND

# The Predictive Mind

JAKOB HOHWY

**OXFORD**
UNIVERSITY PRESS

Great Clarendon Street, Oxford, OX2 6DP,
United Kingdom

Oxford University Press is a department of the University of Oxford. It furthers the University's objective of excellence in research, scholarship, and education by publishing worldwide. Oxford is a registered trade mark of Oxford University Press in the UK and in certain other countries



First Edition published in 2013

Impression: 5



Published in the United States of America by Oxford University Press
198 Madison Avenue, New York, NY 10016, United States of America

British Library Cataloguing in Publication Data
Data available

Library of Congress Control Number: 2013953488

ISBN 978–0–19–968273–7 (hbk.)
ISBN 978–0–19–968673–5 (pbk.)

As printed and bound by
CPI Group (UK) Ltd, Croydon, CR0 4YY

# *Contents*

## Part III The Mind

# *Preface*

My work on this book was made possible through invaluable research support from the Australian Research Council and from Monash University.

I am grateful to many researchers from around the world for inspiration, fruitful discussion, and generous comments.

My colleagues at Monash have influenced me, worked with me, and trained me in science; thanks in particular to my co-authors Bryan Paton, Colin Palmer, and Peter Enticott, to Steve Miller and Trung Ngo for including me in many projects and discussions, and to Naotsugu Tsuchiya, Anastasia Gorbunova, Mark Symmons, George van Doorn, Andrew Paplinski, Lennart Gustavsson, and Tamas Jantvik. Thanks also to my colleagues in philosophy, many of whom have repeatedly been roped in to do pilot studies, and to our participants and the patients who have endured many hours of rubber-hand illusion tapping in the lab.

Andreas Roepstorff's group in Aarhus are expert navigators in blue ocean research, and in many ways initiated and enabled my interest in this field. In addition to Andreas, Josh Skewes deserves thanks for many hours of discussion. Chris and Uta Frith, also sometimes at Aarhus, remain great, generous influences; they are the paradigm of the open-minded academic, especially when data are in the offing.

I am fortunate to have friends in philosophy and neuroscience who are prepared to endure lengthy discussions on predictive coding and the brain. Tim Bayne very early on encouraged me to push on with the book, and he read and commented extensively on the manuscript at various stages; I am extremely grateful for his academic generosity. Thomas Metzinger likewise went well beyond the call of duty and offered generous comments on a draft of the book; I also greatly benefited from many discussions with Thomas' group of colleagues and students while visiting Mainz. During a week at University of Tokyo's Centre for Philosophy I enjoyed very valuable discussions on the book with Yukihiro Nobuhara and his colleagues and students. I have benefited greatly from many stimulating and encouraging discussions and comments on my writings and ideas from Andy Clark. Ned Block offered fruitful and needed resistance to parts of the story. Tim Lane and Yeh Su-Ling and colleagues from Taipei generously discussed many aspects of the book with me. I have had fruitful discussions with Floris de Lange, Sid Kouider, and Lars Muckli. Anonymous reviewers from the Press offered a host of insightful comments and criticisms.

I am especially grateful to Karl Friston whose work in so many ways has inspired the book. On numerous occasions, Karl has patiently offered feedback on my work. He read and commented extensively on every chapter of this book, he has endured long-haul flights to participate in interdisciplinary workshops, and has in many ways contributed to my work and furthered my understanding of the hypothesis-testing brain. It is very encouraging to experience the open-mindedness with which Karl approaches my attempts to translate the framework into philosophy, even as much of the mathematical rigour and detail is lost in translation. I of course remain responsible for any shortcomings.

The book is dedicated to my family: Linda Barclay, for encouraging me to write it, for predicting my errors, and for being with me; and Asker and Lewey, for being terrific rubber-hand guinea pigs and neurodevelopmental inspirations.

# Introduction

A new theory is taking hold in neuroscience. The theory is increasingly being used to interpret and drive experimental and theoretical studies, and it is finding its way into many other domains of research on the mind. It is the theory that the brain is a sophisticated hypothesis-testing mechanism, which is constantly involved in minimizing the error of its predictions of the sensory input it receives from the world. This mechanism is meant to explain perception and action and everything mental in between. It is an attractive theory because powerful theoretical arguments support it. It is also attractive because more and more empirical evidence is beginning to point in its favour. It has enormous unifying power and yet it can explain in detail too.

This book explores this theory. It explains how the theory works and how it applies; it sets out why the theory is attractive; and it shows why and how the central ideas behind the theory profoundly change how we should conceive of perception, action, attention, and other central aspects of the mind.

## THE ARGUMENT

I am interested in the mind and its ability to perceive the world. I want to know how we manage to make sense of the manifold of sensory input that hits the senses, what happens when we get it wrong, what shapes our phenomenology, and what this tells us about the nature of the mind. It is these questions I seek to answer by appeal to the idea that the brain minimizes its prediction error.

My overall argument in this book has three strands. The first strand is that this idea explains not just that we perceive but *how* we perceive: the idea applies directly to key aspects of the phenomenology of perception. Moreover, it is *only* this idea that is needed to explain these aspects of perception. The second strand in my argument is that this idea is attractive because it combines a compelling theoretical function with a simple *mechanical* implementation. Moreover, this basic combination is of the utmost *simplicity*, yet has potential to be applied in very nuanced ways. The third strand of the argument is that we can learn something *new* from applying this idea to the matters of the mind: we learn something new about the mechanics of perception, and about how different aspects of perception belong together, and we learn something new about our place in nature as perceiving and acting creatures.

The overall picture I arrive at from considering the theory is that the mind arises in, and is shaped by, prediction. This translates into a number of interesting, specific aspects of mind:

> Perception is more actively engaged in making sense of the world than is commonly thought. And yet it is characterized by curious passivity. Our perceptual relation to the world is robustly guided by the offerings of the sensory input. And yet the relation is indirect and marked by a somewhat disconcerting fragility. The sensory input to the brain does not shape perception directly: sensory input is better and more perplexingly characterized as feedback to the queries issued by the brain.
>
> Our expectations drive what we perceive and how we integrate the perceived aspects of the world, but the world puts limits on what our expectations can get away with. By testing hypotheses we get the world right, but this depends on optimizing a rich tapestry of statistical processes where small deviances seem able to send us into mental disorder. The mind is as much a courtroom as a hypothesis-tester.
>
> Perception, action, and attention are but three different ways of doing the very same thing. All three ways must be balanced carefully with each other in order to get the world right. The unity of conscious perception, the nature of the self, and our knowledge of our private mental world is at heart grounded in our attempts to optimize predictions about our ongoing sensory input.
>
> More fundamentally still, the content of our perceptual states is ultimately grounded not in what we do or think but in who we are. Our experience of the world and our interactions with it, as well as our experience of ourselves and our actions, is both robustly anchored in the world and precariously hidden behind the veil of sensory input. We are but cogs in a causally structured world, eddies in the flow of information.
>
> The theory promises not only to radically reconceptualize who we are and how aspects of our mental lives fit into the world. It unifies these themes under one idea: we minimize the error between the hypotheses generated on the basis of our model of the world and the sensory deliverances coming from the world. A single type of mechanism, reiterated throughout the brain, manages everything. The mechanism uses an assortment of standard statistical tools to minimize error and in doing so gives rise to perception, action, and attention, and explains puzzling aspects of these phenomena. Though the description of the mechanism is statistical it is just a causal neuronal mechanism and the theory therefore sits well with a reductionist, materialist view of the mind.

A theory with this kind of explanatory promise is extremely exciting. This excitement motivates the book. The message is that the theory delivers on the promise, and that it lets us see the mind in new light.

I am confident that many other aspects of this approach to the brain and the mind can and will be explored. This book by no means exhausts the impact of this kind of approach to life and mind. I focus on key issues in perception but largely leave out higher cognitive phenomena such as thought, imagery, language, social cognition, and decision-making. I also mostly leave aside broader issues about the relation of the theory to sociology, biology, evolutionary theory, ecology, and fundamental physics. This still leaves plenty of work to do in this book.

## PLAN

The book has three parts. Part I relies on the work of researchers in neuroscience and computational theory, in particular that of Karl Friston and his large group of collaborators. In a series of chapters the prediction error minimization mechanism is motivated, described, and explained. We start with a very simple Bayesian conception of perception and end with a core mechanism that makes Bayesian inference sensitive to statistical estimation of states of the world as well as their precisions, while making room for context-sensitivity and model complexity. The overall view is attractive in part because it appeals to just this one mechanism—this is thus a very ambitious unificatory project.

This area of research is mathematically heavy, and this is indeed part of the reason for its increasing influence: the mathematical equations provide formal rigour and the possibility of quantifiable predictions. However, my exposition is done with a minimum of technical, formal detail. I appeal to and explain very general Bayesian and statistical ideas. This neglects mathematical beauty but will make the discussion accessible and more easy to apply to conceptual and empirical puzzles in cognitive science and philosophy.

My main concern is to bring out the key elements of the prediction error minimization mechanism, in particular, the way prediction error arises and is minimized, how expectations for the precision on prediction error are processed, how complexity and context-dependence factor in, and how action is an integral part of the mechanism. Furthermore, I set out how this mechanism is re-iterated hierarchically throughout the brain. These are the elements needed to explain everything else and they can be fairly conveyed without too much formal detail. I do provide a brief primer of Bayes' rule at the end of Chapter 1, and describe some rudimentary formal detail in the notes to Chapter 2. I also at times provide some very minimal formal expressions, which mainly serve as reminders for how the more complex points relate to simpler Bayesian expressions; these more formal elements are not essential to the flow of the overall argument but they do serve as an indication of the vast mathematical backdrop to this theory.

The prediction error minimization framework can also be generalized to a basic notion of *free energy minimization.* I do obliquely appeal to this notion when I go beyond the simple, epistemically focused version of the problem of perception in terms of prediction error minimization, but I do not in general use this broader notion of free energy in my discussion, nor have I delved much into the wider consequences of it. This is because the aspects of mind I concentrate on make best sense by first and foremost appealing to the more directly epistemic notion of Bayesian hypothesis testing. Fundamentally however there is no difference between these formal frameworks.

Part II looks at the consequences of the basic prediction error minimization mechanism for some long-standing debates in cognitive science having to do with our perception of states of affairs in the world: the binding problem, and the debate about how much our prior beliefs shape perception. The hypothesis-testing brain theory is able to chart interesting routes through these debates. This part of the book then sets out a multifaceted view of reality testing and fine-tuning of prediction error minimization, which is in turn related to mental disorder.

I will be dealing with these issues at a level of detail that is fine-grained enough to establish the framework as fruitful for understanding them, though I do not give full accounts of every aspect of the vast literature on the binding problem, cognitive impenetrability, mental illness, and so on. I illustrate many of these discussions with examples of empirical research from psychology and cognitive neuroscience, including some that I have been directly involved in myself.

This Part of the book demonstrates that even though there is just one, basic mechanism in this account of the mind, the explanatory reach is both very impressive and illuminating. The final chapter in Part II continues this project in a set of more squarely philosophical debates about misrepresentation, rule-following, representation, and understanding.

In Part III, I explore what the prediction error minimization mechanism can tell us about some intriguing aspects of our mental lives that have fuelled deep and recalcitrant debates in philosophy and cognitive science. Again, given the extreme explanatory ambition of this theory—it is supposed to give the fundamental principle for the brain—we should expect it to apply to all aspects of the mind.

First I apply it to attention and its ill-understood relation to conscious perception. Then I appeal to the theory in an account of the unity of conscious perception, which is an intriguing and puzzling aspect of our perceptual lives. In the penultimate chapter I explore how the theoretical framework can give a sense of our overall place, as perceiving and acting creatures, set over against the world. Finally I loosen the reins more and speculate about how the framework might be extended to emotion, introspection, the privacy of consciousness, and self.

The simple notion of prediction error minimization at the heart of the theory is capable of both addressing these kinds of deep issues with interesting results, and, importantly, seems able to unify these very diverse aspects of our mental lives under one principle.

Overall, this edges us closer to a unified, naturalistic account which affords a new and surprising understanding of many puzzling aspects of the mind. Conceiving of the brain as a hypothesis tester enables us to re-asses, re-calibrate, and reconceive a whole host of problems and intuitive ideas about how the mind works and how we know the world.

## BACKGROUND

Although the formal machinery surrounding the prediction error minimization account has been developed only recently, the core ideas are not new. It was anticipated a millennium ago by Ibn al Haytham (Alhazen) (ca. 1030; 1989), who developed the view that "many visible properties are perceived by judgement and inference" (II.3.16). There is certainly also a distinct Kantian element to the idea that perception arises as the brain uses its prior conceptions of the world (the forms of intuition of space and time, and the categories etc.) to organize the chaotic sensory manifold confronting the sensory system (Kant 1781). The relation between our thinking (or inference) and the manifold content delivered from the senses is captured in the Kantian slogan that thoughts without content are empty, intuitions without concepts are blind: "The understanding can intuit nothing, the senses can think nothing. Only through their unison can knowledge arise" (A51/B75).

But it was Hermann von Helmholtz who first seized on the idea of the brain as a hypothesis tester, in a direct reaction to Kant. He was worried about how it is, on a Kantian way of thinking, "that we escape from the world of the sensations of our own nervous system into the world of real things" (Helmholtz 1855; 1903; for the relation to Kant, see Lenoir 2006). His answer was, basically, that we are guided by the answers nature delivers when we query it, using unconscious perceptual inference based on our prior learning (Helmholtz 1867). It is this kind of inference that anchors perception in the world.

This brilliant and very simple idea remains the core of the modern, formal and empirical explorations of the hypothesis-testing brain. Helmholtzian ideas were taken up and developed in various tempi throughout the 20th Century. Jerome Bruner's 'New Look' psychology considered the influence of prior beliefs on perception (Bruner, Goodnow et al. 1956), which was in turn challenged by Jerry Fodor and Zenon Pylyshyn, though they both accept the basically Helmholtzian notion of (low-level) unconscious inference (Fodor 1983; Pylyshyn 1999). Ulrich Neisser (1967) developed the notion of analysis by synthesis, which has a distinctive Kantian feel; Irvin Rock (1983) developed such ideas further, and Richard Gregory (1980) explicitly modelled his account of perception on Helmholtz's appeal to hypothesis testing (see Hatfield 2002 for overview and discussion). The formal apparatus for harnessing these ideas was presaged by Horace Barlow (Barlow 1958; Barlow 1990) and developed by many working in computational neuroscience and machine learning, in particular Rao, Ballard, Mumford, Dayan, Hinton, and others, while Bayesian approaches to perception were explored and developed by Kersten, Yuille, Clark, Egner, Mamassian, and many others (useful introductions and texts include (Knill 1996; Dayan and Abbott 2001; Rao, Olshausen et al. 2002; Doya 2007; Bar 2011)). There are also recent expositions and discussions of the framework in work by for example (Bubic, Von Cramon et al. 2010; Huang and Rao 2011; den Ouden, Kok et al. 2012). Chris Frith's terrific *Making Up the Mind* (2007) discusses many aspects of the hypothesis-testing brain and provides very many examples of relevant empirical studies.

A related historical undercurrent to the prediction error minimization story concerns developments in our understanding of causation and inductive inference. David Hume is a pivotal character in this regard, as he defined "a cause to be an object followed by another, and where all the objects, similar to the first, are followed by objects similar to the second. Or in other words where, if the first object had not been, the second never had existed" (Hume 1739–40: 146). To Hume, causation is thus both about extracting statistical data and about imagining what happens when the world is intervened upon in a controlled manner. This dual definition was emphasized by Lewis in his counterfactual treatment of causation (Lewis 1973) and developed in a full-fledged analysis of causation in terms of invariance under intervention by Woodward (2003), in tandem with Pearl's seminal works on both aspects of Hume's basic idea (Pearl 1988, 2000). The notion of extracting statistical regularities and the notion of modelling intervention both loom large in the notion of unconscious perceptual inference.

Perhaps it is the confluence of modern developments of both the causal story and the hypothesis-testing story that has made it possible to develop and now apply the notion of prediction error minimization to such a degree that we can see it transform our conception of the mind.

Though there has been discussion of aspects of this kind of theory in philosophy of mind and cognition throughout the last 60–70 years, very little philosophical work has been done on the newest incarnations of the theory. Working partly on the basis of Dretske's influential approach (Dretske 1983), the pioneers in terms of connecting the statistical idea of representation with traditional philosophical debates have been Chris Eliasmith and Marius Usher (Eliasmith 2000; Usher 2001; Eliasmith 2003, 2005). Rick Grush has contributed in a similar vein and developed compelling theories, for example, of temporal consciousness on this basis (Grush 2004, 2006). Andy Clark is currently developing the framework in extremely interesting ways, showcasing its wide ramifications and in crucial ways taking the framework in different directions than what I argue for in this book (Clark 2012a, 2013). Within epistemology, there is an interesting, related line of research focused on Hans Reichenbach's (1938) example of inferring the existence of the external world from inside a cubical universe, discussed recently by Eliott Sober (2011) in Bayesian and causal terms that anticipates key elements of the framework.

The prediction error minimization theory is in many respects difficult to classify: it is both mainstream and utterly controversial. On the one hand, with al-Haytham and Helmholtz and others it sits at the very historical core of psychology and neuroscience, and with Gregory, Rock, Neisser, and many others this kind of approach has major contemporary support. On the other hand, it has such extreme explanatory ambitions that there are relatively few who would support it beyond accepting that our expectations and prior knowledge do shape or guide perception. Many would agree with the general idea that predictions play a role in perception but few would agree that prediction error minimization is all the brain ever does and that action and attention is nothing but such minimization. Fewer still would agree that this is all an expression of the way organisms like humans self-organize, and, further, that this is something that essentially is founded in variational free energy with a direct link to statistical physics!

Within neuroscience research it is rare to see any fundamental concession to the notion; instead textbook accounts explain perception largely in terms of feature detection in the bottom-up sensory signal, without any strong role for the overwhelming amount of backwards connections in the brain, which are thought to mediate predictions on the prediction error scheme. In contrast, textbooks in computational neuroscience and machine learning routinely include chapters on representational learning that in detail go far beyond the aspects of the theory I discuss here. Judging by the increasing number of published studies that are inspired by the idea, or that discuss their results in the light of the idea I think it will not be many years before some version of the theory will dominate in neuroscience, but this prophecy is of course hostage to empirical fortune.

Within cognitive science and machine learning, versions of the prediction error minimization scheme are, as mentioned, widely acknowledged. Parts of the scheme have roots in connectionism, in particular in the construction of neural networks with back-propagation algorithms, which are error correcting ways of classifying incoming data (Rumelhart, Hinton et al. 1986). However, it differs in central respects from back-propagation in not being supervised (so it does not need labelled training data). Prediction error minimization uses models that generate data in a top-down fashion rather than classify the bottom-up data, in addition use of generative models works much better in a deep hierarchical setting (Hinton 2007). These aspects clearly mark out the scheme as different from earlier connectionist ideas, and they are behind many of the discussions I focus on throughout the book.

The prediction error scheme seems reasonably well-positioned between two opposed trends in cognitive science. On the one hand there is a top-down approach, which begins with conceptual and functional analysis of cognitive processes and then seeks to reverse-engineer a model of the brain. On the other hand there is a bottom-up approach, which builds biologically inspired neural networks and seeks to learn about which cognitive functions such networks implement (Griffiths, Chater et al. 2010; McClelland, Botvinick et al. 2010). As a philosopher, I am naturally inclined to begin with conceptual analysis and indeed the book begins in this vein. However, one of the great attractions of the scheme is that it lends itself to a very mechanistic approach. Though more evidence is needed it sits well with overall anatomical and physiological facts about the brain and how it works. In particular, it is inspired by the overall flow of relatively distinct forwards signalling in the brain, which is met with massive and more diffuse backwards signals; it sits well with the brain's functional segregation and connectivity; and the different functional elements suits the different kinds of plasticity of the brain very well. This appeals to the scientist in me. The combination presents an attractive package.

My own journey towards the hypothesis testing brain began when Ian Gold and I worked on theories of delusion formation (Gold and Hohwy 2000), and took off when Andreas Roepstorff and I began collaborating in Aarhus around 2001. Together with a motley interdisciplinary group we began deciphering the framework, appreciating its explanatory potential, and began thinking about how it would apply across a number of different topics. Inspired by work by Chris Frith I first explored it through issues in neuropsychiatry (Hohwy 2004; Hohwy and Frith 2004; Hohwy and Rosenberg 2005), before looking at broader issues such as self (Hohwy 2007b) and the general consequences for our conception of cognitive and perceptual function (see the special issue of *Synthese* (Hohwy 2007a) with key contributions from Eliasmith (2007) and Friston and Stephan (2007)). Since then I have looked at core functions of visual perception, introspection, and emotion, as well as attention (Hohwy, Roepstorff et al. 2008; Hohwy 2011; Hohwy 2012). In all these cases I have relied on work by Friston, Frith, and others, and developed the consequences for specific issues. The time has clearly come to not only unify many of these themes but also to stand back and get a more overall sense of what the framework says about the mind.

## ABOUT THIS BOOK

The book is intended for philosophers, neuroscientists, psychologists, psychiatrists, and cognitive and computer scientists and anyone interested in the nature of the mind. Readers who are not familiar with the framework can gain an appreciation of it through my simplified rendering of the basic mechanism at its heart, and by seeing how it applies to a range of different problem cases. Readers who are already familiar with the framework will be in interested in how it can connect to a wide range of topics in psychology and cognitive science at large as well as with philosophical problems.

I have sought to explain philosophical debates without too much philosophical jargon. Topics from empirical philosophy and neurophilosophy permeate the book, but I have collected much of the more directly philosophical debate in Chapter 8. Sometimes I provide argument in some detail and sometimes more in the shape of promissory notes, or invitations, for further work. The strength of the book, I hope, lies just as much in the particular suggestions as in the combined package of suggestions. I have also made an effort to describe neuroscientific and psychophysics studies in straightforward and accessible terms. Although I do not provide new empirical evidence for the theory here, I believe my treatment does support the theory by providing a broad-ranging, unifying explanation, which resolves and illuminates some recalcitrant problems and debates in philosophy of mind and cognitive science.

At the end of each chapter I have placed Notes. These provide references and suggestions for further reading as well as textual sources and brief reviews of relevant, additional empirical evidence. Some notes contain brief discussions that are not crucial to the main argument of the chapters in question though they do concern important further aspects of the broader topics discussed. I have included them as notes to indicate how they may relate to the main theme of the book. Finally, some notes provide basic descriptions of some of the formal and mathematical machinery on which the conceptual framework rests.

# Part I

# The Mechanism

# 1

# Perception as causal inference

Our senses are bombarded with input from things in the world. On the basis of that input, we perceive what is out there. The problem that will concern us is how the brain accomplishes this feat of perception.

This chapter pursues the idea that the brain must use inference to perceive—the brain is an inference mechanism. The first aim is to show why we should agree with this and what the key ingredients of such perceptual inference are. The second aim is to show how inference could underpin the phenomenology of perception.

A very basic and useful formulation of the problem of perception is in terms of cause and effect. States of affairs in the world have effects on the brain—objects and processes in the world are the causes of the sensory input. The problem of perception is the problem of using the effects—that is, the sensory data that is all the brain has access to—to figure out the causes. It is then a problem of causal inference for the brain, analogous in many respects to our everyday reasoning about cause and effect, and to scientific methods of causal inference.

The problem of perception is a *problem* because it is not easy to reason from only the known effects back to their hidden causes. This is because the same cause can give rise to very different effects on our sensory organs. Consider the very different inputs we get from seeing rather than merely touching a bicycle, or seeing it from different perspectives, or seeing it in full view as opposed to being partly obscured behind a bush. Likewise, different causes can give rise to very similar effects on our sense organs. Consider the potentially identical sensory input from different objects such as a bicycle or a mere picture of a bicycle, or a whole bicycle occluded by a bush as opposed to detached bicycle parts strewn around a bush, or more outré possibilities such as it being an unusually well-coordinated swarm of bees causing the sensory impression as of a bicycle.

In our complex world, there is not a one-one relation between causes and effects, different causes can cause the same kind of effect, and the same cause can cause different kinds of effect. This makes it difficult for the brain to pick the one effect (sensory input) that goes with the one cause (object in the world). If the only constraint on the brain's causal inference is the immediate sensory input, then, from the point of view of the brain, any causal inference is as good as any other. When the input is different, as in the seen and felt bicycle case, the brain would not know whether to infer that the cause of the inputs is the same, or if there are distinct causes, and whether one type of cause is more likely than another.

## CONSTRAINTS ON PERCEPTUAL INFERENCE

The key issue is then that without any *additional constraints* the brain will not be able to perform reliable causal inference about its sensory input. We can in fact engage in such inference, since we can perceive. So there must be such additional constraints, but what could they be?

One possibility is that the additional constraints are *mere biases*. Even though the brain cannot reliably infer that it is one rather than another cause, it simply happens to be biased in favour of one. It just so happens that it decides in favour of, say, the bicycle being the cause when it gets a certain kind of input. No doubt there is a describable, law-like regularity in nature such that, in certain to-be-specified conditions, if a system like the brain were to have a certain kind of sensory input caused by a bicycle, then it would be biased towards perceiving it as a bicycle. In principle, various branches of science would be able to discover these biases by systematically exposing systems like the brain to bicycle inputs and tracking the causal chain of events throughout the brain. The brain would seem to cut through the problem of perception by just opportunistically favouring one among the intractably many possible relations between cause and effect.

But even if at some level of description there are these regularities it would not solve the problem of perception as we have conceived it. Such regularities do not afford an understanding of perception as causal *inference*. Inference is a normative notion and brute biases cannot lead us to understand how there could be a difference in quality between an inference back to bicycles rather than, say, swarming bees being the cause of sensory input. What brute regularities in nature give us is a story about what the system *would* do, not what it *should* do in order to get the world right. What is needed, then, is a normative understanding of the role of such regularities. We need to see the additional constraints on causal inference in normative terms.

There is a clear first candidate for an additional constraint with normative impact. It seems obvious that causal inference about things like bicycles draws on a vast repertoire of *prior belief*. This could be what allows us to rank lowly some candidate causes such as it being a swarm of bees that is causing the current sensory impression. Our prior experience tells us that bees are actually extremely unlikely to form such patterns of sensory input in us. There is in fact little doubt that perceptual causal inference needs to be buttressed with prior knowledge, but doing so is no trivial matter. On the one hand, if the story we tell is that we just find ourselves with a stock of prior beliefs, then we have not after all moved beyond the mere biases type of story. On the other hand, if prior knowledge is itself a product of prior perceptual, causal inference, then we are presupposing what we set out to explain, namely perceptual causal inference—the bump in the carpet has merely shifted.

We can now see what a solution to the problem of perception must do. It must have a bootstrapping effect such that perceptual inference and prior belief is explained, and explained as being normative, in one fell swoop, without helping ourselves to the answer by going beyond the perspective of the skull-bound brain (Eliasmith 2000; Eliasmith 2005). The contours of just such a solution are now beginning to emerge. It is based in probability theory—Bayesian epistemology—which is normative because it tells us something about what we should infer, given our evidence.

## PERCEPTION AND BAYES' RULE

Consider this very simple scenario. You are in a house with no windows and no books or internet. You hear a tapping sound and need to figure out what is causing it (Figure 1).

This illustrates the basic perceptual task. You are like the brain, the house is the skull, and the sound is auditory sensory input. As you are wondering about

**Figure 1.** The basic perceptual inference problem: figuring out what caused a sound. This is analogous to the situation for the brain.

the cause of the input, you begin to list the possible causes of the input. It could be a woodpecker pecking at the wall, a branch tapping at the wall in the wind, a burglar tampering with a lock, heavy roadworks further down the street, a neighbour's loud music, or those kids throwing stones; or it could be something internal such as loose water pipes banging against each other. Let your imagination rip: it could be that your house has been launched into space over night and the sound is produced by a shower of meteorites. There is no end to the possible causes. Call each of these possibilities a *hypothesis*. The problem of perception is how the right hypothesis about the world is shaped and selected.

Set aside the problem that once we begin generating hypotheses, there is no clear principle for when we should stop. Consider instead the fact that we *can* generate hypotheses, and that not just any hypothesis will seem relevant. For example, we would not accept that the tapping noise on your house could be produced by a distant mathematician's musings on Goldbach's conjecture, or by yesterday's weather. This means we are able to appreciate the link between a hypothesis and the effects in question. We can say "if it is really a woodpecker, then it would indeed cause this kind of sound". We can say something about how likely it is that the hypothesis fits the effects. This is *likelihood*: the probability that the causes described in the hypothesis would cause those effects. It is clear that assessing such likelihoods is based on assumptions of causal regularities in the world (for example, the typical effects of woodpeckers). Based on our knowledge of causal regularities in the world we can often rank hypotheses according to their likelihood, according to how close their tie is to the effects we are seeking to explain. Such a ranking can be said to capture how good the hypothesis is at accounting for, or *predicting*, the effects. For example, the woodpecker hypothesis may have roughly the same likelihood as the banging pipes hypothesis, and both have higher likelihood than the hypothesis concerning those stone-throwing kids.

We could simplify the problem of perception by constraining ourselves to just considering hypotheses with a high likelihood. There will still be a very large number of hypotheses with a high likelihood simply because, as we discussed before, very many things could in principle cause the effects in question. Just going by the hypothesis with the very highest likelihood does not ensure good causal inference. Here is a hypothesis with very high likelihood: the sound is caused by a tapping machine especially designed by cunning neuroscientists to use you to illustrate perceptual causal inference. This hypothesis fits the auditory evidence extremely well, but it does not seem like a good explanation in very many actual situations. The problem is that the cunning neuroscientist hypothesis seems very improbable when considered in its own right and before you heard the banging sound.

Therefore, we need to take the independent, prior plausibility of hypotheses into consideration, in addition to their likelihood. We need to consider the probability of the hypothesis prior to any consideration of its fit with the evidence. This is then the *prior probability* of the hypothesis. Perhaps there is some objective truth about how probable each hypothesis is, based on the frequency of the events it describes. This kind of knowledge would be useful but mostly it is not something we have. Instead we will assume you assign probabilities to hypotheses based on your own background beliefs and subjective estimates (making sure the probabilities sum to 1, to make the ranking meaningful).

By appealing to your prior beliefs we have given you two tools for figuring out the cause of the sound: likelihood, which is the probability of the effect you observe in the house *given* the particular hypothesis you are considering right now; and the prior probability of the hypothesis (or just the "prior"), which is your subjective estimate of how probable that hypothesis is independently of the effects you are currently observing.

It seems rational to pick the hypothesis which best fits the observed effects but weighted by the independent probability of that hypothesis. Likelihood and prior are the main ingredients in Bayes' rule, which is a theorem of probability theory and thought by many to be a paradigm of rationality. This rule tells us to update the probability of a given hypothesis (such as the woodpecker hypothesis), given some evidence (such as hearing some tapping sound) by considering the product of the likelihood (which was the probability of the evidence given the hypothesis) and the prior probability of the hypothesis (normalized so probabilities sum to 1). The resulting assignment of probability to the hypothesis is known as the *posterior probability*. The best inference is then to the hypothesis with the highest posterior probability. (A brief primer on Bayes' rule is included at the end of this chapter).

Return now to the sound you hear in the house. With likelihoods and priors you can arrive at a good hypothesis: the one that achieves the highest posterior. If you have experienced many woodpeckers in your area and only a few burglars, and if you don't really think your house is likely to have been launched into space over night, and so on and so forth, then you should end up inferring to the woodpecker hypothesis (Figure 2).

Even on this very simplified presentation, Bayesian inference provides a very natural way to think about perception. Of course, the drawback with illustrating the problem as I have done here is that there is no intelligent little person inside the skull consciously performing causal inference. On the story we shall develop, which goes back to Helmholtz, what is really going on is that the neural machinery performs perceptual inference unconsciously. As Helmholtz says about the "psychical activities" leading to perception,

> [they] are in general not conscious, but rather unconscious. In their outcomes they are like inferences insofar as we from the observed effect on our senses arrive at an idea of the cause of this effect. This is so even though we always in fact only have direct access to the events at the nerves, that is, we sense the effects, never the external objects (Helmholtz 1867: 430).

**Figure 2.** Prior probability of hypothesis $h_i$: $P(h_i)$. Likelihood that the evidence e would occur, given $h_i$ is the true hypothesis: $P(e|h_i)$. Posterior probability of the hypothesis $h_i$, given the evidence $e$: $P(h_i|e)$. Simplified version of Bayes' rule that puts it together: $P(h_i|e) = P(e|h_i)P(h_i)$.

So what we will be talking about is *unconscious perceptual inference*. The job before us is to see how what the system does can be usefully conceived as a form of inference. We just need to accept the Helmholtzian idea that the brain is capable of unconsciously going through the same kind of reasoning that we described for figuring out the cause of the sound heard inside the locked house. The brain infers the causes of its sensory input using Bayes' rule—that is the way it perceives. The core idea is fairly clear and has a pleasing air of generality to it: the problem of perception is not inherently special, something for which an entirely new branch of science is needed. It is, instead, nothing more than a version of the kind of causal inference problem that we are often confronted with in both science and everyday life.

While the Bayesian, inferential approach to perception is attractive many questions quickly arise. Straight off, aligning perception with ideally rational, probabilistic, scientific-style reasoning seems rather intellectualist. It is difficult to learn probability theory and to implement Bayesian inference but perception is unconscious and effortless—it is something adults, children, and animals can do without knowing anything about Bayes. Moreover, there is evidence that we are not very good at explicit Bayesian reasoning—Bayes' rule takes some explaining and exercise so does not seem to come naturally to us (Kahneman, Slovic et al. 1982). There is also something slightly odd about saying that the brain "infers", or "believes" things. In what sense does the brain know Bayes, if we don't?

For that matter, a Bayesian approach to perception does not seem to directly concern the full richness of perceptual phenomenology as much as mere conceptual labelling or categorization of causes of input (it could seem to be not so much about visually experiencing a bicycle as merely labelling some sensory input "bicycle"). Nor does this approach, with its focus on assigning subjective probabilities, immediately begin to provide a satisfactory explanation of where prior beliefs come from. As we will see in this and the following chapters, the theoretical framework can be developed to deal with all of these issues.

The contrast to the inferential picture of perception is a picture on which perception, rather than being the upshot of inferential processes in a hypothesis-testing brain, is the result of an analytic, bottom-up driven process where signals are recovered from low-level sensory stimulation and gradually put together in coherent percepts. On this alternative, non-inferential approach, perception is driven bottom-up by the features the brain detects in the input it gets from the world. Crudely, changes in input drive changes in perception, and so top-down inference in any substantial, normative sense is not needed.

There is much discussion about the relative virtues of the feature detection approach vs. the more inferentialist, Bayesian approach (for a review and discussion, see Rescorla (in press). One reason for not adopting the feature-detection approach is that it is not very clear how it can help with the problem of perception as we have set it out above. This theoretical debate cannot be resolved conclusively here but in the next section I will give what I think is a very good example of a perceptual effect demonstrating the need for inference.

## PERCEPTUAL INFERENCE AND BINOCULAR RIVALRY

In 1593 the Italian polymath Giambattista della Porta reported an intriguing visual phenomenon:

> Place a partition between the eyes, to divide one from the other, and place a book before the right eye, and read; if another book is placed before the left eye, not only can it not be read, but the pages cannot even be seen, unless the visual virtue is withdrawn from the right eye and changed to the left (Porta 1593; quoted in Wade 1998: 281).

Some centuries later Charles Wheatstone invented the stereoscope, which uses mirrors to help split the images presented to the eyes, and in 1838 also described this kind of perceptual alternation between different letters shown to each eye (Wade 1998; Wade 2005). This fascinating effect is known as binocular rivalry and remains, 400 years after Porta, a vibrant focus of much research in vision science. The neural mechanism behind it is still unknown and it keeps throwing up new and intriguing findings. As Porta delightfully puts it, what makes "visual virtue" alternate between the eyes?

It is a surprising effect because one would think that if two different images are shown to the eyes they should just somehow blend in with each other. If a picture of a house is shown to one eye and a picture of a face is shown to the other, then one should surely just see a face-house. But this is not what happens, as Porta and Wheatstone and many others have described. The brain somehow seems to *decide* that there are two distinct things out there, a face and a house—and perception duly alternates between seeing one or the other every few seconds, sometimes with periods of patchy rivalry in between.

We shall return to binocular rivalry on a number of occasions later in this book but for now notice that it puts pressure on the idea that perception is purely stimulus driven, bottom-up feature detection. During rivalry, the physical stimulus in the world stays the same and yet perception alternates, so the stimulus itself cannot be what drives perception. It is very difficult not to impute to the perceptual system some manner of inferential power here. It is as if the perceptual system refuses to accept that a reasonable solution to a confusing input could be a face-house mishmash out there in the world.

To put it in the Bayesian vernacular, the prior probability of such a mishmash cause of my perceptual input is exceedingly low. Instead, very "revisionary" hypotheses are selected, each of which effectively suppresses a large part of the incoming sensory signal. It is as if when a face is seen the visual system says "it is most probably a face, never mind all the parts of the total input that the face hypothesis cannot explain"; and *vice versa* when perception then alternates and the house is seen. How exactly this inferential process proceeds is a further matter but it is difficult to see how we could even begin to explain this effect without appealing to some kind of inference.

Recall the worry that the Bayesian, inferential approach to perception seems rather intellectualist. The initial response to this is then that some degree of inference seems to be necessary at least in some circumstances. It is of course possible that the brain only has to resort to this kind of inference in special cases like rival input to the eyes. However, it would be odd if the brain had evolved a highly sophisticated inferential process to deal with a perceptual situation it encounters mainly in highly artificial laboratory settings (though there is debate about how uncommon it is, see Arnold 2011; O'Shea 2011). It seems reasonable to work on the assumption that the brain always uses some sort of inferential process to perceive the world, and that rivalry is an effect that simply makes the brain's everyday inferential processes easier to spot.

Some of the wonderful special aspects of binocular rivalry strengthen the supposition that the brain is engaged in quite sophisticated inferential work. In 1928 Emilio Diaz-Caneja (Diaz-Caneja 1928) discovered that if the two images are cut in half and combined such that one eye sees, for example, half a house and half a face, and the other eye sees the other halves of the house and the face, then there is not rivalry between what is presented to each eye,

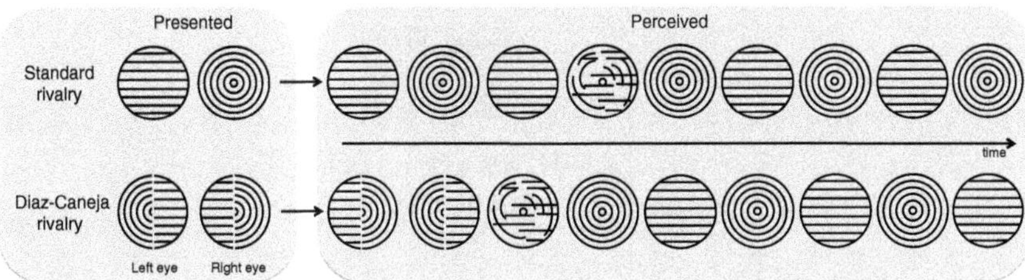


**Figure 3.** Top panel: standard rivalry. Bottom panel: rivalry with Diaz-Caneja stimuli; the different halves of the stimuli are grouped together, so that perception often resembles standard rivalry.

there is instead rivalry between the full, uncut images of the face and the house (Figure 3 illustrates this for the type of stimuli Diaz-Caneja used).

This is a remarkable feat by the brain. It is also a stunning thing to experience for oneself. It shows that even if rivalry is to some extent is the result of very low-level brute competition between processing from each eye this cannot be the whole story since half an image is taken from each eye and grouped in coherent, rivalling percepts.

In the same vein, work in the lab of leading neuroscientist Nikos Logothetis has demonstrated that if the images to the eyes are swapped from eye to eye a couple of times every second, rivalry continues in a relatively normal fashion. So, if you're currently seeing the face, as shown to the right eye, then you will continue to see the face, even if the image of the face in the right eye is swapped to an image of the house (Logothetis, Leopold et al. 1996). The brain very dramatically overrules the actual input in order to make sense of the world.

With Andreas Roepstorff and Karl Friston I have suggested a simple Bayesian story about why only one image is seen at a time in binocular rivalry. The visual system receives an unusual total input in the shape of, for example, a house image to one eye and a face image to the other. There are three relevant, candidate hypotheses to explain what may have caused this sensory input: it is a house only, it is a face only, or it is a face-house blend. The system will pick one of these hypotheses based on (i) their likelihood, that is, how likely it is that a house, face, or face-house blend would have caused this input, and (ii) their prior probability, that is, how likely it is that you should be seeing a house, a face, or a face-house now, irrespective of the actual sensory input. The Bayesian story then goes like this. The combined face-house blend hypothesis has the highest likelihood, because it accounts for more of the sensory input than the face or the house hypotheses on their own. But this high likelihood cannot overcome the exceedingly low probability that a face and a house could co-exist in the same spatiotemporal location (you might on occasion come across a transparent image of a face positioned in front of a house but it is

| | |
|---|---|
| Input: I |  + |
| Hypotheses | F+H: "It's a face-house"<br>H: "It's a house"<br>F: "It's a face" |
| Likelihoods | $P(I/F) = P(I/H) < P(I/F+H)$ |
| Priors | $P(F) > P(H) >> P(F+H)$ |
| Perceptual inference | $P(F/I) > P(H/I) > P(F+H/I)$  |

**Figure 4.** The selection of one of two presented stimuli for perception in binocular rivalry, interpreted in Bayesian terms (adapted from Hohwy, Roepstorff et al. 2008).

very difficult to conceive of fully opaque faces and houses in the very same location in space). So the hypothesis that is selected, and which determines perception, is either the face or the house hypothesis; Figure 4 (Hohwy, Roepstorff et al. 2008).

Some empirical support for this hypothesis is emerging. If the Bayesian story is correct it follows that, if the prior probability for one of the hypotheses goes up, then that enhanced hypothesis should dominate in rivalry. Rachel Denison and colleagues (Denison, Piazza et al. 2011) used lines at different orientations to each eye to induce rivalry and successfully biased prior probabilities in favour of one or the other eye's stimulus by briefly showing rotating lines that would stop at either the horizontal or vertical position just before rivalry would begin. As predicted, participants are more likely to select for their first percept the stimulus with the highest prior probability. Zhou Wen and colleagues (Zhou, Jiang et al. 2010) induced binocular rivalry by presenting participants with images of text markers and roses. They increased the probability of it being the roses by adding olfactory evidence and letting participants smell roses too. As predicted by the Bayesian story, the participants consequently spent more time perceiving the rose image.

As we will see later, more needs to be done on this simple Bayesian account. For one thing, it does not explain why there is continued *alternation* between images in binocular rivalry (Chapter 10 returns to this issue, and somewhat revises the proposal given in Hohwy et al. 2008). As presented so far, the account only explains how it can be that only one image is selected for perception. Nonetheless the basic Bayesian idea at least begins to make sense of some essential features of rivalry.

The jury is still out about how much the Bayesian approach can contribute to the understanding of binocular rivalry and sensory processing in general (for a review, see Blake and Wilson 2011). While I am not suggesting the appeal to rivalry will end this debate once and for all, it strongly suggests that even if none of us consciously know and apply Bayes' rule in perception, the perceptual system in our brains somehow unconsciously follows Bayes' rule. What the brain does for us is indeed inferential. I think binocular rivalry provides a particularly good case in defence of perceptual inference, though Hermann von Helmholtz and many others since have appealed to a number of additional phenomena in their defence of the notion of unconscious perceptual inference.

## HOW DO NEURONS KNOW BAYES?

The proposal is that the brain unbeknownst to consciousness is engaged in sophisticated probabilistic reasoning. This may sound as if neuronal populations in the visual cortex and throughout the brain know and apply Bayes' rule. Putting things like this carries a risk of what we might call neuroanthropomorphism—inappropriately imputing human-like properties to the brain and thereby confusing personal level explanations with subpersonal level explanations. As we saw, there are strong reasons to think perception is unconscious inference, carried out by the brain, so the question is how we should understand this idea without succumbing to crass neuroanthropomorphism.

A huge theoretical issue lies buried here, which we will not resolve fully. But since I will continue to talk in terms of the brain "inferring", "believing", and "deciding" things it may be useful to briefly explain why I do not think this usage is particularly problematic. Hopefully, in the balance of the book, it will then come to seem natural.

An analogy to the problem comes from computer science and research in Artificial Intelligence: the components of a computer chip do not in any ordinary sense "know" the concepts of the program they are executing. Accordingly, there is a theoretical debate about how software really stands to hardware. This kind of debate plays out in philosophy of mind too, where *functionalists* about mental states hold that mental states are defined by a functional role that specifies a certain kind of input-output profile, given a certain internal state. A toy example: you are in the mental state of pain if you have an input of bodily damage and an output of screaming and pulling your hand from the fire, given you're in the internal state of desiring to avoid bodily damage and believing that moving your hand will help. Functionalists then discuss the relation between this functional role and the physical stuff that plays the role, which in us is an extended network in the brain often labelled the pain matrix.

Various terms such as "implementation" or "realization" can be used for the relation between the role and what plays the role, as well as for the relation between computer program and computer chip (I will tend to use "realization" in this book). There is debate about what these notions mean exactly but for our purposes this laxness is not critical. There is also debate about the extent to which functionalism is independent of neurobiological detail. Some functionalists argue that it is the functional role and not its realization that is crucial to understand a phenomenon, others insist the realization is crucial. There is further debate about how computational approaches relate to functional roles, and to neurobiological mechanisms (for a nice discussion that resolves this debate, see Kaplan 2011). Even though there are heavy functional considerations behind the framework that is discussed in this book, there is also a direct motivation from the neurobiological detail of the brain's structure, namely in terms of its hierarchical structure and the nature of message passing within the brain; this strongly suggests a Bayesian brain, implemented with prediction error minimization, as we will see in the next chapter.

Very few people would claim that computers do not engage in computation because the hardware inside them does not *know* the concepts and rules employed in the program. Similarly, we should not claim that brains do not engage in probabilistic inference because the neurons making them up do not know Bayes' rule. What we should claim, rather, is that we can only understand how computers engage in computation if we understand how the hardware is able to realize the functional roles set out in computer programs. Similarly, we can only understand how brains engage in probabilistic inference if we understand how neurons can realize the functional roles set out by forms of Bayes' rule. Getting to fully understand this is not going to be a trivial task but putting it like this somewhat defuses the worry that the Bayesian approach to perception is crudely neuroanthropomorphic: if it was, then so too would be the claim that computers compute.

Of course, this is a fairly brief defence of the application of Bayesian vernacular to the brain. Underlying it is a more substantial view based on the rather uncontroversial idea that the brain is involved in information processing, and that information theory is cast in terms of the probability theory from which Bayes' rule is derived (see the last section of this chapter for a primer on this derivation). It would be odd, therefore, if the brain's processing could not be understood in ways that could at some level of description smoothly involve Bayes' rule. This kind of sentiment is captured well by Chris Eliasmith in an argument that our conception of the mind is ready to move beyond metaphors of symbol manipulation, connectionism, and dynamics: "We are in the position, I think, to understand the mind for what it is: the result of the dynamics of a complex, physical, information processing system, namely the brain" (Eliasmith 2003: 494).

In many ways, this broad line of reasoning is the impetus for this book: there is converging evidence that the brain is a Bayesian mechanism. This evidence comes from our conception of perception, from empirical studies of perception and cognition, from computational theory, from epistemology, and increasingly from neuroanatomy and neuroimaging. The best explanation of the occurrence of this evidence is that the brain *is* a Bayesian mechanism. So, by inference to the best explanation, it is. I find the appeal to inference to the best explanation attractive as a way through this debate—not least because this inference type is itself essentially Bayesian.

## FROM INFERENCE TO PHENOMENOLOGY

So far, this chapter has built up the case in favour of using unconscious probabilistic inference as an approach to perception. Now it is time to consider how such rather austere looking inference can construct the richness of perceptual experience.

I used binocular rivalry to illustrate the need for a notion of inference in perception. Rivalry can also be used to start the discussion about perceptual phenomenology. What happens in rivalry is not that what one sees is an unchanging, confusing mishmash of the two pictures while one's conceptual judgement alternates—it is not that you will *see* a face-house blend and *think* "it's a house . . . no, it is a face . . . wait, no, it is a house . . . ". What makes rivalry so intriguing is that what changes is what you actually see, that is, the inferential process drives perceptual content itself.

My own first experience of rivalry was when doing a kitchen table experiment. I placed a blue and a red toy car (a Porsche and a van) on the table, viewing each through a cardboard toilet paper roll and trying to free-fuse my eyes to make the cars appear in the same location in the visual field. After some trial and error it worked and took my breath away. There are periods of patchy rivalry where I see bits of blue car and bits of red car, as if the three hypotheses of what is out there in the world (mentioned in the previous chapter, see Figure 4) are fighting each other. Then one of the blue patches begins to spread and suddenly I see only the blue Porsche, nothing is left of the red van even though I know full well it is presented to one of my eyes. A few seconds later, a red corner of the van pops up and spreads to suppress any hint of the blue car.

Rivalry is characterized by this very dramatic change in actual visual consciousness. It is as if the brain uses vibrant mental paint to paint over the image from one eye. What you see may cause you to issue a conceptual judgement such as thinking "this is a blue Porsche" but it is the visual perception itself that is changing so dramatically in rivalry. In the words of Helmholtz, rivalry is a "wonderful theatre" ("ein wunderliches Schauspiel") (Helmholtz 1867: 776). It is that perceptual phenomenology that we are trying to explain in terms of probabilistic inference.

Straight off, it can seem that the notion of perceptual inference, in its simple Bayesian clothing, is just a labelling exercise that may allow us to recognize or categorize objects. It is more difficult to cast it as a process that can yield the rich perceptual content of actually seeing a blue Porsche, or all the features of a face. There only seems to be competition between labels for what is seen ("should I categorize this input as 'blue Porsche', 'red van', or 'blue-red Porsche-van'?"). So the task now is this: show that the inferential approach to perception can accommodate differences in perception as such, rather than only differences in conceptual categorization.

This is an important task, and central to the message of this book. It seems the Bayesian moves we just made would do fine if we were only interested in explaining conceptual thought about perception, rather than explaining perception itself. So what makes this an account about perception specifically?

There is an answer to this question. To see this it is necessary to appreciate a *hierarchical* notion of perception. Bayesian perceptual inference applies to all levels of sensory attributes, and perception normally simultaneously takes in a wide range of these levels. These levels of sensory processing are ordered hierarchically and this is a crucial aspect of the account of the hypothesis-testing brain.

Specifically, this hierarchical notion of perceptual inference seems able to capture something central about perceptual experience, which sets it apart from mere categorization or labelling, namely that perception is always from a *first-person perspective*. It is not just that we see a car but that we see it, as a car, from our own perspective. Different levels of our perspectival experience change in concert as the movement of eyes, head, or body changes our perspective on the world. Perceptual content is embedded in the cortical, perceptual hierarchy and there can be dramatic changes in this content as our first-person perspective changes. This teaches us that what we say about how things are, how we end up categorizing them, depends on how things more transiently seem to us during perspectival changes. I now set out the notion of a perceptual hierarchy and attempt to capture these aspects of our perceptual phenomenology.

## A HIERARCHY OF CAUSAL REGULARITIES

The world is rife with regularities. Day follows night, seasons follow one another, most power corrupts, milk goes sour, faulty brakes are often followed by accidents, many marriages are followed by divorce, and so on. These regularities are of a causal nature: faulty brakes cause accidents, the planet's spinning in the solar system cause the succession of day and night, and lots of hidden causes can contribute to divorce. There is also irregularity, or noise. The milk goes sour but there is some variability in exactly when it happens, power corrupts but how much can be difficult to say. Even in the best of circumstances we have to accept a level of irreducible noise. Perception requires us to extract the regularities from the irregularities, the signal from the noise. In science this normally happens by controlling for interfering factors in the lab and intervening judiciously in the causal chain. In normal perception it mostly happens by keeping track of and modelling relevant interfering factors (and with the help of action, attention, and other tricks, as we will discuss in Chapter 4 and 7).

Regularities come at different time scales, ranging from tens of milliseconds to hundreds, to seconds, minutes, and upwards towards regularities or rules that are stable over weeks, months, and years. Fast time-scale regularities include things like how shadows change as you move an object in your hands, slower ones concern the trajectory of a balloon you're trying to catch, slower still concern the way people tend to respond to your requests, and still slower how people tend to vote in years of financial unrest.

Mostly, there is a trade-off between time scale and level of detail. Fast changing regularities are good for detail; slower regularities are more general and abstract. This makes sense when we consider what regularities allow us to predict. If I want to predict something with great perceptual precision then I cannot do it very far into the future, so I need to rely on a fast changing regularity (exit polls are better estimates of voter behaviour than polls a week before the election but allows less time for action). On the other hand, predictions further into the future come at a loss of precision and often detail (on our current form curve I may predict that we will lose next Sunday's game against the Vikings but I will only be able to predict exactly by how much we will lose a few seconds before the final whistle). The relation is intricate because there may well be longer-term regularities about patterns in detailed behaviour. For example, I can predict that every year in September newspapers in Melbourne will be full of words about Australian Rules Football, even if I don't know exactly what those words will be.

Regularities can be ordered hierarchically, from faster to slower. Levels in the hierarchy can be connected such that certain slow regularities, at higher levels, pertain to relevant lower level, faster regularities (for example, slow regularities about aussie rules footy word frequency during the yearly news cycle pertain to faster regularities about the words I end up reading; if I know the slower regularity then I am less surprised by the occurrence of those words). A complete such hierarchy would reveal the causal structure and depth of the world—the way causes interact and nest with each other across spatiotemporal scales.

Causal structure and depth is important to perception in at least three ways. Causal interactions are what make perceptual inference difficult by preventing simple one-one relations between the causes of my sensory input and the sensory input itself, discussed earlier in this chapter. Causal interactions between objects, and between the perceiver and objects, shape our first person perspectival experience (for example, the way a shadow may disappear and reveal the true shape of an object when we hold it out in the sunlight). Finally, causal structure allows us to plan our own causal interactions with the world on the basis of what we perceive.

The brain responds to this importance of causal, hierarchical structure in a very comprehensive manner: it recapitulates the interconnected hierarchy in a model maintained in the cortical hierarchy of the brain. Fast regularities are processed early in the sensory processing stream (for visual perception, this happens in area V1 at the back of the brain) and then increasing time scales are processed as the sensory signal works its way up through the primary sensory areas and into higher areas.

The hierarchy also has a spatial dimension, which sits naturally with the temporal focus we have had so far. The fast time scale regularities represented in low levels of the hierarchy (such as in V1) have small, detail-focused receptive fields of only a couple degrees whereas later areas of processing have wider receptive fields (e.g., 20–50 degrees in the temporal cortex). Receptive fields are also characterized by interconnections, such that wide receptive fields take in sets of smaller receptive fields processed lower down in the hierarchy.

Perceptual inference happens in this highly interconnected, cortical hierarchy and can as such avail itself directly of its representation of myriad causal relations in its attempt to get the world right, in its construction of a first-person perspective, and in its ability to orient itself for action in the world (Friston 2008; Kiebel, Daunizeau et al. 2008). I will first explore some of the properties of this *perceptual hierarchy* and then, in the next chapter, explain how it is thought to arise in the brain, and how it is shaped.

## PERCEPTUAL VARIANCE AND INVARIANCE

Fast regularities occur in perceptual inference in the shape of the *variant* aspect of experience: perception captures our immediate and constantly varying first-person perspective. Every time there is a difference in first-person perspective, for example as your eyes or head move or objects of perception shift around, the brain needs to process fast causal regularities for very basic sensory attributes such as contour, shading, and orientation. Some of these changes are suppressed, such as those arising from quick saccadic movement of the eyes. But many changes are consciously experienced, such as those caused by moving your head to scan a scene in front of you.

At the same time, slow regularities occur in perception in the shape of the *invariant* aspect of experience: perception depends on our ability to abstract from our immediate fluctuating first-person perspective and focus on states of the world that are less sensitive to the concrete way the world is being sampled by the senses right now. For example, even though there are dramatic differences in fast regularities as you perceive a child playing a basketball match, you perceive an enduring object throughout the game rather than just a rapidly changing series of jumbled, perspectival scenes. As Edmond Rolls, who is the architect of an impressive computational model of invariant object recognition, puts it concerning visual perception:

> One of the major problems that is solved by the visual system in the cerebral cortex is the building of a representation of visual information which allows object and face recognition to occur relatively independently of size, contrast, spatial-frequency, position on the retina, angle of view, lighting, etc. These invariant representations of objects, provided by the inferior temporal visual cortex are extremely important for the operation of many other systems in the brain, for if there is an invariant representation, it is possible to learn on a single trial about reward/punishment associations of the object, the place where that object is located, and whether the object has been seen recently, and then to correctly generalize to other views, *etc.* of the same object. (Rolls 2012: 1)

The difference between variant and invariant perception, as defined here, is best conceived as a matter of degree, with somewhat vague endpoints. As perception becomes more and more dependent on slower regularities it becomes more and more invariant. For example, our perception of people as enduring objects is more invariant than our perception of the change of facial features as a person smiles at us.

It is not entirely clear how fast the time scales are at the variant end of the scale, or exactly how fast the regularities are that we can become conscious of even if we do process them (there is some computational evidence that very basic and fast-changing sensory attributes are dealt with in a Bayesian manner, such as features of line orientations and lengths, see Rao and Ballard 1999). Neither is it clear how slow the regularities are at the invariant end of the scale. For the sake of illustration, a maximally slow regularity could be a Big Bang–Big Crunch cycle of the entire universe but it is very unlikely that this regularity, though we can represent it in various ways, plays any role in modulating ongoing perceptual inference. On the other hand, the rather constant regularity that light normally comes from above does influence perceptual inference of convexity and concavity (for experiments on this, see Adams, Graf et al. 2004; Morgenstern, Murray et al. 2011). Similarly, the slow regularity that captures how our bodies grow and change as we age is factored into our perception of other people over time, and may modulate our levels of surprise when we see them after a long absence. For example, I am surprised at people who don't seem to age.

It is thus possible to think of degrees of invariance in perception in terms of the spatiotemporal hierarchy of represented causal regularities. This yields a nice conception of your first-person perspective, namely as your actual perceptual inferences ordered and connected according to invariance. Your first-person perspective and mine will differ in as much as we engage in different short time-scale, variant inferences, and they will overlap in as much as we engage in similar inferences over more extended time scales.

This helps explain a key feature of perceptual experience—that it always has a first-person perspective—and thus helps us see how the notion of Bayesian perceptual inference pertains to perception rather than mere object categorization. If Bayesian perceptual inference happens in a recapitulation of the causal hierarchy, spanning a wide spatiotemporal range, then it can encompass both the invariant perception that matters for recognition and planning, and the variance characteristic of the more transient first-person perspective.

The causal hierarchy is thus crucial for a plausible account of perceptual inference. It provides the first step in combining variant (first-person perspectival) and invariant perception within one type of process. This aspect in turn relates to more epistemic issues concerning our ability to know the states of affairs of the world and how we ourselves are placed in it. Sometimes we get to doubt that our perceptual inference is correct because we learn that it depends too much on our variant perspective. That may lead us to reality test, and explore some state of affairs better, more deeply, from different perspectives. The aim of reality testing in such cases is to arrive at more confident perceptual inferences, which are anchored more solidly in invariant perception. Similarly, our perceptual knowledge of states of affairs in the world depends on our personal trajectory through the world and this is something variant perception gives us information about. The flow of variant information allows us to track how we are positioned over against objects in the world. The perceptual hierarchy thus plays a role for how we conceive of our own epistemic role. These epistemic matters belong with the deeper facets of perceptual phenomenology and they seem also to relate to the perceptual hierarchy. I will pursue some of these issues in more detail in Chapter 7.

## MESSAGE PASSING BETWEEN HIERARCHICAL LEVELS

The basic idea for the hierarchy of perceptual inference is that for every level of the hierarchy we probe deeper into the causal structure of the world. But structure is not just a matter of piling levels of ever increasing time scales on top of each other. A key element of causal structure has to do with the *interactions* between regularities at different time scales. This interaction works in a bottom-up fashion such that, for example, the fast changing regularities governing contour, orientation, and so on help you become more confident that what you are looking at is really a nose belonging to an enduring face. It also works in a top-down fashion such that the longer-term regularities governing faces (e.g., they tend to be attached to headed bodies) assist in recovering fast scale changes in the input from the face (for example, the shadow cast by the nose as the body moves). For there to be such interactions, there must be extensive passing of messages up and down the different levels of the hierarchy. Understanding these messages is crucial to understanding how perceptual inference works (Lee and Mumford 2003).

Using a development of the Bayesian story, Friston and his colleagues (Friston and Kiebel 2009) provide a computational model that exemplifies message passing across levels. A bird listening to another bird's song is extracting the fast time scale modulations of the song and can use that over time to extract slower time scale regularities about the size and strength of the other bird; perhaps stronger birds sing more distinctly and more forcefully for longer. But conversely, if an assumption is made about the size and strength of the singing bird, then that will help extract nuances in the fast time scale dynamics of the song, which could otherwise be lost in noise. Low-level, fast scale regularities help choosing among hypotheses higher up and higher-level hypotheses about slower regularities work as control parameters on low-level regularities.

Top-down and bottom-up message passing of this type tie the levels of the perceptual hierarchy together. It is not as if the phenomenology of visual or auditory perception itself is just as of a causally shallow sensation that we can then subsequently label with categories for progressively deeper causal structures—this is the kind of picture one would expect if processing at each level was in some sense complete and message passing was only a matter of sending a fully processed product to the next level for categorization. The picture is instead much more interactive with strong top-down modulation of lower level activity. That is, variant perception itself is steeped in causal structure. We find it hard to completely divorce the perception of the changing light and shadows from perception of which object it is, and the message passing throughout the perceptual hierarchy reflects this.

This picture of how the levels of the perceptual hierarchy connect thus depends on extensive message passing between levels. There are top-down expectations given slower time scale regularities and faster time scale processing

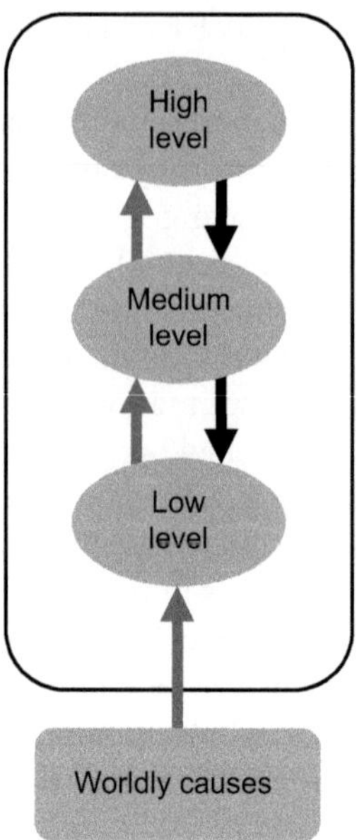


**Figure 5.** The perceptual hierarchy, first version. Processing of causal regularities at different time scales influence each other in a bottom-up–top-down fashion. Sensory input (dark grey arrows pointing up) is met with prior expectations (black arrows pointing down) and perceptual inference is determined in multiple layers of the hierarchy simultaneously, building up a structured representation of the world. This figure simplifies greatly as there are of course not just three well-defined hierarchical levels in the brain. A later version of the figure will nuance the description of message passing between levels; in particular, the dark grey arrows will be re-labelled as "prediction error".

somehow sends messages in a bottom-up fashion that can guide higher-level processes. Figure 5 provides a schema of this initial idea; in the next chapter, more sophisticated versions will explicate what happens in the meeting between input and expectations, where prior expectations come from, and what happens next.

This busy pattern of concurrent message passing is central to the hypothesis testing mechanism that will emerge in the next chapters, and only then can the force of the perceptual hierarchy really be appreciated.

## ADDITIONAL CONSTRAINTS ON HIERARCHICAL INFERENCE

In the light of the notion of the perceptual hierarchy, we can now revisit the issue concerning the need for additional constraints on perceptual inference.

In order to prioritize between different hypotheses about the causes of sensory input, the system needs to appeal to prior belief. But prior belief needs to be better than raw guessing, and our account of it will be circular if the story reduces to prior belief being directly based on the very thing we are trying to understand, namely perceptual inference. The problem was, that is, to account for prior belief without circularity. With the reciprocal message passing in the perceptual hierarchy we can do something to situate prior belief, without yet solving the problem.

Some prior belief is embodied in the expectations passed down from higher levels. To use the birdsong example again, if the bird expects the birdsong to come from a strong singer then inference for the extraction of individual notes at faster time scales lower down in the hierarchy can be guided along by those longer term expectancies. The prior expectations are therefore pulled down from what has previously been learned best at higher levels of the hierarchy (this is called empirical Bayes; for a brief introduction, see Bishop 2007: Ch. 3.5). This can happen in a cascading manner where very high-level expectations help shape many levels below but filtered through intermediate levels. This means the required additional constraint is not extracted directly from the sensory signal, which would lead to the threatening circularity or hopeless attempts at bootstrapping the process.

Helmholtz mentions an interesting case of a prior that can serve as an illustration, in this case of learned long-term term visual expectations of depth and colour in different parts of our visual field. He observes that the clouds in the sky have less depth perspective than objects on the ground, and that the colours of the objects on the ground appear to change depending on whether they are close by or far away. He rather charmingly seems to have tested this by sticking his heads between his legs:

> It appears that, when the head is turned upside down, the clouds get real depth while objects on the ground appear more like a painting on a vertical surface, much like the clouds in the sky [normally look]. In this case, colours also lose their relation to near and far objects and appear to us with their original differences. (Helmholtz 1867: 432)

That is, when the clouds appear in the lower visual field they immediately gain more perceived depth, and when objects normally on the ground appear in the upper visual field they lose depth and also the modulation of colour that is determined by depth cues. Many will have experienced this kind of effect when flying above the clouds and noting the unusual depth and beauty they seem to acquire when viewed from this perspective. The long term expectation for depth in the lower part of the visual field allows extraction of information from objects placed there, and the lack of this expectation for the upper half restricts our ability to extract depth information, even for familiar objects placed there.

This idea of hierarchical, nested inference provides the first step for explaining the needed additional constraints on perceptual inference. It is a version of a standard move in discussions of Bayes when the question arises "where do the priors come from?" (Kersten, Mamassian et al. 2004; Friston 2005). It is not very satisfactory if priors are set entirely subjectively, and if not set entirely subjectively, then it seems we must go beyond the Bayesian framework to provide them. With the hierarchy, and the notion of empirical Bayes, we can just say they are extracted from higher levels.

But obviously, this can only be the first step of the explanation. The second step has to concern how these top-down priors are arrived at and how they are shaped over time. That step of the explanation has to show that the prior knowledge embedded in higher hierarchical levels is not given over to raw guessing. The explanation, as we will see in the next chapter, is that the priors are themselves guided by a particular kind of feedback signal stemming from processing of the incoming sensory signal.

A neat explanatory circle then seems to transpire: top-down priors guide perceptual inference, and perceptual inference shapes the priors. Couched in such simple terms, this circle is clearly not fit for underpinning perceptual inference: messages can be passed around in a completely idle fashion, never leading to perception of the world. The trick is to conceive of the two steps as being performed consecutively (it is not a circle as much as a spiral, as it were), and to give a particular, predictive flavour to the whole story. This is the job of the key prediction error minimization mechanism, which I will discuss in the next chapter and which will explain from where the priors come.

## ON BAYES' RULE

Bayes' rule is a simple result in probability theory and at the same time an extraordinarily powerful idea. It may be helpful to see first how this simple result comes about, and then see why it is co-opted as a paragon of rationality and scientific inquiry. This section then sets up some very minimal formal notation, which is used in later chapters.

Say we are interested in the joint probability of two random variables $D$ and $C$ taking the specific values $d$ and $c$. As an example, say we are interested in how probable it is that the drought will break this year *and* that my computer breaks down this year. We can write this joint probability as

$$P(d, c)$$

One way of transforming this expression is like this:

$$P(d, c) = P(d|c)P(c)$$

This makes intuitive sense because it just says that the probability of both events happening is the same as the probability that one event happens given the other one happens, times the probability that that other event happens. The probability that the drought breaks and my computer breaks can be found if we first find out how probable it is that the drought breaks given that we're in a year where my computer breaks, and then adjust that probability with the probability that my computer breaks in the first place. It is a way of chaining up the probabilities.

The order in which we chain up probabilities in this kind of expression does not matter. That is, we could just as well ask how probable it is that my computer breaks given we are in a year where the drought breaks, and then adjust that conditional probability with how probable it is the drought breaks in the first place. Thus we could say

$$P(d,c) = P(c|d)P(d)$$

But now we can combine the two right sides of these equations, because they are both equal to $P(d, c)$, thus

$$P(d|c)P(c) = P(c|d)P(d).$$

It is simple then to divide with $P(c)$ on both sides

$$P(d|c)P(c)/P(c) = P(c|d)P(d)/P(c),$$

and then cleaning up the left side

$$P(d|c) = P(c|d)P(d)/P(c),$$

which is none other than Bayes' rule itself. For our example, it says that the probability that the drought breaks given the computer breaks is equal to the probability that the computer breaks given the drought breaks, multiplied by the probability that the drought breaks in the first place, and then divided by the probability of the computer breaking in the first place.

This rule could well have lingered as just a result of probability theory but Bayes, Laplace, and others focused on it in attempts to think about how one should update belief in the light of new evidence. The next step is then to understand why this simple result should be seized upon for these purposes. We will distinguish between a *model* and a *hypothesis* in the sense that a model can entertain a number of competing or alternative hypotheses. For example, I could model outcomes in terms of the toss of a coin or the throw of a die. The coin and die correspond to models of observed outcomes. For each model there are a number of hypotheses—for example, the best hypothesis for explaining my observations under a coin model is that the coin came up tails. Throughout this book, we will be dealing largely with hypotheses, $h$, under a model, $m$, that is assumed by the agent in question. For present purposes, we set aside models and focus on hypotheses.

So, for application of Bayes' rule, we want to consider two things, a hypothesis, $h$, and some evidence, $e$. How strongly is the hypothesis supported by the evidence? Intuitively, that depends on two things. First, how tightly the evidence fits with the hypothesis, and second, how probable the hypothesis is in the first place. These two elements mirror the way we think critically about such matters, even if we often get the actual computations wrong when trying to do it.

Say we are confronted with a conspiracy theory about the 9/11 World Trade Centre attacks. The hypothesis of a massive, covert, state-driven conspiracy explains the evidence incredibly well: it is highly likely that we would have observed the bombings and much of the other related evidence, *given* there really was such a conspiracy. That is, the probability of the evidence is high, conditional on the conspiracy hypothesis, $P(e|h)$. This is presumably why some people begin to consider this kind of conspiracy theory.

But then we quickly think of how probable it is that there would be such a conspiracy in the first place, without considering this particular evidence. Of course, this probability, $P(h)$, is absolutely minuscule. So we say that even though the conspiracy hypothesis would certainly explain a lot, including snippets of evidence that competing hypotheses cannot explain, we should not believe it because it is just so very unlikely in the first place. But this is just a way of running through Bayes' rule: we multiply the (high) *likelihood* of the evidence given the hypothesis by the (minuscule) *prior probability*. We are interested in whether we should believe the conspiracy theory, $h$, given the evidence at hand, $e$ (*i.e.*, the attacks and so forth), that is, we ask "$P(h|e)$?", and we answer "$P(e|h)P(h)$".

Bayes' rule thus captures the two key elements we employ when we adjust our belief in a hypothesis given some new evidence. It may be instructive to run through for yourself an example where the likelihood $P(e|h)$ is very low, but where the prior probability is very high, as well as an example where there is both high likelihood and high prior.

The next step is then to compare the resulting *posterior probability*, $P(h|e)$, with the posteriors for other hypotheses, $h'$. Then we can rank hypotheses and end up believing, and acting upon, the one with the highest posterior probability.

It is fortunate that this natural way of reasoning about belief is captured by a result from probability theory because it tells us that doing so is in some way rational (for example, in a betting scenario, relying on probability theory ensures one doesn't irrationally accept certain bets guaranteed to lose one money).

Notice that the denominator ($P(e)$) of Bayes' rule is ignored in this heuristic treatment. This is because it is normally written in a slightly different way, such that its role is to normalize the resulting posterior probability to a value between 0 and 1, as required in probability theory (this is why probabilities are normally reported as for example, 0.1 or 0.8 but never as 7 or 42). This technical detail can be brought out by noticing that $P(e)$ is the *marginal probability*, that is, the sum of the probabilities of $e$ conditional on all hypotheses.

For the purposes of perception, and the main themes of this book, the key idea is that $e$ is the sensory input and $h$ and $h'$ are competing hypotheses, maintained in the brain, about the state of the world. The hypothesis that is selected determines perceptual content, and therefore belief and action are determined by how the brain assesses likelihoods and weighs that by priors; the next chapter looks at the mechanism for achieving this.

## SUMMARY: HIERARCHICAL NEURONAL INFERENTIAL MECHANISMS

This chapter presented the problem of perception in terms of causal inference, and presented a Bayesian approach to this problem. The idea that perception is inferential may seem rather intellectualist but I motivated the need for inference by noting the phenomenon of binocular rivalry, which seems impossible to explain without use of inferential mechanisms. I also briefly indicated why I think it is appropriate to describe the brain as engaged in inference-making.

I then argued that the Bayesian notion of perceptual inference has the resources to capture not just our ability to use perception to recognize and categorize states of affairs in the world but also to capture the phenomenological richness of perceptual experience. The central tool for this is the notion of the perceptual hierarchy.

The reciprocal, top-down–bottom-up message passing in this hierarchy seems able to accommodate the variant and invariant aspects of perception as well as the first-person perspectival nature of our perceptual experience. Finally, the perceptual hierarchy allows us to situate the prior beliefs that perceptual inference must avail itself of in order to guide its selection of the best hypothesis. This hypothesis corresponds to the parameters of a probabilistic model encoding beliefs about hidden states in the world. This model has a hierarchical form such that its parameters are selected to provide an explanation for the world, at multiple levels of description. We noticed also the distinction between selecting the parameters of a model (as in the perceiving brain that selects a hypothesis) and actually selecting a model that could contain different parameters (selecting a brain). The latter may be a long-term process at a developmental or even evolutionary timescale. In this book, we will focus primarily on selecting the parameters of a particular model (brain), where each setting of the parameters represents a distinct hypothesis.

The perceptual hierarchy will play a central role in many of the discussions in the following chapters. It is built up out of replications of the prediction error minimization mechanism we will see in the next chapter, and the message passing is a crucial part of how this mechanism works.

This chapter has prepared the ground for the main message of this book. Once we see that perception is inferential and happens in a causal hierarchy we will be able to see how perception is a matter of prediction error minimization. The task that lies ahead in the next two chapters is then to explore how the neural machinery in the brain can realize probabilistic, causal inference. An important step is to reconceive this kind of inference such that it becomes more obvious that an organ like the brain can be an *inferential mechanism*, and how this speaks to the full richness of perceptual experience.

## NOTES

*Page 14.* ["One possibility is that the additional..."] By referring to these mere regularities I have in mind the kind of law-like statements proposed as a model of non-inferential knowledge by Armstrong and discussed as candidates for a theory of content by Fodor (Armstrong 1973; Fodor 1990).

*Page 14.* ["But even if at some level of..."] The idea that there is a normative aspect to the problem of perception is put most forcefully by (Kripke 1982) in his discussion of linguistic meaning; Chapter 8 will have more discussion of this work.

*Page 15.* ["Consider this very simple scenario..."] The simple scenario of someone trying to make sense of the external world from inside a room by extracting statistical regularities might be called the "Reichenbach Room" after Hans Reichenbach's example of the "cubical universe" in his *Experience and Prediction* (1938). Eliott Sober (2011) discusses this case and anticipates elements of the notion of active inference, discussed in Chapter 4 below.

*Page 18.* ["While the Bayesian, inferential approach..."] So far the account of Bayesian theories of perception is greatly simplified. Researchers have extensively worked out theoretical aspects of Bayesianism as applied to perception and cognition, and tested many of them in the lab (for reviews, see Clark and Yuille 1990; Knill and Richards 1996; Kersten, Mamassian et al. 2004; Chater, Tenenbaum et al. 2006). In addition to Bayesian theories that focus on perception, there are influential, more cognitive applications of Bayes to how we learn concepts, acquire language, and grasp causal relations, and more generally how the brain manages to generalize from sparse samples and apply that knowledge under uncertainty (Tenenbaum and Griffiths 2001; Tenenbaum, Kemp et al. 2011).

*Page 19.* ["Some centuries later..."] Helmholtz argues for the need for inference in perception on similar grounds as I do here. He does not use rivalry as his initial example but instead the ambiguity of movement of light on the retina when we look to the side in the normal way vs. when we forcibly use the fingers to push the eyeball (Helmholtz 1867: 428). Helmholtz discusses rivalry in attentional but also rather inferentialist terms towards the end of this edition of *Physiological Optics*, beginning at page 766. Ibn al Haytham acknowledges the need for perceptual inference because he is aware that there are optical distortions and omissions of the image hitting the eye, which without inference would make perception of similarity and difference, colour, transparency, and written language impossible (Lindberg 1976; Hatfield 2002). Thus al-Haytham (ca. 1030; 1989) says "not everything perceived by the sense of sight is perceived by pure sensation; rather, many visible properties are perceived by judgement and inference [syllogism] in addition to sensing the visible object's form, and not by pure sensation alone" (II.3.16); "the shape and size of a body... and suchlike properties of visible objects are in most cases perceived extremely quickly, and because of this speed one is not aware of having perceived them by inference and judgement" (II.3.26).

*Page 20.* ["It is a surprising effect..."] Rivalry was as lively a topic of discussion around the mid-1800s as it is today. Wheatstone for example chastizes the experimental philosopher Thomas Reid for claiming he experiences something like a fused blend and not rivalry (Wheatstone 1838: §14). Helmholtz comments on the controversies and remarks on the significant individual differences in bistable perception (Helmholtz 1867: 437–8).

*Page 23.* ["As we will see later..."] Helmholtz beautifully anticipates the core Bayesian story about rivalry and bistable perception in general. He notes that sometimes "numerous comparisons and their corresponding interpretations are possible for the sensory impression. In such cases the explanation [of the impression] vacillates such that the observer has different experiences, one after another, for the unchanging retinal image" (Helmholtz 1867: 438; my translation).

*Page 23.* ["The proposal is that the brain..."] A good place to begin on the difference between personal level and subpersonal level explanation is (Davies 2000). There is a useful overview of functionalism in (Braddon-Mitchell and Jackson 2006) and a comprehensive study of the philosophy of science of neuronal mechanisms and levels of explanation (Craver 2007). Different interpretations of "realization" of a functional role by some physical property leads to different metaphysical conclusions (Melnyk 2003; Kim 2008).

*Page 24.* ["Very few people would claim..."] For further discussion of the worry about being too intellectualist and about neuroanthropomorphism, see (Chater, Tenenbaum et al. 2006); for criticism (Colombo and Seriès 2012); for a kindred defense see Rescorla (in press); see also (Phillips 2012) who responds to this kind of challenge in a discussion of Jaynes' early approach to probability.

*Page 25.* ["In many ways, this..."] The relation between inference to the best explanation and Bayes is discussed in the second edition of Peter Lipton's classic book (2004) on the topic.

*Page 26.* ["This is an important task..."] There is a deeper way to engage this kind of issue about the determination of perceptual content, which has to do with whether the perceptual relation determines perceptual content or whether it is a more austere relation to things in the world; see (Schellenberg 2010) whose views seem to me congenial to the view argued for here; see also discussion in Chapter 11.

*Page 28.* ["The brain responds to this importance of causal . . . "] For some evidence of the perceptual hierarchy in the auditory domain, see (Wacongne, Labyt et al. 2011) who showed that a low level absence of sensory input can be surprising and more surprising than a merely different low level input, a pattern which is best explained by reciprocal message passing between low level input and expectations anchored in higher level representations of slower regularities. Evidence is also given by Harrison et al. (Harrison, Bestmann et al. 2011), who finds "that visual and parietal responses are released from the burden of the past, enabling an agile response to fluctuations in events as they unfold. In contrast, frontal regions are more concerned with average trends over longer time scales within which local variations are embedded. Specifically, [there is] evidence for a temporal gradient for representing context within the prefrontal cortex and possibly beyond to include primary sensory and association areas." For the temporal structure of the prefrontal cortex, see also (Fuster 2001).

*Page 28.* ["Perceptual inference happens in this . . . "] In this section I describe aspects of what I call the perceptual hierarchy. In addition to the work by Friston and colleagues that I focus on there are important developments of Hierarchical Bayesian Models (HBM), which speak to many of the issues and examples I have mentioned here (Tenenbaum, Kemp et al. 2011).

*Page 30.* ["It is thus possible to think of . . . "] For the notion of first-person perspective and perceptual content see (Metzinger 2009) as well as the discussion in (Schellenberg 2008; Jagnow 2012).

*Page 30.* ["The causal hierarchy is thus . . . "] Here I propose that our tendency to reality test is anchored in the different levels of the perceptual hierarchy. More abstractly, this seems to relate to our sense that there is a difference between appearance and reality, between how things seem and how they are. Metzinger describes this in terms of the emergence of a degree of opacity in our representational content and suggests in a way congenial to my treatment that hereby "[t]he difference between appearance and reality itself becomes an element of reality, and it can now be acted upon or thought about, attended to, and made the object of closer inspection." (Metzinger 2004: 176).

*Page 33.* ["Helmholtz mentions an interesting . . . "] My translation of Helmholtz, the original quote is "Ja es kommt wohl vor, dass bei umgekehrtem Kopfe die Wolken richtige Perspective bekommen, während die Objecte der Erde als ein Gemälde auf senkrechter Fläche erscheinen, wie sonst die Wolken am Himmel. Damit verlieren auch die Farben ihre Beziehung zu nahen oder fernen Objecten, und treten uns nun rein in ihren eigenthümlichen Unterschieden entgegen."

*Page 34.* ["Bayes' rule is a simple result . . . "] There is a mountain of literature and research on Bayes' rule. It all begins with this simple intuition, that it captures something basic about weighing evidence and adjusting belief (two good places to start are Howson and Urbach 1993; Bovens and Hartmann 2003). There is also much research on how poor we are at conscious Bayesian reasoning (Kahneman, Slovic, et al. 1982; Gigerenzer and Selten 2001).

# 2

# Prediction error minimization

Unconscious Bayesian perceptual inference is an attractive way to begin to deal with the problem of perception. Inference is needed to overcome the brain's encapsulation in the skull, and to account for phenomena such as binocular rivalry. It can withstand some initial worries that it may be too intellectualist, and it can be harnessed in a hierarchical structure of causal inference of regularities at different time scales. If the levels of this hierarchy somehow engage in prolific bottom-up and top-down message passing, then it can begin to capture otherwise elusive aspects of the phenomenology of perceptual experience.

All these elements were discussed in the previous chapter, and they allow us to be more concrete in addressing the problem of perception. In this chapter we will see that the central mechanism for hierarchical perceptual inference is prediction on the basis of internal, generative models, revision of model parameters, and minimization of prediction error.

The problem of perception begins, as we saw, with the observation that there is not a one–one relation between our sensory input and its causes in the environment. The same input can be caused by different things, and different input can be caused by the same things. To illustrate, when you see someone waving their arm, it can be because they want to greet you or because they want to hail a taxi, and so on, and they can greet you in many different ways such as nodding, lifting their eyebrows, waving, and so on. Just going by the sensory input alone, it is impossible to be sure one has hit on the right hypothesis about the causes. This problem was approached with the help of Bayes' rule: if somehow we have a prior ordering of hypotheses, then we can chose the highest ordered hypothesis and weight it with its likelihood, with how well it fits the incoming sensory signal.

The issue now is: how is this process constrained, or supervised? As described so far, it would be very easy to begin with a pathological ordering of prior probabilities of hypotheses and infer the existence of entirely fabricated events in the world. This is the issue broached earlier, that there would have to be some additional constraints on this Bayesian process.

If the constraints come from some authority that already knows the correct answer, then we just move the problem of perception to this authority. For example, if a computer programmer trains a neural network to classify apples and pears, then we would ask how the programmer has formed the right fruit-related perceptual inferences and how she has coded this. Of course, much of what we do and learn throughout life is supervised by wiser people around us but we also manage to extract information directly from the environment without such supervision. Moreover, external supervision is only beneficial if we can form perceptual inferences about the meaning (and thus causes) of the messages from the supervisor on the basis of behavioural, verbal, and written messages from them, so supervision itself is hostage to an initial solution to the problem of perception. But if the constraints are not coming from something that already knows the correct answer where could it come from?

This is a problem that philosophers and many others working in cognitive science and artificial intelligence have grappled with extensively. From a purely engineering point of view, a supervised system is perfectly fine. But, in typically philosophical fashion, we will not rest satisfied until we have a reductive analysis of perceptual inference. The dialectic is this: either the inferential process is constrained or not. If it is *not* constrained, then there is no robust difference between right and wrong inference, and inference as a normative phenomenon remains unexplained. If it *is* constrained then the source of the constraints either is already engaged in correct perceptual inference or it isn't. If it is so engaged, then positing the source of the constraints as the explanation of perceptual inference does not amount to a reductive analysis since it is circular or leads to a regress. If it is not so engaged, then again there is no difference between right and wrong inference. So it seems we cannot explain perceptual inference at all, without ending in circularity or regress.

## A STATISTICAL ILLUSTRATION

*Prediction error minimization* can begin to solve this problem—or at least it transforms it in interesting ways (see Chapters 4 and 8 for discussion of whether it solves or transforms the problem). The basic idea is simple and can be illustrated by the most basic statistical idea.

In statistics, statistical models are fitted to data. In general, the better the fit the better the model. For example, the mean (or average) of some dataset is a model (e.g., given some rain samples I can model the daily rainfall with the mean of those samples). If many of the values of the dataset are far away from the mean then this means-model is a poor fit, whereas if they are close to the mean it is a good fit. What this implies is that the difference between the model and the data—the *error*—should be small. So, in general, the data is equal to the model estimate *plus* the error between the model prediction and the data. This means that the more we can minimize the error the better the model fit will be.

The error can be minimized in two ways. One way is by changing the model. For example, change from the simple mean, which is a constant and thus a horizontal line through the data (Figure 6a) to a model that charts a straight but sloping line through the data points (a first-order polynomial); this model might represent how rainfall tends to decrease throughout the year and thus reduces somewhat the large error that afflicts the means-model (Figure 6b). The other way to reduce error is by sampling more carefully. For example, by controlling for a confound or noise source that makes data points fall far away from the model predictions. In the rainfall example, this could be controlling for poor sampling methods; for example moving the gauge away from the sprinkler system. I focus more on the first way of reducing error here, and will discuss this second way more in Chapter 4.

Statistical models can be compared in a quantitative way. A very simple statistical method is to measure the distance from the line representing the model to each data point above or below this line, square these measurements to make sure they are all positive, and then sum them. The model that has the least sum of squared error is expected to have the better fit. In our case the mean rainfall model has a larger sum of squared errors than the first order sloping line representing a model saying that rainfall decreases. The latter model is closer to all the data points but a third-order polynomial would fit the data even better (Figure 6c).

Applying this to our case of perception, we get that the data in that case is the sensory input and the statistical model is the hypothesis, maintained in the brain, about the causes in the world. So simply put, the aim is to find a mechanism that can minimize the error between the incoming sensory data and what the hypotheses say the data are.

The statistical picture so far has been rather static and backward looking. But a model, such as a statistical regressor, which is a function, can help us more dynamically *predict* what comes next. For example, a regressor might help us accurately expect decreasing rainfall.

A good statistical model will predict with much accuracy, a poor one with less accuracy. For example, my statistical model of car movement allows me to predict with some accuracy whether I can make it over the street. In contrast, my hapless model of cricket balls and bowlers does not allow me to predict with any noteworthy accuracy how to bat. The error between a statistical model's predictions and the data collected when things actually happen is then the model's *prediction error*. This will be the central term of this book. I test the quality of my hypothesis by seeing how much prediction error it generates, and the less prediction error I can make it generate the better the hypothesis

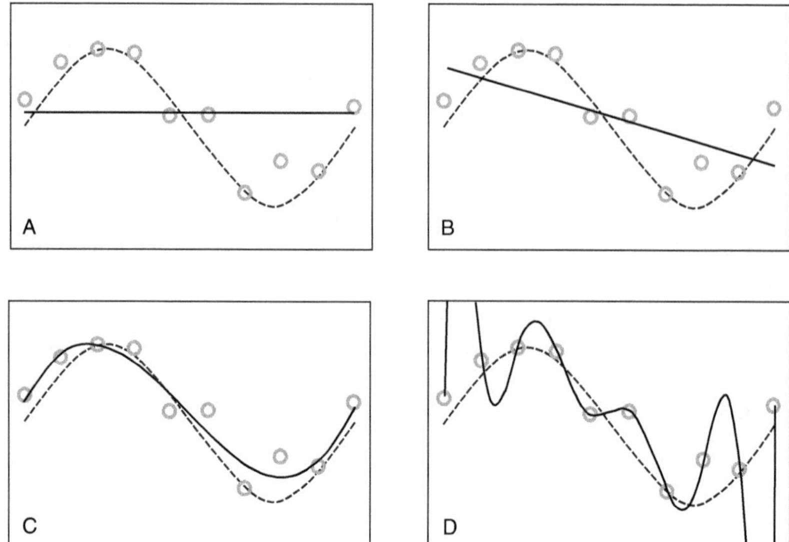


**Figure 6.** Model fitting. The function generating the dashed line is the actual cause of the 10 light grey data points. The solid black line plots the statistical model. In *A* the model is the mean of the data points, giving a large average difference between the data points and the line. In *B* a first-order polynomial is fitted, which gives a sloping line with smaller error. In *C*, the error is further minimized by using a third-order polynomial. In *D*, there is overfitting to the 10 data points with a ninth-order polynomial that leaves no error at all but which seems unable to predict an 11th data point with any accuracy (figure adapted from Bishop 2007: 7).

can be assumed to be (or, in Bayesian terms, the higher its posterior probability will be).

When the statistical version of the problem of perception is put in these more dynamical terms then the aim is to actively use hypotheses to predict what will happen next and to find ways to minimize the ensuing prediction error.

This way of thinking also allows us to focus on an important problem with fitting statistical models through error minimization. In the rain example, the moral was that we should find the model with the least squared error. This model will be the model on which the error is zero, which would be represented by a very squiggly line that goes through all the data points (Figure 6d; mathematically *n* data points can be fitted perfectly with an *n-1* order polynomial). This would however not be a good model because of *overfitting*. The model behaves as if the data points are completely noise free so tries to fit them perfectly. But data are always noisy so the better, truer, fit will be a less squiggly line (in Fig. 6 the grey data points are generated by the function illustrated in the dashed plot, with added noise).

One way to see this is by considering the consequences for prediction error. Though the error in fitting the existing data is zero or close to zero, an overfitted model will almost certainly provide a poor prediction of the next data points. The way to project the model will be highly sensitive to the noise in the existing data set and thus it will be prone to miss the underlying pattern generating the data (as in Figure 6d). When choosing between models one therefore has to be careful to weigh up error minimization vs. overfitting issues such that prediction error will remain low. Crucial to this process is one's expectations about the level of noise in the sample data because that influences the judgement of when a model begins to be overfitted. Heuristically, a model that fits data perfectly is itself highly implausible, because it violates our prior beliefs that noise is always greater than zero. This is a theme we will return to at length in Chapter 3 as well as in later chapters.

Some very simple statistical ideas can thus be used to capture the essence of prediction error minimization and thereby perceptual inference. The application of these simple ideas to perception is then this: use prior beliefs harnessed in an internal model to generate predictions of the sensory input and then revise the model's prediction (hypothesis), or change the input, to minimise the prediction error (subject to expectations of noise). This repeats the basics of the Bayesian approach but adds the all-important predictive element, which allows an iterative step-wise procedure where a hypothesis is chosen, and predictions are made, and then the hypothesis is revised in light of the prediction error, before new and hopefully better predictions are made on the basis of the revised hypothesis. This process then continues until prediction cannot be improved upon any further, where this involves sometimes difficult decisions concerning overfitting and expected levels of noise.

If this is all done in a reasonably optimal fashion, the resulting hypothesis must then be close to the real world's state of affairs, at least as signalled in the sensory input: nothing is a surprise, given the hypothesis, which means that everything is fully known (compare, if I am not at all surprised by the present you give me, then I already *knew* what it was going to be—perhaps because I checked the credit card statement).

This iterative edging towards accurate models makes sure that perceptual inference is not going around in the threatening explanatory circle where the prior expectations guide perceptual inference and perceptual inference in turn guides the formation of priors. Hypothesis revision guided by prediction error signals shapes priors, and makes sure I do not simply see what I predict and predict what I see: the reason is that the prediction error is an objective corrective caused by the objects in the world, which shapes inference. In other words, my predictions are always nuanced by sensory evidence.

The claim is then that perception arises as prediction error is minimized. This is the more substantial way of fleshing out perceptual inference. Importantly, we can begin to see how a mechanism in the brain could do this, because now there is a concrete quantity, prediction error, which can be measured and minimized. In what follows I will give a heuristic explanation of this mechanism, which shadows some of the formal and mathematical aspects of it. To begin, I give the gist of how this idea connects to the simple Bayesian scheme of Chapter 1.

The idea of prediction error minimization is to create a closer fit between the predictions of sensory input based on an internal model of the world and the actual sensory input. This corresponds to being less surprised by the evidence given through the senses. This tells us that we should look at the likelihood term in Bayes' rule, $P(e|h)$, where $e$ is the evidence and $h$ is the hypothesis. Basically, if the prediction error is minimized then the likelihood has been maximized, because a better fit between the hypothesis and the evidence has been created. This in turn will increase the posterior probability, $P(h|e)$, of the hypothesis, which was the aim of Bayesian perceptual inference. This idea of maximizing the likelihood makes sense if we conceive it as a likelihood function, plotted as a curve for all the values it can take. Wherever this curve peaks is where the hypothesis fits the data best, and determining this then becomes mathematically tractable. This is not just likelihood-focused, since the hypothesis chosen will be the one with the highest posterior, $P(h|e)$, which is proportional to $P(\mathrm{e}|h)P(h)$ and thus weighted by the prior $P(h)$. Moreover, for every step in this iterative process, the old posterior in effect becomes the new prior, such that the prior can change with each step. As I said, this only hints at the formal technique and the Bayesian ideas; in a later section I add a little more complexity to the description.

The basic idea is then that minimizing prediction error is the perceiving brain's overarching objective and the principle by which perception must be understood.

There is, naturally, much more to say about how the brain accomplishes prediction error minimization and what it means for our conception of the mind as such. This idea is rapidly gaining influence in computational neuroscience and machine learning (see the notes at the end of this chapter for some of its sources); I rely on and interpret this work as I now begin to unfold the basic idea in more detail.

## RECONCEIVING THE RELATION TO THE WORLD

Once we have accepted that perceptual inference is not an overly intellectualist notion, it may appear an innocuous and even unsurprising proposal for the mechanism that ensures perception. It is just the idea that the brain uses a kind of scientific-style trial and error method, and learns from its errors. This is indeed the broad kind of analogy used by Gregory, one of the main architects of the notion of the hypothesis-testing brain:

> Following Hermann von Helmholtz, who described visual perceptions as unconscious inferences from sensory data and knowledge derived from the past, perceptions are regarded as similar to predictive hypotheses of science, but are psychologically projected into external space and accepted as our most immediate reality. (Gregory 1997: 1121)

This analogy is central to the framework and we will later pursue it in various ways. However the idea goes beyond a simple analogy with trial-and-error practices. In fact, it profoundly reverses how we conceive our relation to the world through the senses. A standard conception is that the senses convey a rich signal that somehow represents worldly states of affairs, which the brain is passively soaking up in a bottom-up manner. If there is any top-down interpretation of the incoming data, then this is mere feedback from the cognitive system on the key bottom-up signal. On the prediction error minimization view, this picture is reversed. The rich representation of worldly states of affairs is signalled in the top-down predictions of sensory input, maintained by the perceptual hierarchy in the brain. These predictions, as it were, *query* the world and dampen down predicted sensory input. The result is that only prediction error is propagated up through the system in a bottom-up fashion, and aids in revision of the model parameters (so we need to re-label the bottom-up sensory input, associated with the light grey, upwards arrows in Figure 5, 'prediction error'). The functional role of the bottom-up signal from the senses is then to be *feedback* on the internal models of the world:

> Cortical hierarchies are trying to generate sensory data from high-level causes. This means the causal structure of the world is embodied in the backward connections. Forward connections simply provide feedback by conveying prediction error to higher levels. In short, forward connections are the feedback connections. (Friston 2005: 825)

This is a challenging and intriguing idea (see also Mumford 1992; Lee and Mumford 2003). Think of what happens when we wake up in the morning, and the sensory data starts flooding in in the shape of the morning sun, the cosiness of the warm doona, the smell of coffee, the sound of the bins being emptied out on the street. The prediction error story compels us to think of all that as mere feedback on neural models of the world. What happens when waking up, rather, is that the brain increases the range of feedback to its hypotheses, which are beginning to predict all those inputs (for this take on sleep and waking, see Hobson and Friston 2012).

Within the camp of researchers who view backwards connections in the brain as important, and who work within the broadly Bayesian framework there are different views about the idea that the feed-forward signal in the brain comprises *only* prediction error. One such view is that backwards connections serve to sharpen the incoming signal, rather than only suppress it with prediction (for discussion, see Kersten, Mamassian et al. 2004; Friston 2005; Kok, Jehee et al. 2012). As we will see in the next chapter, I think the kinds of processes (in particular precision-optimization and attention) involved in sharpening are best understood in terms of hierarchical prediction error minimization.

There is a sense in which this reversal of the standard picture leaves perceptual phenomenology at one remove from the world. Whatever you perceive is the way it is by virtue of processing an error signal. Interspersed between you and the world is a process of using models to explain away sensory input. You open your eyes and see a bird flying past: this perceptual content arises by predicting the sensory input and, on the fly, being sensitive to how the prediction error landscape changes.

This means that perceptual content *is* the predictions of the currently best hypothesis about the world. Perceptual inference is always trying to use its prior knowledge to predict and suppress the sensory input the system is receiving. This is a theme we will return to repeatedly throughout this book. This kind of indirectness is suggested already in the simple statistical illustration above. The hypothesis with the least error is the hypothesis that determines perceptual content (the black line in Fig. 6c) and this hypothesis is internal, subject to statistical decisions and expectations of noise, and different from the hidden causes (the dashed line in Fig. 6c) of the samples making up sensory input.

Perception is of course not indirect in the sense that there is an inner representation somehow emblazoned on a mental screen observed by some homunculus. That is not a very attractive conception of how representation occurs. It is indirect in the sense that what you experience *now* is given in your top-down prediction of your ongoing sensory input, rather than the bottom-up signal from the states of affairs themselves. Or in our simple statistical terms, it is indirect in the sense a statistical estimate is a mathematical representation of hidden causes, extracted from samples (this theme of indirectness is pursued more in Chapter 11).

## BEING SUPERVISED BY THE WORLD

On the prediction error minimization scheme, perception must be at one remove from the world. But this kind of indirectness does not imply that perception is somehow unsupervised, and wide open to sceptical attack. Recall from the discussion above that perception needs additional constraints, it needs to be supervised somehow. Recall also that for an explanation of perception to be satisfactory this supervision cannot come from an external perceiver—like a computer programmer who already knows the answer. Neither can it come from the perceiver itself (a *hermetically* self-supervised system is not properly constrained). How is this issue dealt with on the prediction error minimization approach, with its indirect notion of perception?

The answer emerges from what I deemed the profound reversal of the way we think of our relation to the world through the senses. The predictions of the internal models that determine perception are supervised by the world itself. This follows from the re-conception of the bottom-up sensory signal as prediction error—as feedback to the model of the world. The prediction error is essentially a feedback signal that informs the brain that it has not yet gotten things right.

On alternative, more traditional conceptions of the sensory signal as a bottom-up driving signal in which features of the world are detected, we cannot discern this essential notion of a supervisory learning signal. Hence we look for supervision either by employing external learning analogies, such as the computer programmer, or we look in vain for some kind of bootstrapping self-supervision. In contrast, supervision only emerges once we operate with a comparison of predicted and actual input since revision of our internal model parameters can happen in the light of the difference between them.

This is a particularly elegant attempt to resolve the problem of perception. We find the required additional constraints, the knowledgeable supervisor, in the world itself. And of course, this is the optimal solution because, to put it in a glib slogan: The world *is* the truth. The feedback signal is the actual statistical regularities caused in us by the world itself. Perhaps the mistake, in earlier conceptions of the problem of perception, was to look for a supervisor (a programmer or the system itself), which somehow *knows* the truth (for discussions of such mistakes, see Eliasmith 2003; Eliasmith 2005). The prediction error minimization approach cuts out the middleman and lets the supervisor *be* the truth itself.

Prediction error driven supervision by the world can happen via representations of quickly changing states of the world and via representations of more slowly changing parameters of the world. The former is thought to occur in the brain's synaptic activity (the way neurons interact in the short term), and the latter in synaptic efficacy (the way connection strengths are set over the longer term) (Friston 2010). A third way concerns the precisions, or variability of prediction errors, that relate to synaptic gain (the intrinsic excitability of a unit; Chapter 3 will explain this notion; Chapter 9 will relate it to attention).

This means that perceptual content, though indirect in the sense explained earlier, is supervised very closely and on a moment-to-moment basis by the world. The indirectness is then not an immediate threat to our relation to the world because perception is harnessed very tightly. But the indirectness is there nevertheless: perceptual content is given in our predictions and this is precisely what allows the world to deliver a *supervisory* signal. Later we will see that this matters for our ability to reality-test our perception and for how robust we think our perception of the world is (Chapters 7, 11).

Now we can return to the theme of additional constraints in the context of the perceptual hierarchy and the way prior knowledge is drawn upon. In Chapter 1, we saw that additional constraints are drawn down from higher levels of the hierarchy—that's where the priors come from. But we noted that this is not itself enough of an explanation because there must be some constraints on these priors too. Something must be shaping them in a way conducive to perceptual inference.

We can now see that the priors are shaped by the prediction error their predictions generate when exposed to feedback from the actual world. Rather than having the idle explanatory circle where inference shapes priors and priors determine inference we have a process where prior expectations are shaped progressively in the light of the *quality* of the perceptual inferences they give rise to. Prediction error allows us to break into the explanatory circle and turn this into a substantial solution to the problem of perception.

For this to work, prediction error must be an objective quantity that the brain can access and assess. This seems possible because the brain does have access to the predictions of sensory input generated by its own hypotheses, and the brain does have access to the sensory data that impinges on it. All it needs to do is compare the two, note the size of the difference, and revise the hypotheses (or change the input through action) in whatever way will minimize the difference. Given that the two things that are compared are accessible from within the skull, the difference between them is accessible from within too. There is no need to, as it were, impossibly jump outside the skull and compare percepts to the causal states of affairs in the real world. These causes remain hidden behind the veil of sensory input and can only be inferred.

The basic idea here is in a way very simple. If a certain state of the brain is to represent a certain state in the world, then it should carry information about it. That is to say, if some neural population *n* is to represent some cause *c* in the world, then the ideal situation would be that *n* fires pretty much when and only when *c* occurs. In that situation *n* and *c* would be strong predictors of each other—their *mutual information* would be very high (I provide a brief explanatory note on this information theoretical notion at the end of this chapter). On the other hand if they were completely independent of each other, so that the occurrence of one had nothing to do with the occurrence of the other, then their mutual information would be zero. Clearly, given noise, ambiguity, and uncertainty in the world and the brain, the mutual information will always be less than perfect (these ideas were explored philosophically in Dretske 1983; for critical discussion and development, see Eliasmith 2000; Usher 2001; Eliasmith 2005; Piccinini and Scarantino 2011).

To represent the causes in the world as well as possible, the brain would be well served to employ a method that entails maximization of mutual information—get it as high as feasible in the context. But the brain has access only to a proxy of $c$, namely the sensory input, $u$. So at best it can hope to do something that will entail maximization of the mutual information between $n$ and $u$. It is a trivial consequence of a system that minimizes prediction error that it maximizes mutual information: the smaller the prediction error generated by the hypotheses embodied in $n$, the better $n$ predicts the occurrence of $u$—that is, the larger their mutual information and the better the representation. Hence, if hypotheses are revised such as to minimize prediction error, then they are properly constrained with respect to representation of the world (on the anti-sceptical assumption that the external world is revealed through the senses).

We can see here that if we begin with a prediction error minimization story, then we get a system that increases mutual information. In this respect the account has something in common with other information theoretical accounts of perception and learning (for example, Barlow 1961; Linsker 1988). It is different however, in terms of the mechanism by which mutual information is attained, namely the prediction error minimization engendered by the generative model in the backwards connections in the brain. Note also that the principles describing such a prediction error minimization system cannot be derived directly from information theoretical notions of mutual information. Here we therefore focus especially on the properties of the prediction error minimization mechanism.

## A DEEPER PERSPECTIVE

It is necessary to add a level of complexity to this story. Otherwise, we will miss a crucial bit of its attraction. To do this I will offer a greatly simplified version of Friston's take on perceptual inference (Friston and Stephan 2007; Friston 2010). Above we invoked the notion of mutual information in order to describe the perceptual task, now we go further into some information theoretical aspects. The nervous system is an information channel, and a sensory state thus should be describable in information theoretical terms. One way of doing this is to describe the *self-information* or *surprisal* (Tribus 1961) of the current sensation. This is a measure of how surprising some outcome is. Intuitively, this quantity should be high for improbable outcomes and low for very probable outcomes. So surprisal is a declining function of probability: as the probability goes to zero the surprisal goes up, as the probability goes to 1 the surprisal goes down. (Formally, it is the negative log of how probable the outcome ($e$) is, under a given model of the world $P(e|m)$, where each model ($m$) can entertain multiple hypotheses ($h$) in terms of its parameters.)

Think of this now from the perspective of an organism like us. Your sensory state ($e$) itself is, in the sense described, more or less surprising. But the surprisal must be relative to who you are ($m$). The sensory state of a particular sperm whale and of you will be vastly different, but they could be equally surprising to you both. Hence, we need to define the creature's expected states first, and then deem as surprising those states that take the creature away from its expected states. Put in terms of probability, if we look at creatures like us and all the states we can find ourselves in, then we find that it is much more probable to find us in some subset of those states than others. To illustrate, it would be highly improbable to find you at the depth of 1,000 metres, wrestling a giant squid. The trick is then to turn this around and define who we are—our phenotypes—in terms of the set of states that we most probably occupy.

Now we get a handle on the surprisal. You are in a 'surprising' state if you are moving outside of the set of states you are expected to be in precisely because there is a low probability of finding you in that state. This is the sense of 'surprise' in surprisal. The state you are in (e.g., encountering another person) determines your sensory input because it determines the causal input to your senses from the world, so now we have an information theoretical characterization of that input. This is consistent with the causal outlook on perception even if it is described relative to who you are, that is, relative to your phenotype as defined by your expected states ($P(e|m)$).

If surprisal depends on sensory input, then we should be able to see perceptual inference as somehow a function relating to surprisal. What could that function be? Given that there is a sense in which surprisal is unexpected for the creature, and given we have talked about minimizing prediction error, perhaps the creature should directly minimise surprisal? This is however not possible. There is no way the creature can assess directly whether some particular state is surprising or not, to do that it would have to do the impossible task of averaging over an infinite number of copies of itself (under all possible hypotheses that could be entertained by the model) to see whether that is a state it is expected to be in or not. It is for this reason that a move to prediction error minimization is necessary: it allows an indirect, tractable way of dealing with the uncertainty of the current state.

We can replace the problem of evaluating surprise with optimizing something that is possible to evaluate and which is always bigger than surprise. This is *free energy* or—under some simplifying assumptions—the prediction error described earlier. Prediction error is always greater than surprise, such that *prediction error = surprise + perceptual divergence*. It is always greater than surprise because the perceptual divergence is non-negative (formally, it is a Kullback-Leibler divergence; see the notes at the end of the chapter for an explanation of this notion). This divergence measures the difference between the hypothesis currently selected and the true posterior beliefs under our model,

$P(h|e, m)$. Expressed in this way, minimizing prediction error can be seen as minimizing perceptual divergence, thereby ensuring our selected hypotheses are as close as possible to the true posterior. Crucially, at the same time, the bound on surprisal gets smaller and the prediction error then becomes a proxy for surprisal—something that we would otherwise not have been able to evaluate (Friston and Stephan 2007; Friston 2010). I expand on these formulations in the next chapter, in the second half of Chapter 4, and in Chapter 8.

This is then how perceptual inference relates, as it should, to the description of a creature's sensory input in terms of surprisal. Since surprisal is the information received from the environment, prediction error minimization will make the overall prediction error approximate this information. In other words, sensory input becomes increasingly stronger evidence, $P(e|m)$, for the internal model of the world (a notion I will return to in Chapter 11).

This is a central part of the attraction of prediction error minimization. Minimizing prediction error (or free energy) does two things at the same time. First, it approximates surprise so that a given organism tends to sample the sensory evidence that defines its phenotype. Second, it obliges the phenotype to select plausible hypotheses about the causes of its sensory input. Prediction error minimization does not just describe what is *required* for representation to occur but gives a tractable *task* for the brain to perform, on quantities that are accessible to it. This in turn opens up the possibility for us to find a *mechanism* in the brain that performs this task, namely the cascading top-down predictions that dampen down bottom-up prediction error (with some twists to the story, as we will see in the next two chapters). I know of no other account of representation that can accomplish this to this degree: a formal account of perception, a tractable optimization task that is mandated by the existence of an agent, and a plausible mechanism that can realize it.

Notice that strictly speaking perceptual inference as explained so far does not do anything to change the surprisal itself—it just creates a tighter prediction error bound on it. To actually change surprisal the system needs a way to change the very input it receives, and in this way ensure it can remain within its expected states. This is the role of action and we will see in Chapter 4 that action can also be dealt with in terms of prediction error minimization. Moreover, much of the discussion in Parts II and III will concern the very close coupling of perception and action in prediction error terms.

## RECOGNITION AND MODEL INVERSION

The problem of perception was introduced as an inverse problem: how to infer back from the effects on the sensory system to the causes in the world. We have tried to implicitly solve this problem in virtue of how minimizing prediction error reduces the difference (divergence) between the hypotheses selected and the true posterior $P(h|e, m)$ that maps from hypotheses or causes to sensory input. This solution harnesses a number of the Bayesian moves in a prediction error minimization scheme. There is one related aspect to look at to round off this discussion.

What we have so far is an internal model that generates a hypothesis—we might call it a fantasy—about the expected sensory input. This is the generative model, which has a number of different parameters that together produce the fantasy (hypothesis) down through the hierarchy. A particular fantasy might do a fine job at matching the incoming sensory input, and thus should determine perception. But this leaves things only half done. In order to *recognize* the causes of the input, the generative model needs to be inverted, such that the system can identify the distinct parameters of the model that produced the fantasy. If the system cannot perform recognition, then inference is rather shallow: All the system knows is that certain input was received but not what causes conspired to produce that input.

In some cases recognition is easy. Inversion of the generative model occurs when Bayes' rule is applicable in a straightforward sense because it inverts expressions concerning likelihood $P(e|h, m)$ to get posteriors $P(h|e, m)$. But problems arise when the generative model has parameters that interact in a non-linear fashion. Then it is immensely difficult turn things around like that. The problem is that there is an intractably large number of ways that the many interacting causes assumed by the generative model could give rise to various constellations of fantasized sensory input, and trying to explicitly sort out or deconvolve these interactions seems to be an impossible computational task for the brain. In this way, recognition presents a problem, which the brain has created for itself in its attempt to deal with the problem of minimizing surprisal. But because everything has now been moved inside the brain, the situation is not hopeless.

The solution is to delegate out the work hierarchically and let the inversion of the model be implicit in minimizing prediction error at all levels of the hierarchy. Predictive units at each level of the processing hierarchy predict something relatively simple, and each unit is guided by prediction error from the level below and makes its inference available for predictions from the level above. If all prediction units are doing this, then the overall result is that the brain's current hypothesis or fantasy is distributed throughout the perceptual hierarchy and, when its predictions are viewed together, this constitutes an implicit inversion of the model (Friston 2008; Friston and Kiebel 2009). There is no extra computational step of inferring inputs from possible causes; the specific model of sensory input emerges in the distributed, individual predictive steps that are internally consistent at every level of the hierarchy, right down to the sensory level. Perceptual representation of the world is not then something that comes together in any specific area of the brain devoted to inversion of generative models. Representation emerges in the ongoing predictive activity of the entire hierarchy of prediction error minimization mechanisms.

There is a sense in which, in spite of being Bayesian, this is more mechanical than it is inferential. Each prediction unit is just trying to stem the flow of sensory input, and anticipating input as well as possible turns out to be a good strategy for doing this. In the course of stemming this flow, the brain happens to represent the world. This allows us to revisit the neuroanthropomorphism issue whether and in what sense the brain must "know" and "apply" Bayes' rule. Using the notion of prediction error minimization, it is easy to see how the brain perceives and why this is best conceived as an inferential process: it fits with the normative constraints of Bayes. But the "neuronal hardware" of the mechanism itself is not literally inferential: neuronal populations are just trying to generate activity that anticipates their input. In the process of doing this they realize Bayesian inference.

## SUMMARY: PERCEPTION IN PREDICTION

Perception arises in prediction error minimization where the brain's hypotheses about the world are stepwise brought closer to the flow of sensory input caused by things in the world. This is an elegant idea because it gives the brain all the tools it needs to extract the causal regularities in the world and use them to predict what comes next in a way that is sensitive to what is currently delivered to the senses.

This idea can be explicated in more complex terms terms of minimizing surprisal to ensure agents sample sensory inputs that are characteristic of their phenotype. This can be cast in terms of minimizing the divergence between hypotheses or probabilistic representations of the world and the true posterior probability, given sensory evidence—a minimization that necessarily invokes a Bayesian brain perspective on perception and places the role of probabilistic representations centre stage. This perspective provides an account in terms of the overall way prediction error bounds the creature's surprisal. This idea of a bound on surprise is something we will return to a number of times.

The next chapter discusses ways in which neuronal populations can optimize this process by relying on contextual information from other neuronal populations and by optimizing the precision of the sensory signal. Chapter 4 broadens the perspective to the role of prediction error minimization in agency. At the end of that chapter we will have a description of the core parts of the complete prediction error minimization mechanism. This will then inform Parts II and III of the book.

## NOTES

*Page 46.* ["The basic idea is then that minimizing prediction . . . "] This section has set out the key notions of prediction error minimization. There are many sources of this idea, and it has been developed in different formal ways. As mentioned, I take my cue mainly from the work of Karl Friston and colleagues. Their work develops and extends important work by Mumford and colleagues (Mumford 1992; Lee and Mumford 2003) and by Hinton, Dayan, and colleagues (Hinton and Sejnowski 1983; Dayan, Hinton et al. 1995), and others working in the field of machine learning. An important development was Rao and Ballard's model of extra-classical receptive fields (Rao and Ballard 1999). The ideas also rest on work on the notion of 'analysis by synthesis' in Neisser (1967) and as mentioned in the text, Gregory—much of which is heavily indebted to Helmholtz. Other early work is in Jaynes, discussed and developed in (Phillips 2012); as well as in work by Barlow (1958) and Mackay (1956); a kindred contemporary version is developed by Hawkins and George (Hawkins and Blakeslee 2005; George and Hawkins 2009).

*Page 46.* ["Once we have accepted . . . "] The analogy to scientific reasoning is also a main driver behind Jaynes' kindred formal probabilistic framework, which has recently been developed ways similar to the prediction error minimization scheme, see e.g. (Phillips 2012).

*Page 47.* ["This analogy is central to the framework . . . "] Here I contrast the perceptual inference with a more passive bottom-up account, which goes back to classic empiricism, such as Locke (1690). This also relates to an even earlier debate in vision, going back to Lucretius and Ibn al-Haytham's defence of intromission theory and objections to the extramission theory of Aristotle and other philosophers, see (Lindberg 1976). Ibn al-Haytham thus argues that vision comes about as a result of light hitting the eye, not as a result of some ray emitted from the eye. As mentioned in the notes to the previous chapter, he also realized that unconscious inference was nevertheless needed for perception.

*Page 48.* ["This means that perceptual content *is* the predictions of . . . "] There is some empirical evidence for these ideas though more laboratory work needs to be done. One prediction is that low-level activity should be dampened down when perceptual inference occurs and one model wins. There is evidence for this in a study of the difference between perceiving disjointed line segments and perceiving coherent geometrical figures; for the latter there was an accompanying reduction in activity lower in the visual stream (Murray, Kersten et al. 2002; Fang, Kersten et al. 2008); see also (Lee and Mumford 2003). See also (Summerfield and Koechlin 2008) and (Muckli, Kohler et al. 2005; Alink, Schwiedrzik et al. 2010; Smith and Muckli 2010). Further references to empirical research are given in Chapter 3 and 4.

*Page 50.* ["The basic idea here is in a way . . . "] Here I mention the information theoretical notion of *mutual information*, the idea being that a system that minimizes prediction error increases mutual information. It may be useful to introduce this and a couple other notions slightly more formally (the pared down formal notation used here is for heuristic purposes; I have ignored differences between discrete and continuous probability distributions and other distinctions; see e.g., Dayan and Abbott 2001: Ch. 4, 8, 10; Cover and Thomas 2006: Ch. 2).

First, consider a very basic notion of what makes some event surprising. If it is something that happens very frequently, then it is not surprising. If it is a rare event, then it is surprising. So a high probability event, like the sun rising tomorrow, is not surprising. In contrast, a low probability event, like the sun exploding in a supernova, is surprising. This kind of surprise-as-unpredictability should be captured in a function that goes down as probability goes up. Second, consider an intuition about the surprise of more than one event. If two events are independent (you get a pay rise, and the ice melt in the arctic has stopped), then the surprise from learning about both should just be the sum of their individual surprises. That is, we should be able to add surprises. It turns out that the logarithm satisfies these two constraints. That is, the surprise, labelled *h*, of an event, *r*, is

$$h\Big(P(r)\Big) = -\log P(r)$$

where it can be seen that as the probability goes up, the negative log of the probability goes down. This notion, *h*, is *surprisal*, and is discussed more in the main text. It is desirable to average surprisal by how probable events are, to reflect the idea that we don't expect improbable events to happen very often. Hence, an overall view of surprise can be achieved when we multiply surprises, captured by $h(P(r))$, with the probabilities $P(r)$ of the events, and then summing them all, which gives entropy, *H*:

$$H = -\sum P(r) \log P(r)$$

Entropy does not in itself say anything about how much information some observations (such as those conveyed in kinds of neural activity) carry about something else (such as sensed events). For that, the notion of mutual information is needed. To link observations or neuronal responses, *r*, with the states of affairs, *z*, we consider the conditional entropy of *r* given *z*, and formulate the *noise entropy*

$$H_{noise} = -\sum P(z)P(r|z) \log P(r|z)$$

This captures variability in the observations *r* that are due to noise rather than due to the presence of *z*. *H* is then the total amount of uncertainty or variability in *r*, and $H_{noise}$ is the amount of uncertainty or variability in *r* that is due to noise (i.e., due to its limitations as a detector of *z*). If we were to subtract $H_{noise}$ from *H* we would then get the amount of variability in *r* that is due to the occurrence of *z*. This is then a measure of the *mutual information, I,* between *r* and *z*

$$I = H - H_{noise}$$

(Incidentally, *I* is symmetric, so *z* carries the same degree of information about *r* as *r* carries about *z*).

Mutual information is therefore a useful concept for understanding in a quantitative way what it is for something like a pattern of neural activity to carry information about something. We should be interested in increasing the mutual information between our heads and the world. This chapter describes the trivial point that a mechanism that minimizes prediction error will increase mutual information between the predictor and what it predicts.

*Page 51.* ["It is necessary to add a level . . . "] Here I discuss the notion of 'surprisal'. See the previous note for some basic exposition of this notion.

*Page 52.* ["Put simply, we can replace the problem . . . "] Here the notion of free energy is linked to prediction error. The simplifying assumption that allows this has to do with the Gaussian shape of the encoding of the recognition density and the equations this allows.

*Page 52.* ["Put simply, we can replace the problem . . . "] The Kullback-Leibler divergence (KL divergence, ($D_{KL}$); also sometimes called relative entropy) is central to the formal treatment of prediction error minimization because its formal properties (i.e., that it is always zero or positive) ensure that prediction error is an upper bound on surprise. Since this is a notion that often occurs in the formal literature it may be useful to give the gist of these formal properties in a few more details (see, e.g., textbooks such as Dayan and Abbott 2001 Ch. 4, 8, 10; Cover and Thomas 2006: Ch. 2; Bishop 2007: Ch. 1, 9, 10; Trappenberg 2010: Ch. 10). The KL divergence is a measure of the divergence between two probability distributions (or densities) ($P$ and $Q$):

$$D_{KL}(P \,||\, Q) = \sum P(r) \log\left(\frac{P(r)}{Q(r)}\right)$$

The KL divergence is 0 when the two distributions are the same, and else it is positive (i.e., $D_{KL}(P|| \, Q) \geq 0$). It is a divergence and not a distance measure since it is not symmetric, so that the divergence between $P$ and $Q$ need not be identical to the divergence between $Q$ and $P$.

Intuitively, the KL divergence works like this because the kinds of function we are interested in (e.g., $-\log x$) have more or less u-shaped plots so that a chord connecting two points on such a plot can never be below the portion of the u-shaped plot that it caps. Hence the KL divergence is equal to or larger than zero, which is the property crucial for serving as an upper bound on surprise, as described in the main text.

The KL divergence can be described in terms of the entropy expression introduced in a previous note. If entropy is a measure of the information required on average to describe a random variable $P(x)$, then, if some other variable $Q(x)$ is an approximation to it, its entropy should be the information required to describe the first variable plus the difference between them (see Cover and Thomas 2006: Ch. 2). In this way, if one minimizes the KL divergence between $Q$ (e.g., the selected hypothesis) and $P$ (e.g., the true posterior) the information required to describe $Q$ must be approximating the information required to describe $P$. The KL divergence is then the difference in entropy, or average surprise.

*Page 55.* ["There is a sense in which . . . "] Having said that the neural machinery does not know Bayes, I need to remark that there is a way to continue this debate, which I will touch on briefly in Chapter 8; this concerns a deep link between information theory and statistical physics that would invite the thought that in fact the hardware is information theoretical, and as such engaged in inferential activity (for discussion of this kind of issue, see Norwich 1993).

# 3

# Prediction error, context, and precision

Perceptual inference is a matter of hierarchical prediction error minimization. Top-down predictions are compared to the actual sensory signal, or with the inference of the level below, and the difference, the prediction error, is used as a feedback signal for the internal models generating the predictions.

This sort of scheme sounds very much like linear predictive coding that was invented in the 1950s to compress data. However, these linear schemes would only work if the world was populated only with very simple, linearly interacting causes. Of course, the world is replete with causes that interact non-linearly—this is part of what makes us worry about the relation between causes and effects not being one–one. Examples range from simple perceptual interactions like a cat being partially occluded by the fence, to deep and complex regularities such as the impact of the global financial crisis on the effort to combat climate change.

Crucially, there is not only an interaction among hidden causes in the production of sensory data but an interaction between different states of the world and the uncertainty or noise associated with sensory evidence generated by those states. For example, visual input is more reliable during the day than at dusk, and a low whisper at a cocktail party is an unreliable guide to what is said, relative to exchanges on a quiet moonlit night.

Perceptual experience is steeped in these effects and therefore the prediction error minimization mechanism must have the capacity to deal with context dependence and context sensitive uncertainty too. Otherwise the prediction error minimization idea will be unrealistically austere.

There is a guiding constraint in the attempt to accommodate context and noise: since we are talking about a system that is supervised solely by the delivery of input from the world through the senses, the system has to *learn* both about different interactions in different contexts, and learn about varying levels of noise and uncertainty. Importantly, this learning about context and noise and uncertainty has to be based only on the sensory resources available—we don't want to generate a new iteration of the problem of perception.

## CONTEXT AND UNCERTAINTY

In fact, with the perceptual hierarchy we have already seen some of the tools for explaining context dependence. Consider for example, the task of perceiving the cat in the context of the picket fence. The evolution over time and space of this sensory input depends in a nonlinear way on the causal interactions between the cat and its context (as well as the observer's position relative to them). The system cannot use the assumed properties of the cat alone to predict the input, it needs to take the context of the fence into consideration.

*Recognition* of this state of affairs requires the ability of the mechanism to unmix the two causes on the basis of the mixed sensory input such that the winning hypothesis is the one that predicts a cat and a fence, and not, say, a fence and some detached cat-slices aligned between the pickets. At the same time, *generation* of predictions depends on the ability of the system to perform a nonlinear mixing of the two higher-level model parameters representing the whole cat and the fence such that the prediction fits the actual, mixed sensory input, down through the hierarchy, caused by the partially occluded cat as it walks behind the fence.

In a completely static world, there is no problem with nonlinear mixing and unmixing of causes because there is no evolution in time and space of the input—no difference between the whole cat hypothesis and the detached cat slice hypothesis. But in the actual world, the different hypotheses about the world have different predictions for the evolution of the input. For example, on the whole cat hypothesis there will be expectations of unseen, continuous cat parts becoming visible as the cat moves relative to the fence. Should a bit of the landscape in the background rather than a bit of cat become visible, then a large prediction error is generated. The whole cat hypothesis will then be favoured if it is really a whole cat but not if instead of a real, whole cat it were the set of detached cat-slices lined up nicely between the pickets of the fence. The evolution of the prediction error landscape is then what helps with recognition: the right hypotheses will over time emerge as the best predictors.

In this process, a higher-level regularity is utilized and finessed, concerning the interaction of spatial trajectories of objects like cats and fences. This regularity can predict sensory input over relatively long time scales but not in much detail. It can predict that some cat parts will become visible but not what those parts will exactly look like. These top-down predictions work as the priors for the activity at lower levels and this facilitates the needed generation of mixed causes to match the nonlinear layout of the sensory input. That is, at lower levels there is high prior probability of seeing bits of cat between the pickets and this favours certain activities of prediction units at lower levels over others, and thereby implicitly a certain mixing of some causes over others.

Context dependence is then in large part dealt with via the spatiotemporal properties of the perceptual hierarchy and the message-passing between levels described in terms of empirical Bayes (recall, empirical Bayes is where the priors are learnt and shaped over time from the incoming signal). Low levels are relatively 'myopic' and cannot easily see the context but are helped out by the relatively 'hyperopic' higher levels that in turn tend to ignore fine detail. When levels begin to send messages to each other, predictions at lower levels become hyperparameterized, that is, their activity becomes partly determined by higher levels, and higher-level regularities become finessed in terms of longer-term interactions of distinct causes.

It is likely that lateral connections within the same hierarchical level serve to decorrelate prediction units such that when a particular hypothesis begins to emerge as having the highest posterior probability other units are progressively prevented from influencing inference (Friston 2002a; 2002b). In an uncertain situation, such as when there is ambiguous context or noise, a number of different hypotheses can concurrently seek to predict the input, which can be a more efficient strategy than searching through hypotheses one by one. However, when one hypothesis is deemed good enough the activities of other hypotheses should begin to recede because whatever they can successfully predict is most likely just noise—those hypotheses are *explained away*.

Similarly, bottom-up prediction error is favoured from units that "feed" well-performing prediction units. That is, an evolving prediction error signal that can continually be explained away well by a particular hypothesis can be assumed to be reliable and should thus be weighted more in the message-passing economy. As we will see later, this notion of weighting prediction error according to their reliability is central to how the system deals with noise and uncertainty, and in turn, to the nature of attention (for background and discussion of the structure of the hierarchy, see Friston 2002a; Friston 2003; Lee and Mumford 2003; Hinton 2007).

Collectively, these mechanisms serve to accentuate the best predictors and the most reliable parts of the prediction error signal within the perceptual hierarchy. It still holds that it is just the prediction error that is shunted upwards in the system, but there are mechanisms that help the right parts of the prediction error meet the right predictions. Positing these further mechanisms does not go beyond the notion that all the brain is involved in is prediction error minimization. Rather, they reflect what prediction error minimization requires in order for a noisy and context-dependent sensory input to reveal the world. To see this, it helps to recall from the previous chapter the statistical core of prediction error minimization and how statistics relies crucially on assessing levels of uncertainty and confidences.

## PLUGGING THE LEAKY DAM

An extended illustration might convey some of the central ideas about how recognition and generation emerge implicitly in hierarchical prediction error minimization, such that the causal structure of the world is recapitulated within the brain.

Imagine being charged with plugging holes in a large, old, and leaking dam. There are many kinds of leaks: big ones and small ones, leaks that persist and others that come and go, and so on. The occurrence, frequency, and nature of the leaks all depend on the water pressure on the other side, the water levels, consumption on this side, the state of repair of the dam, and so on. But you do not know anything about that. Your job is just to minimize overall leakage. You run around frantically with a limited supply of different materials to plug different kinds of leaks.

After a while you begin noticing patterns in the leaks: some leaks are big gushing ones, others more trickly, some occur in certain orders ("every time a big gusher with jagged edges occurs in location A, about ten tricklers occur a bit later in location B"). As you learn you might also see more general patterns ("big gushers tend to intensify en masse"). All such knowledge of leakage patterns will allow you to be better at anticipating where leaks will be and plug up in advance. You might even make somewhat Rube Goldberg-esque contraptions with plugs, cogs, wheels, string, and long arms that can plug different patterns of leak profiles. In the long run you may be able to make the workings of the contraption depend on long term patterns throughout months and years. This will capture long term seasonal patterns such as droughts, wet seasons, and so on, though of course you don't know that these are the causes of the long term patterns. Then you can make the contraption follow rules such as "if prediction of pre-plug to gusher at B, also pre-plug ten tricklers around B, unless overall leakage has been low for the past few years" and so on.

You can tinker with the contraptions every time that, in spite of your best predictions, water leaks through. Sometimes the tinkering will be in local arms of the contraption ("plug 11 tricklers around B, not 10"), sometimes the tinkering involves its more global features ("leakage is down on the long term average so don't bother about tricklers"). Eventually you will have very efficient patterns of leak plugging, and the structure of the mechanical contraption will then carry information about the causal structure of the causes impinging on the other side of the dam, including both the impact of local currents and eddies and more long term, hidden causes such as seasonal changes and droughts and how they modulate the concrete leak patterns. The flow of information in the multilayered contraption will be in both directions: persistent leak patterns will increase the activity of the long-term seasonal part, which will in turn begin anticipating changing patterns of leaks.

We thus get representation that is highly context-dependent in virtue of learnt regularities and associations of leaks. It furnishes a rich model of the causal structure and depth of the watery world beyond the dam.

The crucial bit, however, is that in achieving this successful representation of the causal structure of the world beyond the dam, you didn't have to *try* to represent it. All you had to do was plug leaks and be guided in this job by the amount of unanticipated leaks. Similarly, all that is needed to represent the world for the human brain is hierarchical prediction error minimization. Recall here the more information theoretical version of the problem of perception from the previous chapter. This was the idea that prediction error is a bound on surprise, such that minimizing error stems surprise. That is the idea we see illustrated here. The brain is somewhat desperately, but expertly, trying to contain the long and short-term effects of the environmental causes on the organism in order to preserve its integrity. In doing so, a rich, layered representation of the world implicitly emerges. This is a beautiful and humbling picture of the mind and our place in nature.

The leakage illustration is beginning to get strained, as it were, but we will stay with it just a little longer. The notion of context-dependence, that we encountered earlier, falls out naturally from your ability to minimize leaks efficiently, using all the statistical information available in the patterns of leaks. The illustration thus helps to show that context-sensitivity is not something extraneous to prediction error minimization.

Of course, prediction error minimization does not happen from scratch. First evolution and neurodevelopment has selected and shaped a brain, that is, a model ($m$) under which hypotheses ($h$) can be selected according to their prediction error minimization prowess (as described in the previous chapter). Similarly, we imagined the leak-plugger as issued with some means to plug the leaks, and then these had to be selected and applied efficiently. A fuller illustration would issue the leak-plugger with not only tools to plug leaks but also a series of connected dam locks that must be controlled and plugged in a hierarchical fashion.

The illustration however has limitations. One limitation is that we imagine someone—you—doing all the plugging and statistical inference. In the brain, there is no agent doing the predicting. It is instead a self-organized system obeying the simple rule to minimize prediction error in order to keep input (or entropic disorder) at bay. (I will return to this issue at the end of Chapter 8).

The illustration is also limited because it does not capture the idea that we actively explore the environment to check our predictions and thereby through our actions change the very input we get. In the dam analogy, this would correspond to changing the location of the dam and the direction of flow of rivers and so on. We return to the crucial issue of action and prediction error minimization in Chapter 4.

For now, we will look at another important limitation of the illustration. A central part of your job as leak-plugger would be to do the plugging as precisely and efficiently as possible and you would need to be able to determine whether a given leak is part of a pattern or just a more accidental occurrence. Also, because your plugging is based on statistical rather than deterministic inference you need to decide how to use your plugs based on how confident you are and on what else you expect to happen in the overall patterns of leaks. This suggests that prediction error minimization needs to be augmented with a way to assess the confidence of perceptual inference, and thus to handle precision, noise, and uncertainty, as we anticipated at the beginning of this chapter. This is the topic of the next section.

## EXPECTED PRECISIONS

Let us turn to the more austere illustration in terms of statistical inference. Prediction error could be explained in terms of how a (generative) statistical model may capture some but not all of the variability of a sample. The uncaptured part corresponds to the prediction error. Another way to conceive prediction error is in terms of statistical inference on the difference between two distributions, where one is the expected distribution (e.g., the null hypothesis), the other is the test distribution. If the test distribution is far enough from the expected distribution, then that is evidence that a certain experimental intervention, for example, made a difference. Here, the difference between distributions can be conceived as prediction error, relative to the null hypothesis (to illustrate, "if this substance is not carcinogenic, then we predict there will be little difference in longevity between the treated and untreated mice; but there was a large difference").

This is a standard statistical story, which bears resemblance to the concept of prediction error. What we need to focus on however is the confidence with which we infer that two such distributions are different or not. We need to not only assess the central tendency of the distributions, such as the mean, but also the variation about the mean. Large variation is what often occurs in very small sample sizes and poorly designed experiments, or experiments using poor instruments. A large amount of variation in a sample should make us less confident in judgements about differences between the distributions (Cox 1946). Graphically speaking, the bell curves for two very variable distributions can be so broad that we are not confident that they are really different (or the same). Difference judgements are easier to make with very narrow, *precise* distributions. This is then what we should aim for: precision in our sampling of the world.

What this statistics-illustration brings out is that assessments of prediction error are hostage to how confident the system is that a prediction error is genuine and something worth minimizing. If the variability in the sensory input and its processing were always the same, then there would not be much of a problem concerning confidence: then the mean of the distribution would be the only thing that shifts around. But there is much variability in the levels of variability: the noise and uncertainty in the signal from the world depends on, and varies with, the varying states of the world and the organism. In one context, the variability of a signal may be enough to deem something a genuine prediction error, whereas in another context the same absolute amount of variability may undermine our confidence that it is a genuine prediction error. Similarly, the same difference in means can be interpreted differently, depending on noise, such as if we say "yesterday I was confident that these two sets of measurements were different, but today there are added levels of extraneous noise so even though the new measurements have the same means as yesterday I am not confident they are different".

What determines such inference about variability is which expectations for variability we have in different contexts. This can be put in the model-fitting terms used earlier. Recall that, in an attempt to fit a statistical model to a set of data, the error between the model and the data should be minimized. But if there are no prior expectations about the variability of the data set (the inverse of which is the same as its precision), then there is no way to reasonably decide how much or how little fitting is enough. If this decision is not optimal, then predictions on the basis of the model will not be good.

Putting all this together under the prediction error minimization approach we get the following picture. (i) To achieve confident and efficient perceptual inference, prediction error minimization should aim for precision. (ii) Precision is achievable only if we generate expectations for the precisions of prediction errors. (iii) Precision expectations must be based in an internal model of precisions in the world.

That is, in order to optimize prediction error minimization, we need to learn about and predict precisions. This means being able to predict when, given the context, a prediction error signal is likely to be precise. It is a kind of second-order perceptual inference because it is inference about perceptual inference. It is still a perceptual inference problem, however, so the brain is required to extract regularities having to do with precisions and use these to optimize the passing of messages back and forth in the perceptual hierarchy. By doing this it can optimize its expectations of precisions. This includes, as we have seen, the way certain contexts afford precise signals and others not. Other examples include the way the precision of one signal predicts the precision of the next (for example, if I implore you to "look over here!" then that lets you reasonably predict that the next signal over there, whatever it is going to be, will be quite precise too).

## PRECISIONS AND PREDICTION ERROR GAIN

So far, we have seen that to minimize prediction error, the brain needs to engage in second order statistics that optimizes its precision expectations. This is a matter of perceptual inference about perceptual inference. But we also need to see how, at a more mechanistic level, this happens and how it fits in with the basic prediction error minimization mechanism described earlier. Here, the guiding idea is that learning about precisions cannot just be more of the "basic" prediction error minimization described for recognising causes in the world. It should be conceived in terms of a mechanism that independently modulates the way prediction errors are processed in the perceptual hierarchy.

The fundamental purpose for precision processing is to enable the activities of internal models of the world to be driven by reliable learning signals: if there is confidence in a signal then it should be allowed to revise the hypothesis and if there is less confidence then it should tend to carry less weight. The assessment of confidence should therefore impact on the strength of the prediction error message being passed up through the system. Precision expectations are thus thought to be realized in systems that regulate the *gain* on prediction error units in the brain (Feldman and Friston 2010). The more precision that is expected the more the gain on the prediction error in question, and the more it gets to influence hypothesis revision. Conversely, if the reliability of the signal is expected to be poor, then the prediction error unit self-inhibits, suppressing prediction error such that its signalling is weighted less in overall processing.

The resulting mechanism makes very good sense from the point of view of a prediction error mechanism that implicitly represents the world. The basic idea is that imprecise prediction error cannot be used to refine models of the world if such revision is supposed to enable those models to generate ever better predictions. Such imprecise signals should be more brusquely suppressed than relatively more precise prediction error, which is then allotted more influence on the overall model. In both cases, however, there is overall minimization of prediction error since brusque suppression also minimizes prediction error. For this reason, the ability to deal with noise and uncertainty is not something over and beyond prediction error minimization.

The minimization of imprecise prediction error was presented as 'brusque': the signal is not explained away as much as deemed less informative and therefore dampened down. However there is a deeper connection with the idea that the perceptual hierarchy recapitulates the causal structure of the world. The overall pattern in the way prediction error is afforded gain or is inhibited will, if precision expectations are optimized, mirror the actual state-dependent levels of noise and uncertainty in the world. Even though the suppression is brusque and not accompanied by recognition of distinct hidden causes in the world, it adds to the idea that the brain maintains a rich, multi-layered model of the world. That is, the model even encompasses the quality of the causal commerce between the causes in the world and the organism.

Looked at from the outside, the brain will then have a complicated interplay between top-down suppression of prediction error and bottom-up facilitation of prediction. This makes it hard to predict what one might observe with various brain imaging techniques and physiological recordings. Top-down activity elicits activity as it suppresses prediction error, and precision optimization works against the suppression and in turn elicits more top-down predictive activity. To tease out patterns of activity for various perceptual inference situations researchers should then ideally consider full-factorial designs taking into account the factor concerning predictability and the factor concerning precision (for examples in this vein, see work by Floris de Lange and colleagues; Kok, Rahnev et al. 2011; Kok, Jehee et al. 2012).

## THE BASIC MECHANISM: MATTERS ARISING

The key parts and processes of the basic mechanism have now been introduced: prediction error is minimized via top-down predictions in response to precision weighted prediction errors. This basic mechanism links any two levels and is repeated as a basic building block of the perceptual hierarchy throughout the brain, schematically represented in Figure 7.

This constellation of prediction error mechanisms then forms the perceptual hierarchy, which maintains a rich representation of the world. To achieve this, each level of the perceptual hierarchy in the brain does not need to "attempt" to represent the world, nor does it need to be supervised by itself or by external perceivers. It just needs to minimize prediction error relative to the level below it, which ensures it is supervised by the statistical regularities caused in it by states of affairs in the world—thereby the brain comes to represent the causal structure of the world.

What we have seen is that all these parts are directly motivated by the imperative to minimize error; none of the parts need to appeal to different, independent principles. We can stick to just the one rule. This extreme parsimony is one of the greatest attractions about the whole framework.

The remainder of this chapter anticipates five interesting matters that arise from considering the workings of this basic mechanism. In later chapters, these matters will then recur as they are put into context and explored.

*Bottom-up vs. top-down: getting the balance right.* The basic mechanism for prediction error minimization is repeated throughout the perceptual hierarchy in the brain. It connects every pair of cortical processing levels with each other such that the best predictions for one level provide the prediction error input

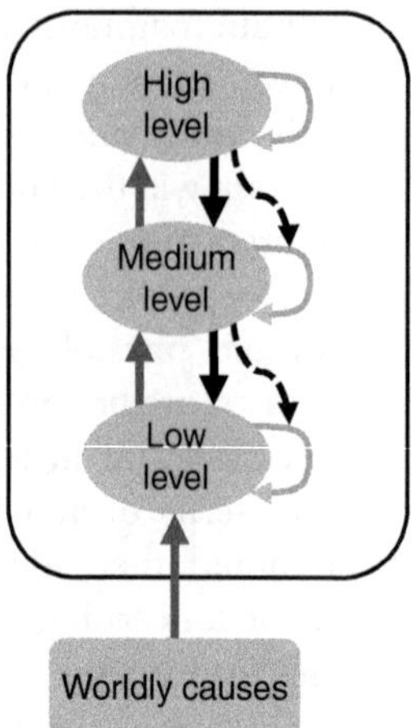


**Figure 7.** The perceptual hierarchy, second version. Dark grey arrows signify prediction error from world or from error units, black arrows arrows signify predictions from state units, the curved light grey arrows signify self-inhibition on error units as a function of expected precision, and dashed arrows signify contextual modulation from other units encoding predictions about precisions. Anatomically, the sources of forward connections are thought to be superficial pyramidal cells of the cortex and the sources of backward connections the deep pyramidal cells; for the full picture see, for example, (Friston 2010). This figure does not include arrows from the system to the worldly causes, representing action; this will be discussed in the next chapter.

for the next level up. In this way there is a cascade of precision-weighted messages passing between processing levels, spanning from the local and short-term to the global and long-term.

A number of things control the flow of messages between levels. On the one hand predictions are generated that explain away and literally suppress bottom-up messages. Predictions at low level can be (hyper-) parameterized by models much higher up in the hierarchy. What we also see is that the prediction error gain associated with precision expectations works to control the flow of prediction error up through the system: prediction error that is expected to be precise is allowed more weight than imprecise, poor quality prediction error messages.

This suggests something very fundamental about inference in the perceptual hierarchy. When a given level is confronted with prediction error, the gain on error units at that level determines how strongly that error should drive changes in prediction units at higher levels. A large gain will ensure a strong response somewhere higher up, a smaller gain will leave much of the revision to be done at the current level and lower down. Our expectations for precisions, which control that gain, therefore modulate the division of revisionary labour in the perceptual hierarchy.

This translates to a top-down vs. bottom-up balancing dynamic. More global, long-term, and general representations will tend to respond to prediction errors with large gain. In contrast, more local, short-term and particular representations will respond to prediction errors with less gain. Here, prediction error is conceived as a learning signal, where the gain modulates how learning proceeds. A large gain biases in favour of learning in a global sense, where the brain seeks to encompass what happens in relatively sweeping, detail-poor generalizations that see patterns rather than individual differences. A smaller gain, in contrast, biases more towards localized learning patterns, where the individual characteristics of particulars are the focus at the expense of fitting them in to larger patterns. These themes are discussed more in Chapter 7.

But prediction error gain can also be conceived as weighting the factors in Bayesian inference. When there is low gain on a prediction error, then the empirical prior expectations generating predictions will be weighted more in perceptual inference. For example, assume I am in a noisy or ambiguous situation where I don't expect to trust the incoming signal from the world much—a boisterous cocktail party, say. Assume also I cannot afford to dispense with inference, I must arrive at a perceptual conclusion (perhaps I am trying to maintain a conversation with someone I like). Then I'll give the sensory input little gain due to the noise, and perceptual inference will then be driven relatively more by prior expectations ("he is genuinely amused by my little joke; good, this is going well"). Or, to give a more sinister example, if you expect people to be talking about you, then you'll be more likely than not to experience your name being spoken out loud by someone at the noisy cocktail party.

*The urge to explain away.* An extreme example of the bottom-up–top-down dynamic may be seen in a well-known hallucinatory effect: cut a table tennis ball in two halves and put them on each eye, and listen to white noise on the radio and relax for a while (e.g., 30 mins). Many people will experience a range of different auditory and visual hallucinations such as simple auditory experiences (beeping, dripping, low grumbles, rustling, hissing), complex auditory experiences (trains, laughter, waterfall, roller-skates, music, party), as well as simple visual experiences (mist, dark patches, flashes of light, blue and yellow lights) and complex visual experiences (ambulances, planes taking off, faces, rising water). People also have bodily experiences (tilting, sinking, weightlessness, being squashed, detached from the body, floating) (Lloyd, Lewis et al. 2012).

This effect is often labelled 'sensory deprivation' but in reality there is still stimulation of the senses by white noise and the creation of a diffuse bright, visual Ganzfeld (i.e., the expanse of the table tennis balls filling the entire visual field). What does happen is that signal quality is severely deteriorated. Viewed from a prediction error perspective, this drives the participant to expect imprecision and shut down the gain on prediction error. In turn, top-down predictions are given an inordinate weight in perceptual inference. These inferences are now not supervised precisely by the current sensory input and therefore become hallucinations. It seems that even under extremely poor conditions of sensory input, there is an urge to engage in perceptual inference, even if it is almost completely unsupervised. The brain will jump to any conclusion to make sense of its environment.

This aspect of the prediction error minimization mechanism seems to me to be extremely important for understanding the workings of the mind. Expectations for precisions are central to learning styles and strategies, and to the way we weight prior belief against the incoming sensory signal in perceptual inference. It relates to the way we make sense of the world; for example, cases where we cannot "see the forest for trees". It also relates to the extent to which we in different situations are slaves of the senses, or caught in our own preconceptions. Moreover, different individuals may differ in how they set their gain and this may help explain individual differences in perceptual inference. For example, in the sensory deprivation study mentioned above (Lloyd, Lewis et al. 2012), people scoring high on a hallucination questionnaire concerning their everyday experiences also hallucinated more under sensory deprivation. Finally, it relates to the way we should conceive of the mind–world relation in the most basic terms.

We will return to these ideas in Chapters 7, 8, and 11. Notice for now that even though we are still working just with the fundamental imperative to minimize error, we can begin to see quite wide-ranging and deep consequences of this simple idea for our understanding of the mind. Note again that the posterior expectations about precision are optimized in exactly the same way as posterior expectations about hidden states of the world; namely using prediction error. In the case of precisions however, the prediction errors are the differences between the expected amount (sum of squared) of prediction error about hidden states and the amount predicted on the basis of current beliefs about precision. In other words, the imperative to minimize prediction error plays out again, when forming posterior beliefs about state dependent precision.

*Precision expectations and attention.* The complex, precision-weighted play between top-down prediction and bottom-up prediction error messaging marks out a particular functional role. Expectations of precision modulate where and how the perceptual system is focused. In particular, it determines which signal is given preponderance and it determines the extent to which there is a worldly focus, rather than an internal, more general, thoughtful or meandering focus. It turns out that this functional role fits *attention* extremely well. This gives rise to the idea that attention is nothing but optimization of precision expectations in hierarchical predictive coding (Friston 2009). We will pursue this idea in more detail in Chapter 9. It will turn out that prediction error minimization can begin to provide a unifying framework for understanding conscious perception and attention, and their relation to each other.

*A regress of higher order statistics?* Notice that precision optimization is presented here as an inference problem. Somehow the brain must extract regularities about precisions from the sensory signal its processing is confined to. There is something unsettling about this.

Recall that the need for precision optimization arises because the input from the world has state-dependent levels of noise and uncertainty, which must be extracted to enable the second-order statistics of assessing confidence in perceptual inference. If we cannot assess confidences, then we cannot use perceptual inference to learn about the world. If the system is engaged in this way in inference about confidences, then it seems it should also be engaged in third-order inference about confidences of confidences: how confident is it that it is getting a certain precision expectation right? But this proliferation of statistical orders has to bottom out before a regress ensues in which the system's capacity for perceptual inference is stifled because it never is completely satisfied in its confidence assessment.

By analogy, in ordinary statistical inference the means are assessed, and then the variations about the means are assessed in order to determine whether the distributions should be deemed distinct or not. If we also begin to worry too much about our assessment of the variation, then the regress of inference threatens. This is where hierarchical Bayesian inference comes to the rescue: at some level the prior beliefs become uninformative and there is no need to consider any further levels. This is illustrated nicely in the estimation of precision, where, generally, the precision of the precision of the precision is assumed to be a broad (uninformative) probability distribution. Prior beliefs about the precision of the precision are sometimes called hyperpriors. In short, an infinite regress implies an infinitely deep hierarchical model, which itself would be highly improbable and therefore highly unlikely to be embodied in a Bayes optimal brain.

This suggests that processing of precisions is more brutish than first-order prediction error processing in itself. The way gains are set in different contexts is more likely to be off-track because it is not itself subject to as stringent, hierarchically deep constraints as first-order statistical inference. This is a consequence of the perceptual system being a statistical machine that only has the input from the world to work on. If something goes wrong in estimating precision then this will be manifest in a decreased ability to minimize error in the long-term average. But this may be hard to correct, simply because there are less checks and balances on that part of the machinery.

Put differently, if there are problems with precisions, then there is less reality testing to resort to in order to resolve those problems. Specifically, there could be a tendency to explain the problems in terms of states of affairs in the world (first-order statistics) rather than issues having to do with the information channel (second-order statistics). This should make us expect that precision expectations (and hence attention) are involved in mental illness that pertains to reality-testing in various ways, such as schizophrenia. This will be part of our discussion in Chapter 7 on ways of getting the world wrong, and of schizophrenia and autism.

*Percepts, concepts, expectations.* It is normal for us to distinguish between on the one hand perception and experience, and on the other hand belief and thought. Similarly, we distinguish between percepts and concepts. When I see and hear the kookaburra in the tree in the garden I am not thinking it, I am experiencing it. When I afterwards consider whether it was a kookaburra or a cockatoo I am no longer experiencing it, I am thinking or believing something. Experiences are composed of percepts, thoughts are composed of concepts, as we might say.

There seems to be a qualitative difference between these ways of representing the world. Yet the perceptual hierarchy does not suggest that there is such a difference. It seems to incorporate concepts and thinking under a broader perceptual inference scheme. Moreover, it seems to connect percepts and concepts in an intimate way in the hierarchical modulation of prediction error signalling.

There are some deep and vexed philosophical issues buried here, which I cannot begin to resolve (see, e.g., McDowell 1994; for philosophical discussion of empirical issues, see Chadha 2009). But I do want to hint at how the distinctions look from a committed prediction error perspective. It seems the difference between percepts and concepts comes out in terms of a gradual movement from variance to invariance, via spatiotemporal scales of causal regularities. There is thus no categorical difference between them; percepts are maintained in detail-rich internal models with a short prediction horizon and concepts in more detail-poor models with longer prediction horizons. In the middle there are representations where we may be more uncertain and in some contexts label them 'percepts' and in other contexts 'concepts'. Of course, we can ask ourselves whether we have concepts for very low-level percepts (say the distinctive call of the kookaburra) and philosophers have trouble coming up with distinct answers. I suspect this is because there is no sharp distinction between these supposed categories.

The more fundamental category, underlying both perception and belief, is *expectation*. Representations are anchored in the expectations of internal models, and expectations are based directly on probability functions. Percepts are then basically shorter-term expectations and concepts longer-term expectations. This suggests that they are fundamentally the same kind of thing but it also gives some principled tools for making distinctions that may or may not fit with our propensity to label states percepts or concepts. Probability functions can be discrete distributions or continuous densities, and it may be that representations we are inclined to deem thought and belief are more tied to discrete distributions (over categorical entities) whereas continuous densities sit more naturally with what we call perception and experience (over continuous or parametric quantities).

Another difference between perception and belief is often said to be that I can have beliefs about things that are not there, such as the kookaburra I saw before or unicorns, but I cannot perceive such absent things. Again, I am not sure this is the best way to think about mental processes in the absence of sensory input. Thinking about things that are not there is not so different from trying to imagine (picture in my mind's eye) such things. In both cases it could be a matter of generating predictions in the absence of prediction error, albeit they are predictions at different time scales, harboured in different levels of the cortical hierarchy. This provides an interesting take on dreaming, as a generative process that proceeds in the absence of precise sensory constraints.

The important point for my purposes is that the perceptual hierarchy is best conceived as incorporating states we like to label concepts, and as sustaining beliefs, in addition to percepts. On this view, concepts and beliefs are fundamentally the same as percepts and experiences, namely expectations. Moreover, percepts and concepts interact in a complicated top-down–bottom-up manner and modulate each other, subject to how prediction error is best suppressed throughout the hierarchy. This opens the question of how and to what extent concepts can alter percepts and thereby determine what we perceive. This will be the focus of Chapters 5 and 6.

## SUMMARY: PASSIVE PERCEIVERS?

Now a point is reached where all the parts and processes of a basic prediction error minimization mechanism for perception have been marshalled. We have seen how hierarchical prediction error minimization can address the problem of perception and the sense in which representation of the world emerges in this process.

But the system is oddly passive as I have described it so far: it is standing back waiting to be exposed to sensory input. It is like an unmoving barnacle, stuck to a rock and able only to register and represent the world as it flows past. In so far as I have worked with a more active element, I have not explicitly made room for it in the mechanism.

For example, at the very beginning, I gave an example in which predictions of the evolution of sensory input caused by a bicycle were tested by actively walking around it to see if the input changed in the way predicted by the parameters of a bicycle hypothesis, rather than the very different way the sensory input would evolve if it was merely a cardboard poster of a bike. This is more than passive observation of the world, it is *active engagement* with the world, where one's sensory input is changed depending on one's own movement. Bayesian perceptual inference, and prediction error minimization is not yet obviously kitted out to deal with this.

This limitation is crucial because it is so natural to think of perceptual inference in active hypothesis-testing terms. For example, the analogy with science, which Helmholtz and Gregory both cultivate, strongly suggest a role for the kind of active intervention in the world characteristic of experimentation. As we will see next, there is indeed a natural but also profound role for action within the prediction error minimization scheme.

## NOTES

*Page 67.* ["Looked at from the outside . . ."] Here I discuss the difficulties in predicting patterns of brain activity for prediction error minimization given the opposed functions of prediction and precision weighted gain. Though the full picture is still emerging I think the mentioned studies are consistent with precision weighted prediction error minimization, see also Fang, Kersten et al. 2008; Summerfield and Koechlin 2008; Alink, Schwiedrzik et al. 2010; Todorovic, van Ede et al. 2011; de Witt, Kubilius et al. 2012.

*Page 69.* ["The urge to explain away . . ."] Here I am speculating about the sensory deprivation phenomenon. Note that there is considerable discussion about what happens in these conditions, and why; for discussion, see (Metzinger 2004: 102). This effect is relatively easy to try out for oneself.

*Page 70.* ["This aspect of the prediction error minimization . . ."] Evidence for the precision-weighting of prediction errors comes for example from a study that looked at base-level activity in the brain under conditions that manipulated precision expectations by presenting visual and auditory stimuli in varying levels of noise (Hesselmann, Sadaghiani et al. 2010): when precision was expected, gain appeared to be turned up, whereas gain was turned down and top-down prediction facilitated when imprecision was expected.

# 4

# Action and expected experience

A picture has emerged of prediction error minimization as the mechanism the brain uses in perceptual inference. This is in many ways an extremely attractive framework, which includes the following features:

(1) It can begin to deal with the problem of perception. The prediction error minimization framework can respond reasonably to the challenge of providing additional constraints on perceptual inference in a non-circular way, without vicious regress, and without being too intellectualist.
(2) By appealing to the notion of the perceptual hierarchy, prediction error minimization can begin to accommodate aspects of the phenomenology of perceptual experience, such as the mixture of variant and invariant representation in our first-person perspective.
(3) When the notion of precision expectations, and the corresponding notion of gain on prediction error, is built into the mechanism, it becomes possible to see how different overall processing patterns could arise, and how there can be modulation in the engagement of prior beliefs in different situations.
(4) The framework is extremely parsimonious, with a simple mechanism at its heart, replicated throughout the hierarchy and yet able to fulfil a number of computational functions.

The key idea in all this is to give the brain, skull-bound as it is, access to not only the incoming sensory data but to a comparison between this data and expectations about what the data should be, under a model of the world. The difference between these two is the prediction error, which is then a measurable quantity for the brain, and something that can act as a feedback signal on the way its models of the world are chosen and their parameters revised.

At the end of the last chapter, we noted that this presents a rather worrisome, passive picture of us as perceiving creatures. The picture seems to leave us completely hostage to our respective starting points. It is a trivial observation that we use our powers of agency to improve our position in the world and that we, of course, use the way we perceive the world to inform and guide agency. Without agency we would be stuck at our starting point, wouldn't be able to improve our situation in the world, and it would be difficult to see why we would be expending energy representing the world in the first place.

This suggests that the prediction error minimization idea should, at the very least, be consistent with the presence of agency. But more than that, perceptual inference should be seen as providing an essential part of what makes us beings with agency. We are engaged in perceptual inference at least in part *because* we need to act on the world.

In fact, however, there is a much deeper connection between perception and agency, which springs from the very idea of prediction error minimization. Perceiving and acting are but two different ways of doing the same thing.

The plan for this chapter is first to connect perceptual inference with action. This serves to strengthen the idea that perceptual inference is much like scientific hypothesis testing. An important part of this story concerns the idea that our model of the world includes representation of ourselves. Next, however, some issues arise, which prompt a more involved and challenging information theoretical approach. This second part of the chapter serves to show why action is so central to our fundamental understanding of why and how we engage in prediction error minimization. This is followed by an exploration of matters arising from this prediction error minimization take on action. This serves to show how perception and action are unified in the same prediction error minimization framework.

The chapter ends on a more general note, by summarizing the prediction error minimization mechanism and commenting on why the framework presented throughout Part I of the book is attractive, as well as on what challenges it confronts.

## ACTIVE INFERENCE IN PERCEPTION

Perceptual inference has been presented as a matter of selecting and adjusting hypotheses about the world in response to the prediction error they engender. It follows trivially that the upshot of the brain's prediction error minimization activities is to increase the mutual information between the mind and the world—to make the states of the brain as predictive as possible of the sensory input caused by events in the world. This account has largely suppressed a very obvious point, namely that the mutual information can also be increased by making the sensory input from the world more predictive of the states of the brain's model, that is by changing the input to fit the model rather than changing the model to fit the input.

The notion of prediction error minimization encompasses both directions of fit. That is, the model predictions will also be less erroneous the more the sensory input is made to fit the predictions. Given the basic idea that the main aim of the brain is to minimize prediction error, we should expect it to exploit this different direction of fit too. That is, we should expect that the brain minimizes prediction error by changing its position in the world and by changing the states of the world, both of which will change its sensory input. This can be captured in the expectation that the brain uses *action* to minimize prediction error.

Indeed, it falls natural to look for a role for action in perception. We are clearly very active in the way we go about perceiving the world. We explore, check out, test, look closer, feel, and so on, all of which are ways of actively engaging with the world and thereby changing the sensory input we receive. This is how I found it natural to describe perception from the very beginning. In Chapter 1, I used as the initial example perception of a bicycle where the posterior probability that it is a bicycle in front of me came about by predicting how the input would change if I *walked around* it and it really was a bicycle rather than a cardboard poster of a bicycle. Finding an example of perception that did not have an active element required the somewhat contrived cases of an individual locked in a room and trying to infer the source of a sound, or the idea of plugging a leaky dam. This was useful because I began by focusing on perception in fairly representational terms. But now action needs to be restored to its central place in our understanding of perceptual inference and prediction error minimization.

Another reason to focus on action in perception comes from the long-standing analogy, stressed as we saw earlier by both Helmholtz and Gregory, between perception and scientific hypothesis testing. Scientific hypothesis testing is paradigmatically a matter of experimentation, that is, active intervention by the scientist in causal chains in order to reveal causal relations. If perception is like hypothesis testing we should expect a similar notion of intervention in perception.

More broadly, this connects to contemporary debates about the difference between merely associationist, statistical inference, and properly causal inference, with the latter being based on interventions where independent variables are manipulated in a controlled fashion. Though statistical associations are necessary for causal inference, there is a limit to how much causal knowledge associations alone can provide us with. Passive observation can allow us to guess at causal relations between random variables *A* and *B*, but it is not until we actively test them that we will know whether *A* causes *B*, or *B* causes *A* or whether they perhaps have a common cause *C* (Pearl 1988; Pearl 2000; Woodward 2003).

So there must be a role for action in the story told so far: mutual information can be enhanced through action and action is obviously involved in perception. The basic idea would be that the brain uses a specific hypothesis about the world, predicts what the sensory input would be like were this hypothesis true, and then actively samples the world selectively to get this predicted sensory input. In other words, the brain generates a fantasy, a set of predictions that now do not fit with the current sensory input. This induces a prediction error that can be minimized by turning the fantasy into reality, that is, by acting to bring oneself into the predicted situation.

There is an immediate challenge here. Relying on action is relying on making the sensory input fit with our expectations, which seems to turn the proposal into a more unattractive analogy to *bad* scientific hypothesis testing. If the brain can do its job by using action to make the world fit its expectations, then it should just adopt expectations that are easy to make come true. For example, if you predict darkness then you will have minimized prediction error very nicely by closing your eyes. Clearly, in the long run, adopting such a strategy will not be beneficial. If the tiger is approaching and you minimize prediction error by closing your eyes, your success will be short-lived—and you may experience other prediction errors, when your predictions about not being eaten are violated. We therefore need to figure out how to accommodate this direction of fit for prediction error minimization without making the whole account implausible.

Luckily, it is easy to answer this challenge. Recall that simple examples of Bayesian inference rely on ordering hypotheses or models according to their prior probability, and then weighing this with the likelihood of a given model actually producing the sensory input in question. Here prior probabilities provided the needed additional constraint on that kind of inference. In the present case, additional constraints are also needed lest we adopt poor models that are too easy to confirm by changing our sensory input in the myopic and implausible ways exemplified above. The difference is that this time, the system needs to use the hierarchical hypothesis with the highest posterior probability and project it to actively test the world according to it.

The process is therefore first to rank hypotheses according to their posterior probabilities, delivered from perceptual inference of the type described in the previous chapters. Then the system actively samples the world to see if new sensory evidence can be produced, which is in accordance with the preferred hypothesis. In other words, we should selectively sample sensory input that conforms to our predictions; where, crucially, we predict that these sensations will minimize the uncertainty that persists about our hypothesis. If predictions are confirmed then the cycle continues—otherwise, the hypothesis generating those predictions is discarded in favour of a more plausible hypothesis that better minimizes prediction error.

For example, the brain receives some sensory information and by using Bayes' rule, implemented with prediction error minimization, it ranks the hypothesis that it is looking at a face higher than any other hypothesis, given the input. Clearly, it will have failed in prediction error minimization if it sidelines this hypothesis in favour of another, for example, that it is observing utter darkness. This is why active testing of hypotheses should proceed on the basis of predictions from the hypothesis with the currently highest posterior probability, in this case the face hypothesis. This rules out the implausible and dangerous case of minimizing prediction error in action by adopting the hypothesis that it is dark, then predicting darkness and successfully closing one's eyes to confirm this. That hypothesis has a very low posterior probability (unless it is bedtime) and will therefore not be a good basis of active sampling.

The situation is then this. Perceptual inference allows the system to minimize prediction error and thus favour one hypothesis. On the basis of this hypothesis the system can predict how the sensory input would change, were the hypothesis correct. That is, it can test the veracity of the hypothesis by testing through agency whether the input really changes in the predicted ways. The way to do this is to stop updating the hypothesis for a while, and instead wait for action to make the input to fit the hypothesis. If this fails to happen, then the system must reconsider and eventually adopt a different or revised hypothesis. For example, if the highest posterior goes to the hypothesis that this is a man's face seen in profile, then the system may predict that by moving visual fixation down towards the chin, a sample will be acquired that fits with this hypothesis. If it does, then this further enhances the probability that this is a man's face; if it does not fit then the system may have to go back and revise the hypothesis such that it expects the cause of its input to be, say, a woman's or a child's face (for computational modelling of face perception, see Friston 2012; Friston, Adams et al. 2012).

The question arises, why does the system need to engage in this kind of active inference if it has already settled on a hypothesis as having the highest posterior probability? What more is there to do than ranking hypotheses? There are two answers to this, which both have to do with reducing uncertainty, that is, with prediction error minimization.

The first answer is that in these cases, action enhances the posterior confidence in the inference. Action makes decent inferences better. For example, I am more confident I am looking at a man's face after successful active sampling of the world according to this hypothesis. This helps decrease uncertainty especially in cases where the winning hypothesis did not have a very much higher posterior than its competitors at the outset. In other words, action can help create much stronger minimization of prediction error than mere passive observation.

In this sense, action can make predictions more reliable—it can make the hypothesis stand out more distinctly against its competitors. Mere perception alone cannot do this, it is hostage to the whims of the incoming sensory data and cannot focus on one hypothesis and ask whether it is really true. As usual, Helmholtz aptly anticipates this idea: "We are not leaving ourselves passively only to the [sensory] impressions intruding upon us, rather we *observe* ["*beobachten*"], that is, we bring our organs into those conditions under which the impressions can be most precisely distinguished" (Helmholtz 1867: 438).

Notice that there is nothing un-Bayesian about this. Bayes' rule tells us how to update belief in the light of new evidence. What we do here is update belief in the hypothesis, which previously got the highest posterior, in the light of new evidence, namely the evidence attained by, for example, actively moving our eyes around.

The second answer to the question why the system should bother with processing of already favoured hypotheses is that it is efficient and quick to do so. What I have described so far sounds slow and laborious: I sit passively for a long time, amass as much sensory evidence as possible, patiently rank my hypotheses according to their priors and likelihoods, and then I actively test the best one by sampling the world according to its predictions. But often it is much quicker to form a quick impression of what the ranking might be and then actively test the hypothesis I merely surmise is best. In active testing I can pick a prediction that is made very likely by the hypothesis but very unlikely to occur by chance. If this prediction holds, then the likelihood term is weighted highly and the posterior probability is reinforced. In contrast, in passive observation I have to wait for observations to occur that are strongly predicted by the hypothesis.

There is a related, more systematic reason why action can help reduce uncertainty. In many cases of contextual interaction and other causal relations, observation alone will not distinguish between hypotheses where there is causation between two random variables and hypotheses where there is a common cause of covariation amongst the variables. The statistical associations can support either hypothesis equally well and only differences in prior probability allow one to get a higher posterior. Even though there is a favoured hypothesis in these conditions, it may not be favoured strongly. This leaves the system lacking in confidence that its inference is reliable. This is a type of uncertainty that can be efficiently reduced by intervening actively. For example, I can rule out that there is a causal relation from *A* to *B* if intervening on *A* fails to invariantly change *B*. Given that we can in fact engage in causal inference, and given that observation alone cannot distinguish between such causal models, we can see that we must be relying on intervention, that is, on active inference.

What we have so far is this. If the system can act on the world to change its own sensory input, then it can test its own hypotheses. It can do this in a Bayesian way by testing primarily those hypotheses that have high posterior probability, endowed from passive perceptual inference. Conditional on the evidence attained in action (for example, as one's eyes move around) a given hypothesis can increase its posterior probability. Through action, already selected hypotheses can be made much more reliable in the sense that they minimize prediction error very efficiently. Action in this sense of testing perceptual models is therefore a moment of prediction error minimization—it is *active inference.*

## MODELLING THE AGENT, AND ACTING

Putting action in these Bayesian terms makes it sounds as if there is a clear-cut distinction between perceptual and active inference. This is true in the sense that they are associated with very different functional roles: they have different directions of fit between models and sensory input. It is also very clear that the system must keep distinct its updating of models from its acting on those models to sample the world. But it is not as if the system needs to have distinct periods of inactivity and activity. As long as the functional roles associated with direction of fit are respected, we can accept that the system is moving around most of the time. Thus, viewed as a whole, the probability of getting a certain sensory input is conditioned on causes in the world jointly with the actions of the system itself. This allows perceptual inference to take into account change in sensory input that is due to the creature's own action.

This point is important because if the system has agency, then it can interact as a hidden cause with other hidden causes in the world. Therefore the system's model of the world needs to include a model of itself and its trajectory throughout the world just as it needs to model other hidden causes.

In this sense there is not much difference between the system's model of itself and its model of other interacting causes, such as the cat and the occluding picket fence we considered earlier. Just as there is a non-linear relation between cats and fences, there is a non-linear relation between acting systems like us and objects in the environment. For example, the simple occlusion of the cat by the fence can be modulated in many different ways by the perspective of the perceiving system (for example, the inference that it is a cat behind the fence takes into account the agent's shifting perspective as he or she walks past).

Here it is again necessary to invoke the perceptual hierarchy. Agency happens at many different time scales, from the very short micro-saccades where the eyes quickly fixate a new place, over hand-reaching movement, to long-term endeavours like climbing a mountain. Actions at these time scales each have different, interacting effects on the sensory input the system will receive. Therefore the internal representation of the agent needs to accommodate this hierarchy such that the effects of its actions on its sensory input can be predicted; in other words, so that its own movement does not inadvertently increase prediction error.

It is hard to resist the temptation here to think of this multilayered, internal model as in some sense a model of the *self*—of who and what the agent is (for discussion, see Metzinger 2009). I will indeed briefly pursue this intriguing thought later, in Chapter 12. The important point for now is the requirement that the internal, generative model needs to include a model of itself such that it can explain away its own sensory input, even when changes in that input are partially caused by itself. This means that the system can learn, and come to expect, patterns in how its sensory input would change given certain actions. For example, it can come to expect how things would change if the eyes fixate in a certain way, given it is a face one is looking at. These learned patterns can fuel action because they are essentially predictions of what the sensory input will be, given a generative model that includes parameters for hidden causes in the world including the hidden cause that is oneself.

Now consider how action comes about in a system that models itself and which can act. The representations of predicted sensory input are counterfactual in the sense that they say how sensory input *would* change if the system *were* to act in a certain way. Given that things are not actually that way, a prediction error is induced, which can be minimized by acting in the prescribed way. The mechanism for being a system that acts is thus nothing more than the generation of prediction error and the ability to change the body's configuration such that the antecedent of the counterfactual actually obtains and error is suppressed. Action therefore does not come about through some complex computation of motor commands that control the muscles of the body. In simple terms, what happens is instead that the muscles are told to move as long as there is prediction error. The muscles of the body are thus at the mercy of the prediction error generated by the brain's model of the way the world is expected to be like but isn't. Prediction error is then the simple mechanism that controls action.

An immediate objection to this story about what generates action is that it implies great variability in our routes to distal goal states. You might predict what your sensory input is like if you have moved your arm from location *A* to location *B* (or engaged in more complex action such as climbing a mountain) but there will be multiple ways of getting to the goal-state. In fact, there is in principle an infinite number of ways the organs of the body can be brought into any given condition. And yet we are able to move swiftly and in fairly uniform ways. The response to this worry must be that the brain represents not only the goal state but whole flows of expected sensory states, that is, how our sensory states will change as behaviour unfolds. In this way, behaviour can be controlled by prediction error in an online fashion, leaving little gap between the present state and the goal state.

Before moving on, I will make four brief comments to support this idea of action controlled by expectations for the flow of sensory states.

First, the modelled flow of sensory input concerns not only the kinds of exteroceptive input we have been focusing on so far, namely visual, auditory, and tactile input. It also concerns interoceptive input such as states of arousal, heartbeat, and proprioception and kinesthesis. This means, for example, that if proprioception is not as predicted, then the body is not configured in the right, predicted kind of way, and prediction error will then persist until reflex arcs have successfully fulfilled the predictions. Hence prediction error can control the body directly, in virtue of these more inner sensory channels. I will discuss this sort of control in abstract terms but notice that it essentially concerns reflexes and homoeostasis that are fundamental for survival, and that can be cast easily in terms of minimizing prediction errors or deviations from set points. A key future, explanatory task for the notion of active inference lies in connecting the ideas of sensorimotor predictions to more long term, abstract notions of motivation and action.

Second, at very low levels in the control hierarchy, which oversees movement at short time scales, it is likely there is a very restricted and therefore automated repertoire of parameters for how the body could be configured. This will facilitate inference because the expectations for how the sensory input changes will be harnessed in such simple reflexive patterns rather than having a full range of possible movement patterns to choose from. This may not be so different from the way perceptual inference at low levels seems to rely on rather restricted classes of model parameters (for example, what seems to be expectations for a restricted range of line orientations for different cells in early visual cortex).

Third, even though action is controlled through prediction error minimization based on expected flows of sensory states there may also be room for exploratory behaviour. Thus it is possible that movement sometimes begins with apparently random "jittering" or itinerant wandering about in different directions to figure out which direction produces best minimization of prediction error. This direction will then be favoured and will eventually lead to the goal state.

Fourth, this overall account creates a puzzle about how action is triggered, that is how the agent shifts from perceptual to active inference. This is because there will be competition between assessment of the actual proprioceptive input and the counterfactual proprioceptive input. Rather than changing the world to fit with the counterfactual predicted input, the system could just adjust its proprioceptive prediction in the light of the actual input—it could realize that it is not actually in that state. This would prevent action from arising. A mechanism is thus needed to ensure agency. One intriguing proposal is that this mechanism is attentional, focused on the precisions of proprioceptive input (Brown, Adams et al. 2013). Briefly put, action ensues if the counterfactual proprioceptive input is expected to be more precise than actual proprioceptive input, that is, if the precision weighted gain is turned down on the actual input. This attenuates the current state and throws the system into active inference. Being an agent then reduces to a matter of optimizing expected precisions of proprioception, which is a far cry from our commonsense idea of what makes an agent. If this is correct, then active vs. passive movement should be marked by attenuation of self-generated sensory input. There is evidence for this in many domains, such as our famous inability to tickle ourselves (Blakemore, Wolpert et al. 1998). This tickle effect ought then to be a very fundamental aspect of being an agent, and not something that can be easily upset by more superficial changes in how the tickling sensation is experienced. Recently, George van Doorn, Mark Symmons, and I (2014) found evidence of this by observing how the tickle effect can survive very extensive, unusual changes in body image: you cannot tickle yourself even if you have swapped bodies with someone else.

## BOUNDING SURPRISE

What we have thus far is a fairly simple account of how prediction error minimization can explain action when the direction of fit is that sensory input is changed to match predictions. Action enhances the reliability of favoured models of the world and ensues when prediction error is minimized for expectations of the evolution of sensory input, under a generative model of hidden causes that includes the acting system itself.

There is something slightly odd about this proposal. It is phrased in terms of testing predictions through sensory sampling of the world but the process seems more like engaging in self-fulfilling prophecies. For example, the system's prophecy is that it is viewing a face, this prophecy induces a prediction error that causes the system to selectively sample the world until the error is minimized. That is, by the very act of prophesying that it is a face, the system will do what it takes to bring itself into a condition where the prophecy is fulfilled.

Building perception on a basis of self-fulfilling prophecies sounds wrong-headed. However, at the level of proprioception and interoception, it is the very stuff of survival—it is the basis of physiological homeostasis and biological self-organization (e.g., maintaining body temperature and heartbeat); I will discuss this more later in this section. At the level of exteroception, we have already seen that even if there is such an element of self-fulfilling prophesying, this is not immediately damaging. Firstly, the prophecies on the basis of which the world is sampled are not pure, unfounded prophecies, or wishful thinking. They are hypotheses about the world with evidence in their favour. Secondly, the prophecies are not guaranteed to be self-fulfilling. It may be that the world does not cooperate to satisfy the predictions. For example, as I visually sample what I think is a face emerging from the bushes, I might encounter surprise—where the eyes should be there are just leaves. In that case I could persist *ad nauseam* until the prediction error is eradicated, for example by asking a friend to stick her head out from among the bushes in the right location. But the brain more often revisits perceptual inference, readjusts in the light of the new sensory input it has generated in active sampling, and elevates a new hypothesis, which then becomes the new and better prophecy.

However, there is a deeper level of understanding, on which it is much less obvious that the worry about self-fulfilling prophecies can be met in this straightforward way. To see this, recall from Chapter 2 that the prediction error minimization framework has been presented in terms of a computational mechanism that works with the aim to minimize surprise (that is, the long term, average surprisal or negative log likelihood of the sensory input). Because surprisal cannot be assessed directly, the mechanism manages to do its job by generating predictions and minimizing prediction error. Mechanistically, this is done by suppressing prediction error at multiple levels of the temporally ordered hierarchy.

This suggests that the mechanism should be able to change the surprisal. However we noted earlier that, as long as we operate with strictly passive, perceptual inference it is in fact unclear how surprisal itself can be made to change. Surprisal is a measure of how surprising it would be to observe the system in question being in certain conditions, or having a certain sensory input. It is clear that this can only be assessed relative to its normal state, the state we are most likely to find it in. This quantity cannot be changed by perceptual inference because perceptual inference changes the hypotheses about the sensory input and not the sensory input itself. Crudely put, perceptual inference can make you perceive that you are hurtling towards the bottom of the sea with something heavy around your feet but cannot do anything to change that disturbing sensory input which is fast taking you outside your expected states. In this sense, ironically, perceptual inference on its own is impotent as regards what was stated as its main purpose.

The obvious candidate for changing surprisal is agency. A creature endowed with agency can make useful predictions and act on its environment and its position in the environment to ensure it stays within the expected bounds. A more unlucky creature who cannot act would in principle be able to represent its environment but could not change the input it receives.

But is agency, in the sense we have described it so far, really sufficient to minimize surprisal? Action in the form of selective sampling on the basis of probabilistically favoured models can *change* the surprisal by changing the sensory input, but it is difficult to see how selective sampling can minimize surprisal. The problem is that surprisal is defined in terms of the expected states of the creature and if the creature is found outside of those states, then selective sampling cannot bring it back, it can only use active sampling to make its model of the high surprisal environment more reliable.

There seems to be only one way to solve this problem. The creature needs to be endowed with prior beliefs that tie it to its expected states. If it chronically expects to be in what are in effect its low surprisal states, then it will sample the world to minimize prediction error between those expectations and the state it actually finds itself in. To the extent it is able to minimize this error it will minimize surprisal, though of course it may be so far from low surprisal that it cannot make its way back (for example, deep in the sea with something heavy around its feet). These expectations are defining of the creature, because they tell us its expected states and thereby its phenotype.

There is no doubt that this idea is an ambitious and challenging part of the prediction error minimization framework. It asserts that at some level of description all creatures of the same phenotype share the same prior beliefs about what their sensory input should be and that this explains why we tend to find these creatures in certain states and not others. But, in a circular sounding way, the idea also asserts that the fact that we tend to find these creatures in certain states and not others explain why they have the expectations they have. Intriguingly, the upshot is that phenotypes are predictors (models) of their low surprisal states. Creatures chronically expect to be in those states so they must have a model of them on the basis of which they can generate predictions of sensory input that will maintain them in low surprisal. This is the tenet of self-organization and the "good regulator" hypothesis proposed by Ashby and colleagues nearly half a century ago, namely that from a formal point view, a system like the brain that maintains minimal entropy (or surprise) of an environment must model its environment (Conant and Ashby 1970).

It is again tempting to describe this in terms of self-fulfilling prophecies. Because of who we are we expect to be in certain states. So we prophesy that we will be in those states, and by the very act of prophesying those states we induce a prediction error that causes us to end up in those states. By predicting it we make it so. A related objection is that it presents us as fundamentally conservative creatures. We are inexorably drawn to the unsurprising states we expect to find ourselves in, never to new and exciting states. This may sound obviously false, since we have explorers, thrill-seekers, and curious people among us. It may also sound obviously false because it seems to predict we will rather forego normal, non-thrilling pleasures of life such as a good meal and a cocktail party in favour of a dark room (Friston, Thornton et al. 2012).

But these objections miss that it is in a rather trivial sense that we are conservative. Consider all the possible states we could be in, where these states can be defined in terms of their causal impact on our senses. There is no doubt it is more probable on average to find us in some of these states and not others (we are rarely going down in the sea with something heavy around the feet). To say that we are fundamentally conservative is then just to say that we tend on average to be found in some sensory states and not others. If we were not conservative in this sense we would be expected to be found in all sorts of conditions, which we clearly are not. A similar response applies to the objection concerning self-fulfilling prophecies. If we could make any old prophecy and if they were all self-fulfilling, then we would expect to find us distributed across all states of the world.

All sorts of exploratory, thrill-seeking, and curious activities are consistent with this kind of conservatism. It seems likely that we expect that in order to remain in low surprisal states on average we need to engage in exploratory behaviour even if such risky behaviour temporarily increases surprisal. For example, in order to protect myself from wind and weather I might explore different kinds of clothing material and lodgings, not always with luck.

Exploratory behaviour seems especially called for in creatures like us, with deep, complex perceptual hierarchies embodying long time scale representations. In order to obtain a distal goal state, highly complex and context-dependent expectations of sensory flows must be learned. For example, in order to test a scientific hypothesis, or in order to climb a high mountain, a long series of sensory inputs will be expected each of which can be confounded in innumerable ways by other sensory contingencies. It may be that learning such complex priors is facilitated by exploratory, itinerant behaviour.

Similarly, this kind of conservatism does not predict that we will seek out dark rooms over all other activities. If we were dark-room creatures, who were expected on average to be found in dark rooms, then that would be what we would expect and hence gravitate towards (if we were like marsupial moles, this would be our story, perhaps). But *we* are not defined by dark-room phenotypes, so we don't end up in dark rooms. We end up in just the range of situations we are expected to end up in on average. It is true we minimize prediction error and in this sense get rid of surprise. But this happens against the background of models of the world that do not predict high surprisal states, such as the prediction that we chronically inhabit a dark room (I return to the dark room issue in Chapter 8, where I relate it to the philosophical debate about misrepresentation).

This discussion began by worrying about the air of self-fulfilling prophesying in the initial story about the role of action in prediction error minimization. The worry could be dealt with in fairly simple, Bayesian terms but prompted a deeper and much more challenging and ambitious framework in which to understand prediction error minimization.

It may be tempting to keep the simpler, more straightforwardly Bayesian account of perceptual and active inference and leave aside the deeper story about minimizing surprisal through self-fulfilling prophesying. In many respects, the remainder of this book can be read in this less ambitious vein. This is because I primarily use the simpler story about the neuronal prediction error minimization mechanism when I apply the framework to problems in cognitive science and philosophy of mind. However, we cannot *understand* how this mechanism works without the idea that the brain does what it does because it needs to minimize surprisal. Specifically, prediction error bounds surprisal and the only reason for minimizing the error through perception and action is that this implicitly minimizes surprisal.

This issue goes to the heart of why this framework is so attractive. The prediction error framework builds on the mathematical idea that prediction error bounds surprisal and this is what yields a tractable target for a system like the brain. As expressed in Chapter 2, all the brain has to do is to minimize the divergence between probability distributions (or density functions) given by the sensory input predicted given its generative model and that given by the sensory input (or the recognition model). This sounds sophisticated and complex but can be achieved in a mechanistically simple way by organizing neuronal activity such that it in the most efficient way counteracts sensory input, on average and at multiple levels of the cortical hierarchy. For the first time we can see and describe in precise mathematical terms not only what the brain needs to do, we can also see that this is something the brain can actually do, as the neuronal machine it is. This is what we lose if we throw out the more ambitious story about surprisal, phenotypes, and self-fulfilling prophecies (for computational models and more background, see Friston and Stephan 2007; Friston, Daunizeau et al. 2009; Friston, Daunizeau et al. 2010; Friston 2012).

At this stage it is clear that one could embark on an exploration of some of these ideas in terms of adaptation and fitness. How is it that some creatures end up with the phenotypes they have, why do we have different species, why do some species have more exploratory behaviour and deeper cortical hierarchies than others? (For discussion relating to evolution, see Badcock 2012). It is also obvious there can be discussions of the genetic bases for the kinds of expectations that help keep us in low surprisal states, as well as of what those expectations might be. Similarly, it is tempting to expand into discussion of the mentioned ideas of self-organizing, dynamical systems (for an early statement, see Ashby 1947).

I will not engage these types of question directly here. I am primarily interested in what the account says about our understanding of the world and our place in it as perceivers and agents. For this project, we mainly need the following ideas: the brain is only concerned to minimize prediction error; prediction error can be minimized in perceptual inference, where hypotheses about the world are updated in the light of their ability to predict sensory input; and prediction error can be minimized in active inference, where the confidence in hypotheses is updated in the light of the way sensory input can be brought to fit their predictions. In short, we update our models of the world in the light of sensory input, and sample sensory input in the light of our models of the world. When harnessed in an organ like the brain, with an appropriate hierarchy, with a structure for message passing between levels, and ability to change in response to changing input (i.e., plasticity) this can explain the nature of perception and action in a unified way.

## ACTIVE INFERENCE: MATTERS ARISING

Action is described as an inferential process because, just as perception, it proceeds by prediction error minimization. Hypotheses with high posteriors are strengthened probabilistically if the selective sampling of their consequences for sensory input come out true. Acquiring those samples implies that the sensory system in question moves around or changes the environment, which is action. In this section of this chapter I note some topics of interest that arise from these ideas. These topics anticipate discussion in subsequent chapters.

*Desire and belief.* Action is mostly described in terms of how we act in accordance with our wants, intentions, and desires, given our beliefs. The question then arises how the description of action in terms of prediction error minimization can accommodate those kinds of mental states. This question is not easy to answer quickly. What drives action is prediction error minimization and the hypothesis that induces the prediction error is a hypothesis about what the agent expects to perceive rather than what the agent wants to do. If this idea is expanded to standard examples of desires, then desiring a muffin is having an expectation of a certain flow of sensory input that centrally involves eating a muffin. This means the concept of desire becomes very broad: any hypothesis associated with a prediction error can induce a want or an intention or a desire, simply because such prediction error in principle can be quenched by action.

What makes the desire for a muffin a desire and not a belief is just its direction of fit. Both are expectations concerning sensory input, and the "motivator" is the same in both cases, namely the urge to minimize prediction error. For action specifically, it is not obvious that a notion of reward, value, or utility is needed to explain action. The way we learn to act through reinforcement can be explained in terms of prediction error minimization rather than a desire for reward (Friston, Daunizeau et al. 2009). It is then tempting to say that strongly desired states are states associated with much and reliable prediction error minimization. There is an element here of mere redescription. Reinforcement learning and optimal control theory are not substantially revised by the prediction error minimization framework. Rather, their notions of reward and cost-functions are shown to be absorbed into the priors of the prediction error minimization mechanism. The point of this is to unify perception and action and to show how one mechanism, namely prediction error minimization, can account for both.

It may seem odd that all action reduces to a kind of inferential process akin to perception. But this way of putting things is in fact a little disingenuous, since we could just as well have said that perception reduces to a kind of agency. In fact, early formulations of some of these ideas came from computational theories of motor control, which can be generalized to encompass perception (Kawato, Hayakawa et al. 1993; see further work on forward models, e.g., Wolpert, Ghahramani et al. 2001). This worry is then somewhat misguided because the starting point is that the system in question needs to minimize its prediction error, and then the observation is made that this can be done in different ways. There is a reason for sticking with the sensory idiom, however. The key element in both ways of minimizing prediction error is what happens at the sensory interface between the mind and the world (either exteroceptively or interoceptively).

I think one price to pay for this approach to desire is that in the most fundamental sense we do not get to choose our desires—rather, our desires chose us. Our phenotype determines the kinds of states we expect to be in on average, and these expectations ensure, through the inferential process of prediction error minimization, that we end up in those states. I think this price is worth paying because there is ample scope for individual differences in the many highly context-dependent state trajectories we need to learn and chose among to obtain those fundamental goals. Our individual starting points and our learning histories are different and this predicts many different choices of strategies to get our distal goals. As we saw, this allows both exploration and avoidance of low sensory input states, like the dark room.

The picture of the human mind that goes with this appears very *indirectly* related to the world. As mentioned, there are many different ways to achieve distal goals and so agency depends on learning ways to get there, ways that are consistent with long-term average minimization of prediction error. In active inference, this calls for prior beliefs about the flow of sensory input one can expect to receive. For both belief and desire, what matters is how things look 'from the inside': as long as the sensory input is as expected and internal prediction error is minimized it matters little whether a state is a belief or desire, or what the external world is like, or what things we desire. In this sense organisms like us do not really "appreciate" what the model represents or what things we expect to happen. We do not purposefully aim to represent the world or to desire the world to be in a certain way. We just minimize prediction error and thereby attain beliefs and desires. However, though this is a very 'internal' perspective on the mind, it does not come with the disconcerting notion of self-fulfilling prophecies that drift apart in costly ways from what is true. When we update hypotheses and act on the world we are deeply in tune with the states of affairs in the world—this is what the prediction error construct gives us. Prediction error increases when we organize the brain, our bodies, or the world poorly and that forces us away from those states.

*Balancing perceptual inference and active inference.* In this chapter a particular vision of action is presented, based on existing neurocomputational theories. The underlying mechanism is one of prediction error minimization, though with a different direction of fit than we saw for perceptual inference. Now I want to draw attention to the combination of action and perception, and note what seems a very fundamental combination of processes emerging from the prediction error minimization ideas.

Prediction error is a bound on surprise that organisms can assess and try to minimize through perceptual inference (revising the models and predictions of the world). Perceptual inference can lead to a tight bound on surprise but cannot itself reduce the surprise. Conversely, action can reduce surprise by compelling us to occupy unsurprising states but cannot itself make us select good hypotheses about the world (since the hypotheses stay the same for the duration of action). Acting on beliefs does not ensure the truth of the beliefs but can reduce the uncertainty about them by minimizing prediction error.

The different directions of fit suggest that to optimally engage in prediction error minimization, we need to engage in perceptual inference and active inference in a complementary manner. Perceptual inference is needed to create a tight bound on surprise, so that active inference has a sound starting point. This is obviously crucial since engaging in active inference on the basis of an inaccurate conception of what the world is like is unlikely to land the organism in unsurprising states in the long run. If you want to dodge the bullets rather than stay put you'd better know exactly when the shots are fired.

Action alone is not enough. Often action induces new prediction error, because the world is a complex and uncertain place. Therefore it pays to suspend active inference and revert to perceptual inference so that the bound on surprise can be readjusted, before action is again taken. As you are hit by a surprise bullet you might pause, briefly, to update your model of when they are fired and then reconsider your strategy for action. Perception alone is not enough either. In the long run it is not efficient to aim for only correctness of our generative models—it will do nothing to place us in low-surprisal states.

We should therefore aim to alternate between perceptual and active inference. This alternation of inferential activity seems to me a very fundamental element of who we are and what we do. Getting the weighting of these inferential processes right is crucial to us: if the bound on surprise is not minimized enough by perceptual inference, then action suffers. If we persist with minimizing the bound for too long before we act, then we become inactive and end up spending too much time in states that are too surprising in the long run. If we persist with active inference for too long without pausing to revisit perceptual inference, then inaccuracy mounts and action becomes inefficient. If we react too soon to mounting prediction error during active inference then we get lost in overly complex and detailed models of the world.

It is easy to imagine that people differ significantly in how they manage this delicate alternation between perceptual and active inference—and that this variability depends upon the precision of beliefs about active sampling of the world. Different genetic set-ups, different developmental and learning patterns, and different contexts can sway us towards quick action, slow learning, and different oscillations between them. Perhaps such matters are involved in some developmental disorders and mental illnesses, such as autism, where patients seem to get stuck in perceptual inference, and schizophrenia where patients may operate with less than optimal generative models. We will revisit some of these questions in Chapter 7.

There will be an intricate relation between how perceptual and active inference is dealt with and other processes that emerge from the prediction error minimization framework. One such process concerns expected precisions. The extent to which we expect precision in prediction errors determines (modulo other contextual factors) how deeply we sample the world and how much we rely on prior beliefs. Hence, if expected precisions are far from optimal, then we may over- or under-sample the world and fail to engage active inference in an efficient manner. Another process concerns optimizing the complexity of models and how to balance complexity against their accuracy of internal models. We touched on this issue in the discussion of overfitting in Chapter 2. A very accurate model of the world will have states and parameters for every little thing that happens. But such a model will be extremely complex, expensive to maintain, and it may end in overfitting. In other words, it will fail to generalize to new settings and, over time, produce more prediction errors. Moreover, many of the represented states of affairs will be irrelevant for subsequent active inference. So it pays to deploy some version of Occam's razor such that the simplest model that will facilitate active inference in the long run is chosen without oversimplifying so much that the sensory input during action becomes poorly predicted. This requires us to engage in some kind of Bayesian model selection, which has an implicit penalty for complexity. Again, getting the balance of complexity and accuracy right will be a complex, context-dependent affair.

Our current state of mind will depend on how we attend to all these dimensions of perception, action, precision, complexity, and context-sensitivity, and on how the combination of them all enables prediction error minimization in a particular situation. As a very rough characterization of a normally functioning mind, the average mental state would be such that if engaged in action, perceptual re-assessment is never far away, and if engaged in perception, action is often imminent; the fineness of perceptual grain is rarely extreme nor exceedingly abstract; and our perceptual and active inferential processes are mostly drawn towards precise rather than imprecise sensory input.

## PREDICTION ERROR MINIMIZATION: CHALLENGES

With these last comments, the discussion of action is concluded, and together with the previous chapters of this Part I of the book, I have brought everything to the table we need for the discussions in the remainder of the book. It presents an attractive package, which obviously has great explanatory potential and can be explored in a wide variety of ways.

There are of course challenges to the prediction error minimization framework as presented so far. These challenges cluster around two themes, which I will address in turn below:

1. What is the *evidence* that the brain is (only) engaged in prediction error minimization? How can the idea be tested? What does it predict? Why should we believe it?
2. How *much* can the prediction error minimization principle explain? *How* (given its level of generality) does the prediction error minimization scheme explain anything?

A primary challenge for the framework is accommodating the multitude of different empirical findings from the many different fields of research it applies to. The danger here is that the framework is phrased in such general terms that it is easy to fit in all sorts of evidence in a just-so manner. By assuming convenient priors and likelihoods it is possible to make Bayesian "sense" of pretty much any kind of behaviour ("why do some people commit suicide? Because that's how they minimize surprise"). This means that the theory can appear unfalsifiable.

A similar problem could be mounted for the most abstract formulation of evolutionary theory. But this does not make us think Darwin was fundamentally wrong. There are mountains of evidence in favour of evolution coming from its more specific predictions (and the theory has itself evolved in the light of the data) (Dawkins 2009).

Something similar potentially holds for prediction error minimization and the more general idea of the free energy principle (which basically says that creatures act to minimize the amount of prediction error over time). It will be tested in specific terms, based on quantitative predictions from specific computational models. Of course, such testing has already begun. I have mentioned quite a few studies in the previous chapters and notes, and there are further, concerted efforts to, for example, use dynamic causal modelling in brain imaging to discern whether the brain deals with prediction error in associative learning in the way predicted by prediction error minimization (den Ouden, Friston et al. 2009; den Ouden, Daunizeau et al. 2010), repetition suppression (Todorovic, van Ede et al. 2011) and mismatch negativity (Garrido, Friston et al. 2008; Garrido, Kilner et al. 2009). Similarly, there are now numerous quantitative computational models, sometimes complemented with psychophysical tests of their predictions, of specific phenomena such as reinforcement learning (Friston, Daunizeau et al. 2009), attention (Feldman and Friston 2010), eye movement in face perception (Friston, Adams et al.

2012) and occlusion (Adams, Perrinet et al. 2012), and illusion perception (Brown and Friston 2012).

There is a way to turn around the challenge about whether there is evidence for the network. We know that the brain's organization is extremely complex and bewildering, with hundreds of cell types, multitudes of neurotransmitters, and intricate patterns of long and short range neuronal connections. This is evidence against a simple mechanism, re-iterated Lego-block style throughout the brain (Koch 2013). I am hopeful that in time, more and more evidence will come in that will show how this complex organ is in fact engaged in prediction error minimization (for example, in terms of extracting the top-down and bottom-up pattern of activity and their time course in the cortical layers of microcolumns of the visual cortex; perhaps in the style of electrophysiological work using multi-contact transcortical electrodes; for an example of this methodology, see Maier 2008). The challenge can also be met by noting the many aspects of the prediction error scheme, which I have focused upon throughout this first part of the book. Even though the basic idea of prediction error minimization is simple, the implementation of the mechanism is highly complex in a way that calls for many different types of parts and processes: there is a need for first order and second order statistics in the brain's attempt to optimize precisions; there is a need to distinguish perceptual from active inference, and their different directions of fit; there is a need to maintain hypotheses across multiple timescales, calling for different kinds of plasticity; and there is a need to maintain some overall balances, for example between perceptual and active inference. It seems likely that very many different neuronal parts and processes have evolved to maintain these many functions, which enable prediction error minimization and which allow us to fine-tune it in perception, action, and attention.

The other type of challenge flows from the explanatory ambition of the framework. It is meant to apply to all aspects of perception, attention, and action. This means it should be able to provide attractive solutions to recalcitrant problems in cognitive science and philosophy of mind. The challenge in doing so is to avoid just-so stories. That requires avoiding priors and likelihoods that are posited only in order to make them fit an observed phenomenon. To avoid just-so stories any particular ordering of priors and likelihoods should be supported by independent evidence, which would suggest that this ordering holds across domains. Mostly, I shall seek to avoid just-so stories by building specific accounts on just the tools provided by the prediction error minimization mechanism rather than relying on any specific ordering of priors and likelihoods.

Explanations can be attractive for many different reasons. Perhaps they explain a lot of evidence, or key evidence, or they can explain some evidence with great precision, or they can be fecund in terms of generating new research questions, or they are simple, or they are unifying, or integrate well with prior knowledge, and so on. So often one must weigh up such explanatory virtues when deciding which explanation is best. It is not always obvious which assessment policy is best, and different contexts and interests may call for different approaches and trade-off between virtues. But in general, one should be able to do this kind of weighing of explanatory "bestness", and then engage inference to the best explanation (for an excellent treatment of inference to the best explanation, see Lipton 2004). Inference to the best explanation is capturable in Bayesian terms: namely in terms of which hypothesis best explains away the evidence. So Bayes' rule applies to the Bayesian brain hypothesis. Indeed, like natural selection, the principle of free energy minimization can be applied to itself. In this meta-theoretical approach, models and hypotheses about ourselves should minimize free energy through a judicious balance between maximizing accuracy (explaining empirical observations) and minimizing complexity (thereby providing a parsimonious and unified account of the facts).

The concrete challenge is to pick the right assessment of the explanatory project pursued in this book. Clearly, the project cannot be expected to excel at all explanatory virtues. Personally, I am attracted to the framework because it appears to explain key, philosophical issues mechanistically and as unified under one neuronal mechanism. The explanation is sometimes mechanistic, showing how a phenomenon arises from the properties of the mechanism, and sometimes the explanation is unifying, redescribing a phenomenon to bring it into the prediction error fold, and showing how it connects to other phenomena. Of course, I do not provide much in terms of alternative explanations here. Part of the reason is that I don't know any other theory that can as much as begin to solve the problem of perception—competing theories do not appear to pass the very basic "bestness" hurdle for candidates for inference to the best explanation, namely that of being explanations in the first place. The burden of the book is then to demonstrate that the prediction error minimization scheme is not merely the best out of a poor bunch of explanations, but is good in its own right.

## SUMMARY: TOOLING UP FOR UNDERSTANDING THE MIND

Now we can begin to form a systematic picture of the nature of the prediction error minimization mechanism that is iterated throughout the brain. This allows us to "tool up" for the project of Part II of this book, where the framework presented in Part I is put to work.

The mind works by minimizing prediction error. This explains perceptual inference and, in the shape of active inference, action too. The emerging picture is that the organism needs to alternate between perceptual and active inference; it needs to assess precisions optimally so as to efficiently balance sensory sampling against reliance on prior belief; it needs to balance the complexity of its models against their accuracy and usefulness in active inference. All of these processes involve context-dependence and depend on prior learning. Architecturally, generative models are maintained in a perceptual hierarchy that makes sense of our first-person perspective and which reconceives sensory input as, functionally speaking, a feedback signal on the predictions based on the generative model.

As a whole, this presents the sophisticated implementation of the simple prediction error minimization idea. It delivers a complex, layered functional role for perception and action, for which neuroscience can provide the realization in terms of hierarchical, interconnected patterns of synaptic connectivity, synaptic plasticity, and synaptic gain.

There are weighty reasons to find this framework attractive. It has great unificatory power, it promises to explain in detail, it can be modelled in precise mathematical terms, and evidence is coming in that the brain is in fact working this way, though much empirical work needs to be done. From a philosophical point of view it is attractive because it offers to explain perception, action, and attention on the basis of a naturalistic mechanism that seems up to the task. There are also, as we just saw, challenges to respond to and pitfalls to avoid.

With these few but powerful tools it is possible to re-asses, recalibrate, and reconceive many issues in philosophy of mind and cognitive science. In some cases this allows us to see new kinds of solutions to long-standing problems.

## NOTES

*Page 75.* ["At the end of the last . . ."] Here I say that we use perception to guide action. This is a commonplace but is in fact controversial because there is discussion of the extent to which we use *conscious* perception to guide action. Visual illusions for example have surprisingly little effect on movement (Aglioti, DeSouza et al. 1995). I discuss this a little further in Chapter 7.

*Page 76.* ["Perceptual inference has been presented . . . "] Formally, mutual information is symmetric so that the mutual information between $P(a)$ and $P(b)$ is the same as the mutual information between $P(b)$ and $P(a)$. Mutual information is the KL divergence between $P(a, b)$ and $P(a)P(b)$, and whereas the KL divergence is not in general symmetric, it is in this instance (see notes to Chapter 2).

*Page 77.* ["Indeed, it falls natural to look for a role for action in perception . . . "] Here I focus on the active element in perception. This idea has been taken up and made central to an understanding of perception under the heading of enactive perception, and related to embodied, situated cognition. This is sometimes taken to be a severe challenge to the idea of internal representations on which prediction error minimization is based (O'Regan and Noë 2001; Noë 2004). It seems clear however that the prediction error approach can encompass the active element of perception without relinquishing internal representations. Conversely, though there is much to admire in the enactive approach, I think it is doubtful it can ultimately do without just the kinds of prediction-generating internal models described here (see, e.g., Block 2005).

*Page 77.* ["Another reason to focus . . . "] The quote from Helmholtz is my translation. The original in full is "Wir überlassen uns nämlich nicht nur passiv den auf uns eindringenden Eindrücken, sondern wir *beobachten*, das heisst wir bringen unsere Organe in diejenigen Bedingungen, unter denen sie die Eindrücke am genausten unterscheiden können".

*Page 82.* ["Before moving on . . . "] Predictions of the flow of sensory states occur as prior beliefs in the prediction error minimization scheme. They play the role of control functions in optimal control theory but when interpreted as priors they can be treated in the same way as perception (Friston, Samothrakis et al. 2012). There are many further aspects to learning and shaping these expectations of flow, including exploratory elements, learning from action behaviour and ideas such as that some goal states are obviated in a way that triggers renewed exploration and action (Friston, Daunizeau et al. 2010).

*Page 90.* ["Balancing perceptual inference and active . . . "] The importance of oscillating between perception and action is also discussed by Metzinger (2004: Ch. 6–7), within his framework of theoretical and practical 'phenomenal models of the intentionality relation'.

*Page 91.* ["We should therefore aim to alternate . . ."] Here I describe the importance of not getting stuck with one active or perceptual inference. This is consistent with recent work on autovitiation of the states visited by self-organising systems, in other words it relates to "a delicate balance of dynamical stability and instability" (Friston, Breakspear et al. 2012: 2).

*Page 92.* ["There will be an intricate . . . "] The notion of complexity reduction has given rise to an interesting approach to sleep and dreaming as essentially the brain taking the opportunity to engage in complexity reduction during periods where the light tends to be bad so that the precision of visual input diminishes the reliability of normal prediction error minimization through perception and action (Hobson and Friston 2012).

*Page 92.* ["Our current state of mind . . . "] This view of medium level fineness of perceptual grain seems to me compatible with proposals concerning consciousness on which experience is a kind of middle level affair, neither too high nor too low in the perceptual hierarchy; see discussion in (Jackendoff 1987; Koch 2004; Prinz 2012).

# Part II

# The World

# 5

# Binding is inference

The prediction error minimization framework described in Part I is extremely ambitious—it gives the organizing principle for brain function as such. It should then encompass and illuminate all aspects of perception and action, including aspects that cognitive science and philosophy of mind view as problematic or poorly understood. In this second Part of the book, the prediction error minimization mechanism is therefore applied to long-standing discussions in cognitive science and philosophy of mind. These discussions primarily concern the mind's grasp of the world—how we manage to represent states of affairs in the world, and how we sometimes misperceive the world.

In this chapter, the focus is the binding problem, how the brain manages to discern properties of objects in the world and correctly bind these properties together in perception. The next chapter looks at the extent to which our perception of the world is penetrated by our prior beliefs, and later chapters look at misperception, reality testing, and mental disorder. Part III delves into the structure and nature of the mind, with a focus on attention, consciousness, the deeper nature of perception, and the self.

The project in this chapter is to build a reasonably detailed response to the famous binding problem entirely from the perspective of the prediction error minimization scheme. The binding problem concerns the ability of the brain to bind together sensory attributes in spite of processing them in different regions throughout the brain. It turns out that prediction error minimization dissolves this problem by virtue of what I in Chapter 2 called the profound reversal of the way we normally conceptualize the role of sensory input. Instead of binding disparate sensory attributes, the brain assumes bound attributes on the basis of sparse input and prior learning, and queries the sensory input on the basis of this assumption—the disparate parts of sensory input are feedback to the brain's unified hypothesis. This provides an attractive understanding of perceptual binding: it is just the kind of causal inference that the brain is involved in in any case. Specifically, binding is inference to common causes, located at the shallow end of the causal hierarchy of the world. It is also an important testing ground for the framework. If it applies satisfactorily here, then we have more reason to believe it is a correct account of perceptual experience.

## THE BINDING PROBLEM AND CAUSAL INFERENCE

In Part I, perceptual inference was presented as a matter of using learned statistical regularities and prediction error minimization to infer causes in the world from their sensory effects on us. There is a sense in which this can seem to leave the job half done. Perception is not just the flooding of perception with representations of sensory attributes. Somehow these attributes are ordered and synthesized so that they all belong together in the right way and with the right objects. For example, when I look at a red ball and a green cube, the sensory attributes for colour and shape are at least in part processed in different parts of the brain and yet the sensory attributes are bound together neatly in a percept of a red ball and a green cube, rather than a green ball and a red cube, and rather than four separate sensory attributes that just float about. The problem of how the brain accomplishes this binding of sensory attributes is known as the *binding problem* (von der Malsburg 1981; Treisman 1996).

However, we should expect some reasonable accommodation of binding in the prediction error story. When the perceptual hierarchy was introduced (in Chapter 1), it was taken for granted that attributes are bound to their proper objects because at higher levels of the perceptual hierarchy there are representations of causal regularities governing objects, such as the relation between the fitness of a bird and its singing pattern. Such representations were claimed to work as top-down control parameters on faster changing regularities concerning the succession of the individual notes of the song. Here a number of sounds are bound under one percept, for example, under the percept of a fit bird—each individual note is not processed in splendid isolation. A similar story can be told about visual binding where longer term expectations shape perception of low-level sensory attributes. So there seems to be some element of binding coming automatically with the perceptual hierarchy, but it is not yet clear what it is or how it connects to the binding problem.

There are a number of ways to approach the binding problem (Roskies 1999). Commonly, it is the idea that sensory attributes are processed separately but perceived as bound, and so that some mechanism in the brain must be responsible for binding. However, there is no agreement on the kinds of mechanisms people have suggested for doing this job. For example, it could be a top-down attentional mechanism that goes through the possible binding combinations in a scene one by one before it decides which are spatiotemporally overlapping, and that then binds the ones that are overlapping (cf. the type of theory proposed by Treisman and Gelade 1980; Treisman and Schmidt

1982). This is an influential and promising approach but it does seem to predict a slow and computationally cumbersome mechanism at odds with the mostly effortless and quick process of binding. A different approach relies on a hierarchical, bottom-up process of object recognition where higher-level units code for invariant object recognition and are activated by preferred lower levels representing spatiotemporally sensitive (variant) information. This allows extraction of invariant object recognition in spite of the proliferation of features at lower levels, and since the higher-level units pick out a subset of lower level features it can be said to bind them (Riesenhuber and Poggio 1999; Rolls 2012). This is also influential and promising but seems to require higher-level units for any possible bound percept, which seems highly demanding.

From the point of view of the prediction error minimization scheme, both approaches are relevant. The top-down, attention-based theory would relate to both prediction activity and to precision optimization of prediction errors. The bottom-up, hierarchical theory obviously relates to the perceptual hierarchy and accommodates not only invariant object recognition but also variant, view-dependent perception of bound features. The question is then whether the prediction error approach brings anything new to the debate?

Here is what I will take as the explanatory target. What we are after is some reasonable prediction error related mechanism that can explain why and how, in perception, sensory features are bound together even though they are processed in a distributed way and at different processing speeds in the brain. Ideally this should be explained by prediction error minimization without incurring explanatory burdens elsewhere.

The basic idea will be this. Distributed sensory attributes are bound together by the causal inference embodied in the parameters of the current hypothesis maintained in the perceptual hierarchy. The hypothesis is, for example, that there is a red, bouncing ball out there so the prediction will be that the redness and the bouncing object co-occur spatiotemporally—that they are bound. The binding problem is then dealt with by default: the system assumes bound attributes and then predicts them down through the cortical hierarchy. If they are actually bound in the states of the world (if the ball is indeed red), then this top-down activity will minimize prediction error (within expected levels of noise), and they will be perceived as bound (this story was hinted at in (Hohwy 2007a; Hohwy 2012); the proviso about expected levels of noise is going to be important as we will see towards the end of this chapter). This as it were turns the binding problem inside out because bound percepts are predicted and evidence sought in the input that will confirm the prediction. I will flesh out that story below.

In principle, there is ambiguity when the system is presented with something red and something round: either they could be independent causes (a red thing and a round thing) or they could be dependent causes—causes that are bound in some way (a red, round thing). This means that activities of two hypotheses will be competing to explain away the sensory input: we can call them the independence hypothesis and the binding hypothesis. Resolving this competition is at the core of the binding problem, from a causal inference perspective. Of course, we can make things more complex by introducing all the many more sensory attributes characteristic of a natural scene. Then we would get an even more difficult causal inference to perform because this would increase the number of ways things could be bound together (so if there is also something green and something square then we need more competing models to decide between red balls and red squares and green balls and green squares). But the basic case of two competing hypotheses will do here.

The kind of ambiguity inherent in a binding scenario is not different in principle from other kinds of ambiguity confronting the perceptual system. There are then the two basic ways to try and resolve it in favour of one of the two competing hypotheses. Either one hypothesis has higher likelihood (is better at explaining away the input), or one of the hypotheses has higher prior probability (the "or" here is inclusive, so both can of course hold).

Having higher likelihood means being able to explain away more of the sensory input and explaining it away better. That means exploiting all the information about each sensory attribute and comparing which hypothesis accounts for most. The input that one but not the other can explain will be the disambiguating information. So, for example, the binding hypothesis will predict that the attributes will have constant spatiotemporal overlap and the independence hypothesis will predict that they don't overlap much (only when, say, the trajectories of independent entities intersect). As this prediction is tested on the input it may turn out that prediction error is minimized only on the binding hypothesis, and its posterior probability will go up. Though this is not conclusive proof that they are bound it may be enough to disambiguate the signal and substantiate the bound percept. If doubts persisted about which hypothesis is right, then active inference could be brought in more fully: for example, trying to catch the ball and bounce it to see if the colour sticks to the ball. As with the standard Bayesian moves, there will also be a selection among hypotheses based on prior probabilities, for example the very much higher probability of a bound red ball hypothesis than disjoint sensory attributes (as one might have when phosphenes or afterimages are rife).

This process is no different to other attempts to disambiguate signals in perceptual inference. It exploits a statistical regularity, namely that bound attributes tend to travel together in space and time, and conversely, that if two attributes are independent it is a rather considerable coincidence if they are persistently synchronized in space and time.

One of my favourite illusions can be used to illustrate the reliance on spatiotemporal cues when trying to disambiguate sensory input. In the rubber hand illusion, a touch sensation administered on your own hand, which is hidden from view, is experienced as bound to a rubber hand lying on the table

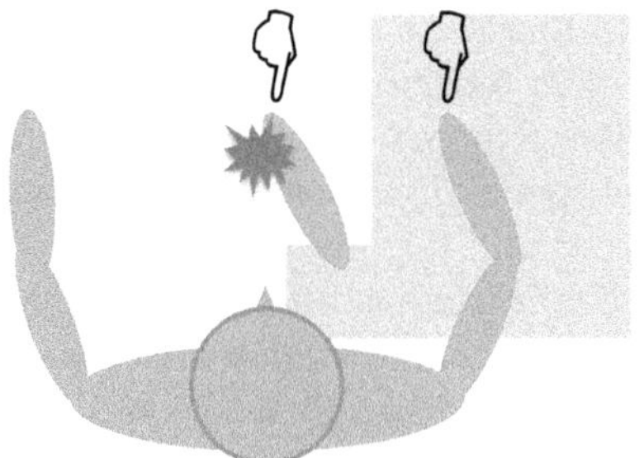
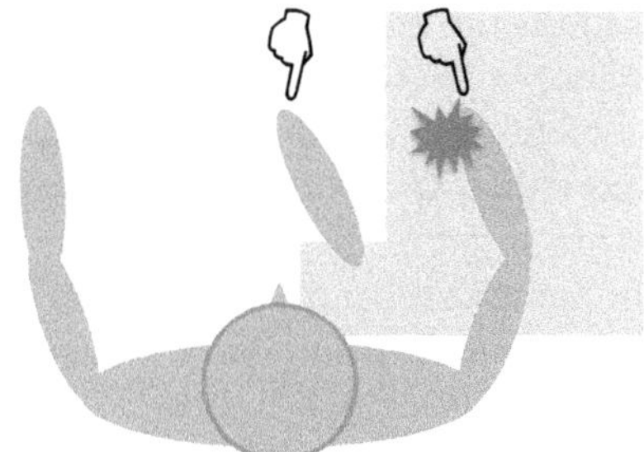

**Figure 8.** Rubber hand illusion. The star represents the sensed location of touch. During synchronous touch the touch is felt on the separate, seen rubber hand (left figure); during asynchronous touch the touch is felt on the real, hidden hand (right figure).

in front of you. This is a striking experience, where the touch is dislocated to an object that manifestly does not belong to your body (see Figure 8). The rubber hand illusion was discovered by Botvinick and Cohen (Botvinick and Cohen 1998) and has since been explored and developed in numerous ways (we will revisit some of these developments in subsequent chapters). For present purposes it is the basic illusion that matters.

When inducing the illusion, the real hand and the rubber hand are both touched in synchrony. The sensory input is then like this: there is visual input of contact between a tapping finger and a rubber hand at location *R*, there is tactile input that one's real hand is being tapped, and there is proprioceptive input that one's real hand is at location *H*. The situation is then ambiguous in the sense described above: there are a fairly large number of binding/independent combinations of these sensory features, and the brain needs to determine which is the most probable. For example, an independence hypothesis will be that you are watching a rubber hand being touched but it has nothing to do with the touch you can feel on your hidden hand. A binding hypothesis is that the touch you can see being administered to the rubber hand at location *R* is also the touch you can feel. Both are consistent with the input except that the synchronicity of the input is much more expected on the binding hypothesis than on the independence hypothesis. This is because, as I mentioned above, it is very unlikely that truly independent properties will be systematically related. That is, we have a strong expectation that there is a *common cause* when inputs co-occur in time. This makes the binding hypothesis of the rubber hand scenario a better explainer, and its higher likelihood promotes it to determine perceptual inference and thereby resolve the ambiguity. The result is that the illusion is experienced.

Conversely, when the seen and the felt touch are out of synch, a bound (or common cause) hypothesis is not preferred over the independence (or separate causes) hypothesis. When you feel the touch on your hand, the rubber hand is not touched, so it is easier to accept that there are two independent causes in the world, one touching you, the other touching the rubber hand.

Notice that when experiencing the illusion, temporal overlap is weighted more than spatial overlap. There is after all spatial discrepancy between the visual input of the rubber hand being touched and the proprioceptive input from the real hand and the usual binding of touch to that estimate (typically the rubber hand and the real hand are separated by about 10–20 centimetres in these experiments). But the perceptual inference disregards this discrepancy and goes with the temporal overlap instead. In fact, this gives rise to a subsequent binding scenario: should the proprioceptive estimate of the hand position itself be bound to the location of the newly bound visuotactile estimate? This is a separate question, but it seems that with stronger visuotactile estimates—the more you are taken in by the illusion in the first place—the more you will tend to have proprioceptive experience that overlaps in space with the location of the rubber hand. Proprioception is often re-mapped onto the visuotactile location.

All this doesn't mean that temporal information is always weighted more than spatial information, it all depends on the situation. There may be decreased or no visuotactile binding if the distance between the real and rubber hand is increased, in spite of the synchrony between them (Lloyd 2007; see also Aimola Davies et al. 2013). In contrast, we have shown in our lab that if there is no distance between them, for example if a virtual reality goggle is used to create spatial overlap between the real and the rubber hand, then the illusion is strengthened (Paton, Hohwy et al. 2011). The winning hypothesis about the world is the one that achieves the best balance of all these parameters. Inducing the illusion then depends on exploiting this balancing process in the right kind of way.

This is the beginning of an explanation of binding in terms of the evidence favouring a common cause hypothesis over an independent causes hypothesis: there is binding when the cause of two sensory attributes are deemed to be common, rather than independent, and when overall the sensory input is predicted more successfully on the basis of the binding hypothesis. More needs to be said about this idea, to make it reasonable and to bring out how it connects with the specific concerns of the binding problem.

## INITIAL PLEAS FOR THE BAYESIAN STORY

The explanation appeals to the idea that we have a strong prior expectation of common causes when there is spatiotemporal overlap. This is a very strong expectation because it overrides other aspects of the situation which have low prior probability, such as that touch cannot be felt on a rubber hand. As we remarked at the end of Chapter 4, when invoking a Bayesian framework, there is always a danger of telling just-so stories: it is always possible to find a hypothesis that fits the data or a story about why some hypothesis just happens to have higher prior. It is therefore important to have independent reasons for positing a particular ordering of priors. We do in fact have a very strong tendency to look for common causes when there is spatiotemporal overlap; in fact it is so strong that often we are unable to accept that something was just a coincidental overlap in space and time. This is, for example, part of the explanation of widespread attraction to superstitious belief: we are unaware of how often we would come across coincidences so when we do come across one we prefer outlandish explanations to chalking it up to chance (see, for example, Gilovich 1993). For example, I might just have had a thought about Yogi Berra, and then I see a relevant tweet quoting one of his delightful sayings ("when you come to a fork in the road, take it"), suggesting to me his spirit is guiding my thinking.

I will now sketch out the Bayes optimal (prediction error minimization) explanation for the rubber hand illusion. Later, we will revisit many of the important themes this explanation appeals to, in terms of constraints on active inference and the crucial role of precision in hierarchal inference. At the moment, we have to ask why the common cause hypothesis succeeds over the different causes hypothesis. The answer lies in the relative precision afforded to proprioceptive signals about the position of my arm and exteroceptive (visual and tactile) information—suggesting a synchronous common cause of my sensations. By experimental design, I am unable to elicit precise information about the position of my arm because I cannot move it and test hypotheses about where it is and how it is positioned. Conversely, by experimental design, the visual and tactile information is highly precise with rich fluctuations in sensory signals. In other words, the precision of my arm position signals is much less than the precision of synchronous exteroceptive signals and it is these that succeed in getting themselves explained away—by selecting the common cause hypothesis.

Thus, from the study of multisensory illusions like the rubber hand, it transpires that perceptual inference is biased towards efficient suppression of prediction error over complying with conceptual prior beliefs. It is as if the perceptual system would rather explain away precise sensory input with a conceptually implausible model than leave some precise sensory evidence (e.g., the synchrony) unexplained. This is especially so if other cues push in the direction of the illuded hypothesis; for example, evidence suggests that the illusion is enabled when the rubber hand is (visually) hand-shaped (Tsakiris, Carpenter et al. 2010).

A related lesson from this interpretation of the illusion is that certain kinds of prediction error seem to be deemed very reliable (precise) signals and are therefore weighted very strongly in inference. In the illusion, the temporal overlap in the synchronous tapping condition seems to be a signal the system cannot ignore, and this makes it favour the common cause hypothesis over the independence hypothesis. This happens even if the favoured hypothesis radically misconstrues reality. Within that false hypothesis about the world, more fine-grained priors about the shape of the hand and other characteristics may then play a role (I return to the wider significance of these radical misconstruals of reality in Chapter 7 and 11).

This overall story about binding is analogous to aspects of binocular rivalry. Such an analogy would help dispel just-so worries because rivalry is, superficially, different from binding: in rivalry, spatiotemporally co-occurring stimuli are separated from each other rather than bound together. However, in spite of this difference, there is an analogous starting-point. In the rubber hand illusion, there is temporal overlap in the synchronous condition that the system seems unable to ignore; in rivalry there is spatial overlap of the images that the system seems unable to ignore. The spatial overlap makes the system adopt a hypothesis that radically misconstrues reality as having alternating objects in the same location, even though in actual fact the objects do not alternate at all. Within this misconstrued model of reality, more fine-grained prior beliefs can then be seen in action. This happens in interocular perceptual grouping, during rivalry conditions induced with stimuli such as those shown in Figure 9 (see also the example in Figure 3 in Chapter 1).

What happens in interocular grouping is that, after a period of confusion, perception settles into alternation. However, alternation is not between the presented images. Instead, the brain tends to concoct two percepts that it is not physically presented with, namely those in Figure 10.

**Figure 9.** Perceptual grouping in binocular rivalry. The stimuli actually presented to the eyes.

**Figure 10.** Perceptual grouping in binocular rivalry. The resulting percepts that alternate.

This is a striking effect. It is as if the brain has neuronal scissors, cuts the images its eyes are presented with in half and then binds the "right" halves together to make more sense of the world. When I present this in a class of students they are often not aware that they were presented with the images in Figure 9, they believe they only ever were presented with the images represented in Figure 10. To make sense of the conflicting input in the same visual space, it is as if the perceptual system is saying (allowing a bit of neuroanthropomorphism): "I can't do away with the spatial overlap, so instead I'll impose a lack of temporal overlap by making the images alternate". But, then the brain grows unhappy with this solution because the prior probability of seeing half-house-half-face objects is low, so it constructively re-binds everything so it perceives the more commonly seen whole faces and whole houses. One way to interpret this is that the brain first sees how it can suppress as much as possible of the incoming sensory input while respecting the prior belief that objects cannot overlap in space. This initiates rivalry. Having done this, the hypotheses are then refined according to more fine-grained priors, which induces the grouping. In this example, we have a trade-off, not between the precision of different sensory modalities (as in the rubber hand illusion) but a trade-off between the precision at high and low levels of the perceptual hierarchy: binocular rivalry suggests that there are certain high-level beliefs that are held with conviction (high precision) that will induce prediction errors at lower levels—in this instance retinotopically mapped visual cortex in one hemifield. In this way, I think it is possible to establish other cases where the system, as claimed for the rubber hand illusion, has a penchant for suppressing hierarchically deployed prediction errors, even if it leads to misperception.

## FROM COMMON CAUSE TO SENSORY BINDING

I have attempted to reduce the binding problem to a matter of resolving ambiguity in favour of a common cause explanation. Under a wide definition of binding this is not unreasonable as it binds properties together when they are deemed the effects of a common cause (and separates them when not, as seen in rivalry).

However, common cause inference in general seems too broad to capture the perceptual aspects of paradigmatic examples of binding such as the red, bouncing ball. For example, when we infer that the barometer reading and the storm are both effects of a common cause such as a low-pressure system, we have little inclination to say the barometer and the storm are bound in any perceptual sense.

To address the worry, we need to focus on the idea that common cause inference is a hunt for *hidden* causes—causes behind the veil of sensory input. Our evidence (the sensory input, for example) may be influenced by the workings of some cause we cannot directly observe. Inferring to the right hidden cause of the evidence will help us predict and control our environment better. Sometimes the cause is deeply hidden, like the way subprime mortgages explain many otherwise independent aspects of the perfect storm of a global financial crisis. Sometimes it is shallower, like the way the cold snap explains both why I have cold feet and why the dough failed to rise. The difference between common cause inference in general and sensory binding in particular is then that the cause in the sensory binding case is very shallowly hidden. The kind of binding we experience in perception is when the hidden, common cause of sensory input is available in the objects around us, that is, when there is a very direct causal fork from the object to the different attributes of our sensory perception.

In the rubber hand case, this amounts to binding of the visual and tactile attributes on the "surface" of the perceptible world, in this case, the rubber hand. This is then an illusion because it derives from a misguided common cause inference. In reality, the synchrony *is* ironically explained by a common cause, namely the mischievous experimenter controlling the tapping. But this common cause is hidden deeper in the causal order than the more superficial common cause of touch on the rubber hand.

Of course, we then need a story about why the fundamentally implausible, superficial story is favoured over the deeper, true story. One possibility is that, while experiencing the rubber hand situation, both stories explain away the sensory input equally well but the true story is more *complex* than the illusory story. As discussed in Chapter 3, there is a bias away from complex, potentially overly parameterized hypotheses and towards simple hypotheses with fewer levels and parameters. If both hypotheses can explain away the sensory input then it is better to opt for the simpler hypothesis, which in this case happens to lead to illusory inference to a superficial, hidden cause. For this appeal to complexity vs. simplicity to work it is crucial to constrain it to a particular situation. In the rubber hand illusion this constrained situation is what happens while one follows the experimenter's instructions to sit still at the table and passively receive sensory input. Sticking to the simple but illusory hypothesis of transferred touch after escaping the lab into the outside world would increase prediction error massively, making the more complex hypothesis about what happened more attractive after all.

Returning now to the general notion of non-illusory, perceptual binding, the basic idea is then that binding is inference to a relatively superficial hidden common cause. We can cash some of this out in terms of variance and invariance. When the hidden common cause is deeply hidden, then there is no *perceptual* binding because the object representations that one needs in such inferences are relatively invariant, not dependent on one's first-person perspective (as in the example of subprime mortgages and financial crisis). In contrast, when the common cause is superficial, then there is sensory binding because the object representations that one then needs are variant, captured in fast-changing dynamics, and dependent on one's first-person perspective. Perceptual binding then boils down to inference to a hidden, common cause under rather variant object representations.

This notion can be rephrased so that perceptual binding occurs when the best explanation of sensory input stems from a common cause model that predicts first-person perspective dependent sensory attributes. In contrast, non-perceptual types of binding occur when the best explanation of sensory input stems from a common cause model higher up in the hierarchy, which predicts more perspective-independent sensory attributes. This makes sense due to the way we used the perceptual hierarchy in Chapter 1 to accommodate the notion of the first-person perspective in general. First-person perspective relates to the extent to which predictions can capture detailed, fast time scale regularities of the type that typically impinge directly on our senses, and which are relevant for the notion of perceptual binding.

## BINDING, ATTENTION, AND PRECISION

So, if we use the tools available through prediction error minimization, then it is possible to explain how sensory binding could arise. The key is to treat binding as just a kind of perceptual inference. The account shares aspects with the bottom-up hierarchical account of binding, mentioned earlier. It relies heavily on the hierarchical nature of object recognition, treating perceptual content as given by a number of levels and encompassing both invariant and variant object representation. But perceptual inference relies on prediction "backwards" in the hierarchy, so it is not a purely bottom-up process. It is instead a process where lower, variant units are modulated by higher, more invariant units such that binding depends on learned associations and the expectations that flow from them. The account also shares aspects with the top-down, attentional account of binding in so far as there is a selection process between different possible hidden causes. However, on the prediction error minimization account, top-down processing is not attentional as such. It is a matter of unconscious inference to the best explanation of sensory input—a process that employs Bayesian notions of priors and likelihoods.

There is however room for a role for attention in explaining perceptual binding. This is because a part of prediction error minimization concerns optimization of precision (this was foreshadowed in Chapter 3 as the basis of attention, and this link between precision and attention will be the topic of Chapter 9). With respect to the role of attention in the binding problem, we will for now just assume that attention is basically the same as precision optimization in prediction error minimization, and then briefly see which role attention in the shape of such precision processing might have in binding.

We introduced the idea that binding is a type of perceptual inference by considering cases of ambiguity. For example, the input might be ambiguous between a common cause hypothesis, which leads to binding, and an independent causes hypothesis, which does not lead to binding. Of course, in perhaps the majority of cases, our prior exposure to bound attributes means processing can be very fast and effortless. We choose the right hypothesis quickly partly because the prior probability of the competitor is very low. In some laboratory cases, ambiguity is manipulated by removing contextual cues that would swiftly suggest one model over another, and by showing visual displays very briefly. In Treisman and Schmidt's classic study (Treisman and Schmidt 1982), arrays for differently oriented line segments in different colours were shown for about 200 ms. Under such conditions participants begin to perceive illusory binding where, for example, a green colour is bound to a horizontal line even if no horizontal lines were in fact green. If binding is the upshot of perceptual inference this is not surprising, since this is a situation in which prediction error minimization is put under pressure.

Treisman reasonably argues that the reason for such binding failures is that in such cluttered displays, and under those time constraints, attention cannot be deployed. Attention therefore seems necessary for binding. A more guarded conclusion would be that attention becomes increasingly necessary for binding as ambiguity increases but that in relatively unambiguous, everyday cases, attention as such is not needed. Here I say attention "as such" because the prediction error approach allows a way to reconcile these two interpretations.

On the prediction error approach, attention is precision optimization of prediction errors, and this would be a process that applies across all degrees of ambiguity. For example, in Treisman and Schmidt's study, the brief presentation time curbs attention's role in precisifying spatiotemporal estimates in cluttered scenes—one cannot be very confident in the orientation and spatial location of the figures. Importantly, precision optimization mechanisms would also have a role to play in everyday cases, such as seeing a bouncing red ball. Movement and colour are processed with different fidelities and therefore there will be a degree of imprecision when trying to get them to bind with each other.

This gives a learnable pattern of imprecision ("for balls and colours under these types of conditions, there is this amount of uncertainty about the estimated means"), and this pattern gives rise to expectations of precision in the sensory signals (that is, in the prediction error signal) from the states of affairs in the world. Mechanistically, these expectations are thought to modulate the synaptic gain on prediction error units. Basically, the idea is that there is more prediction error shunted up in the system when the errors are expected to be precise than when they are expected to be imprecise (we touched briefly on the importance of getting this balance right towards the end of Chapter 3). The effect of this prediction error mechanism is that when the system has learnt to expect imprecision, then the bottom-up, driving signal is given less weight in perceptual inference and top-down expectations are given more weight.

I am building up to the idea that during typical binding situations, there is relatively high imprecision due to the different variability of each estimate. This variability is often expected and so the gain on prediction error decreases—prediction error is gated. Instead, prior and more "cleaned up" hypotheses of the relative spatiotemporal whereabouts of these sensory attributes are allowed to dominate inference. This model allows neat perceptual binding, for example, the redness is mapped precisely on to the bouncing ball. The binding is maintained in spite of the uncertainty about the individual estimates. Precision optimization—the use of accurate expectations of precision—thereby allows binding to happen in everyday situations by glossing over some degree of uncertainty. By relying on prior beliefs, binding thus sharpens representation of the individual sensory attributes in the process of binding them—and judiciously exploits expected precision.

In contrast, when the uncertainty in a binding situation is higher than expected, then this top-down controlled perceptual inference might go astray and result in illusory binding (illusory conjunction). This might be what happens in Treisman's cases of binding failures described above. In such cases it would be natural to direct the attentional searchlight—endogenous attention—at the stimuli in order to re-calibrate expected precisions and get binding back on track. This would make sense from the perspective of prediction error minimization because endogenous attention, according to that theory, consists of volitional increases of the gain on prediction error units in the expectation they will be precise (see Chapter 9). With this we can return to Treisman's theory that attention is necessary for binding, and the more guarded view that volitional, endogenous attention is necessary for binding under conditions of relatively high uncertainty only. The combination view (or vindication of Treisman) is that attention is needed for all binding, on the understanding that attention is optimization of expected precisions for prediction errors.

I used metaphors—"cleaning up" and "sharpening"—when I claimed binding depends on precision optimization. I will give an example of what I have in mind, though I am not aware of any studies that have looked at this for paradigmatic examples of binding. The basic claim is that the brain can anticipate its own signal-to-noise levels and adjust perceptual processes accordingly, sometimes so that noise (and uncertainty) is reduced. Just this has been argued for in perception of orientation patterns such as those in Figure 11 (Morgan, Chubb et al. 2008; Ross and Burr 2008).

Pattern (b) differs as much from pattern (a) as pattern (c) differs from (b). Yet we perceive (a) and (b) as pretty much identical, with all elements aligned with each other, and (c) as very different from the other two, with its elements pointing in different directions. Processing of noise in perceptual inference therefore is non-linear. The effect concerning our perception of (b) in particular is described by Ross and Burr as a default condition, where "the visual system, in the absence of evidence to the contrary, opts for clean solutions—sharp edges, unmottled surfaces, 'good' *Gestalten*; and [. . .] it knows its own noise". Moreover, consistent with my account above, this process relies on "regularizing assumptions, which are, in effect, Bayesian priors". I particularly like the way Ross and Burr link this evidence for sharpening with perception as an inferential process: "The sting in the tail [. . .] is that it implies that what we see is not worked-up versions of retinal images (as Marr's representations

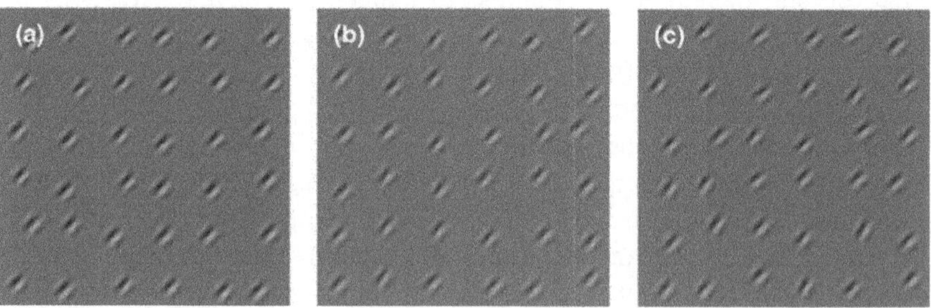


**Figure 11.** Random patterns of Gabor patches at 45 degree orientations with an amount of jitter (noise) about them such that (a) has jitter around 45 + 0 deg., (b) has jitter around 45 + 2 deg., (c) has jitter around 45 + 4 deg. See text for explanation (see Morgan, Chubb *et al.* 2008; figure adapted from Ross and Burr 2008).

are), but things we construct or imagine, from a statistical description of what images contain" (2008: 363).

## SUMMARY: BINDING IN ERROR MINIMIZATION

This chapter has been a test case for the prediction error mechanism presented in Part I. There we relied on developments in computational neuroscience to build up an ambitious account of brain function, centred on perceptual inference, and fully encompassing action.

The core properties of this framework have been wielded here to re-frame much of the discussion about a particular, fundamental problem in cognitive science, namely the binding problem. This has been a speculative account, and empirical and theoretical research is needed to bear it all out. It does seem to show that the prediction error account does apply, at least in principle, to this specific thorny issue. But it also seems to me that we get a promise of a deeper understanding of the binding phenomenon through the prism of prediction error minimization.

We can unify binding with perceptual inference in general, we can use the perceptual hierarchy to understand how binding differs from other examples of common cause inference, and we can use expected precisions to explain why binding seems so neat, why it breaks down, and how attention fits in to the whole story. We ended with the idea that binding is essentially a statistically based inner fantasy, shaped by the brain's generative model of the world.

Another aim of this chapter has been to see the prediction error account in action and learn about it from considering different kinds of cases, such as paradigmatic cases of binding and more obscure, illusory cases of crossmodal binding and perceptual grouping in rivalry.

In the next chapter, prediction error minimization is applied to the debate about cognitive impenetrability.

## NOTES

*Page 105.* ["Conversely, when the seen and the felt touch . . . "] There might be other illusory effects happening in the rubber hand illusion when tapping is asynchronous but the illusion is generally less compelling under asynchronous touch. In our lab we find that some participants can have odd feelings of numbed rubber limbs or other more mysterious sounding experiences. I discuss these issues further in Chapter 11.

*Page 106.* ["Notice that when experiencing the illusion . . . "] Experimentally, proprioceptive changes in the rubber hand illusion are assessed with a drift measure, where participants indicate the felt location of their real hand. When they experience the illusion the location tends to drift towards the rubber hand. However, the illusion and the drift can dissociate, supporting the idea that these are related to different perceptual inferences, see (Rohde, Di Luca et al. 2011).

*Page 109.* ["This is a striking effect . . . "] In this discussion of the Bayesian account of binocular rivalry I am drawing on some of the ideas from our earlier work (Hohwy, Roepstorff et al. 2008). In particular I appeal to the notion of general priors (sometimes informally labelled "hyperpriors"), such as that two objects are not expected to have spatiotemporal overlap, and that fused "face-houses" have low prior; another hyperprior that helps explain rivalry is a standing expectation that the world changes (or that priors diminish). This is where just-so worries arise, as discussed at the end of Chapter 4; see also Clark's (2013), where the use of such general priors is criticized: it could seem that these priors are not only ad hoc but also false. I answer the ad hoc charge in the main text, by appealing to analogies across different perceptual phenomena. But I also do not think the suggested priors are false beliefs. Of course we can see one object with two spatiotemporally coinciding *properties*, such as the red ball; and we can see transparent images of faces superimposed on images of houses. But this only occurs when there are cues to suggest that there are not two opaque, distinct objects there. It is well-known that rivalry begins to cease when contrast drops off, allowing an interpretation in terms of superimposition; similarly, rivalry ceases and fusion takes over when local and global elements of the images together allow an interpretation in terms of one object and co-existent properties (e.g., eyes and mouth in the right eye and nose in the left eye). But for full contrast images with strong local and global overlapping elements, the cues are strong that here there are two distinct objects, and for them the prior seems to reasonably hold. Similarly, whereas it is true that in normal viewing conditions we can see objects persist over a long time, this objection to the prior that we expect things to change overlooks that perception actually fades surprisingly fast when active exploration and fixation is curbed, as seen in Troxler fading and stabilized retinal images. It is under such conditions of staid inference that the prior seems to hold. This makes good sense under rivalry conditions where active inference can also be expected to be curtailed since it would require the eyes to move independently of each other (I return to this idea in Chapter 10). If active exploration is allowed, for example in the shape of attentional fixation, then dominance periods can be prolonged significantly. So this prior, when understood right, also seems plausible. In general, it is an empirical question whether a prior holds so our hypothesis that these priors exist is best tested experimentally. Notice, for comparison, that there are other examples of priors that we discover and explore experimentally, and whose application conditions we can learn about through experiment (for example, the general expectation that light comes from above, or that things move slow rather than fast, discussed briefly in the next chapter. (Thanks to Colin Klein for discussion of these issues).

# 6

# Is predicting seeing?

If perception depends on prior belief, does it follow that we perceive what we expect to perceive? Is our perceptual experience a product of our predictions, and if so, to what extent can our perceptions be anchored in our predictions rather than the states of affairs in the world?

These are obviously important questions for the prediction error minimization framework. The framework says that perceptual experience depends on top-down prediction of sensory input, so it seems to imply that if the predictions change then the perceptual inference will change too, even if the input stays the same. But it is equally obvious that the final story cannot be a simple one. Not any old prediction will be able to determine perception, and no prediction can determine it fully. This is because perceptual inference is guided by prediction error such that prediction error shapes the hypotheses available for generating the predictions, and because perceptual content is determined by the hypotheses that best suppress prediction error. Therefore a randomly picked hypothesis will have little chance of determining what is perceived. In addition, there are strong independent reasons to suspect that in some respects perception is in fact impenetrable to higher level expectations—often beliefs are prevented from determining perception.

We should therefore expect it will be less than straightforward to address these questions. The significance of the questions, and the difficulty in answering them, was noted already by Helmholtz, who relates the questions, naturally, to the key debate in the history of philosophy between empiricism and nativism: "[We should] acknowledge the extensive influence experience, training and habit have on our perception. It may be impossible to completely and sufficiently demarcate how extensive this influence really is" (Helmholtz 1867: 431).

These questions keep recurring in philosophy and are still with us today. They are central to philosophy of science and epistemology: is observation theory-neutral, or is it theory-laden? If the latter, in what sense can science be an objective endeavour, and how can we really know the world as it is?

Neuroscience, psychophysics, and cognitive science should be able to throw light on this debate, since they focus on the mechanisms underlying perception.

There has indeed been extensive theoretical and empirical research, often centred on the question whether perception is *cognitively penetrable* or *impenetrable*. However, Helmholtz' prophecy has proven correct, as there is no clear solution at hand and there is much confusion about what it would take to answer these questions scientifically. For this reason, experimental research into the questions can often be interpreted in multiple ways.

This chapter explores what the prediction error minimization framework can say about the extent to which prior beliefs determine perception. The framework has clear roles for both top-down expectations and bottom-up prediction error, and this allows it to chart a reasonable route through the questions; moreover the way these two seemingly opposing processes interact lets us see why these questions have been so difficult to answer. On the basis of the framework, there is a way in which our expectations in interesting ways modulate our perception. This however happens mainly under conditions of mounting uncertainty and under a definition of cognitive penetrability that is more inclusive in some respects than the standard definition.

## COGNITIVE PENETRABILITY: INITIAL MOVES

Does what we believe to some degree determine what we perceive? If you answer yes, then you believe in cognitive penetrability; if you answer no, then you believe in cognitive impenetrability. That is the simple version of the question of cognitive penetrability. The question rose to prominence in debates between Fodor (1983) and Churchland (1979), and in discussions centred on Pylyshyn's development of these topics (1999). (Hohwy 2009 briefly delves into the question from the prediction error perspective; for recent discussion, see Macpherson 2012; Stokes 2013).

There are several things that could be meant by penetrability, which are not central to the debate I want to focus on here. As a toy example, take the situation where two physically similar individuals both are confronted with a red strawberry. Person *R* expects strawberries to be red whereas person *B* for some reason expects them to be blue. The question is whether these differing expectations make a difference to their respective perceptual processes; in particular, is there a way in which *B's* blue-strawberry expectations could begin to influence the way the sensory input from the strawberry is processed, perhaps such that it begins to appear blue-ish? In this section I will go through four possible cases, discuss their interesting aspects, but ultimately sideline them; on the basis of this a fifth case emerges as our target case, which I discuss in the next section.

Here is one case that most people would agree is not a case of cognitive penetrability. Person *B* expects the strawberry to be blue and perceives it as blue, but this is only because a tumour somehow causes someone with that expectation to have that perception. This case is of course a philosopher's thought experiment but the point matters: even though there is a causal relation between the expectation and the perception it is of an uninteresting kind for our purposes. What is needed as a coherent or meaningful relation such that the content of the expectation and the content of the penetrated perception stand in some reasonable relation (for discussion, see Pylyshyn 1999). Note, though, that this still permits many different kinds of cases. For example, if my psychosis causes me to believe I am stranded in the land of inverted colour and this causes me to perceive the strawberry as blue we might accept it as a case of penetration.

Next consider a case where *R* and *B* merely *judge* the cases differently. They both have the conscious experience as of a red strawberry but afterwards *B* makes a conceptual judgement that the strawberry is blue, whereas *R* when asked about this confirms that it was red. Most people would agree that cases like this happen, though perhaps rarely in cases as dramatic as the strawberries. There are interesting questions in the vicinity, such as how much self-deception can be involved in such cases. For example, I strongly expect my favourite horse to come first and judge that to be the case, even though the next punter saw the race too and came to a different judgement—am I being honest to myself? But, on the face of it at least, this kind of case leaves perceptual experience itself unaffected, so it is not the kind of case we are interested in here.

As the third kind of case, consider a situation where *B* because of her expectation moves the strawberry into different lighting conditions, which are conducive to seeing the strawberry as blue, and accordingly sees it as blue. Obviously, this is not an interesting kind of case, because the very input to the senses now differs between *R* and *B*. In general, we should not count as cognitive penetrability cases where the input is made to change and the perceptual experience thereby changes too. This will rule out a great many cases because it does not take much to change the sensory input in some way. For example, if I attend more closely to something because I expect it to be a certain way, then I might change both the sensory input and the perceptual experience.

Notice that if we adhere strictly to this as a condition on cognitive penetrability, then the prediction error minimization framework almost certainly rules out any real kind of penetration. Perceptual inference works in tandem with active inference to such an extent that internal models normally generate predictions on the basis of the perceiver's movement, including eye movement, head movement, and movement of the body in the environment. It will be difficult to find any cases where perceptual inference is utterly unaffected by movement and thus any cases where there is no change in the sensory input. This is more so because we should expect different perceptual inferences to be embedded in different trajectories of active inference and different prediction error landscapes.

At this stage we could simply conclude that the prediction error minimization framework almost certainly rules out any kind of cognitive penetrability. However, this would prematurely curtail the discussion. The reason is, as I noted at the very start of the chapter, that it seems the framework must induce penetrability of some kind. It is better then to adopt a more lax stance on this particular condition on the debate. That is, we should accept the in-principle possibility of interesting cases of penetrability even if there is some degree of difference in the sensory input of the cases we are comparing. In other words, we should accept as a possibility that predictions can modulate perceptual experience even if such modulation also has as a consequence that the perceivers seek to confirm these predictions by changing their input in different ways. It will then be more of a judgement call than a matter of principle whether a given change in the sensory input rules in or rules out a case as an interesting change in perceptual experience. This is the way we will run the discussion from now on.

As the fourth kind of case, consider the role of expectations in low-level perceptual inference. A good example here is the light-from-above expectation that plays a role in whether we see objects as concave or convex. If the system assumes light comes more or less from above, then shadows will fall on the underside of objects that pop out and on the upper inside of objects popping in, see Figure 12.

Even people who strongly oppose the notion of widespread cognitive penetrability (i.e., Fodor) tend to allow top-down modulation of perception within low levels of the perceptual hierarchy. For these commentators, the case that is up for discussion is whether and to what extent higher level belief can penetrate this kind of low level process and change perceptual inference down there. In the example of the light-from-above prior, it is reasonable to assign

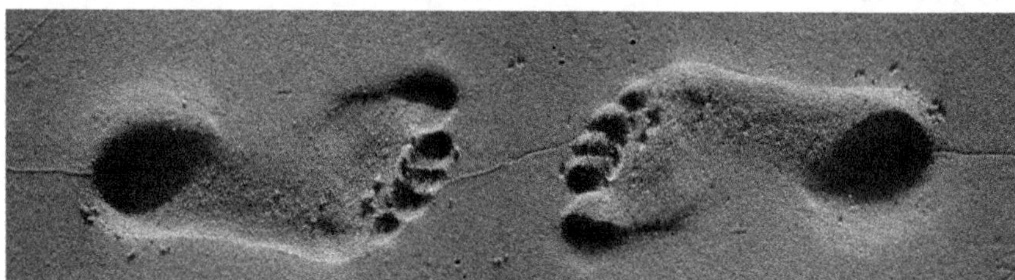

**Figure 12.** Illustration of the light from above prior. The left and right footprints are identical images but are perceived differently due to the light from above prior; (adapted from Morgenstern, Murray et al. 2011); photo courtesy of Manuel Cazzaniga (flickr.com/ezioman).

this prior to such low-level sensory processes. This means that as that example is described it is not really an interesting case of cognitive penetrability.

The strongest argument for cognitive *im*penetrability comes from cases where higher-level belief is strikingly unable to change perceptual inference, even in cases where those inferences are known by the perceiver to be illusory. We will discuss these cases in detail later. For now, we need to set aside cases of low-level penetration, those are not the interesting cases that the debate focuses on. Most people also believe low-level penetration does not mean observation is in any strong sense theory-laden or subjective. It can be reasonably assumed that we all pretty much share our low level expectations, and those expectations are assumed to be extracted from real world regularities (such as that light mostly comes from above) and thus to facilitate rather than hinder objective inference. The problematic case would instead be where more subjectively held higher-level beliefs, which are more easily changed on a whim, penetrate down, and load perceptual experience with theoretical content.

This in fact presents a nice challenge for the prediction error minimization framework. The observation from the opponents of penetrability is that, even though there is a kind of top-down penetrability within low-level processing, there seems to be impenetrability of those low-level processes to higher-level beliefs. It is not clear why there should be such impenetrability between higher and lower level processing within the perceptual hierarchy that accommodates prediction error minimization.

There is a related distinction to take into account here, concerning the time frame for cognitive penetrability. The most dramatic case of cognitive penetrability would be a *synchronic* case where current perceptual experience is directly dependent on a given higher-level belief. I see what I see now because of my current high-level belief. A less dramatic case would be a more *diachronic* case where perceptual experience over a longer time frame is shaped by beliefs, where those beliefs are themselves changing in a dynamic way (for discussion, see McCauley and Henrich 2006). For example, if you were moved into an environment where light predominantly comes from below then you would over time come to acquire the belief that light comes from below and your perception of convexity and concavity would also change accordingly. But these changes happen in concert with each other, as the parameters throughout the perceptual hierarchy are reset in response to prediction error processing. The diachronic case is less obviously an interesting case of cognitive penetrability because it does not seem as if it is a high level belief that penetrates deep down and changes perceptual experience. There is an interesting question in the vicinity, of course, namely whether there are some low-level expectations that cannot be changed as a result of entering a new environment.

In what follows I will focus mostly on more synchronic cases. I will restrict discussion of diachronic cases to the observation that, from the perspective of prediction error minimization, we should expect some possibility of diachronic tuning of low level, general expectations, such as the light-from- above prior. At the same time we should expect limits to such tuning at least for individuals put in radically new environments. This is because we defined phenotypes in terms of a set of basic expectations and therefore should not expect a great deal of plasticity at that level of description, except perhaps on evolutionary time scales.

## COGNITIVE PENETRABILITY UNDER MOUNTING UNCERTAINTY

We have so far considered four candidate types of case for cognitive penetrability and found all four wanting. All this brings us to the fifth case, which finally lets us define a relevant, interesting kind of penetrability. Here, the two people *R* and *B* differ in their relatively higher-level beliefs about the colour of strawberries and via an appropriately semantic, top-down route these beliefs influence their current perceptual experience of the strawberry in front of them. In particular, even though *B* is confronted with a red strawberry, she experiences it as being blue. She does not experience a red strawberry, and judge it to be blue; and she does not in any dramatic way change the circumstances such that the berry is experienced as blue rather than red.

This fifth kind of case is the one we are primarily interested in: it is where your more or less subjective prior beliefs directly change your very perceptual experience of the world. As I noted at the beginning, the prediction error minimization framework seems torn on what to say about such cases. On the one hand, there is an argument that goes like this:

1. Perceptual inference always depends on top-down prediction of sensory input.
2. There is no theoretical or anatomical border preventing top-down projections from high to low levels of the perceptual hierarchy.
3. Cognitive penetrability occurs when the influence of sensory input is changed by top-down input from high to low levels of processing.
4. So, cognitive penetrability should be expected.

This is the kind of case that opponents to cognitive penetrability argue is very rare or impossible. On the other hand, there is an argument that goes like this:

1. Perceptual experience is a matter of how top-down predictions suppress prediction error in perceptual and active inference.

2. Hence, if there is a difference in the expectations that drive perception, then there must be a difference in the prediction error, that is, a difference in the bottom-up input.
3. Different expectations and similar bottom-up input are needed for cognitive penetration.
4. So, there can be no cognitive penetration.

I claimed above that the second argument is probably too restrictive. In particular premise 3 should be relaxed such that cognitive penetrability can in principle occur when there is difference in beliefs and with some difference in the sensory input. It will then be a judgement on a case-by-case basis whether a difference in sensory input is of a character that rules out cognitive penetration.

There is however a second way of escaping this argument, which takes issue with premise 2. This premise rests rather implausibly on equating bottom-up sensory input with prediction error, leaving out a role for uncertainty and noise. Under relatively noisy and uncertain conditions, the perceptual input may underdetermine perceptual inference and give rise to situations where expectations make perceptions differ without much systematic suppression of prediction error. I shall pursue this thought more below.

Now a clear set of challenges to the prediction error minimization framework begins to transpire from considerations of cognitive penetrability. We need to find a way of specifying the framework such that we can explain why cognitive penetration is possible and even highly expected but nevertheless often restricted so it does not occur too pervasively. Importantly, this specification needs to respect the idea that the way the prediction error minimization mechanism works makes it less than straightforward to find cases where the expectations differ and the input stays the same.

Luckily, there is a parsimonious way to discharge this multifaceted task. This focuses on the afore-mentioned idea that there is more scope for top-down modulation under increasingly uncertain conditions.

Recall, from the end of Chapter 3, that in situations where the system has learnt there are high levels of uncertainty the synaptic gain on prediction error units decreases. That is when the system gets to expect the signal from the world to be imprecise and thus not an efficient supervisory signal on perceptual and active inference. Perhaps sometimes we can afford to suspend inference and as it were acquiesce in the uncertainty. But often inference must nevertheless be engaged. In that case, higher levels of the perceptual hierarchy are given increased weight: you cannot trust the signal from the world, but must arrive at a conclusion, so you rely on your prior knowledge. This is the rational thing to do, given an imperative to do something—the worse alternative would be to merely guess.

This gives a principled class of cases for which we should expect interesting cases of cognitive penetrability to emerge. When uncertainty is high, we should expect an increase in the ability of ever higher-level prior beliefs to determine conscious experience. I think this is borne out by the types of case often used as examples of cognitive penetrability: these cases often involve noisy or otherwise unexpected sensory inputs, or sensory inputs that have not been properly learned yet, or illusions, most of which are based on inherently ambiguous stimuli. At the end of this chapter I will substantiate this claim by discussing a number of typical cases. The first task is however to explain how this proposal can make room for cases of cognitive impenetrability, even in cases where there seems to be some degree of uncertainty.

## MAKING ROOM FOR COGNITIVE IMPENETRABILITY

The proposal is that interesting cases of cognitive penetrability tend to happen under mounting uncertainty. However, this does not make it any easier to make room for cases that appear to favour impenetrability. In fact, since there is always some uncertainty in perceptual inference it seems there is always some degree of cognitive penetrability, even if it is only very mild. So, what would make impenetrability occur?

Here we can use an example that has been at the centre of the debate, namely the Müller-Lyer illusion, Figure 13. The two vertical lines are really the same length but one is perceived to be longer than the other. Even if we have a

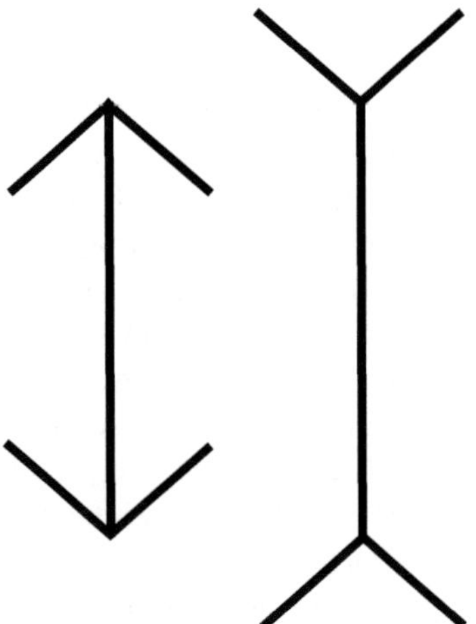

**Figure 13.** Müller-Lyer illusion.

strong prior belief that they are of equal lengths, we still perceive one to be longer. So the conscious experience here seems impenetrable: the higher-level belief fails to modulate perception. What can prediction error minimization say about this?

The first observation about this kind of case, which we remarked upon earlier, is that there is probably cognitive penetrability in this illusion occurring at relatively low-level sensory processing. There are a number of different proposed explanations of the illusion but one of the most popular ones, the inappropriate size-constancy explanation, treats it as an upshot of prior belief about depth cues that determine conscious perception. The outwards pointing wings on the right vertical line in the illusion suggest to the visual system that it is closer to us than the left line, and should therefore be perceived as slightly bigger than the left line whose inwards pointing wings make it seem further away. See Figure 14 for an illustration.

There is not universal agreement on this type of explanation, but it has some traction (see Gregory 1998; McCauley and Henrich 2006). The explanation turns the illusion into a case of low-level cognitive penetrability, where the relevant priors occupy levels of the hierarchy within the early visual system itself.

However, the depth explanation does not in itself answer the question with which we began, as to why the higher-level prior belief in equal lengths cannot penetrate and create veridical experience of the lengths? This is however something the prediction error minimization account can deal with.

In the Müller-Lyer illusion there is ambiguous input: either the lines are the same length or they are not. The context provided by the wings trigger fairly low-level priors, which lead to the inference that they are of different lengths

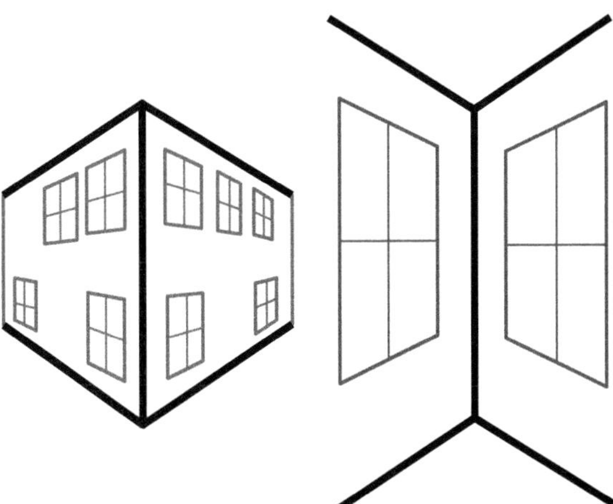

**Figure 14.** Illustration of the inappropriate size-constancy explanation of the Müller-Lyer illusion.

rather than to the competing inference that they are of the same length. This means that the uncertainty induced by the ambiguity is dealt with relatively early on in the visual system. This is indicated by the robustness of the illusion, which suggests that people have high confidence (precision) in their perceptual inference. The consequence of the early resolution to the ambiguity is that very little residual prediction error is shunted upwards in the system, and that therefore there is little work for any higher-level prior beliefs to do, including the true belief that the lines are of equal lengths.

The proposal is then that cognitive impenetrability occurs when prediction error is sufficiently suppressed at relatively early processing stages. Even if the higher-level belief is part of a model generating predictions, these predictions generate little prediction error because activity at lower levels is already very low. There is no special mechanism or anatomical architecture needed to explain impenetrability, it just so happens that given a certain level of uncertainty and certain priors, prediction error is efficiently suppressed very earlier on. One prediction flowing from this proposal is then that if more noise were introduced into the situation, for example by degrading the stimuli or providing a context suggesting added ambiguity, then the prior high-level belief in equal lengths could be allocated more weight.

I have tried to indicate why cognitive penetrability is stymied in the kinds of cases brought out by the Müller-Lyer illusion. But I think there is a deeper and important way of strengthening this story. The prediction error minimization story comes with a principled way of saying that not all beliefs can cognitively penetrate perception in all circumstances. In short, prediction error minimization constrains which prior beliefs can penetrate and when.

Let us return briefly to the rubber hand illusion, discussed in the previous chapter. There it is also striking that people are rather poor at using their prior belief to destroy the illusion. It is obvious to participants that there is something odd going on in this illusion (we do not tend to keep the set-up a secret from them). Yet this prior belief does not in general tend to penetrate down and keep the observer anchored in reality.

What we do get a lot in our lab is people who have an overwhelming urge to move their hands, remove the goggles, or otherwise intervene on the process. For example, one person we tested physically had to hold her hand fixed with her other hand to prevent it from moving. Other people are frantically looking for clues that would allow them to not experience the illusion, such as minute differences in the texture of the surface on which their hand and the rubber hand rest. Some people complain that the experimenter's touch is ever so slightly misplaced, or needs to be harder. What this suggests is that people are trying hard to let their prior veridical belief about the situation penetrate and change their conscious experience. But they can't because the experimenter has prevented all ways of doing this. That is, we prevent the participant from engaging active inference driven by some specific prior beliefs, which happen to be veridical. That means that people are left with whatever other hypotheses of the world will instead best minimize error—and that happens to be a more low-level, illuded hypothesis.

The same thing holds of the Müller-Lyer. We might try engaging the veridical prior belief in equal length of the two lines but we fail because the situation is constrained. That is, we might try to make predictions on the basis of the belief concerning what would happen to sensory input if the belief was true and we intervened in a certain way. But none of those predictions can get traction on the decontextualized line drawings in a proper, controlled experimental set-up. If these conditions are relaxed, then we can destroy the illusion by intervention; see Figure 15 for one possible method.

What we can see in both of these illusions is that even if the prior, true belief about the world is there, circumstances might prevent it from being confirmed by active inference. The true belief is therefore never tested and is denied access to the sensory prediction errors that would have otherwise confirmed it. This prevents it from determining conscious experience and thus provides cases of cognitive impenetrability. Importantly, this impenetrability co-exists with cognitive penetrability by other beliefs somewhat lower down in the hierarchy, which are able to engage prediction error.

This idea generalizes. For any higher-level state in the perceptual hierarchy to cognitively penetrate, or as I prefer to say, explain away prediction error coming up from below, it must be able to predict at the right fineness of spatiotemporal grain. It must be able to make predictive contact with sensory

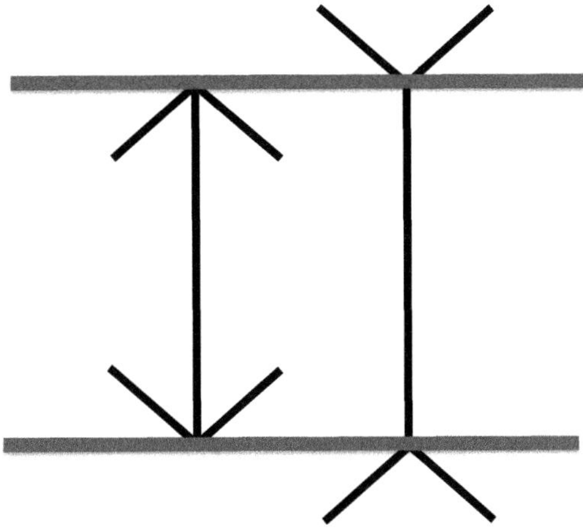

**Figure 15.** An attempt to destroy the Müller-Lyer illusion. I have actively tested my prior belief that they are of the same length and thereby changed my conscious experience.

input. If not, then it will be probabilistically idle. This is an idea I have considered elsewhere, in the context of a discussion of delusions, where patients get stuck with beliefs such as "a demon is controlling my movements", "my doctor thinks my thought", "people enter my body unless I carry a purple pillow", "I smell of faeces" (Hohwy and Rosenberg 2005; Hohwy 2009). The current idea can be illustrated with these cases: some patients are aware that somehow their beliefs are very bizarre and that they might actually be mentally ill. But they cannot get this rather coarse (invariant) true prior belief about their mental illness to make proper contact with the fine-grained (variant) prediction error thought to give rise to these illusions. The trouble is that it is difficult to figure out precisely how the top-down belief that "my brain is damaged" can explain away something like, for example, the subtle mismatches in my sensorimotor system thought to underlie some kinds of delusion formation. (We will return to delusions in Chapter 7).

The general lesson is then that belief revision is hostage to prediction error minimization throughout the cortical hierarchy. This means we can be stuck with false beliefs because they can explain away prediction error more efficiently down through the hierarchy—they provide better control over the actual sensory input than do the competing true beliefs. This speaks to the kind of dissonance one may feel in disputed cases of cognitive penetrability or impenetrability: on the one hand I am stuck with a false or even bizarre belief, and on the other hand I have a reasonably well-supported belief that things cannot be this way (for example, I know I am committed to a psychiatric hospital, or I know the rubber hand set-up is deceiving me). Crucially, the way we normally resolve such dissonance is through the interventions on the world delivered by active inference. But if active inference is hampered, then no resolution can be found and the dissonance persists (and keeps recurring in philosophical debate).

We can then accommodate impenetrability within the prediction error minimization scheme. The key ingredient is the idea that prediction error can be suppressed to different extents at different levels of the perceptual hierarchy, and by noting the stricture that top-down explaining away must match the spatiotemporal fineness of grain at lower levels, especially as active inference seeks to increase the accuracy of disputed hypotheses.

In a very general sense the proposal stresses the point, which we will return to a number of times later in the book, that our mental states and how we represent the world and ourselves are deeply hostage to our ability to minimize prediction error in a given situation. It is easy to generate situations where that ability is curtailed (illustrated with the rubber hand illusion, Müller-Lyer, and perhaps delusions) and where we are then landed with experiences of the world that are more rooted in some rather than other of our prior beliefs.

## POSSIBLE CASES OF COGNITIVE PENETRABILITY

The view of cognitive penetrability I have advocated predicts that we will find interesting cases of penetrability when the perceptual situation is rather riddled with uncertainty: when we are still learning, or when there is noise or ambiguity. Because of this ambiguity there will tend to be low confidence in the perceptual inference, so the proposal also predicts that in those cases there will be scope for introspective uncertainty and alternative interpretations about what is actually experienced. The following cases illustrate this. They also illustrate the very wide range of situations where interesting cases of cognitive penetrability may arise. In each case I will try to show why I am inclined to think they are interesting cases of cognitive penetrability.

*Scale errors.* Children between 1.5 and 2.5 years can be brought to display perplexing errors of scale. In Judy Deloache's (DeLoache, Uttal et al. 2004) delightful study, children of this age were first given an opportunity to play with full scale toys like plastic chairs to sit on, slides to slide down, or cars to sit in and drive around in (the 'Little Tikes Cozy Coupe'). Subsequently, they were given the opportunity to play with a miniature model of the same toy. Now they display *scale errors*: they will sometimes behave as if they have not noticed the change in scale. In the case of the Cozy Coupe, they try to climb in to the miniature car and will persist in this behaviour for some time, somewhat perplexed that their nice toy is not cooperating any longer.

It is difficult to say exactly what causes these errors to occur. Deloache and colleagues reasonably interpret it in terms of dissociations between perception and action pathways in the brain. I mention the study here because it seems that, in some way, the prior learning obtained when playing with the full scale model persists in guiding their perception of the world in spite of the object dramatically changing scale.

It is tempting to say this reveals cognitive penetrability: they experience the car as bigger than it is because they harbour the belief that it is big. However, as expected, the interesting cases are hard to interpret, and it is very hard to say what the conscious experience could be that changes with the changing beliefs. Perhaps, in the situation, the children experience a full scale car, or experience themselves as having the same size. These seem like very drastic changes of experience, however. Or perhaps they simply fail to notice the change in their experience from a full-scale car to a miniature. Then the story would be that they believe, of the miniature car, that it is full scale—and it would not be a case of penetrability after all. But somehow it is difficult to believe that another child, who merely pretends to try to stick her foot in a miniature car, experiences the world in *exactly* the same way as a child who makes the scale error and really believes that she can get in the car. The scale error behaviour seems too dramatic to merely come down to pretend vs. belief. There seems no easy way to determine whether this is a case of cognitive penetrability or something else.

*Bistable figures.* In the literature on cognitive penetrability the duck-rabbit often makes an appearance, together with other bistable figures such as the young/old woman, and the whale/kangaroo, see Figure 16 (Churchland 1988; Fodor 1988). This is no wonder, given that bistable figures are inherently ambiguous and so a situation where we should expect cognitive penetrability. If I believe it is a rabbit, then I see it as a rabbit and if I believe it is a duck then I see it as a duck. However, this is where the worry arises that different eye movements and attentional states bring with them different sequences of input, ensuring it is not penetrability by the original definition. As Fodor objects to Churchland's use of the duck-rabbit as an example of penetrability:

> One doesn't get the duck rabbit (or the Necker Cube) to flip by 'changing one's assumptions'; one does it by (for example) changing one's fixation point. Believing that it's a duck doesn't help you see it as one; wanting to see it as a duck doesn't help much either. But knowing where to fixate can help. Fixate there and then the flipping is automatic. (Fodor 1988)

I have been arguing for a more relaxed definition according to which we may perhaps count these as cases of cognitive penetrability, simply because there are precious few cases where we should expect a new assumption to be entirely unaccompanied by differences in fixation in these kinds of cases.

More generally however, Fodor is arguing that what causes the flip in perception is not the changed assumption but the changed fixation; my argument, via the notion of active inference, is that changed fixation is not a causal factor that in normal circumstances is independent of one's assumptions. Of course, we may side with Fodor in as much as we may judge that on balance the duck-rabbit-style cases may be relatively uninteresting examples of

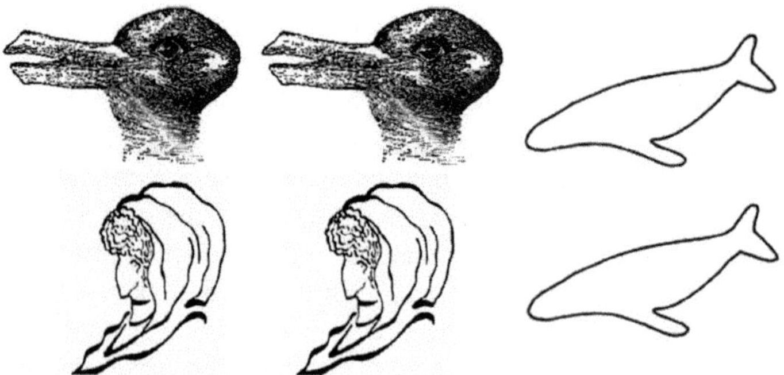

**Figure 16.** Pairs of bistable figures. Does each pair seem to swap in tandem? For further instructions, see main text (figure from Jensen and Mathewson 2011; reprinted with permission from Pion Ltd, London).

cognitive penetrability, depending on how much change in input there is with each shift of fixation.

Quite apart from this discussion, we can do something to induce some degree of interesting penetrability into these kinds of illusion, or so it seems to me. Notice that each pair of figures seems to shift in tandem: either you see two rabbits or two ducks, and likewise for the other two pairs.

If there is cognitive penetrability, perhaps we can change this pattern of flipping in tandem by changing our beliefs about the situation. I will modulate your belief by giving you some extra information: the duck is about to eat the rabbit; the kangaroo is about to bounce on the whale; the young lady is watching the old woman. What happens? Some readers should be able to, perhaps with some effort, stop the tandem alternation and instead see both figures at the same time (Jensen and Mathewson 2011). Speaking for myself, I have fleeting moments of being able to see both the rabbit and the hungry duck at the same time.

Again, it is very difficult to rely on introspection here, as we anticipated for the interesting putative cases of cognitive penetrability. From the point of view of predictive coding, I am inclined to count it as cognitive penetrability. It is as if the new causal information allows the perceptual system for a short while to entertain a new hypothesis about the scenery.

I find this case interesting also because the information that allows some of us to see different figures simultaneously is distinctively causal information (for example, the duck is *eating* the rabbit). The new information thus harnesses the sensory input in a causal context such that more complex, higher-level model parameters can be applied to the initial low-level recognition task. This sits comfortably with the notion of the causal regularities embodied in the perceptual hierarchy.

*Sensory integration.* We have touched on sensory integration before. There are elements of sensory integration in the rubber hand illusion, when the visual input begins to drag the location of the tactile input towards itself, and when the proprioceptive estimate in turn begins to be dragged towards the visuotactile estimate. A very well-described case of integration is the ventriloquist illusion. This is of course well known from actual ventriloquists, where the visual input from the doll's mouth seem to capture the auditory input from the ventriloquist herself. Similar phenomena occur when we watch TV and then locate the source of the sound where we can see the talking head move its mouth rather than at the different location of the loudspeakers.

In the lab a more boring version is explored, where a flash of light and a sound, off-set in their spatial location, appear to come from the same location. This effect obeys Bayes' rule such that the integration of the two inputs weighs the precisions of each and always leads to a more precise integrated location. Normally the sound is dragged more towards the light than vice versa, because vision is more precise in the spatial dimension than auditory estimates. If the visual stimulus is degraded, then the location is dragged more towards the auditory estimate (see the note at the end of this chapter, and see Alais and Burr 2004; this type of Bayesian approach to sensory integration can be accommodated formally within the prediction error framework (Friston, Daunizeau et al. 2010)); (see Figure 17).

There seems to be a degree of cognitive impenetrability here. Even if we harbour the true belief that the doll is not speaking we still experience the sound as coming from it. It seems the prior belief cannot trump the sensory integration.

Even though there is impenetrability in this case, it seems to me that in important respects there is a degree of penetrability too. This is because these illusions, for example, the illusion you experience every time you watch TV, exploit the uncertainty inherent in our sensory estimates. This uncertainty enables the top-down hypothesis that *there is co-location* to play a role in inference. If both our auditory and visual estimates had been incredibly precise, then we would not experience the illusion. This is because we couldn't then be convinced that the causes of the two inputs are co-located in the world—watching TV would then be frustratingly disjointed. Similarly, if the two stimuli are very far apart, we don't experience the illusion. This means that we rely on interactions between prior expectations about precisions of the sensory input and prior learning about the likelihoods of co-location of

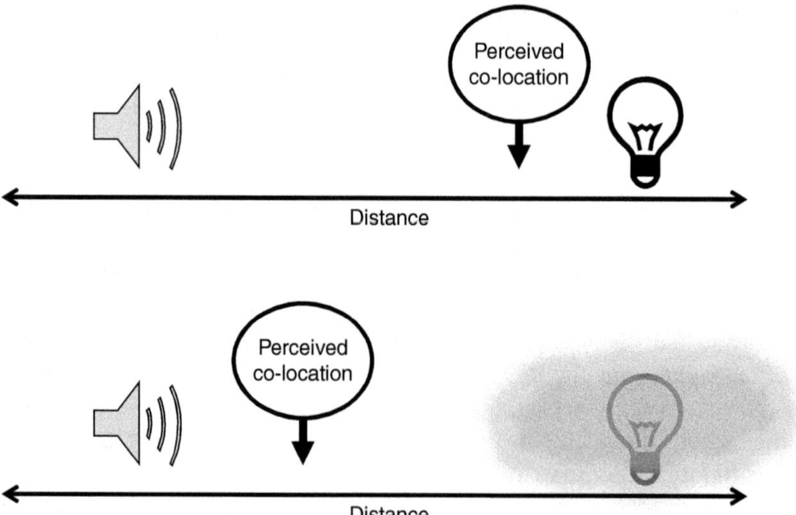


**Figure 17.** The ventriloquist in the lab. The source of the two distinct auditory and visual stimuli is perceived to be co-located at a location between them. The co-location is weighted in an optimal way according to the precision of each stimulus estimation. For example, if the visual stimulus is degraded, then the estimate is dragged towards the auditory stimulus (lower panel).

sensory estimates given temporal synchrony (where the synchrony is that the flash and the sound co-occur in time; or the voice and the mouth movement are synched). If these prior beliefs are triggered, then conscious experience is as of co-location in space, where the co-location is determined by weighting of precisions in unconscious inference. If the prior beliefs are not triggered, then conscious experience is as of differently located sensory attributes, for example, something making a sound over there and some light flashing over here (for discussion, see Körding, Beierholm et al. 2007).

The co-located estimate and the differently located estimates give rise to very different experiences that vacillate depending on which belief is triggered. I am inclined to allow this as a kind of cognitive penetrability. Even though the top-down belief is not at the highest levels of the perceptual hierarchy it is high enough to be multisensory, that is, it is not operational only at low-level unimodal modules. There also seems little doubt that this is a difference in conscious experience: it concerns the difference between enjoying a good ventriloquist and a bad one. Experiencing an illusion such as this is not, that is, just having individually located perceptual estimates, and then merely judging that they are co-located somewhere in between.

But, also as anticipated, it is not so easy to make the case for cognitive penetrability after all, due to the uncertainties in the perceptual situation. In multisensory integration of the type discussed we should expect people to lose access to the individual sensory estimates in favour of the integrated one they are conscious of. Certainly, if this is a case of cognitive penetrability then the change should be in the conscious experience itself such that it is smoothly integrated. But it seems that people can retain some information about the individual estimates, as they were pre-integration (Hillis, Ernst et al. 2002). So, it is not entirely straightforward to just claim that the integrated experience of estimates that are in reality not stemming from the same source is experienced *just the same as* the integrated experience of estimates that are in fact stemming from the same source. For example, experiencing a talking head on TV may not be the same in terms of the phenomenology of the co-location of sound and vision as experiencing a real person talking to you. In the former case, the individual estimates in some circumstances seem to be available in some sense still. For intrasensory integration, on the other hand, there seems no access to the individual, non-integrated estimates. For example, there is no awareness of the binocular disparity that is integrated in 3d vision.

Interestingly, there is a developmental aspect to this. Children have to learn to integrate sensory estimates and, until they do, they have better conscious access to the individual estimates than do adults. So they can outperform adults in assessment of the individual sensory attributes (Nardini, Bedford et al. 2010). The cost is that they cannot reduce uncertainty by integration: they do not benefit from the optimal Bayesian weighting of precisions characteristic of sensory integration. This suggests that the priors concerning co-location, which modulate integration, are learned from the statistical regularities of the world. This is of course consistent with the prediction error story and suggests that conscious experience changes with learning those priors.

Again, the question whether this is a case of cognitive penetrability is hard to answer confidently. The balance of reasons favours cognitive penetrability, it seems to me.

*Patterns in noise.* Consider the noisy images in Figure 18. Is there anything there, or is it just noise?

Most people see something in one of them (a boat?) and not much in the other. However, when people are primed with situations when they felt out of control, or primed with ideas like the stock market being out of control, then they are more inclined to see things in the noise that are not there (Whitson and Galinsky 2008). Intriguingly, people who believe in extrasensory perception (ESP) also see more meaningful patters in noise (Brugger, Regard et al. 1993). Is this cognitive penetrability? The input to the brain is the same but the conscious experience differs, depending on a prior expectation. We should anticipate penetrability, given the noisy and uncertain stimuli. Moreover, we should expect increased penetrability when the initial uncertainty is added to, namely by the priming (here, being out of control suggesting uncertainty).

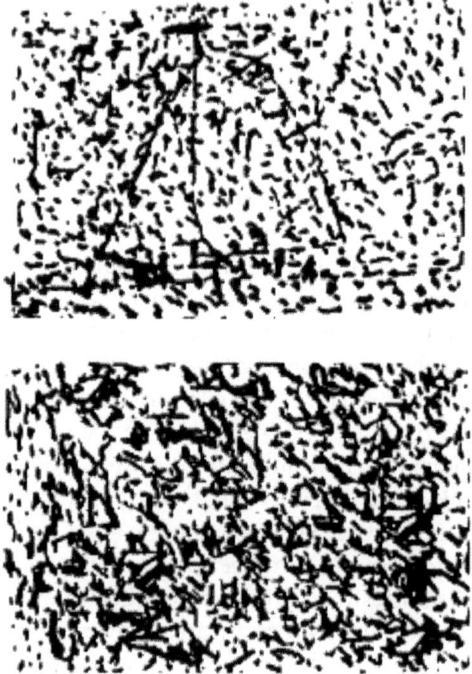

**Figure 18.** Are there patterns in the noise? (Whitson and Galinsky 2008, figure reprinted with permission from AAAS).

But as we have come to expect, there is no simple answer here either. The worry is that there is not a coherent, meaningful link between the prior expectation that things are out of control and the conscious percept of, for example, a house in the noisy image. Recall that this was a requirement for genuine cases of penetrability (Pylyshyn 1999). It may not seem satisfied here. Being primed with being out of control perhaps seem a bit like getting hit over the head and therefore coming to experience something else. In fact, forcibly altering the brain's activity with transcranial magnetic stimulation, which is in some respects tantamount to being hit over the head, can decrease the perception of patterns in noise (Bell, Reddy et al. 2007). Similarly, people see more patterns in noise when the stimulus is merely shown to their left visual field, which again seems somewhat removed from issues of proper cognitive penetrability (Brugger, Regard et al. 1993). If we want to deem the out-of-control case a case of cognitive penetrability, then we need to show that the transcranial magnetic stimulation and left visual field cases are different from the out-of-control case.

Again, the case for or against penetrability is not clear-cut. In prediction error terms the account might go like this. When one is actually in an out of control situation one is failing to minimize prediction error in active inference and failing to revise hypotheses in response—the chosen trajectory causes much error and no better trajectory seems available. It is a situation where there is larger than expected imprecision in active inference and no clear way to fix things. In that situation it makes sense to let prior beliefs guide perceptual inference: instead of being guided by the senses to failure, one should decrease the gain (precision) on the input and rely more on prior belief. In an unconstrained case this may mean cycling through a number of prior beliefs until one is found that has some predictive power, however small. Hence, when primed with being out of control, participants will see more patterns in noise because they, reasonably enough, let their prior beliefs determine more what they see. Whereas there may not be a direct relation between the *content* of the out-of-control belief and the *content* of the ensuing perception (seeing a rat, say, in the noisy image), there is a meaningful, rationally acceptable relation between the out-of-control belief and the perceptual process. So I am inclined to think there is cognitive penetrability in these cases.

*Attentional penetrability.* I will end this list of potential cases of interesting cognitive penetrability by exploring the effects of attention on conscious experience from the point of view of prediction error minimization. This will foreshadow the more full treatment of attention in Chapter 9. Recall that under the traditional definition of cognitive penetrability, changes in conscious experience caused by a change in attentional focus is ruled out as cognitive penetrability. This is because it is thought that a change in attention causes a change in the sensory input itself. Under the broader definition of penetrability I have advocated there are however attentional cases that look

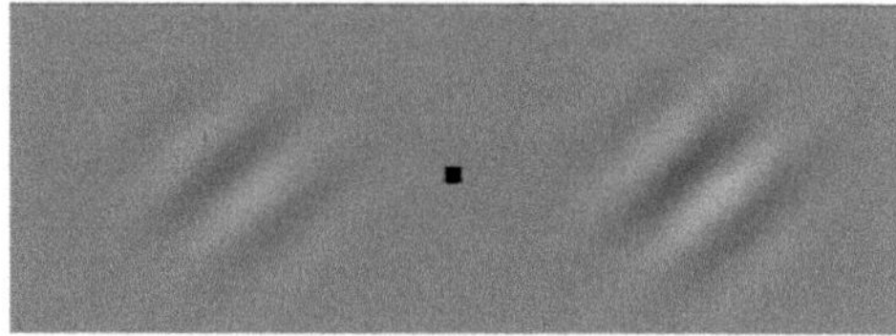

**Figure 19.** Maintain fixation on the black dot; when the weaker grating to the left of the dot is cued attention is attracted to it (even though fixation is still on the dot), and then the cued grating will appear to have a higher contrast than it really has, and the two gratings will appear as of the same contrast (adapted from Carrasco, Ling et al. 2004).

like interesting examples of penetrability. One of these cases come from Marisa Carrasco's lab and is exemplified in Figure 19 (Carrasco, Ling et al. 2004), also discussed extensively in (Block 2010).

The task here is to keep fixating on the central fixation point (the little black dot), and then covertly attend to a cued grating to either side of the fixation point. The effect is that the attended grating increases its perceived contrast strength. Since nothing in the display changes, and eye movement is kept stable, it is hard to argue here that the sensory input itself changes. It is for example different from the case of the duck-rabbit illusion where switches in experience are accompanied by eye movement. There also seems no reason to doubt that Carrasco has identified a difference in conscious experience, so it is not a case of the same conscious experience under different cognitive judgements. So there is a difference in conscious experience that is driven by a top-down cause, namely covert attentional focus. Does this make it a case of cognitive penetration? A reason against would be the idea that a general executive function like attention is not coherently related to the specific content of the experience of the grating in question. On this view, there is here about as much cognitive penetrability as when one decides to close one's eyes and thereby changes one's conscious experience.

By appealing to prediction error minimization, it is in fact possible to argue that there is cognitive penetrability here. This is because there is a coherent, meaningful relation between the top-down attentional mechanism and the content of the experience. As we will see in more detail later on, attention is best understood as optimization of expected precisions in prediction error minimization. The details of this proposal need not concern us right now. The crucial bit is that what drives attention in cases like Carrasco's is *expectations for high signal strength input*, where such high strength input has more precision. These expectations are based on learned or innate regularities tying central high strength cues, for example, an arrow pointing left, to peripheral high strength input, such as the grating. This learned regularity then increases the gain on the sensory input from the cued region, resulting in conscious perception of a stronger contrast grating. It is thus an illusion since the grating does not in fact have the expected high signal strength. It does however seem that the prior expectation is coherently related to the change in conscious experience: an expectation for a strong signal modulates the strength of what is experienced. Now this ticks all the boxes for cognitive penetrability, even though it is an attentional effect. It is also a case in which there would be increased uncertainty, as predicted. Not only is covertly attending to something away from a fixation point a relatively unusual situation (mostly we turn our gaze to things we attend to), the expectation of precision is itself violated by the weak contrast grating in the attended region. I am not claiming that all attentional effects provide interesting cases of cognitive penetrability but it is important to notice that some can reasonably be said to provide such cases.

## SUMMARY: A BALANCED NOTION OF COGNITIVE PENETRABILITY

We have looked at a series of possible cases of interesting cognitive penetrability. The aim has been to show that they tend to occur when input is rather uncertain, noisy, or ambiguous. I am inclined to think that most of the cases are indeed interesting cases of cognitive penetrability. It is also striking how varied these cases are. They range from very basic visual perception to multisensory integration to the perceived scale of things—they even include attentional effects. This variability in the type of cases is no surprise, given my argument has been that interesting cases would occur when uncertainty is high, which it can be in any kind of context. The prediction error minimization story thus seems to provide a different perspective on the issue of cognitive penetrability vs. impenetrability. In particular, it is a perspective that can accommodate both sides in this debate.

A main lesson that I take from this is that beliefs, in the shape of prior expectations, are capable of determining perceptual content in quite profound ways, and that this is especially evident in cases of high uncertainty—in these cases, precision is low and will be estimated as such; thereby attenuating the influence of prediction errors at the appropriate level of the hierarchy. This is not to say that conscious experience is wholly determined by prior beliefs, instead it is to say that conscious experience arises as the upshot of the brain's appetite for making the best sense it can of the current sensory input, even if that means weighting prior beliefs very highly. This fits with the idea that conscious experience is like a fantasy or virtual reality constructed to keep the sensory input at bay. It is different from the conscious experience that is truly a fantasy or virtual reality, which we enjoy in mental imagery or dreaming, because such experiences are not intended to keep sensory input at bay. But normal perception is nevertheless at one remove from the real world it is representing.

Issues surrounding cognitive penetrability relate closely to issues of misrepresentation and reality testing. I will turn to these kinds of issues in the next two chapters, and in the course of that I will return to cognitive penetrability again in order to round off the treatment of the limits to penetrability, that is, to give due weight to the side that insists on cognitive impenetrability.

## NOTES

*Page 117.* ["We should therefore expect it . . . "] My translation of Helmholtz; the original quote is "Dergleichen Thatsachen lassen den ausgedehnten Einfluss erkennen, welchen Erfahrung, Einübung und Gewöhnung auf unsere Wahrnehmungen haben. Wie weit ihr Einfluss aber wirklich geht, dies vollständig und genügend abzugrenzen möchte vor der Hand unmöglich sein" (Helmholtz 1867: 431; see also page 435 and his ensuing discussion of empiricism and nativism).

*Page 119.* ["Next consider a case where *R* and *B* . . . "] I am expressing this case somewhat carefully because the perceptual hierarchy, in which prediction error minimization happens, can complicate our verdict. In particular, on the prediction error story, conceptual judgement and perceptual inference are not clearly separable but merely inferential processes at different levels of the perceptual hierarchy (as discussed in Chapter 3). That means a conceptual judgment about a current perceptual content is expected to filter down and work as a model parameter on lower level perceptual processing. Even a case of post hoc judgement, as the one I gave in the example, is not clearly purely conceptual: perhaps when person *B* judges that the strawberry was blue she automatically generated a perceptual fantasy of a blue strawberry (for a computational model consistent with this idea, see Hinton 2007).

*Page 120.* ["Even people who strongly oppose . . . "] The light-from-above prior can be modulated with a little training (Adams, Graf et al. 2004; Morgenstern, Murray et al. 2011). Similar findings have been published for other priors, such as the less obvious prior expectation we have that motion around us is somewhat slow rather than fast (Sotiropoulos, Seitz et al. 2011). Thus even within some kinds of accepted, low-level cases of penetrability there is room for experience-dependent changes in general expectations.

*Page 124.* ["This gives a principled class . . . "] The proposal here is that top-down modulation is facilitated in conditions of high uncertainty. This kind of proposal is also found in work focusing on conditions of partial awareness, see (Kouider, de Gardelle et al. 2010).

*Page 129.* ["Children between 1.5 and 2.5 . . . "] For the case of scale errors, see the video in the supplementary material to the cited article, also see Deloache's website <http://www.faculty.virginia.edu/childstudycenter/researchprojects.html>. Thanks to Uta Frith for bringing scale errors to my attention.

*Page 129.* ["It is difficult to say exactly..."] In the scale error experiment, children were exposed with the full scale toys first. It should be noted that there are numerous reports from parents of this kind of behaviour arising spontaneously (Ware, Uttal et al. 2010). Scale errors decline rapidly with development, though it is of interest here that adults can also be brought to get the scale of the world wrong, through full body versions of the rubber hand illusion (van der Hoort, Guterstam et al. 2011).

*Page 131.* ["In the lab a more boring version..."] Here I describe Bayes optimal sensory integration. To get a sense of how this works it is worth illustrating the simple rule by which this integration occurs. The integration sums the individual estimates, weighted by their precisions:

$$\hat{S} = w_X\hat{S}_X + w_Y\hat{S}_Y$$

Here, $\hat{S}$ is the integrated estimate, $w_X$ and $w_Y$ are the weight, and $\hat{S}_X$ and $\hat{S}_Y$ are the individual estimates. The individual weights, $w$, are determined by the precisions, that is the inverse of the variances, $\sigma$, of the individual estimates. Thus for computing the weight $w_X$ for the auditory estimate $\hat{S}_X$ we need to estimate the variances of both estimates ($\sigma_X$ and $\sigma_Y$):

$$w_X = \frac{1/{\sigma_X}^2}{1/{\sigma_X}^2 + 1/{\sigma_Y}^2} = \frac{{\sigma_Y}^2}{{\sigma_X}^2 + {\sigma_Y}^2}$$

$$w_Y = \frac{1/{\sigma_Y}^2}{1/{\sigma_X}^2 + 1/{\sigma_Y}^2} = \frac{{\sigma_X}^2}{{\sigma_X}^2 + {\sigma_Y}^2}$$

Precision is the inverse of the variance (that is, the more variable the estimate the more imprecise it is). The weight of one estimate is then determined by its own precision scaled by the precision of the other estimate. For example, the weight of $\hat{S}_X$, $w_X$, will diminish as the precision of $\hat{S}_Y$, namely $1/{\sigma_Y}^2$, in the denominator increases. What this expression tells us is that as the precision of the visual estimate goes up, the weight for the auditory estimate goes down. This then moves the integrated estimate towards the visual estimate, and vice versa. Note that, crucially, the variances or precisions have to be estimated in terms of expected precisions in order to weight sensory evidence in a Bayes optimal fashion.

# 7

# Precarious prediction

Perception and action are driven by the simple imperative to minimize prediction error. This occurs in the perceptual hierarchy described in Part I. Even though the core idea is simple, the mechanism comes with a number of different ways to minimize error. That is, prediction error minimization is not just a matter of prediction that *P* and then waiting to see if *P* occurs. Not only is there the difference between perceptual inference and active inference, but there are also considerations of precision and complexity, and everything can occur at different levels of the hierarchy and in different contexts of causal interactions and levels of uncertainty.

This chapter explores some of the many different ways we must tend to these various, interacting aspects of prediction error minimization in order to prevent misperception. This then elaborates further themes from the previous two chapters, where many of the central cases concerned situations where the world is misperceived, for example in illusory conjunction and multisensory illusions.

It turns out there are a number of balances, and probabilistic "knobs" that can be tweaked such as to optimize, or fail to optimize, the representation of the world. For example, there might be trade-offs that allow some amount of misperception in order to efficiently explain away sensory input elsewhere; there might also be trade-offs between precision and imprecision, between high level and low levels of the perceptual hierarchy, and, as I will focus on at the end of the chapter, there is a crucial balance to get right between passive perceptual inference and active inference.

The overall picture of perception and misperception is thus a complicated one, and getting the world right is not always a matter of just being as precise and accurate as possible at all levels of processing. Perceiving agents chart a precarious route towards the truth, where many things can skew our perceptions.

In the last sections of the chapter, I then consider how this picture of the prediction error minimization mechanism could apply to aspects of mental illness, in particular delusions in schizophrenia and perceptual disturbances in autism.

It transpires that the prediction error minimization framework is surprisingly capable of accommodating a wide range of perceptual errors and ways the system can go wrong. Sometimes, rather small but intractable errors and malfunctions seem able to cascade in dramatic ways, which appears to be a parsimonious way of approaching some mental disorders.

Overall, this strengthens the claim that the prediction error mechanism is more than a computational mechanism underlying perception—it is deeply involved in shaping the very phenomenology of perception.

## TRADING OFF PERCEPTION AND MISPERCEPTION

Illusions result from applications of kinds of perceptual and active inference that by and large, in most situations, would be supposed to issue in veridical representation. Such a situation could for example be the way we routinely integrate auditory speech with visual mouth movement. However, sometimes circumstances conspire to make the perceptual inference a matter of misperception; for example, when we see a ventriloquist in action. Illusions seem to be parasitical on something the brain does, and does well, in non-illusory cases. In this sense, illusory perceptions represent the cost of having fairly low-level, automatic mechanisms for dealing efficiently with noisy or ambiguous types of sensory input (for example, the uncertainty in unimodal sensory estimates, such as locating the source of sound in isolation from other input).

This suggests a trade-off between the kinds of automatic processing one can benefit from and the scale and types of illusions one can live with. We should expect illusions to be so far and few in between that they do not outweigh the advantage of having automatic and fast-working low-level perceptual processing.

This seems the case. Many illusions occur predominantly in well-controlled laboratory conditions (for example, experiencing the rubber hand illusion), or in situations where perceptual inference is not very substantially related to active inference (for example, sitting still watching TV, or watching a ventriloquist on stage). It is characteristic of illusions that they mainly work when active inference in the shape of reality testing is curbed. For example, the participant is not allowed to move their real hand in the rubber hand illusion, or to measure the lines in the Müller-Lyer illusion. This suggests that in real, everyday life, where reality testing is less curtailed, illusory contexts would be more transient and elusive. Our engagement with the world is active and if a low confidence perceptual inference matters to us we have many ways of assessing its accuracy.

This fits with the functional role of active inference as primarily able to sharpen the confidence in a hypothesis (Chapter 4). Illusions thrive in contexts

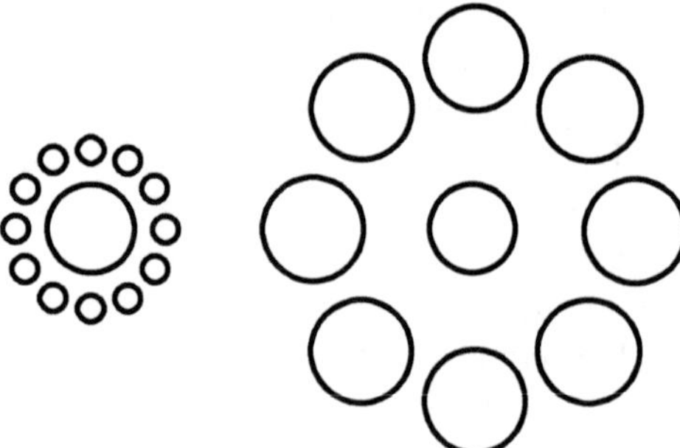

**Figure 20.** Ebbinghaus Illusion. Although the central disk on the left appears larger than the central disk on the right, this difference in visual perception does not influence subsequent reaching movements.

where active inference, if it had been allowed, would fail to make an initial hypothesis more reliable.

In addition, it may be that the perceptual system harbours structures that happen to inoculate itself against some kinds of illusions, and thus make the mentioned kind of trade-off more bearable. I will illustrate this with a speculation about size constancy. Consider the Ebbinghaus illusion (see Figure 20), where the two central disks appear to have different sizes even though they are in fact the same size.

People invariably misperceive the left central disk as larger than the right central disk. This illusion is driven by the context of the surrounding disks. A size constancy explanation of the sort suggested in Chapter 6 for the Müller-Lyer illusion may apply to this illusion too. That is, the illusion occurs because the smaller surrounding disks give a cue that the central disk is further away than do the larger surrounding disks. This makes the visual system represent the former as further away than the latter and compensates for this in size constancy in spite of their identical retinal size.

It would be natural to presume that this visual but illusory perception guides subsequent action such that if a version of the Ebbinghaus illusion is made with slices of wood that can be grasped, then people will wrongly estimate the size of the central disks, as measured with the aperture of their reaching movement. However, this is not what happens. The motor system seems impervious to the illusion: people's reaching movement is not directly influenced by the illusion (Aglioti, DeSouza et al. 1995; see also Skewes, Roepstorff et al. 2011; Plewan, Weidner et al. 2012).

This is an important finding suggesting that *vision for perception* is distinct from *vision for action*. A prominent explanation is that vision for perception is concerned with scene processing for which the entire visual array is important because it can deliver disambiguating cues. In contrast, vision for action is much less concerned with the entire scene and is instead used to provide computations for reach that are centred on the object itself—hence it is less context-dependent and less subject to illusion effects (Aglioti, DeSouza et al. 1995).

This finding is one of the cornerstones of the very influential distinction between the ventral and dorsal visual systems (Goodale and Milner 1992). The segregation between the streams seems to deliver a serendipitous inoculation from the illusion, such that even though one experiences it visually, it does not interfere directly with behaviour.

This is consistent with reasonable trade-offs between on the one hand having low-level, automatic perceptual inference for quite ambiguous stimuli, and on the other hand experiencing the illusions that these mechanisms tend to saddle us with. It seems likely the perceptual system can tolerate quite significant scope for misperception in the shape of illusions as long as there are underlying benefits such as fast, automatic processing, and as long as the illusions do not in the long run infiltrate and increase the prediction error costs of other perceptual and active inference. That is, many illusions generate only transient and fairly locally circumscribed departures from prediction error minimization and can therefore be contained.

Overall, this approach to the presence of illusions also continues a theme we have seen earlier, namely that the perceptual system is not interested in veridicality as such. Rather it is interested in the most efficient route to minimizing as much prediction error on average as possible. In that light it seems quite reasonable for the visual system to tolerate some measure of illusions.

## ACCURACY AND NOISE

A number of the illusions we have discussed rely on sensory integration. In the ventriloquist, for example, there is sensory integration of the estimated locations of the distinct visual and auditory input. In the rubber hand illusion there is integration of visual, tactile, and proprioceptive estimates. Integration is often optimal in the sense that the integrated estimate (for example, the co-location of the source of the sound and the vision) is weighted by the respective precisions of the individual estimates and is itself more precise than either of the original estimates, see Figure 21.

Thus as the precision of the visual estimate goes up, the weight for the auditory estimate goes down (see discussion and Notes in Chapter 6). This then moves the integrated estimate of their co-location back and forth according to their individual precision. There is therefore something to be gained from sensory integration: more precise estimates of the world.

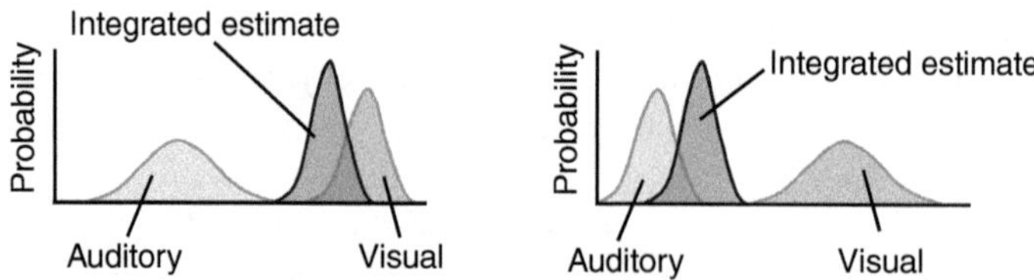


**Figure 21.** Optimal integration of sensory estimates. The integrated estimate is weighted by the precisions of the individual estimates (illustrated as the variance, or width, of the distributions), and is more precise than each of the integrated estimates.

Moreover, these integrated estimates should be accurately tracking hidden causes of sensory input. In the case of audiovisual integration, this is the common (co-located) cause of the two sensory inputs. In the illusory case of integration, the precision is retained but the accuracy suffers. The co-location is not where it seems to be—it is not the doll but the ventriloquist who is the (more deeply hidden) common cause of both the auditory and the visual input.

If the two sensory estimates are extremely precise, or quite far apart, then there is no attempt at sensory integration. This is because we rely on learned or innate regularities about when co-located causes should be expected. As I mentioned in Chapter 6, the prior expectation of co-location is not triggered when the estimates are sufficiently distinct.

Now we can see that correct tracking of hidden causes depends to some degree on precision weighting and precision optimization. On the one hand, the degree of precision in individual sensory estimates low down in the perceptual hierarchy should not be too poor. If it is, then the assumption of co-location will be triggered inappropriately. This is because two noisy estimates are characterized by broad sensory distributions, which are more likely to be considered so close to each other that they likely come from the same common cause. On the other hand, the degree of precision for the individual estimates should not be too high either. If it is, then the assumption of co-location will fail to be triggered when it should be triggered. This is because two very precise estimates are characterized by two narrow distributions, which are more likely to be considered distinct; in other words, two sources are the more plausible explanation for this precise sensory information. Hence, if the overall levels of noise in the low levels of the perceptual hierarchy are estimated to be too high or too low then causal regularities represented higher in the hierarchy will be misperceived. Overly precise or overly imprecise estimates may mask underlying causal structure.

This brings us to a trade-off in the perceptual hierarchy in our attempt at getting the world right, namely the trade-off between low-level precision and high-level precision; in other words, the delicate but crucial balance between precision at different levels in the hierarchy. In some situations, it may be beneficial to assume low-level imprecision; but conversely, sometimes having imprecision at low levels is not beneficial in itself as it can make us miss important distinctions. The overall lesson is the somewhat counterintuitive one that the perceptual system should not automatically strive for maximal precision throughout all levels. In a hierarchical prediction error minimization mechanism, buying precision at one level can come at a cost of imprecision and inaccuracy of representations at other levels.

## PRECISIONS, SAMPLING, AND PRIOR BELIEF

The basic trade-off between low-level precision and high-level precision connects to the fundamental requirement to optimize expected precisions, introduced in Chapter 3. This optimization is crucial to finding the balance between trusting the sensory input and consequently keeping on sampling the world, versus distrusting the sensory input and instead relying more on one's prior beliefs.

The part of the prediction error minimization mechanism that we focus on here is the way the error units gate prediction error according to its expected precision. Prediction error that is expected to be precise is not gated very heavily—it is allowed to drive revision of hypotheses higher up the hierarchy. The effect is that sampling of the world can continue unabated because the signal is trusted. Prediction error that is expected to be imprecise is gated more; it is dampened down with the effect that sampling of the world decreases and instead prior expectations are allowed to determine more the outcome of perceptual inference.

This is a nicely rational approach to inferring the causal structure of the world. When the signal is good, we keep sampling, and use it to drive inference. When the signal is bad, then we sample less, and instead rely on prior expectations to arrive at a conclusion about the world.

This mechanism captures something epistemically essential, which relates to our discussion in Chapter 6 of cognitive penetrability. To what extent is our knowledge of the world driven by the senses or by our preconceptions? Without any preconceptions to marshal the sensory input, it is at best an overly particular, disjointed cacophony and at worst a wholly disorganized, chaotic manifold. But when the preconceptions are given too much weight (or are fed too little sensory input), perceptual inference becomes divorced from the world and we begin to see connections and relations that are not real. Getting the balance between them right is pivotal to the quality of perception. In other words, minimizing prediction error depends on finding the right balance between trusting the sensory input and falling back on priors.

Crucially, the mechanism we are looking at relies on our expectations for precision, and thereby on our ability to learn precision regularities. This will be reflected in the effects on perception from getting the balance wrong. Assume there is an optimal level of overall expected precision at each and every level of the hierarchy: this is when the precision regularities in the world are precisely and accurately learned. Individuals who deviate from this optimum will then misperceive the world in different ways.

Individuals who expect *too much precision* will tend to sample the world more fastidiously, they will strive for more precise low-level sensory estimates in situations where others will allow a measure of imprecision, they will sacrifice representation of some higher-level causal structure (that is, will not be guided as much by higher level prior belief). In short, such individuals will be more slaves of the senses (of low level sensory attributes) than those who have expected precisions that are more optimal in the overall scheme of prediction error minimization. The tendency in such a system will be towards minimizing prediction error for short-term regularities, and poor minimization when longer-term regularities control changes in the short-term regularities.

Contrast this with individuals who expect *too much imprecision* relative to the optimum—people who expect the world to be more noisy and uncertain than it is. They will tend to undersample the world, they will rely less on the senses and more readily rely on prior beliefs in arriving at estimates about the world. In short, such individuals will be more caught in an inner world than people with more optimal expected precisions. Perceptual inference will be biased more towards higher-level causal structure but because such higher-level representation is poorly supervised by sensory sampling it may be poor at minimizing overall prediction error—if that prediction error had been elicited appropriately.

Individuals who fail to optimize expected precisions therefore stand at risk of quite profound and pervasive epistemic shortcomings. This is an interesting and often overlooked perspective on misperception. When we conceive of precision optimization as itself an issue of perceptual inference about (precision) regularities in the world, it also seems a regress begins to threaten (as mentioned in Chapter 3): in order to engage in perceptual inference in the first place, we need to assess precisions, but if assessing precisions depends on higher level perceptual inference, then we should be assessing precisions of precisions (how confident are you that this is the right precision to expect here?); but if that is required then perceptual inference depends on a never-ending process of precision optimization. Obviously, we do not and could not embark on this regress. Instead we must assume we cut the process short—perhaps after one or two levels of statistical inference much like the way things are done in statistical inference in the sciences. However, cutting short the process of inferring precisions should have the consequence that if expected precision is in fact not optimized to begin with, then this can be very difficult to rectify.

So we should expect inference and learning difficulties in the area of expected precisions to be relatively recalcitrant: such estimates are difficult to learn and difficult to revise when not learned right. Moreover, we should expect such difficulties with precision optimization to be accentuated in contexts where uncertainty and ambiguity is high. This is because those contexts are where it matters most to have access to the precisions of one's estimates and where one should be least inclined to just rely on the simple mean. Later in this chapter, this issue is related to aspects of mental illness.

For now I want to point out that we all need to get this balance right. We are often in situations where the uncertainty mounts and yet perceptual decisions must be made. How we react in these circumstances depends on how we process uncertainty and what we consider to be a mounting level of uncertainty. Misperceptions arise when we get this wrong: the overall model of the world begins to carry less information about the actual world when it is biased towards low level sensory attributes at the expense of high level regularities, or vice versa.

The intriguing perspective that arises out of the prediction error minimization approach is then that this kind of misperception can be caused not by faulty processing of the evidence but instead by faulty processing of the evidence about the evidence (for two relevant studies in this area, see Yu and Dayan 2005; de Gardelle and Summerfield 2011).

## REALITY TESTING

Sometimes we come to suspect that perceptual inference has gone awry, and we must then test its veridicality. This can range from the mundane such as shouting hello to a stranger you misperceived as a friend before realizing your mistake, to the more sinister such as a woman hearing voices and checking her house for its source, concluding that she is hallucinating (Hammeke, McQuillen et al. 1983). I will not attempt a full treatment of perceptual reality testing here but will pursue the notion through some of the issues we have already touched upon.

In Chapter 6, I argued that cognitive penetrability can happen when a higher level representation can explain away prediction error lower down at sufficiently fine-grained spatiotemporal scales, especially under conditions of mounting uncertainty. Cognitive impenetrability is then when the higher-level state fails to make this kind of specific contact with the low-level states it is supposed to penetrate. On this view there is no principled obstacle to cognitive penetrability, it just so happens that some hypotheses about states of the world do not fit the spatiotemporal resolution of low-level perceptual content as well as others, so they cannot work as well as explanatory hypotheses.

This simple idea relates to a type of reality testing. Sometimes perceptual content is unexpected, or unexpectedly uncertain; sometimes we subsequently learn from others, or from later evidence, that a perceptual inference was misguided. In those cases, we have to engage in reality testing, we have to test whether things are really as they seem. That is, we have to re-engage inference under a hypothesis that has been revised in light of other information. This new information should then ideally rectify perception. To illustrate, observe Figure 22. It seems just like a constellation of meaningless black and white shapes.

But I am telling you there is really an image of some real middle-sized object in Figure 22. Now that you know there is some object, can you see it? Most people cannot use that bland piece of new evidence to efficiently re-engage perceptual inference (or meaningfully engage active inference). We look around in the image but still cannot see what object it is. So let us improve the situation with more detailed information: it is a banana standing on its tip and bending to the left. That gives you the new evidence that will allow you to re-engage perceptual information under a revised hypothesis.

If you get the 'aha' moment, then your perceptual inference will change and you cannot help but see it as that fruit. (If you struggle, then peek at Figure 23 on page 150). This is a simple example of perceptual reality testing. What makes it work is that the revised parameters of the banana-hypothesis could make appropriate 'contact' with the low level sensory attributes of the image. Your first go at making sense of Figure 22 minimized prediction error well enough, given your impoverished hypothesis back then. But prediction error increased once you were told about the presence of 'some middle-sized object'. Only when you were given semantic and spatiotemporally relevant evidence about the object were you able to minimize prediction error again: your perceptual system was able to work specifically with each black and white

**Figure 22.** A meaningless image? (Frith and Dolan 1997; reprinted by permission of the Royal Society).

blob in the image and bring them under the predictions from a higher-level hypothesis of what bananas rather than mere blobs look like.

We do this kind of thing all the time. We explore the world, revise our hypotheses about it using a multitude of sources of evidence; then we re-explore the world in the light of all the available evidence, and seek to command the sensory input under the richer hypothesis, and under renewed active inference. We try to make sense of the world, given what we know. But this is a highly constrained process, for good reasons. Misperception would be rife if we could modulate perceptual inference on ill-based, misguided whims. For example, if a typo had sneaked in changing 'banana' to 'Dalmatian' in the text above, then it should not allow you to change the very perceptual experience in the direction of only being able to see it as a Dalmatian. The constraint comes, as we have seen previously, from the ability of the new evidence to help generate predictions that can suppress prediction error all the way down in the perceptual hierarchy.

Now we can see how reality testing can fail; how we can fail to make good, veridical sense of the world. This can happen when the independent, reliable evidence that a given perceptual inference is a misperception nevertheless fails to make proper, predictive contact with the low level sensory input pertaining to that inference. This presumably often occurs when the new evidence is too general or abstract (or judged imprecise) relative to a spatiotemporally fine-grained stream of sensory input. That is, when I cannot translate the high-level predictions into predictions for each of the subsequent levels below. In that case there is unrequited prediction error in the system: I know the perceptual inference in question probably isn't true, I know the more probable hypothesis that should be able to explain it away and may highly trust this hypothesis, yet I fail to make the prediction error go away. In this situation, an inferior hypothesis about the state of the world may jump in to minimize prediction error. Let me give an illustration of this, again taken from our own studies of the rubber hand illusion.

If we set up the rubber hand illusion using virtual reality goggles, as in Figure 24, then the illusion is very easy to induce and can be modulated in striking ways (Hohwy and Paton 2010).

In one variation we studied, we simply lifted the finger off the seen rubber hand while maintaining tapping on the participant's real hand, which was hidden from view. So while they felt a tap on their real hand they saw the scenario depicted in Figure 25.

The perceptual inference situation is now this. We have first used synchronous touch to lure the participant into minimizing prediction error by locating touch on the rubber hand, and they duly experience the touch as caused by the experimenter's hand they can see in the virtual reality goggles. Then we have made this illusion completely unbelievable, as judged by all the participants' background knowledge about how the universe works, by introducing a visible

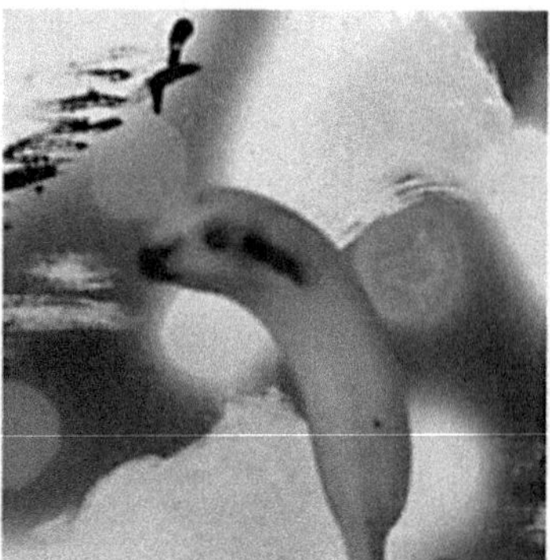

**Figure 23.** The clue to Figure 22 (Frith and Dolan 1997; reprinted by permission of the Royal Society).

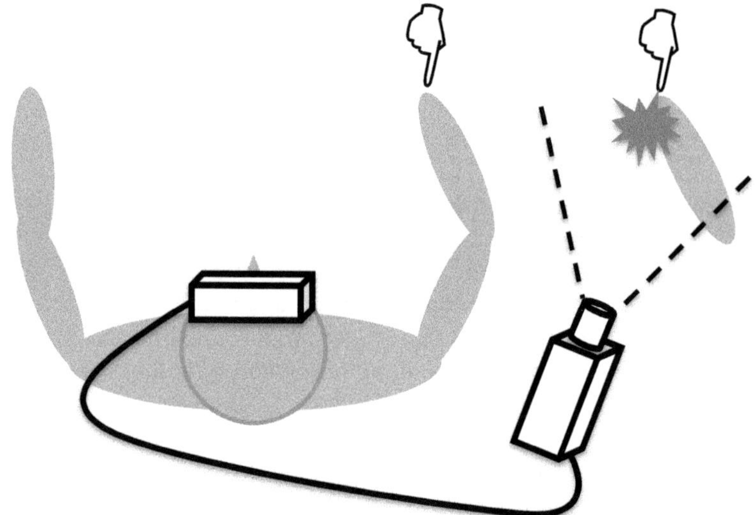

**Figure 24.** Virtual reality rubber hand illusion.

gap between the experimenter's finger and the rubber hand. It is just exceedingly unlikely that causation of touch could happen over such a distance. So the initial (illusory) perceptual inference should now undergo reality testing under the parameter that the seen finger is *not* after all the cause of the touch. This ought to destroy the illusion. Participants should begin to experience what they see in the goggles as something completely unrelated to them—it is just like something they watch on TV, while someone happens to touch their real, unseen hand.

But this is not what happens. If anything, participants get sucked deeper into the illusion, feeling it even stronger. They now report really strange, supernatural-sounding things:

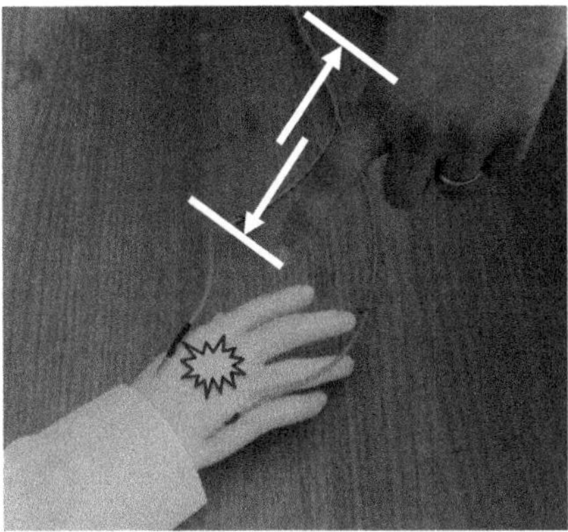

**Figure 25.** Elevated, seen touch in the virtual reality rubber hand illusion. The arrows indicate the up and down movement of the experimenter's finger, which does not make contact with the rubber hand; the star indicates the location of the felt touch.

> "There are opposed magnets on the finger and the skin"
> "It is a magnetic field impacting on my arm"
> "It is witchy . . . it is black magic"
> "There is an invisible extension on the finger"
> "It is ESP"
> "It is telekinetic"
> "A magician makes my muscles contract"
> "The finger is a spectral gun"

Here reality testing has failed. The known and trusted higher-level hypothesis about the true nature of the world has failed to engage the spatiotemporal fineness of grain of the sensory input so it cannot be used to minimize prediction error. Instead a different hypothesis jumps in to take up the prediction error slack: it is a spectral gun, or an invisible extension of the finger extending down to the rubber hand and producing the touch there. Even though this hypothesis would have a very low prior probability it is favoured because it minimizes prediction error better than its competitors—it stems error better at more levels.

Of course, participants in this experiment do not *really believe* in spectral guns and ESP. They are all fully aware of the conflict between their reports of supernatural events and their background knowledge. What makes this intriguing is that, nevertheless, they cannot avoid experiencing supernatural touch. This is then a case where we have cognitive penetrability because the 'supernatural' hypothesis changes the way things are experienced but where we also have cognitively impenetrability since the true belief about the situation fails to change perception in the right way. The debate about cognitive penetrability therefore relates directly to issues concerning reality testing.

## THE COURTROOM OF PERCEPTION

The themes we have discussed so far will be of importance to the discussion of perceptual inference in mental disorder, which will be the topic of the section after this. There is however one aspect of reality testing I want to highlight first, which again relates to cognitive penetrability and reality testing.

I may have given the impression that top-down explaining away is more of a free-for-all than it really is. I have said that the constraint on cognitive penetrability is the ability to predict at the fineness of low-level spatiotemporal grain of available prediction error. This is true but seems to underrate the functional segregation of the sensory system. Different parts of the system specialize in different tasks and seem relatively unimpeded by other processes (this relates to Fodor's (1983) notion of informationally encapsulated cognitive modules). Again and again neuroscience researchers find the same highly specific types of processing in the same areas of the brain, across situations and individuals. If cognitive penetrability was a free-for-all, then perhaps we should not expect such strong regimentation and modularization?

I will try to indicate a partial answer to this worry, from the point of view of reality testing in the prediction error minimization scheme. The aim is to suggest how a kind of partially segregated architecture is beneficial for perceptual inference.

Reality testing is somewhat like engaging an epistemic courtroom. Some perceptual inference is put in a context of doubt and is interrogated in the light of other supporting or contradicting evidence. Similarly, in a courtroom, some defendant's claim is being interrogated in the light of supporting or contradicting witnesses. It is essential for a trial that different witnesses are independent. This is why the witnesses should not be allowed to chat about the case in the corridor or meet with the defendant before being let in to testify. If the witnesses are not independent with respect to the case in question, then we cannot trust their evidence. Similarly, the judge needs to be impartial and the jury needs to be independent too. For example, the jury members should not be bigots and should not have had access to copious media reports before the trial begins; and the judge is not allowed to influence any testimony. If the judge and jury are not independent in this sense then we cannot trust them to evaluate and weigh the evidence in a fair way. This imposes a kind of *evidential architecture* on the legal system: checks and balances are in place to ensure independence. Fairness is violated when this fails.

I think the same holds for reality testing in the brain—indeed, the whole point of prediction error minimization is to maximize Bayesian model evidence with a particular evidential architecture. Different sources of evidence need to be independent witnesses with respect to the event in question, and higher-level expectation needs to evaluate evidence from lower levels in a balanced way. If the evidence from one sensory source (for example hearing), is influenced by the evidence from another source (for example vision), then what you hear should not be used as a guide to reality testing. Let's say you may have seen a dog. You should not use what you've heard to support that perceptual inference if the auditory estimate itself is a least in part caused by the perceptual inference that you *saw* a dog (this is like asking another witness what you should testify). Similarly, if you cannot figure out what is before you, you should not rely exclusively on higher-level expectations in determining perceptual inference (this is like asking the judge what to testify).

This can be applied to some examples we have come across before. In the ventriloquist illusion, estimation of the co-location of the source of the visual and the auditory input will go astray if the auditory estimate of location is caused by the visual estimate of location rather than being an independent estimate of the causal source in the environment. In the study of seeing patterns-in-noise (Figure 18 in Chapter 6), misperception arises for those who see a pattern in the certifiably noise-only image; even though it is reasonable to let prior, top-down expectations resolve uncertainty, it is not correct to do so when there is in fact no information at all to discern.

This suggests that to work efficiently as a reality-testing machine, the brain is well served to implement some evidential architecture. Different sensory modalities in particular and perhaps some intrasensory streams of evidence too, need to be evidentially shielded from each other. This predicts evidential insulation amongst 'vertical' streams. Likewise, sensory processes—the testimony delivered by the senses—need to be shielded from undue influences from higher-level representations; and higher levels need to be able to arrive at a prior expectation without having considered the current evidence. This predicts some degree of evidential insulation between 'horizontal' levels of processing.

The perceptual hierarchy, and the iterations of the prediction error minimization mechanisms implemented at each of its levels, seem apt to deliver evidential insulation between horizontal levels. Each overlapping pair of levels forms a functional unit where the lower level passes prediction error to the higher level, and the higher level passes predictions to the lower level. The higher level is in turn lower level for the next level up: it passes prediction error up and receives predictions from that next level (see Figure 7 in Chapter 3).

In this sense the upper level in each pair of levels only "knows" its own expectations and is only told how these expectations are wrong, and is never told directly what the level below "knows". Similarly, the upper level never tells the lower level what message to pass on, it only ever anticipates what the lower level will tell it. For this reason, the right kind of horizontal evidential insulation comes naturally with the hierarchy, as I foreshadowed in the previous chapter on cognitive penetrability.

As always, there is going to be some relaxation of these conditions. In the courtroom, the judge and jury are allowed to know the gist of the case; lawyers may be allowed to present the case before witnesses are presented and their evidence scrutinized; and the judge is allowed to know what verdicts have been arrived at in similar cases. As the case evolves, all this prior evidence is then revised and weighted in the light of the new evidence. Similarly in the brain, much time and effort would be lost if higher levels had to search the entire search space of hypotheses before hitting on the right one, therefore the gist of the scenario may be available to guide the way the evidence is subsequently interrogated. What determines the eventual perceptual inference is then the fit between the evolving expectations and the fine-grained information delivered by the testimony of the senses. This is analogous to the court case where the final verdict should reflect how the actual evidence from the independent witnesses fits with the competing hypotheses for explaining it away (for example, the guilty vs. innocent hypotheses).

Regarding vertical evidential insulation, there is also a probabilistic story to tell. Having more than one witness delivering evidence of an event can increase posterior probability more efficiently than just using the same sensory modality in the same conditions to collect more of the same evidence over and over again (for discussion, see Bovens and Hartmann 2003). This principle was also reflected in the cases of Bayes optimal multisensory integration (Figure 21 above), where a more accurate estimation was made possible only when two sources of evidence were integrated. This effect of adding witnesses tapers off relatively quickly, so that adding a large stream of witnesses to the same event is not conducive to reality testing. Prediction error minimization would then be greatly aided by having multiple, but not too many, independent sources of evidence. This all fits nicely with our having five main senses—that are each sensitive to different information channels concerning the same events in the environment.

Of course, this general need for independent sensory evidence applies also to cases where there is disagreement with what the senses tell us (just as it applies to witnesses in a court case). Hence, if I arrive at a conclusion about something by feeling it in a darkened room, then much doubt is thrown on this if I get contradictory visual evidence once the light is turned back on. Thus having independent witnesses is crucial to trigger further reality testing.

I am not arguing that the only reason we have the senses we have is that they serve as independent witnesses to perceptual inference. There is no doubt that we also benefit from the way the senses tap into different aspects of the same events such that they can complement each other in different ways in different situations (for example, in clear daylight vs. at dusk). But I think the need for independent witnesses could be an important driver in the evolution of the senses and, indeed, for our ability to rank their individual reliabilities in different environmental contexts.

In cases where perceptual inference depends on only *one* sensory modality, it will be easier to end up with intractably poor perceptual inference. In such cases we can predict there will be diminished scope for reality testing because there are less independent routes to suggest the perceptual inference is wrong, and because posterior probability is not boosted by further independent witnesses. This will apply in cases where reality testing is curbed artificially, such as in laboratory controlled illusions (for example, the rubber hand illusion). It will also apply in cases not governed by the five major senses (hearing, sight, taste, smell, and touch) but that tend instead to be more internal and tap into areas not easily accessible to other senses: proprioception (body sense), balance, acceleration, pain, temperature sense, and interoception in general (senses originating from within the body). Given that mental illness is often characterized by intractable, poor perceptual inference we should expect these inner senses to have a central place in mental disorder; we will discuss this in the next section.

In Chapter 6, I argued that interesting cases of cognitive penetrability tend to occur when uncertainty is heightened. I also provided room for cases of cognitive impenetrability, and I suggested that our understanding of penetrability is related to issues of reality testing. It is now possible to see better how this fits together. Cognitive impenetrability is related to evidential insulation imposed both by the nature of message-passing up and down in the perceptual hierarchy and by the need for independent witnesses in the shape of different senses and possibly individual intrasensory streams. This evidential architecture imposes limits on top-down and lateral modulation—it is not a free-for-all situation. However, what is predicted and how well it is predicted determines what signal is passed up through the hierarchy and thereby what perceptual inference is drawn.

We can turn to the courtroom analogy one more time to illustrate the idea that cognitive penetrability will tend to happen when there is mounting uncertainty. The interesting cases of penetrability are like summary court cases. A verdict must be arrived at in a hurry and the jurors let their preconceptions weigh more than the witnesses' evidence in the verdict they communicate to the judge. Similarly, the low-level prediction error that is passed up through the hierarchy under uncertainty is less influenced by the actual causes in the world and more influenced by the predictions of favoured hypotheses—by our preconceptions. Again, we see that cognitive penetrability and impenetrability appear to be inextricably linked to reality testing and Bayesian inference. This is what the predictive coding framework, and with it the notion of the perceptual hierarchy strongly suggests. This is an attractive view because it gives an epistemological take on the issue of cognitive penetrability.

In the analogy between prediction error minimization and the courtroom, I have focused on perceptual inference and not said much about active inference. Active inference can easily be made to fit, however. A court case has a highly active engagement with the evidence in its attempt to make an inference (reach a verdict) under uncertainty (that is, when there is low confidence in both hypotheses). In turn, the prosecutor and the defence both interrogate the evidence under their each different hypotheses about what happened. The hypothesis that is not only best supported by the evidence but that also most successfully can be used to interrogate the evidence ends up being deemed more reliable. Just as for active inference in the brain, prosecutor and defence must assume a hypothesis about the world and actively seek out evidence in conformity with their hypothesis—not to mention their crucial role in calling expert witnesses (and selecting the jury).

Proponents of unconscious perceptual inference have often compared perception to scientific hypothesis testing. As Richard Gregory puts it in his article entitled "Perceptions as Hypotheses" (Gregory 1980): "Perceptions may be compared with hypotheses in science. The methods of acquiring scientific knowledge provide a working paradigm for investigating processes of perception." What we have seen is that much can also be gained by using the legal context of the courtroom as a working analogy to perception, where both—as argued in this book—are quintessentially evidence-based. I return to the analogy in Chapter 12, where I use it to motivate a view on the privacy of conscious experience.

## MENTAL ILLNESS AND PREDICTION ERROR

So far in this chapter we have marshalled a number of ways in which prediction error minimization can be adjusted and thus ways it may be suboptimal. If we assume that mental disorder is characterized at least partly by more or less systematic misperception, then we could perhaps learn more about such disorder by considering prediction error minimization. Here I exemplify this with specific aspects of mental illness: delusion formation in psychosis and sensory deficits in autism. The objective is to exploit what has been said so far about the prediction error mechanism and explore the extent to which this may begin to cast some much-needed light on mental disorder.

Here are the ways of "tuning" the prediction error minimization mechanism we have looked at so far.

- Some quick and automatic expectations may come with an allowable cost of erroneous inference (leading to illusions, for example).
- Sensory integration relies on a trade-off between precisions at high and low levels of perceptual hierarchies.

- A general balance must be struck between trusting the signal from the world and trusting one's prior belief; this depends on one's expected precisions, which themselves can be difficult to optimize.
- Processes of prediction error minimization are processes of incremental reality testing; this connects to cognitive penetrability and impenetrability.
- Penetrability and thereby reality testing depends on the ability of top-down predictions to match the spatiotemporal grain of low-level sensory input.
- Reality testing relies on hierarchical evidential architecture with distinct, independent sources of sensory evidence.

This gives a rich tapestry of possible error—multiple interacting kinds of tuning failure. In neither case is it easy to give definite rules for how to adjust the various checks and balances on inference. Some of these aspects of inference have been implicated in psychosis and autism. I will pursue some of the themes in the next two sections, first for delusions, then for sensory issues in autism. The aim is to conceptually analyse what the connection might be between prediction error and mental illness and to begin to situate some of the growing body of empirical literature in this area. The prediction error mechanism suggests that for some aspects of mental illness it only takes relatively small but recalcitrant "tuning" errors to initiate severe and disabling cascades of malfunction.

## DELUSIONS AND EXPECTED PRECISIONS

Delusions are unusual, bizarre beliefs that are held on to tenaciously in spite of evidence and testimony to the contrary. It has long been suspected that unusual experiences may trigger delusions (Maher 1974), though there is debate about whether unusual experiences are sufficient for full delusion formation or whether further elements are needed (Davies and Coltheart 2000; Coltheart, Langdon et al. 2011; McKay 2012).

Disturbances to the prediction error framework have been implicated indirectly or directly in some of these theories (Frith 1992; Hohwy 2004; Stephan, Friston et al. 2009; Corlett, Taylor et al. 2010). Prediction error mechanisms are attractive candidates for explaining delusions because delusions seem to concern the delicate interplay between sensory input and the prior expectations we use to make sense of the input. It seems plausible that it is this interplay that has been disturbed when patients believe, for example, that doctor is out to get them, or that they smell of faeces, and perhaps even when they believe such bizarre things as that the Mafia have put a horse in their tooth.

There are different ways one could characterize the kind of prediction error disturbance that leads to psychosis and delusions. It would be desirable to work towards a kind of disturbance such that (i) the disturbance is relatively domain general (i.e., the same mechanism applies across different processing modules), such that the heterogeneity of delusional phenomena seen in schizophrenia can be accommodated in a parsimonious way; (ii) the disturbance is strongly intractable, so it can reflect the trouble in treating schizophrenia and delusional disorder; and (iii) the disturbance is able to capture the hallmarks of delusions, such as their strange content and the way they are tenaciously believed in spite of much evidence going against them. Here I will chart a course towards an account that seems able to satisfy these three constraints. Importantly, this account will rely only on what I have highlighted so far about relatively intractable prediction error aberrances. Specifically, the account will centre on three aspects of optimization of expected precisions.

One thought I have focused on above (and in Chapter 3) is that there may be limits to how much reality testing is feasible for optimization of expected precisions without ending with a regress of statistical inference. It is crucial that the system has a method for assessing the confidence in its perceptual inference, but it seems obvious that there is a limit to how deep the search for confidence estimation can go without the system breaking down. Indeed, it seems likely that very quickly the system must simply trust that it is getting confidence estimation right. It follows that if there is a problem with optimizing precisions, then it will be difficult for the prediction error minimization mechanism to rectify this. That is, problems with precision optimization may easily be chronic and entrenched. Also, attempted solutions by the system may display a fair amount of fluctuation as different policies for assessing confidence are tried out.

As I have noted, expected precisions and the associated confidence estimates play a key role for the very general balance between bottom up sensory evidence and top down expectations: when the prediction error is expected to be noisy, then it is dampened down and instead the system relies on top-down priors. This tells us that chronic problems with expected precisions can generate chronic problems with getting that balance right. Specifically, a persistent, exaggerated expectation for noise and uncertainty would lead to imprecise sensory prediction errors mediated by low gain on sensory input and heightened reliance on top-down priors. An individual who constantly expects the sensory signal to be noisier than it really is will then tend to be caught in his or her own idiosyncratic interpretations of the input and will find it hard to rectify these interpretations. This gives rise to the idea that psychosis and delusions stem from such faulty uncertainty expectations.

I have also highlighted how having independent sources of evidence facilitates reality testing. Hence, even if expected precisions are suboptimal in one sensory domain they could in principle be corrected by the evidence delivered via other sensory sources. For example, if the auditory sense is suboptimal it could perhaps be adjusted via the more optimal estimates from visual and tactile estimates.

One obstacle to such adjustment would be if the problem with optimizing expected precisions is global. In that case, there is little help to get from adding extra sources of evidence, since they are all compromised. Another obstacle may be if the problem persists in a sensory channel for which there are no other relevant sensory sources of information. This speaks to the preponderance of delusions that arguably occur in sensory domains where it is hard to avail oneself of multiple independent sources of evidence that would directly engage prediction error at the right spatiotemporal fineness of grain. Thus, emotional, agency-related, proprioceptive, body, and self-related contents are often delusion prone and fall in this evidentially insulated category. It is also conceivable that as intractable interpretations in these insulated sensory domains become part of one's doxastic bedrock, they can lead to more prolific delusional systems.

Trying to put together these three different strands of precision-related reality testing, we can begin to see the outline of a generic account of delusion formation, which can begin to satisfy the three constraints. The account posits suboptimal precision optimization, such that there are persistent exaggerated expectations for noisy prediction error. This means that prediction error is dampened down and top-down priors are weighted more in inference; in addition, the dampened down error signal is a less efficient supervisor in the ongoing revision of prior belief, making it more likely those priors stray from reality. When such troubled perceptual inference is global or when it occurs in a relatively 'mono-evidential', inner domain other sensory evidence cannot help to correct the failing precision optimization.

In these conditions, prediction error minimization will be compromised by inappropriate weighing of priors. Differences might also emerge as a result of the overall dampening down of the prediction error landscape. For example, relatively small prediction errors, which other people routinely are guided by, may be presented as just noise; this would create problems for learning and for attention allocation. Also, larger prediction error may appear as more exceptional than it would to other people because it occurs against an overall background of more subdued prediction error; this would attract attention more than in other people and make it more imperative to explain it away.

We have also seen that reality testing (and penetrability) depends on the ability of the hypothesis under test to match the fineness of spatiotemporal grain of the low-level prediction error down through the perceptual hierarchy.

A highly trusted hypothesis ("the doctors tell me something is wrong with my brain") may fail in this respect, leaving less trusted hypotheses ("it's a female demon moving my arm") to fill the void and satisfy our appetite for suppressing prediction error at each and every hierarchical level of description. This relates to the inability of patients to use background knowledge and testimony of family and carers to combat their delusions; the background knowledge and the testimony are not parsed at the right spatiotemporal scale to explain away the aberrant error (Hohwy and Rosenberg 2005). It may then be expected that the selection of hypotheses that end up doing certain kinds of error-minimization work will differ between patients with suboptimal expected precisions and healthy individuals. Even though we all occasionally fall in this trap, the way delusional individuals fall in it differs.

Precision optimization is a natural focus for this generic account of delusion formation since it is central to reality testing, and since learning is expected to be particularly difficult in that higher-order area of sensory inference. It is also domain neutral in a specific sense: to assess the precision of a signal we need not know what it is a signal of. This means that the account of delusions is not tied to specific representational contents, and this can go some way to explain the very heterogeneous nature of psychotic symptoms where delusions are elaborated in many different ways.

All this naturally leads to the question how failures of precision optimization could arise. There are intriguing theories that relate precision optimization to the dopamine disturbances that have long been suspected of having an involvement in schizophrenia (Fletcher and Frith 2009; Corlett, Taylor et al. 2010); norepinephrine also seems involved (Yu and Dayan 2005). There is also evidence that there is a genetic component to schizophrenia, which relates to how dopamine regulates signal-to-noise ratio, that is, precision (Winterer and Weinberger 2004; Rolls and Deco 2010).

This generic account of delusion formation suggests that in some cases it may take very little to upset perceptual inference in profound and pervasive ways. Perhaps all it takes is a genetic predisposition to expect the world to be a little bit noisier than most people expect it to be and then having the misfortune of being in uncertain (e.g., abusive) environments (or having other perhaps developmental problems) such that prediction error become unexpected in ways that are difficult to expose to reality testing. One gets the impression, from the prediction error story, that even though perceptual inference is remarkably consistent and closely supervised by the sensory input, it is not very robust. It is hostage to how the uniformity of the world lends itself to statistical inference and to statistical inference itself having a fundamental sense of the reliability of the sensory input. This points to an intriguing understanding of our place in nature; we will pursue this theme of robustness later (Chapter 11).

More would need to be done to substantiate this account. Here it serves to show how suboptimal "tuning" of the prediction error mechanism could lead to a parsimonious understanding of delusions.

## AUTISM AND EXPECTED PRECISIONS

Autism spectrum disorder is a neurodevelopmental disorder characterized by presence of social deficits, stereotypies and restricted interests, language abnormalities, and repetitive behaviour (Frith 2003). In addition, there are a number of less explored sensory and motor differences in individuals with autism (Rogers and Ozonoff 2005; Simmons, Robertson et al. 2009). There is much heterogeneity along this spectrum, with symptoms ranging from heartbreakingly disabled and non-communicative patients to high-functioning individuals.

Much research in this area is devoted to the question of how the sensory and motor differences in the autism spectrum relate to the more prominent social cognition deficits. An influential view, proposed by Uta Frith, Francesca Happé, and their colleagues, is that there is a bias against global, context-dependent processing (Happé and Frith 2006). This kind of *weak central coherence* is marked by a degree of inability to pull different, relatively local estimates of aspects of the world in under higher-level, more global regularities and principles. As such it could then begin to explain some social deficits because getting the social world right depends on being appraised of global, general linguistic conventions and social mores.

This view is attractive from the point of view of prediction error minimization because it directly concerns the balance between bottom-up and top-down processing that is key to perceptual hierarchical inference. It immediately suggests that there may be issues with expected precisions gating the sensory input such that global coherence is impeded.

The basic idea would go like this. A perceiver who expects very precise prediction errors will increase the gain on bottom-up prediction error and will rely relatively more on the senses than on prior beliefs, as compared to a perceiver who expects the world to be somewhat more noisy. This will lead the perceiver to sample the world more and for longer, to appeal less to higher-level parameters in an attempt to generalize over particular perceptual inferences, and so will rely less on contextual influences in attempts to resolve uncertainties in the input. Described like this, the perceiver begins to fit the profile of sensory perception characteristic of the autism spectrum. There is a kind of enslavement by the senses, a pre-occupation with local sensory content, extended sampling, intolerance of change in circumstances, and lack of coherence under global models (that is, ignoring the need to predict longer term regularities and being surprised when they modulate routines).

Hence, what the prediction error account promises here is a fairly parsimonious mechanism that uses just the notion of hierarchical precision optimization to tap into aspects of perceptual inference in autism.

The precision optimization account should be reflected in learning processes and may thus speak to the developmental aspects of autism. In particular, it seems likely that heightened expected precision could lead to a particularist learning style where there is no interpolation between samples based on more general expectations. Each sample is processed in isolation from the next sample, under the expectation that it can be represented very precisely. In support of this, I will briefly consider two theoretical perspectives that are consistent with the idea that precision optimization is a central aspect of autism.

In the predictive coding framework, learning is just longer-term revision of hypotheses in the light of prediction error. Therefore, a difference in learning style should reflect a difference in perceptual inference. An individual who expects more precision than most others will be more guided by particular sensory input and less tempted to try to generalize that input under previously learned more general regularities—indeed it will be hard to ever learn more global regularities. The autistic learning style will be more particular and sensory oriented, and less general and globally coherent. This learning-perspective is important because it speaks to the developmental aspects of autism.

Recently, just this kind of difference in learning style has been proposed as a unifying account of autism (Qian and Lipkin 2011). Qian and Lipkin do not use prediction error minimization to develop their account but instead phrase their account in terms of neuronal tuning functions, which describe the way particular neurons or populations of neurons respond to particular kinds of stimuli, that is, how they carry information about particular stimuli. Their main hypothesis is that typically developed brains are biased towards generalist, interpolation learning (broad tuning curves) and that the brain of an autistic individual is biased towards particularist, lookup table learning (narrow tuning curves). I think this difference in learning bias would be nicely understood in terms of a difference in precision optimization.

Next consider how the prediction error minimization framework would be applied to the specific case of *mentalizing* (getting to know the minds of others). This is a cognitive domain where individuals with autism have very pronounced deficits. Specifically, we want to consider what would happen to mentalizing under the assumption that in autism, precisions are generally expected to be high (and the learning style thus biased towards a particularist lookup table style).

Mentalizing is an exercise in causal inference on hidden causes. Indeed, to many of us, others' mental states are paradigms of the hidden. This is the observation that has fuelled the Other Minds Problem in philosophy for centuries—the sceptical problem concerning how we can know whether other creatures have minds when we cannot observe directly their mental states.

John Stuart Mill famously suggested a solution to this problem, namely that we get to know other's minds by inference from analogy with our own mind and behaviour. We see what the other creature is doing or saying, then we consider what our own mental state would be under that behaviour, and then we infer that the other's mental state is essentially the same as ours would be (Mill 1865). This is an inferential process and the application of prediction error minimization to mentalizing is essentially just an extension of this general idea. We try to predict behaviour of the other person on the basis of an internal model, partly fuelled by knowledge of the trajectories of our own mental states and behaviour (that is, it is fuelled by our model of our self, cf. Metzinger 2009). If the predictions are right, then we ascribe the mental states implicit in the recognition model of the mental states. (This has been worked out in more detail in (Kilner, Friston et al. 2007); see also Wentzer and Frith (in press).)

Perceptual inference works particularly hard in the case of mentalizing: as deception and stage acting teach us, there is no robust one-one relation between surface sensory attributes and mental states; there is also extensive context-sensitivity in linguistic interpretation (like that involved in trying to interpret "Beer? You know where the fridge is!"); and in general there are mental states working as top-down parameters on behaviour at multiple time scales, which makes behavioural patterns non-linear and hard to predict (for example, immediate desire for beer, long-term desire to avoid beer due to the association between beer and card games, combined with fluctuating levels of *akrasia*). This dependence on situation and global context in mentalizing predicts that having a lookup-table learning style for mentalizing is going to be particularly detrimental to normal development in this social domain.

The simple idea is then that in autism there is a bias towards particularist perceptual inference as a result of failed optimization of expected precisions. That is, in autism much of the world is represented correctly but is harnessed by hypotheses that are causally shallow, that miss out on longer-term regularities and that cannot well predict deeply hidden causes. I think this proposal is consistent with a recent proposal by Friston, Lawson and Frith (2013), who phrase it in the converse terms of increased imprecision of top-down predictions (where this amounts to increased weighting to the incoming prediction error, that is, expecting it to be precise).

We can predict that this signature learning style and perceptual difference will be particularly prominent when there are elevated levels of uncertainty. That is because, as we have seen, it is when uncertainty mounts that one should rely less on the senses and more on background knowledge. Individuals with autism should buck this pattern and instead rely on the senses for longer, try to keep sampling the world in spite of the uncertainty, and perhaps occasionally through this extensive sampling eventually arrive at superior particular estimates. The prediction that learning and perceptual inference is especially compromised under mounting uncertainty may go some way to explain why there are often conflicting findings in the study of autism (and schizophrenia). Two studies that both look at perception of the same illusion in autism may get different results because they don't control for levels of uncertainty in the same way.

I think our own work on the rubber hand illusion in people with autism spectrum disorder begins to support the notion of expectations for high precision in autism (Paton, Hohwy et al. 2011). Though much more research is needed in this area, there is now evidence that in schizophrenia the rubber hand illusion has an earlier onset than in healthy controls and in autism it has a later onset and seems characterized by less subsequent multisensory integration of the visuotactile estimate with the proprioceptive estimate (Peled, Ritsner et al. 2000; Peled, Pressman et al. 2003; Paton, Hohwy et al. 2011; Cascio, Foss-Feig et al. 2012). Together this fits with the idea that in schizophrenia the incoming signal is considered imprecise, is trusted less, and sampling is reduced whereas in autism it is the reverse.

We also explored how people, ranked on the autism spectrum scale, would reach for an object after experiencing the illusion. As a proxy for expected precision we measured the jerk of the movement, which is the rate of change of acceleration. The reasoning is that someone expecting a reaching movement to be imprecise would change the rate of acceleration more than someone expecting it to be precise. In terms of active inference, experiencing the rubber hand illusion should induce some uncertainty about where the reach target is relative to the real hand, and thus make participants expect imprecision in the proprioceptive prediction error minimized in the movement. They should in other words cast about more in order to efficiently minimize the prediction error with action, issuing in more jerk. This is what we found; people who are low on the autism spectrum have more jerk after experiencing the rubber hand illusion than after not experiencing it, whereas people higher on the spectrum (but not clinical) have no jerk differences (Palmer, Paton et al. 2013). Though more research is needed in this area, this is some evidence for the hypothesis suggested here.

As it was in the case of delusions, we again see the idea that it may take something very trivial to profoundly disturb perceptual inference. Getting the expected precisions of sensory input slightly wrong can at least in principle trigger a cascade of effects in perceptual inference, effects that seem capable of capturing frightening aspects of autism. Perceptual inference is very good for representing the world, but not much needs to go wrong before inference begins to fall seriously apart.

In this section and the last we have considered how the many ways of misperceiving the world while engaged in prediction error minimization might apply to delusion and autism. In particular we have considered the idea that in delusions there is an exaggerated expectation of imprecision in the sensory input, whereas in autism there is an exaggerated expectation of precision in the sensory input. When these expected precisions modulate the prediction error mechanisms making up the perceptual hierarchy it seems key characteristics of these disorders can be accommodated.

This is far from a unifying theory of psychosis and autism, which are incredibly complex syndromes with heterogeneous constellations of symptoms. It is however an illustration of the intriguing explanatory potential of the prediction error framework.

## BALANCING PASSIVE AND ACTIVE INFERENCE

So far, we have been discussing reality testing and misrepresentation mainly in terms of perceptual inference, setting active inference aside. However, as we have noted a number of places, there does appear to be a very fundamental balance to get right between perceptual inference and active inference. This last section will discuss this balance, and briefly explore how it may relate to mental illness.

Recall that perceptual inference is the passive process of updating one's internal beliefs to best explain away the sensory input. The prediction error is minimized by minimizing the bound on surprise such that the tighter the bound the closer one's hypotheses are to matching the actual input. Active inference does not change the hypotheses to fit the input, instead it takes the prediction for granted and minimizes the prediction error by changing the world and the agent's position in the world and thereby changing the actual input.

Consider that a tight bound on surprise implies accurate perception of the world. On the other hand, a loose bound on surprise implies a somewhat inaccurate model of the world. It is a trivial consequence of this that the more the prediction error the less the information about the world carried by the model. This should mean that if the perceiver acts on a very tight bound on surprise, then she is less likely to encounter surprises. On the other hand, if the perceiver acts on a very loose bound on surprise, then she is more likely to encounter surprise in agency.

It is this balance that I have in mind: how tight does the bound on surprise through perceptual inference need to be before we act? How much optimization of the bound is optimal? Going too early means I will generate more prediction error during action. Going too late may mean I've lost the moment, or that I unnecessarily expend energy making the model overly accurate. Perhaps the balance works the other way too: how tight does the bound on surprise through agency need to be before we go back to perceptual inference? The world is a changing place so persistently sampling the world on the basis of an increasingly out-dated hypothesis may not be optimal on average.

Getting this balance right would be difficult. It seems to demand difficult learning of long-term patterns of overall prediction error evolution. That is, to optimize the way we engage in prediction error minimization we need to represent the way we minimize prediction error and develop strategies to find the right balance. We have to develop expectancies for how prediction error evolves, and learn to swap between perceptual inference and active inference to keep its evolution under control.

What counts as the right balance would be highly context-dependent. In some stable contexts it may be optimal to engage in the same action pattern for a long time, whereas in other, more volatile contexts this may not be optimal. There will be considerable trade-offs between time scales in getting the balance right (for example, exploring minute perceptual detail now may carry a cost in terms of longer term generalization). Similarly, there will be trade-offs in precision: sometimes riding roughshod over imprecision will be beneficial to large accuracy benefits (for example, not bothering with details in order to more fundamentally change one's environment). Marshalling all these elements, across both perceptual and active inference is a massive task. Doing it right also seems to imply representing oneself as an autonomous agent in the world, a self with control over prediction error minimization strategies, with a choice over when to act and when to sit back.

All this may generate the impression that getting this balance right is somehow a very clear-cut switching process guided by a mostly conscious effort. But this cannot be the case. There is constant and fast-switching alternation between perception and action. Consider the way our eyes constantly move in sweeping saccades. Saccades are moments in active inference, which then occur very frequently and at very fast time scales (Friston, Adams et al. 2012). This would lead to very rapid and automatic switching between updating hypotheses and selectively sampling the world to test those hypotheses. The switching would slow down as inference moves up through the perceptual hierarchy. It will be hard to say when conscious deliberation would begin to play a role but the main point is that at any level there will be a balance to get right. Getting it right will be based on learning the prediction error profile in perception and action appropriate for that time scale.

Throughout the book we have operated with the idea that perceptual inference and active inference are both involved in prediction error minimization, albeit with different directions of fit. Now we can see that getting the balance right between these two types of processes is itself a means to successful representation—to sustained suppressing of prediction error (and implicitly, surprise). This broadens the notion of misperception in interesting ways. Successful perception is not just a matter of good Bayesian inference, or of tuning the different aspects of the prediction error mechanism in the right way. It is a matter of acting on an *appropriately* tight bound on surprise (don't act too early and not too late); similarly, perception is a matter of knowing when to stop acting on the world (don't give up too early, don't persist too long).

Of course, there is nothing extraneous to prediction error minimization here. The balance between perception and action is guided by the same one, unifying mechanism for prediction error minimization. For example, it seems possible that there are different equally good (or bad) ways of optimizing this balance for bounded individuals like us. Someone acting on a relatively loose bound on surprise may encounter increasing prediction error earlier in the agentive process than someone who has a more conservative threshold for action. But both may be successful if they adjust their balance appropriately as they go along. For example, the conservative agent should become less conservative as he or she learns that the prediction error generated in action is very small whereas the less conservative agent must spend energy "mopping up" generated prediction error later in the process.

Now we can think about what happens if this balance between perceptual and active inference is suboptimal. Chronic prediction error problems should accrue if the individuals in question are not well placed to optimize the balance between perception and action. If they for example persistently act on very loose or overly tight bounds, then prediction error should be expected to increase over time. Similarly, if individuals sample too much or too little before they return to perceptual inference, then prediction error will tend to rise over time.

It is tempting to speculate that disruptions like these may occur in mental illness. Here is how such a speculation could roughly begin, in line with our speculations above about differences in precision optimization. In schizophrenia there is a tendency to act on a loose bound, which would mean that agency generates much prediction error; perceptual inference is quickly revisited only to be haphazardly revised before new active inference is embarked upon. In autism, there is a very conservative threshold on agency causing a tendency to act only on a very tight bound, and once action is initiated on the basis of the overly precise model it throws up few surprises; therefore perceptual inference is not revisited very much and instead the world is sampled repetitively to fit with the model.

It is attractive to connect mental illness with the active/passive balance because it speaks to something that is puzzling about disorders like schizophrenia and autism. On the one hand they are characterized by perceptual and reasoning problems and differences and on the other hand there is disturbance to autonomy, agency, and sense of self. Research focusing on perceptual disturbances tend to forget about the perplexing forensic and personal disturbances. It is difficult to create a bridge between these two aspects and so perhaps a framework that puts perception and action on the same footing, such as the one proposed here, should be considered.

These ideas are of course rather briefly presented here but what I have suggested so far serves at least to illustrate the kinds of unifying explanatory avenues made available once we consider the entire prediction error minimization edifice. It seems to me to be an overlooked candidate for understanding what contributes to disorders such as schizophrenia and autism—and for what shapes our phenomenology in general.

## SUMMARY: PREDICTION ERROR FAILURES IN ILLNESS AND HEALTH

This chapter has been concerned with an exploration of the prediction error minimization mechanism with a view to explaining the many ways inference can be tuned in order to represent the world correctly, and correspondingly, the many ways that misperception may arise. It turns out to be a rich and complex collection of possible error that we need to navigate in our everyday interactions with the world and each other. The mechanism seems to have rich potential to fit in types of perceptual error and to point out new ways to explain and unify them. It is pleasing that a simple notion like the prediction error minimization mechanism has the resources for such a rich and, it seems to me, phenomenologically and ecologically valid picture of our epistemic interaction with the world.

I then attempted to connect the prediction error framework, and the many ways we can fail to optimally minimize prediction error, to a portion of two key mental illnesses. Of course, I have not presented comprehensive theories of these illnesses, it has been more of a conceptual journey that has partly tried to re-describe aspects of psychosis and autism in terms of prediction error minimization and partly suggested where the prediction error mechanism might go wrong in ways that can explain more chronic ways of misrepresenting the world. In the next chapter, I delve in to some more theoretical and deep philosophical issues about the nature of misrepresentation.

Overall, this chapter has pointed to a picture of precarious prediction. Though most of us get most things right most of the time, it does not seem to take much to disrupt the entire system in profound ways that make it veer off the path of truthful representation. In the background of this is the idea that the neural system seems more interested in suppressing prediction error than in representing the world aright. We will return to these themes in later chapters.

## NOTES

*Page 143.* ["This finding is one of the cornerstones..."] From the point of view of prediction error minimization, it makes sense that the active inference involved in reaching for the central disks in the Ebbinghaus illusion departs from the perceptual illusion: in the context, movement minimizes prediction error better for the central disks than more passive vision. However, this incurs two explanatory tasks. First, why isn't active inference guided more by visual perceptual inference in this case? The best answer seems to me to be that it is so guided, but in more subtle ways consistent with how prediction error is quickly minimized in action. There is evidence for this in the Müller-Lyer illusion (Bruno and Franz 2009; Skewes, Roepstorff et al. 2011). Second, why doesn't the correct conclusion to the active inference penetrate subsequent visual-only perception of the illusion? A version of our method for accommodating cognitive impenetrability, from the previous chapter can be used to answer this. The active inference does not penetrate because it does not have sufficient resources to minimize the prediction error associated with the flanking circles—the hand movement is incapable of updating those parameters. This lets the illuded, visual-based hypothesis back in as the best overall error minimizer because it can take the context of the flankers into consideration.

More generally, it is perhaps not immediately clear why the prediction error scheme should allow the mentioned separation between processing streams for perception and action. Even though perception and action are both in the business of minimizing prediction error it seems reasonable to assume they do so under different constraints, reflecting the regularities incurred by our bodily and sensory configuration as we move about the world. Perception operates with great bandwidth of sensory attributes, which interact at multiple spatiotemporal scales, and often perception needs to dispense with prior assumptions in order to be open to new situations. Bodily action is concerned with getting things done, it needs a smaller bandwidth of sensory attributes, it operates at fewer spatiotemporal scales, it needs to be constrained by more prior assumptions, and can afford only little online clutter as it minimizes prediction error. Conceivably, such a narrower range of possible interpretations of action-orientated situations would serve to avoid costly delays when we, for example, attempt to grasp or avoid looming objects. The overall idea is then that the prior expectations for movement are much more constrained, and thus less context sensitive, than the priors in perceptual inference (Friston, Daunizeau et al. 2010). This predicts that there will be less illusion in action than in perception: there is less scope to go different ways when uncertainty mounts. (Thanks to Josh Skewes and Bryan Paton for discussion of these issues).

*Page 143.* ["This is consistent with reasonable trade-offs..."] Here I suggest that the relation between perceptual and active inference is subtle in a way that explains the illusion findings. Specific aspects of the chosen illusions may strengthen this story by motivating a stronger divide between action and perception. For example, it may be that the causal regularities involved in generating an illusion such as the Ebbinghaus do not apply at the spatiotemporal scales relevant for generating the specific type of reaching behaviour. The size constancy effect, that we are assuming generates the illusion, may be relevant only for relatively large distances and not for the short distances covered in a reaching movement. That is, the depth cues in question may normally govern regularities relating to the sizes of quite distant, out-of-reach objects. That such depth cues for far distance are not relevant for action would be a learnable regularity, which would inoculate the system, in a less serendipitous manner than described in the previous section, from the effects of this kind of illusion.

*Page 143.* ["Overall, this approach to the . . . "] Metzinger presents a similar line on veridicality, though he argues that veridicality is sacrificed to maximize global coherence (Metzinger 2004: 237).

*Page 156.* ["Proponents of unconscious perceptual . . . "] The proposal here has been that there is an analogy between the neural and the legal context. The question may arise whether it is reasonable to portray the court room as a Bayesian mechanism? The answer seems to be yes. Much Bayesian theorizing is performed in quasi-legal terms (Bovens and Hartmann 2003), and, importantly, there is a concerted effort to re-cast legal idioms in Bayesian terms and analyse legal cases accordingly (Lagnado, Fenton et al. 2012; Fenton, Neil et al. 2013).

*Page 158.* ["There are different ways one could . . . "] A very influential model relating to prediction error minimization is based on the notion of forwards models and applies predominantly to delusions of alien control (expressed for example in a belief that "female demons are controlling my movement"). The starting point is that we can predict well the sensory consequences of our own movement but not the sensory consequences when others control our movement (for example, someone pushing your arm from behind). This means prediction error should be very small for own movement but large for other-controlled movement. If there is a problem with comparing predicted and actual sensory consequences of movement, then a spurious prediction error could be generated, which wrongly associates own movement with the kind of prediction error we have learned to expect for movements we are not in control of. This unusual experience is then what gives rise to the delusion that one's movements actually are under the control of others (Frith 1992; Hohwy and Frith 2004; Fletcher and Frith 2009). There is extended debate about how an unusual experience like this can give rise to full-blown delusions. I believe the way prediction error aberrations cascade around the perceptual hierarchy is sufficient to encompass most of the phenomena surrounding delusion formation and other unusual experiences (Hohwy 2009, 2013). I will not attempt to argue fully for this position in this book. Instead, I work towards a more generic account focused on expected precision. It is worth noting that the kinds of predictions of the sensory consequences of own movement that are thought to be implicated in delusions of alien control have been shown to exhibit the kind of imprecision effects that this account predicts (Synofzik, Thier et al. 2010). The account needs to be tweaked to account for the difference between classic monothematic delusions and delusions more typically seen in schizophrenia; for some discussion of this, see Hohwy 2013. See Bortolotti (2009) for a full philosophical discussion of the delusions debate; see Coltheart, Menzies et al. (2009) for one type of Bayesian account.

*Page 163.* ["The simple idea is then that in autism . . . "] Recently, Pellicano and Burr (Pellicano and Burr 2012) have suggested an interesting approach to autism on which perceptual inference in autism is afflicted by attenuated priors ("hypo-priors") which cause their perception of the world to be less influenced by prior knowledge. This is an attractive Bayesian approach, which is in family with both the precision optimization account and the learning style account suggested by Qian and Lipkin (discussed in this section). I think the precision optimization account offers a deeper analysis since it is anchored in a mechanism producing the perceptual pattern; it also predicts that perceptual differences emerge particularly when levels of uncertainty are high or fluctuate, which would address the problem that people with autism often do not show any difference in their perceptual accuracy or precision when tested in controlled circumstances. For an example relevant to the rubber hand illusion, it turns out that people with autism have the same proprioceptive accuracy and precision as controls (Fuentes, Mostofsky et al. 2010), suggesting that their priors are the same in these conditions. Differences may therefore occur only when uncertainty mounts; see also the commentary on Pellicano and Burr by Brock (2013) and by Friston, Lawson, and Frith (2013).

# 8

# Surprise and misrepresentation

Sometimes we misperceive the world. Philosophers are fond of examples such as: you are confronted with a dog at some distance out in a field at dusk when lighting is poor, and you misperceive it as a sheep. We could also use the examples of illusions from previous chapters. When you perceive one of the lines in the Müller-Lyer illusion as being longer than the other you have misperceived the world. Similarly, you may misperceive when you experience weirdly coloured patterns around you, as a result of taking drugs or receiving a blow to the head.

Sometimes we may recognize that something is a misperception and try to get at the truth in a process of reality testing, as discussed in the previous chapter. For example, we may pick things up to have a closer look, or ask other people what they saw. Often, we may presume, we do not realize that we misperceive. For example, I could easily go through life not noting the subtle ventriloquist illusion I experience when watching TV.

This tells us that the brain is not a flawless and ideal prediction error minimizer—in relation to some magical brain that knows how sensations are caused. It also tells us that the internal generative model that must represent the causal structure of the world is not at all times a perfect image of the causal structure of the world. If it was, then misperception would not occur. This is fine and in many ways uncontroversial: we know that humans are bounded by our biology and noisy environment and thus we cannot live up to ideals of rational inference. The prediction error or free energy bound on surprise is never zero.

Philosophers of mind and language are interested in how misperception can be accommodated in various theories of perception. What makes something misperception? This is not just the question how we can come to *believe* that we misperceived (for example, what may make us wait for daylight to check out that dog, or hearing it bark rather than bleat). It is the question of what makes it the case that misperceiving the dog for a sheep was not the introduction of a new, hybrid percept falling under the gerrymandered or disjunctive concept *dog-sheep*. Though we could of course introduce such a new gerrymandered concept it is essential that some perceptual inferences could be misperceptions. If not, then misperception is ruled out and then the account ceases to be about perception at all. This is the point with which we began, back in Chapter 1, namely that the concept of perception is a concept with a normative core.

This is a surprisingly difficult challenge (Kripke 1982; Fodor 1990; Cummins 1991). A satisfactory response needs to show, in a reductive, non-circular manner, how some specific states and parameters of a winning hypothesis determine what environmental causes are referred to by those states, so that we can say that it is a mistake when the perceptual inference is that something is a sheep even though it is really a dog. So we need to consider how this might be done in the prediction error minimization scheme. Crucially, this must be done such that it is clear we that avoid the situation where an alleged misperception is indistinguishable from veridical perception of a disjunctive state of affairs. Luckily relevant work in this direction has been pioneered by Eliasmith and Usher (Eliasmith 2000; Usher 2001; Eliasmith 2005), which I will utilize here.

In the background of this issue is the very general question of how the perceptual hierarchy represents states of affairs in the world. The nature of mental representation has also long puzzled philosophers: by virtue of what is an inner state of the mind referring to or about something in the world? *Aboutness* does not seem to be an obviously naturalistic relation and it is therefore a challenge to explain it in reductionist terms.

Philosophers typically are divided in two camps on representation: either aboutness is said to be a *causal* relation between things in the world and states of the mind, or it is said to be a relation that comes about when the state of the mind uniquely fits or *describes* the way the world is. Even though there is a strong causal element to the prediction error scheme I will suggest that the second type of account is attractive too. This makes the predictive mind emerge as more internal and removed from the world than it may initially appear.

The chapter finishes with a brief discussion of a very famous problem in cognitive science and philosophy of mind, namely Searle's Chinese Room Argument. This argument aims to show that AI-inspired accounts of mental states cannot substantially explain mental states. I think the prediction error minimization account comfortably can be placed within a class of reasonable answers to this problem.

This chapter delves into these rather deep philosophical issues. Though the intention is to make this material broadly accessible, it is the chapter in the book that engages the most philosophical background knowledge. The aim is not to provide comprehensive treatments of any of these issues, which would require much more space. Rather the aim is to indicate points of contact between the prediction error minimization framework and these more austere philosophical issues. This is important because these points of contact serve to tell us what kind of account the prediction error account is—what it tells us about the nature of the mind and the mind's place in the world. It helps place the scheme in the philosophical landscape.

## MISPERCEPTION AS FAILURE OF PREDICTION ERROR MINIMIZATION

Consider the overall picture of a creature engaged in perceptual inference with the goal of minimizing prediction error. This is a moving, ultimately unobtainable goal, because error cannot be zero in a noisy system. But nevertheless, for a creature that succeeds reasonably, there is constant approximation towards this moving goal. Against this picture, misperception can then be perceptual inferences that move the creature away from this goal: misperception is when prediction error increases.

However, this idea cannot work as it stands. The test cases of misperception that we are trying to make room for often arise when prediction error in fact seems to be minimized: the hypothesis that that thing right there out on the field is a sheep minimizes prediction error right here and now better than the hypothesis that it is a dog, so you end up (mis-)perceiving it as a sheep. It is a moment of reasonable perceptual inference. This is the philosophical problem: we want to say that it is a misperception but the process leading to the perception seems to follow all the rules for correct inference. Then we only get to deem it a misperception because we presuppose that that mental state represents dogs and not sheep. The problem is that then the account is ultimately not reductive—to tell the story we had to presuppose basic *semantic* relations.

Within a statistical inference framework, the best way around these issues is to appeal to a difference between the information a model parameter carries about something in a particular set of circumstances (such as seeing a dog in a field at dusk) and the information the parameter carries averaged across all stimulus conditions (Eliasmith 2000: Chs. 4, 5, 8; Usher 2001: 326). This distinction allows misperception: perceiving the dog as a sheep in those specific circumstances is a misperception because, averaged across all conditions *sheep* percepts carry most information about sheep, not dogs. If we align the content or meaning of a percept with a probability distribution in this way, then we get a standard against which we can compare single perceptual inferences. That gives a way to deem some inferences erroneous, namely when they pair percepts with environmental causes they are not on average best paired with. There is a normative dimension to this idea in as much as the ability to carry information on average is an aim for the organism. Hence when an inference fails in this regard it seems in order to deem it wrong.

Recall from Chapter 2 how the ability to carry information is a matter of having mutual information, and that it is a trivial consequence of the prediction error account that when prediction error is minimized then mutual information increases. This relationship means the notion of ranked mutual information can be put in terms of prediction error minimization. What makes the perceptual inference in question a misperception is then that, in spite of being a local minimization of prediction error, on average minimization of prediction error is maximized by perceiving all and only dogs as *dogs*. That is, the perceiver should perceive dogs as *dogs* because that is the perceptual inference that best minimizes prediction error on average over time.

This is a fact about the perceiver: given the perceiver's past inferences concerning certain model parameters, a probability distribution can be described, which sets up an expectation concerning future inferences; for example, that dogs are perceived as dogs. Relative to this expectation, perceiving the dog as a sheep is incorrect. Put differently, in the long run prediction error minimization would suffer if an inference such as that the dog-in-the-dusk is a sheep was allowed to proliferate. For example, that inference will not facilitate the formation of veridical representations of longer-term regularities about the whereabouts of sheep and dogs, respectively; it will also fail to minimize prediction error in many active inferences involving interactions with dogs and sheep. A simple example of failing to minimize average prediction error over time would be if the quadruped—that you thought was a dog—then proceeded to eat grass.

Viewed like this, the response to the problem of misperception is no different from the response to the objection that if the brain is interested in minimizing surprise, then we should always seek out dark rooms (discussed in Chapter 4). The answer to that objection was that chronically seeking out the dark room does not minimize long-term, average prediction error. The key to this was the notion of surprisal, which is defined in terms of the creature's expected states: seeking out the dark room would remove creatures like us from our expected state in the long run. Misperception of the dog as a sheep is similar to the dark room scenario: in the long run, not being able to distinguish dogs and sheep will increase prediction error—it will take us away from our expected states.

Of course, the dog-case is not as dramatic as the dark room-case. But the underlying situation is the same. One is a case of perceptual inference, the other is a case of active inference, and in both cases a transient prediction error win would come at a long-term prediction error cost. Therefore those inferences are both erroneous. In both cases something is true of the creature as it is making those inferences, namely what its expected states are. Misperceptions are inferences that drag the creature away from those states.

This may sound rather teleological, as if the brain aims to maintain the creature in its expected states. This would be problematic since aiming at something seems to presuppose a representation of the goal state. If that was the case, then misperception would have been explained in a non-reductive way after all since the account would piggy-back on a prior coordination of internal representations and their goal states. However, a key element of the discussion in Chapter 2 was that the brain cannot itself directly estimate surprisal, which means it cannot directly represent its expected states as a goal. Instead it maintains a model of its expected states, minimizes error relative to it, and revises its hypotheses in the light of unexplained sensory input. This can be done without already knowing the truth about the external causes of sensory input or being able to represent its aims. There is therefore no immediately threatening circularity in the account. In the next section I will however dig a little deeper in this intricate issue. Before then I will draw out four interesting aspects of this idea of misperception as inferences that undermine average, long-term prediction error minimization.

*Degrees of misperception.* A perceptual inference is a misperception if sticking to it would come at a cost of average prediction error—if it would make for overall worse hypotheses about the world. One way to make this idea more concrete is to consider misperception in terms of the entire model of the world, maintained over time in the brain. Thus, misperception could be minimization of low-level, fast time-scale prediction error, which would be at an average cost to higher-level, slower time-scale predictions (for example, as one predicts where the 'sheep' will be tomorrow). Or it could be minimization of higher-level, slow time-scale prediction error, which would be at an average cost of low-level prediction error increases (for example, collapsing together representation of dogs and sheep undermines prediction in more precisely informed circumstances). Similarly, seeking out the dark room in order to minimize fast time-scale prediction error will come at a cost of longer-term surprise (for example as one gets increasingly hungry). In many cases, identifying misperception seems to require considering overall, long-term average prediction error minimization for the entire model.

Considered in terms of average prediction error minimization for the total internal model, it is clear that misperception must be a matter of degree. The framework is probabilistic and noisy so even the best total model will never carry perfect information about the world. This is a substantial admission since it basically says that all perceptual inference is misperception to some degree. So when we deemed the sheep-inference erroneous what we are really saying is that it is more erroneous than inferring of the dog that it is a dog. In other words, there is bound to be some error in the multilayered perceptual inference concerning even the dog. If they are both errors then the ranking must concern how close to the truth they are—how they are ranked on truthlikeness.

Truthlikeness is a philosophically troublesome notion (Oddie 2008) but it is clear how it can be handled on the prediction error scheme, namely in terms of the average divergence of the probability distribution function describing the true input and the function describing the predicted input. Truthlikeness falls out of this measure in a trivial way: something that predicts perfectly carries perfect information and must be a true representation, so it seems reasonable to say that the better the prediction on average, the closer the representation is to the truth.

*Wrong ways of being right.* Just as we should expect there to be some falsity in most if not all perceptual inference, we should expect there to be some truth in much perceptual inference. In terms of mutual information, many perceptual inferences that we might deem misperceptions will on average have more than zero mutual information with the relevant state of affairs in the world. In the case of the dog misperceived as a sheep there will be elements of the multilayered percept that in fact carry information rather well. In this specific case, there will presumably be some fast time-scale, variant sensory attributes that are correctly perceived (such as the presence of a hazy grey-ish fur); similarly, there might be some slower time-scale, invariant attributes that are correctly perceived (such as the classification of the object as a living quadruped).

The parts of the representation that are correct seem to be parts that taken on their own issue in poor model fits. There is some prediction error minimization for very general models of quite invariant attributes but we know that such very general models come with much prediction error. There is also minimization for very specific models of quite variant attributes but we know that such models on their own tend to be overfitted and poor at minimizing prediction error. So sticking with such models is bad for prediction error minimization in the long run, even if they carry some information. They are the wrong ways of being right.

What seems to be missing from these cases of misperception is good prediction error minimization for relatively mid-level sensory attributes, such as that this is a dog of a certain kind of appearance. In a given situation, the system is somehow misled by low-level inference ("it's grey-ish fur") and high-level inference ("some four-legged animal") to the wrong mid-level inference ("it's a sheep"). Of course, misperception does not have to come about as a result of getting mid-level attributes wrong. It could come about by misclassification at very high levels or low levels too (for example by misperceiving the shadow of some branches as a living creature). But the model-fitting considerations suggest that, in general, correct perception involves minimizing prediction with a model that finely balances between being overly general and overly specific.

In other words, the brain's efforts to minimize average prediction error predicts that the action in its best performing hypotheses will occur throughout the perceptual hierarchy. This prediction revisits remarks made in Chapter 4 and sits well with findings on the neural correlates of consciousness suggesting heavy involvement in medial temporal lobes together with more subtle widespread activity throughout the hierarchy (Leopold and Logothetis 1999; Quiroga, Reddy et al. 2005). It also seems consistent with more theoretical proposals of conscious perceptual content, which highlight mid-level representations (Jackendoff 1987; Koch 2004; Prinz 2012). These brief comparisons suggest that there is potential for connecting quite different approaches to conscious perception with the rather simple idea of model-fitting using a prediction error minimization mechanism.

*Action failure.* In most of the discussion so far, the focus has been on perceptual inference and the ways it can go astray. Only obliquely has active inference made an appearance (for example, in the way reality testing relies on selective sampling). As set out in Chapter 4, perception and action are but two different ways of minimizing prediction error. Therefore, we should expect misperception to have an analogy relating to action.

Such "action failure" should be analysed in terms of prediction error minimization but reflecting the different direction of fit characteristic of action. This seems straightforward. Action is minimization of prediction error by making the sensory input fit the existing hypotheses about the world through manipulating one's position in the world or the world itself. If this is successful, then it follows the behaviour (including the changes caused in the world) carries information about the model. This is analogous to the way the model, in perception, carries information about the world but under the different direction of fit.

Action failure is then behaviour that fails to minimize prediction error, that is, behaviour that reduces the extent to which action can inform hypotheses. Again, we need to analyse this in terms of average, overall prediction error since singular actions can minimize prediction error here and now but fail to do so on average, making it fail in the same sense misperception can fail, albeit with a different direction of fit. This approach thus generalizes the brief comments above about the relation between the classic, philosophical misperception problem, and the dark room problem.

I think that it should be possible to develop analogies, for the case of wrong behaviour, of many of the perceptual ways of having disrupted prediction error minimization, which I discussed in the previous chapter. It would be an attractive aspect of the prediction error minimization scheme if it can unify not only perception and action but also the ways perception and action can fail.

*Insurmountable scepticism.* In spite of all that has been said so far, there is no guarantee that a model implemented with a prediction error minimization mechanism will approximate truth—truthlikeness is not assured. It will be possible to concoct cases where average prediction error is minimized and yet we would intuitively say there is misperception. This happens in sceptical

(*Matrix*-like) scenarios where the sensory input from, say, the dog-at-dusk (misperceived as a sheep) and the real sheep, is deviously indistinguishable. That is, where there is no possible way that a prediction of a sensory attribute of one *would* differ from a sensory attribute of the other. Then the overall model of the world can carry no more information about one than the other, so perceiving the dog as a sheep is not a misperception. I don't believe there is a straight answer to this essentially sceptical problem. I agree with Fodor, Usher and Eliasmith and others that it is reasonable to simply set it aside. In the words of Usher "such a misrepresentation is, by assumption, beyond the power of the agent to detect it and therefore it does not pose the same kind of problem [as the misperception problem discussed in terms of ruling out disjunctive percepts above]" (Usher 2001: 326).

The persistence of this sceptical problem should not surprise us, since we noted repeatedly in Part I of the book that the states of the world are hidden to the observer so that what is directly explained away in perceptual inference are statistical patterns in the proximal sensory input, which is, of course, insensitive to whether it is caused by real distinct objects in the world, or whether they have a deviously disguised common cause in the shape of, say, an evil scientist manipulating my brain-in-a-vat to have just that sensory input I tend to predict. Perceptual inference only discerns the statistical patterns in the stimulation of the sensory system and thereby it gets to carry information about these regularities. We assume, naturally, that what it carries information about are the real distal states of affairs in the world (and in the body). But for all we know, it might be information about a fundamentally sceptical scenario; my states co-vary with the evil scientist's devious machinery.

Even if we decide to set aside full-blown sceptical worries, this picture does present the mind as engaged in an internal struggle to make its states fit with its input, rather than with the world. It might be thought that adding action to this picture will help: if I can manipulate objects to test my hypotheses about the world then they must exist. But this will not help lessen the sceptical worry, or make the mind's engagement with the world less indirect. This is because, of course, action is active inference, which is driven by predictions of sensory input too—it is just as much an internal struggle to make hypotheses and input fit.

## MISPERCEPTION AND RULE-FOLLOWING

The last section interpreted Usher and Eliasmith's accounts of misperception within the prediction error scheme, and showed how this fits nicely with a number of discussions from previous chapters. It therefore appears to be an attractive type of account.

As I flagged above, there is however a nastier, deeper version of the dog-sheep misperception problem. This is associated with a debate that raged in the wake of Kripke's (1982) version of Wittgenstein's (1953) so-called *rule-following considerations* (chronicled and discussed in Kusch 2006). The purpose of briefly delving into this debate is to steer toward some deep issues in the prediction error minimization account, which are important to appreciate.

The debate begins with the same kind of case as before: is there anything nonsemantic about me, right now, which makes it the case that I misrepresent the world when I say that this dog is a sheep? Is there anything nonsemantic about me that makes it the case that I *should* rather say it is a dog? That is, can I tell a non-circular story about what it is that makes my utterance (or mental representation) 'sheep' mean *sheep* rather than *dog-or-sheep*?

The initial answer is clear enough from what we have said so far: it is true of me now that there is more average prediction error minimization purchase by refraining from calling the dog 'sheep', or in the perceptual case, perceptually inferring that it is a sheep. But the problem from the rule-following considerations is nasty because it claims this answer just moves the bump in the carpet. It says the rule I should follow is this: *reduce prediction error*. But what is it about me, right now, that in entirely non-semantic terms can be said to make it the case that I follow that core rule correctly by minimizing prediction error rather than not minimizing it? In other words, why *should* I minimize prediction error? The answer cannot be something along the lines of: you should minimize prediction error because it leads to truthful representations. That answer is couched in semantic terms of 'true representations', so it is circular. In general, attempts at naturalistic solutions to this problem have failed to command much agreement.

There is on the horizon a controversial and challenging but also immensely intriguing answer, which comes with the prediction error minimization scheme when formulated in terms of surprisal, as discussed in Chapter 2. The idea there was that by minimizing overall prediction error the organism self-organizes to occupy a limited range of states, and thus emerges as the phenotype it is by virtue of the expectation of finding it in just those conditions and not others. As mentioned earlier, this idea can be generalized such that the aim is to minimize the overall sum of prediction error, which is a quantity that roughly can be labelled the *free energy*, under a generative model (Friston 2010). Free energy is an information theoretical term that is itself analogous (or perhaps identical) to notions in statistical physics: free energy is a system's average energy minus its entropy. By going along with this analogy we arrive at the idea that for an organism to minimize free energy (and thus prediction error) is for it to organize itself in a far-from-equilibrium state, thereby insulating itself temporarily (and always imperfectly) from entropic disorder described by the second law of thermodynamics. This is a very ambitious but also wonderful idea to think about.

Via this interpretation of the core idea, we get the following solution to the nasty Kripke-Wittgestein problem. I should minimize prediction error because if not then I fail to insulate myself optimally from entropic disorder and the phase shift (that is, heat death) that will eventually come with entropy. Now, on the face of it this sounds teleological since I have the aim of not succumbing to heat death. I don't think a teleological account is attractive, however. It just replaces one normative rule with another (aim at avoiding death rather than aim at truth). But nor is it necessary. There is a more fundamental way of getting an answer. Recall that for a creature to exist is for it to occupy unsurprising states (Chapter 4). That is, I carry information about the world by virtue of being because my phenotype is defined in terms of the states I can occupy. So, most fundamentally, I don't *try* to follow a rule in any normal sense, I just *am*. Since it is a fact about me that I exist, it is a fact about me that I occupy unsurprising states, and thus that I minimize prediction error. Perhaps we can put it like this: misrepresentation is the default or equilibrium state, and the fact that I exist is the fact that I follow the rule for perception, but it would be wrong to say that I follow rules in order to exist—I am my own existence proof.

Moreover, the fact that I exist is a non-semantic fact about me so this answer is truly non-circular and naturalistic. It ties representation directly to statistical physics so it could hardly be more naturalistic! Of course, this also runs in the opposite direction, because this is an information theoretical approach to physics itself. If this speculation about a common information theoretical basis is driven far enough we can see how the line between the descriptive (physics) and the normative (semantics) is becoming blurred and thus how new types of answers to the normative question of how we follow rules begin to emerge. In so far as this makes sense, it implies a radical reconceptualization of what the debate is about. It turns perception into an extremely broad category—so broad that dying becomes the ultimate misperception!

As I emphasized, this is controversial. I do think it is important to have it on the table as Wittgenstein's nasty version of the misperception problem is one of the truly recalcitrant problems in philosophy, which may require more radical reconceptualizations of the overall dialectic to receive a solution. Moreover, these considerations have brought out some of the theoretical heart of the prediction error minimization account: the deep link to statistical physics.

## HIERARCHICAL MODES OF PRESENTATION

We are now in a position to say a little more about how representation is accomplished in the perceptual hierarchy. Philosophers have generally thought about the *representation relation* in two different ways.

On the one hand there are *causal* theories of representation content. On this theory, some string of words, or some internal, neural pattern of activity gets to have the content *there is a glass of cordial in front of me* by virtue of the causal relation between its parts and parts of the world. For example, the word "cordial" gets to mean *cordial* because tokens of it are mainly caused by there being cordial about.

On the other hand, there is the *description* theory of meaning and content. On this theory, some string of words or pattern of neural activity gets to have that content because it is associated with a set of definite descriptions, or *modes of presentation*, which uniquely picks out objects and properties in the world. For example, the word "cordial" gets to mean *cordial* because it is associated with the definite description that includes something like *the coloured, watery stuff, which tastes sweet, which kids love, which is sometimes made from fruit and berries but more often from nameless chemical substances*, and so on. These two theories of representation are generally seen as competitors, though there have been attempts to unify them (for some discussion, and contextualization to the statistical framework, see Eliasmith 2000).

So far, perceptual inference has been cast in causal terms and this of course invites us to see perceptual inference along the lines of the causal theory. There is something right about this because the aim of the perceptual system is to fine-tune the causal relation between states of the internal model and states of affairs in the world as revealed in the sensory input, so that they tend to predict each other's occurrence.

However, with the perceptual hierarchy and the richly structured way it represents perceptual attributes it becomes tempting to conceive of the way it represents states of affairs in the world in terms of the description theory's modes of presentation. For a given object or event in the world, the perceptual hierarchy builds up a highly structured definite description, which will attempt to pick out just that object or event.

For example, the glass of cordial in front of me is the object that has such-and-such low-level, variant properties governed by these fast time-scale regularities, such-and-such medium-level properties governed by these medium-level properties, and such-and-such high-level properties governed by these long-term regularities. That is, when the invariant label 'cordial' is used to recognize the glass of cordial this is driven by the sensory descriptors represented at multiple levels such that a glass of cordial is represented as *the* thing that satisfies just those descriptors. In this sense it is tempting to view definite descriptions as nothing but the hypotheses of hierarchical prediction error minimization.

Importantly, the perceptual hierarchy ties all these individual descriptors together in a causal, statistical structure. This ensures that the mode of presentation of the object is driven by its place in the causal structure of the world, rather than as a mere agglomeration of properties. This idea can be expressed semi-formally like this: The glass of cordial is the thing in the world such that, for properties *x, y, z . . .* , its low-level property *x* stands in such-and-such statistical relation to its medium-level property *y*, and both are governed in that statistical way by the high-level property *z*, and . . . (so on and so forth for other properties). If this is the right way of thinking of representation in the perceptual hierarchy, then it picks out things in the world by way of structural, causally informed definitions. It is as if the brain builds up a model of the world, with a unique description of the causal, inferential role of each object of perception. Of course, this is just the way we have been describing hierarchical prediction error minimization.

This may sound strangely austere and removed from the actual world since we do not actually have to define properties themselves, just their interconnections. For example, we don't have to say as much about what cordial *is* as about how the substance, which is cordial, relates to other things like tasting sweet and being universally liked by children. In turn, those properties, tasting sweet and being liked by children, are also defined in terms of their relational properties. What is left is a *statistical network analysis* for a set of random variables. This is austere indeed, but notice that the elements of the hierarchical model of the world mirrors every sensory attribute of our perception of things like glasses of cordial, such as the reflection of light of the glass and the subtle play of colours in the cordial. This goes some way to avoid being austere since the internal representation of the cordial captures the variant low-level descriptors too.

It also matters here that our construction of this layered model of the world is closely guided by causal input from the world in the shape of prediction error—this is the element that makes us align the story with the causal theory of representation. So the account is not dangerously removed from the world. However, the account in terms of structured modes of presentation does lend itself to a fairly indirect picture of representation. Representations are like queries: the selected hypothesis (mode of presentation) expects there to be a states of affairs, revealed in sensory input, which uniquely satisfies a statistically structured set of descriptors. It goes about its job by testing these expectations. For the representation to be true is for just this state of affairs to in fact have those properties.

As can be seen, the perceptual hierarchy, with its focus on causal regularities, connects to foundational issues in semantics and philosophy of language. Although many of the details remain to be worked out, it is interesting to see that the structure of the internal, perceptual hierarchy potentially can be accommodated within the ways philosophers of language have thought of representation. This is an important topic to consider since it concerns the way our inferentially based percepts make contact with and represent the world: it turns out that this is not just a matter of causal relations but rather a matter of causally guided modes of representation maintained in the brain.

In the last few paragraphs I considered how well this rather austere-looking statistical network analysis notion of representation fits with actual phenomenology. I want to end this section by giving a few more reasons why prediction error minimization in this guise can accommodate phenomenology. This harks back to Chapters 1 and 2, where I emphasized how perceptual inference was meant to elucidate not just discrimination and categorization of states of affairs but the subjective phenomenology that comes with perception.

I will address this issue by borrowing from a different, large, and difficult debate. This is the debate about whether conscious experience is fundamentally representational or not. I do this not because I am here interested in discussing the metaphysics of consciousness but because I want to suggest that the representational structure of the perceptual hierarchy is similar to what researchers claim is the structure of the paradigm of phenomenology, namely conscious perceptual experience. To do this I utilize the discussion of representation and consciousness in Frank Jackson's (2003) defence of representationalism about consciousness.

Jackson sets out five requirements that describe "what is special about the representation that takes place when something looks or feels a certain way [i.e., has a first-person phenomenology and is consciously perceived]" (Jackson 2003: 269ff). Here are the five requirements, each followed by my indication of how they can be satisfied by the prediction error minimization framework:

(1) "such [conscious] representation is rich [i.e., has many perceptual attributes]". This is captured by the variance of percepts from the first-person perspective as represented in the fast time-scale causal regularities in the lower levels of the perceptual hierarchy.

(2) "[such conscious representation] is inextricably rich [i.e., it is not a mere agglomeration of atomistic sensory attributes]". This is captured by the richly hierarchically structured perceptual inference (including binding, penetrability, and sensory integration); there is no perceptual inference without a perceptual hierarchy to accommodate empirical Bayes.

(3) "conscious representation is immediate". This is dealt with via the idea that perception is based on a model whose predictions query occurring sensory input.

(4) "There is a causal element in [conscious content]. [ . . . ] To feel something is to feel in part its contact with one's body. Vision represents things as being located where we see them as being, as being at the location from which they are affecting us via our sense of sight". This is captured in the idea that perception responds to the prediction error generated from the causal onslaught on the senses, given a generative model, and the idea that perception is shaped in the way we predict how

the causal impact on the senses change through acting and moving in the world.

(5) "Sensory experience plays a distinctive functional role [which is best understood in terms of how] a subject's posterior state of belief supervenes on their prior state of belief conjoined with their sensory experience". This is of course captured directly in the hierarchical Bayesian approach to perception.

These remarks provide comforting points of comparison between the kinds of things that are viewed as central to the phenomenology of conscious perception in philosophy of mind, and the offerings of the computational framework we are considering here. Having done some work to establish this connection will make it easier to see that the way prediction error minimization is described in the computational literature does in fact capture how we experience the world.

## IN THE BAYESIAN ROOM

I have argued that the prediction error scheme can account for misperception. And I have set out what representation amounts to on this scheme, and how this seems to embody the phenomenology of conscious experience too. However, there is a deep problem that none of these arguments directly deal with, namely whether the brain really *perceives* or *grasps* the states of affairs of the world it represents. This question harks back to discussions of Artificial Intelligence centred on whether computers really understand. As applied to the brain, the question is whether the brain, conceived as a kind of biological computer, really understands, if it processes input according to some algorithm?

This issue is the focus of perhaps the most discussed philosophical argument in cognitive science, Searle's famous Chinese Room Argument (Searle 1980). In Searle's story English-speaking Tex is locked in the Chinese room, gets only Chinese notes as input, and consults English-language tables or computer programs giving instructions for how to combine Chinese input characters with Chinese output characters. From the outside, it appears as if the Chinese room understands and yet Tex doesn't understand any Chinese at all, even though he implements what looks like an Artificial Intelligence. So algorithms are not sufficient for mental states, and minds are thus not like programs, according to Searle.

Here is how we set this up in our preferred terms of unconscious perceptual inference. Let us say we have Hermann, who is in the Bayesian room. Hermann follows Bayes' rule, but does he truly perceive? Perhaps Searle would say that he perceives just as little as Tex understands Chinese in the original Chinese room. Isn't he just blindly following rules without any idea what any of it means, without any idea of what is really out there in the world?

The debate about the Chinese room is vast and the conceptual landscape has been mined to an extreme degree. So there is no quick and uncontroversial answer I can offer. But it is useful to play out how the story goes for a room in which prediction error minimization is the rule. The starting point for this book was the simple idea that perception has to arise by virtue of how the brain makes sense of its sensory input, from inside the walls of the skull and with no outside help. This is similar to the idea behind Searle's thought experiment. Only here, there is no look-up table or program but instead statistical inference over the sensory input, given a generative model.

Here is a straightforward argument, based on the material in this chapter, to the conclusion that Hermann truly perceives, or grasps, the world. If Hermann in the room minimizes prediction error, then he does perceive because he by virtue of minimizing prediction error would be increasing the mutual information between his model of the world and the states in the world. This is because the basic idea is that representation is a matter of increasing the mutual information (which is entailed by minimizing prediction error). Moreover, we have assumed that for a system to perceive the world there must be a sense in which it can misperceive, and this is when average mutual information decreases. By these criteria of representation, Hermann in the room does represent the world.

If we were to ask Hermann what he perceives, he may be stumped for an answer. This is just like Tex in the Chinese room. If we ask Tex what the Chinese signs he is manipulating actually *mean*, then he will not be able to answer (because he does not understand the Chinese characters he manipulates). Similarly for Hermann. One way to respond here is to say there should be no expectation that the mechanism performing the perceptual inference itself has the phenomenal or conscious feeling of perceiving the world (or of understanding Chinese). The account of understanding, or perception, is not meant to capture *phenomenal consciousness* (Block 1995). Therefore, the objection must be interpreted in another way: it is not just that there is a lack of a conscious sense of perceiving but that there is a lack of perceiving by some other criteria. The objection can then be dealt with by denying that there are any criteria by which Hermann fails to perceive. I think the right criteria are just those we have discussed above (carrying information with a possibility of failing to carry information), and that on those criteria Hermann does indeed perceive.

Of course the underlying mistake here is to think that there is an intelligent perceiver, like Hermann or Tex, in the room in the first place. If we require that the system implementing the perceptual inference is itself a perceptual inference system, then things quickly turn into a regress of homunculi. When we ask whether Hermann perceives, we should therefore not require a homuncular answer. A first stab at a non-homuncular answer could go like this. Over a period of time, Hermann has built an intricate model of the world that predicts well the input to the room. Hermann gets an input, notices how it deviates from the output settings of the hypotheses in question, adjusts the parameters in the hope of minimizing the deviance, cranks the wheels, and gets a new output message predicting what the next input should be (an analogous story can be told for active inference in order to encompass the output phase with prediction error minimization too; perhaps combined with a robotic Hermann). When we ask Hermann whether he truly perceives, all he can do is mutely point to the model of the world he has built. But this picture is still not quite right. There is no explicit inversion of the model going on in the brain, as we saw in Chapter 2. Hermann doesn't have to figure out explicitly what to expect. The inversion is implicit in the actual prediction error minimization. Hermann's model should be conceived more like our Rube Goldberg-esque dam plugging (elaborated in Chapter 3) such that the outputs of the model directly counter the input. This is a matter of self-organization—like a game of survival in an onslaught of entropy—and Hermann is not needed. So the question we need to ask is whether *this system perceives*? Having done away with Hermann and having fixed on a set of criteria for representation and misrepresentation, I see no reason to withhold perception from this neural system.

## SUMMARY: A MECHANISM FOR REPRESENTATION

I have discussed how the prediction error minimization scheme allows for misperception, representation, phenomenology, and understanding. Though these discussions have been brief and more needs to be done, I hope I have said enough to show that this scheme is a viable and interesting contender in this more strictly philosophical domain. In this manner I have added to the credibility of the prediction error minimization framework because we then have some reason to think it can overcome some key philosophical obstacles. Importantly, by showing where there are interesting points of contact between the computational project and stubborn philosophical debates we learn about the prediction error minimization mechanism: about what happens when it goes wrong, about how it manages to capture the world, and about the indirect relation to the world it represents.

## NOTES

*Page 173.* ["This is a surprisingly difficult challenge . . . "] Perhaps the best fit with this account of misperception in the existing philosophical literature is with Churchland (1998), which Usher (2001) discusses.

*Page 177.* ["In other words, the brain's . . . "] Here I suggest a reasonable fit to areas of consciousness science. It is worth noticing, also, that the very general idea considered here (i.e., finding a balance between overly general representations that obliterate specific information, and overly specific representations that are blind to the relations between things) is suggestive of the notion of integrated information. This is an information theoretical quantity that is sensitive to just this kind of balance. Integrated information has been proposed as a key notion of consciousness (Tononi 2010), and it is interesting to see how prediction error minimization pushes towards models that we may suspect are high in integrated information.

*Page 180.* ["The initial answer is clear enough . . . "] Other naturalistic answers to the rule-following problem have been tried. For example, that we should call dogs 'dog' because this corresponds to the proper function of these mental states, where a mental state's proper function is something that is true of me now, and can be analysed in nonsemantic terms; this is problematic partly because the notion of a 'proper function' is difficult to define (this is 'teleosemantics', see discussion in Neander 2006).

*Page 181.* ["We are now in a position to say a little . . . "] Modes of presentation were coined as 'Art des Gegebenseins' in Frege's seminal paper in the field (Frege 1892) and formalized as definite descriptions by Russell (1905); the juxtaposition of these two theories comes out clearly in Kripke's classic (1972/1980) treatment, which spawned an intense research effort about their relative merits. More sophisticated versions of the description theory can be found in Jackson (2007; see also discussion in Schroeter and Bigelow 2009).

*Page 182.* ["Importantly, the perceptual hierarchy ties . . . "] These long structured definite descriptions are *Ramsey sentences* (Lewis 1970), they are arrived at by transforming the predicates in a definite description to property names and quantifying over them. Ramsey sentences can then describe states of affairs in *topic neutral* terms (this term was coined by Jack Smart in his seminal paper 'Sensations and brain processes' (Smart 1959)): we don't need to know what *x* and *y* and *z* etc. stand for in the world, we just need to know how they are related (statistically related in our case).

*Page 184.* ["I will address this issue by borrowing . . . "] Of course, saying that there is similarity between conscious experience and prediction error minimization could also be a first step in an argument that a representationalist about consciousness would be well served to adopt the prediction error minimization framework. A representationalist believes that all conscious perception is representational and that therefore, if we can account for representation we can account for conscious perceptions. This is not an easy view to maintain and a full discussion of it would take us too far into murky metaphysical waters. But it is important to note that the prediction error story as presented so far seems to tick the boxes that Jackson and others have set out as requisites for a substantial representationalism about consciousness.

# Part III

# The Mind

# 9

# Precision, attention, and consciousness

The chapters making up this third part of the book adopt a different perspective than Part II, which focused on explaining how prediction error minimization relates to perceptual representation. The aim now is to turn the gaze more inwards and explore how the prediction error framework can be of use in understanding deep and puzzling aspects of the mind.

In this chapter, I discuss the nature of attention and its puzzling relation to conscious perception. In the next chapter, I link prediction error to theories of consciousness and perceptual unity. Chapter 11 then builds on discussions in a range of previous chapters to identify the sense in which prediction error minimization and thereby perception is marked by fragility and indirectness; the last chapter explores notions of emotion, introspection, the privacy of mind, and the self.

The starting point for this chapter is attention. Our ability to attend to things and to have our attention drawn to things is a key facet of our mental lives. We not only perceive the world, we do so under different degrees of attentional focus and attentional load. It is also a core research area for psychology, neuroscience, and philosophy. There is much focus on the neural mechanisms underlying attention, as well as on uncovering its multifaceted functional role.

The prediction error framework is able to encompass many of the central findings on attention and to provide a unifying framework for them within the broader church of prediction error minimization. This allows us to see attention in a new light and to provide alternative conceptualizations of its functional role in our overall mental economy.

Recently, there has been much focus on the relation between attention and conscious perception. It seems that in some circumstances they have opposing effects, and yet they seem intimately connected. The prediction error framework can resolve this perplexing situation. It therefore suggests a unifying approach not only to attention itself but also its relation to conscious perception.

The prediction error minimization theory of attention is theoretically well-motivated and well-founded, whereas empirical evidence is still relatively scarce. This chapter uses the philosopher's tool of supporting the theory in an inference towards the best explanation. The "best-makers" in such an inference for the prediction error minimization explanation of attention are mounting, making it worth serious consideration (for a list of "best-makers" for an explanation, see the end of Chapter 4; the present chapter draws on (Hohwy 2012), which has additional discussion of a series of empirical studies).

## FROM MENTAL SEARCHLIGHT TO PRECISION EXPECTATIONS

The most famous attempt to capture the essence of attention comes, of course, from William James:

> Everyone knows what attention is. It is the taking possession by the mind, in clear and vivid form, of one out of what seem several simultaneously possible objects or trains of thought. Focalization, concentration, of consciousness are of its essence. It implies withdrawal from some things in order to deal effectively with others, and is a condition which has a real opposite in the confused, dazed, scatter-brained state which in French is called *distraction*, and *Zerstreutheit* in German (James 1890: Vol I: 403–4).

James intends to capture something platitudinous about attention here ("everybody knows what attention is"). There is little doubt that an account of attention that fails to capture at least the spirit of James' conception is not going to be satisfactory. This conception of attention as something that focuses the mind by casting a mental spotlight on some but not other states is evident in very modern approaches to attention too. Thus, as put in the important work by van Boxtel, Tsuchiya and Koch (2010: 2):

> The visual system is constantly bombarded with information, leading to a data deluge that cannot be processed in real time; on the order of one megabyte of raw information exits the retina every second. The prime goal of visual attention therefore is to select information to meet current behavioral goals [ . . . ]. By definition this implies a relative decrease of processing resources for non-attended locations or features.

This is taken to contrast with conscious perception:

> Consciousness is surmised to have functions almost diametrically opposite to those of attention. It does not select information. Rather, consciousness' proposed roles include summarizing all relevant information pertaining to the current state of the organism and its environment and making this compact summary accessible to the planning stages of the brain, detecting anomalies and errors, decision

> making, language, inferring the internal state of other animals, setting long-term goals, making recursive models, and rational thought. (ibid.)

Van Boxtel et al. sum up in this slogan:

> From this viewpoint, we can regard selective, focal attention as an analyzer and consciousness as a synthesizer. To the extent that one accepts that attention and consciousness have different functions, one has to accept that they cannot be the same process, and anticipate dissociations between the two. (ibid.)

There is, as we shall see, some evidence for this dissociation between attention and conscious perception. But the neat division of functional labour is not easy to accommodate, from a commonsense point of view. It is natural to conceive of the relation between the two by saying that we attend to things we are conscious of (how could I attend to something I am unconscious of?) and we are conscious of things we attend to (how could I be aware of something without attending to it?). What this suggests is that our account of attention should allow for both a close connection with conscious perception and also for their distinct functional roles.

There is reason to think our notion of unconscious perceptual inference is well placed to throw light on attention, and that it can accommodate the various aspects of attention. An early clue comes from the main inventor of the notion of unconscious inference, Helmholtz. He proposed attention as the mechanism responsible for binocular rivalry. But he didn't seem to opt for something like a Jamesian conception of attention. Instead he explicates attention in terms of activity, novelty, and surprise, which anticipate the way predictive coding would apply to rivalry (see Chapter 2, and Hohwy, Roepstorff et al. (2008)), and thereby implies that attention and perceptual inference are closely related:

> The natural unforced state of our attention is to wander around to ever new things, so that when the interest of an object is exhausted, when we cannot perceive anything new, then attention against our will goes to something else. [...] If we want attention to stick to an object we have to keep finding something new in it, especially if other strong sensations seek to decouple it. (Helmholtz 1867: 770)

It is tempting to develop Helmholtz's dynamic conception of attention in terms of the conceptual tools provided by the prediction error minimization account. In particular, I believe we need to look at the optimization of precisions.

In the discussion so far, the notion of expected precisions has cropped up numerous times. It is an essential element of perceptual inference (and active inference): engaging in predictive inference without taking account of precision would be as precarious as engaging in statistical comparison of means without taking the variance about the means into consideration. The proposal from the main architect of the contemporary prediction error scheme, Karl Friston and his colleagues, is that attention is just optimization of precisions in hierarchical prediction error minimization ((Friston 2009; Feldman and Friston 2010), see also (Spratling 2008; Summerfield and Egner 2009; Summerfield and Egner 2014)). The key idea is that perceptual inference should concentrate on reliable, precise signalling and that the way this happens maps on to a reasonable functional role for attention. I will try to unpack elements of Friston's idea now.

## LEARNING PATTERNS OF NOISE AND UNCERTAINTY

A statistician may sometimes want to compare means and make an inference about whether they differ. If the samples are very noisy then the confidence in the inference may be low, so having samples with small variance is normally good for inference. That's the lot of statisticians. Imagine instead a world in which all samples have the same variability. In such a world the statistician would be wasting time worrying about the variance of the samples every time a statistical inference is needed. The reason our world is not like this is that noise and uncertainty are state-dependent: different states of the world have different levels of noise and uncertainty. This is why the statistician needs to always estimate the variability of his or her samples.

As it is for the statistician so it also is for the brain. As noted in Chapter 3, the prediction error minimization mechanism needs to take the variability, or precisions, of its sensory estimates into account. If it fails in this regard then it will tend to engage in faulty perceptual inference because it then ignores the reliability of the sensory signal. This is also why expected precision loomed large in the discussion of precarious prediction (Chapter 7).

The job for the relevant part of the prediction error mechanism is to assess the precision of the incoming signal, a signal that is of course conceived as prediction error in this framework. So somehow the precision of prediction errors must be optimized. Mechanistically this is done via groups of neurons making up error units of each level, increasing or decreasing the gain on the prediction error, as we have seen earlier. Precise prediction error is allowed passage up through the hierarchy to a larger extent than imprecise prediction error. The crucial question is on what basis the mechanism sets the gain on prediction error.

As mentioned, prediction error precision is state-dependent. Some kinds of states are regularly associated with more noise than others. That is to say, differences in noise levels are regularities in nature and as such they are in principle learnable (for example, at dusk visual precision is less than in full daylight; or, inebriated people have more sensorimotor uncertainty than sober ones). If these patterns of noise and uncertainty are learned, then they can be used to predict noise levels and thus used to guide how the gain on prediction error is set. The internal model, which generates predictions, therefore needs to represent the expected precisions about the prediction errors. The mechanism is doing two jobs concurrently, first-order statistical inference of what the prediction error is reporting (akin to estimating the mean), and second-order statistical inference of the precision of the prediction error (akin to estimating variance).

Now imagine this layered landscape of prediction error minimization, where the minimization efforts are shaped by expected precisions. Effort is put in where the prediction error signal is expected to be precise. This makes sense because precise signals are reliable and will lead to the best average prediction error minimization, and the best representation of the world. For a system that is able to optimize its precision expectations the pattern of effort will fluctuate in tune with the pattern of state-dependent noise.

The result is that prediction error minimization effort is *selective* within the prediction error landscape. This is, most basically, why it fits with the functional role for attention. Attention is then the process of optimizing precision of prediction errors in hierarchical perceptual inference (Friston 2009). On this conception, attention requires learning state-dependent patterns of noise and precision and then using such prior beliefs to set the gain on prediction error. This proposal implies that experimental findings concerning attention can be explained in terms of expected precisions.

## PATTERNS OF EXPECTED PRECISIONS IN ATTENTION

A paradigmatic experimental set-up for spatial attention is Posner's classic spatial cueing task, often labelled the *Posner paradigm* (Posner 1980). Participants maintain fixation on a central fixation mark, then a cue shows up (an arrow, often) which predicts a peripheral target stimulus in the direction of the arrow 80 per cent of the time; 20 per cent of the trials have invalid cues where the arrow does not point to the target stimulus location (Figure 26).

Valid but not invalid cues allow attention to focus on the target location and speeds up detection of the target. On each trial the input to the eyes stays the same so the explanation for the speeded detection seems to be the spatial attention to the target region afforded by the valid cue. The type of attention involved here is endogenous attention where the cue gives information about where to direct the attentional searchlight.

Here a simple precision regularity is available: the cues predict a high precision stimulus, namely the dot. This regularity can be used to increase the gain on prediction error from the cued region, which speeds up detection

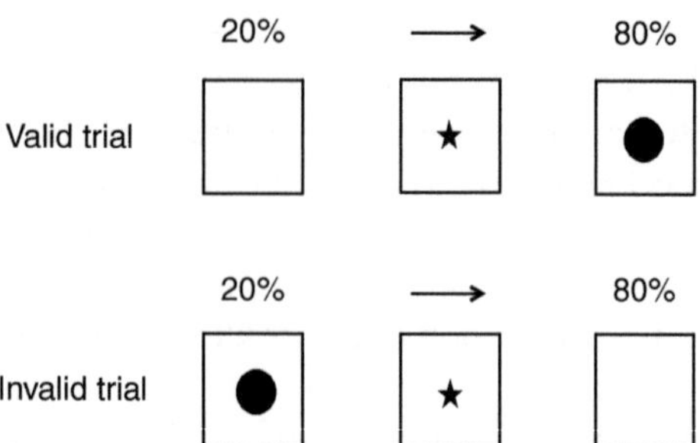


**Figure 26.** Posner task. Participants fixate at the central star at all times; the arrow is a valid cue (80% of the trials) or invalid cue (20% of the trials) for the target dot on either side. Congruent trials speed up detection of the target stimuli.

of targets occurring there. In fact, two things happen. The prior probability of a target occurring goes up and the gain is increased. On invalid trials neither thing happens for the target region and there is no detection speed benefit. In support of this idea, computational modelling of the Posner paradigm using a predictive coding model with expected precision has been shown to replicate nicely psychophysical and neurophysiological findings (Feldman and Friston 2010).

This kind of endogenous attention is thus modelled as driven by the increased prior and the up-weighted prediction error for spatial attributes that are expected to be precise. The stronger prediction error is more likely to drive perceptual inference—leading to subsequent suppression of that prediction error—than competing errors that are not expected to be precise. Similar regularities of precision would hold for feature-based attention where what is cued for precision it is not stimuli occurring in a specific spatial region but specific types of sensory attributes. Precision regularities for cue-target associations can also explain the role of attention in biasing competition when stimuli are presented simultaneously (cf. Desimone and Duncan 1995; see Feldman and Friston 2010).

There is also empirical evidence that directly supports the role of endogenous attention as precision weighting (Kok, Rahnev et al. 2011). As we have seen, without attention, the better a stimulus is predicted the more attenuated its associated signal should be. Attention should reverse this attenuation because it amplifies the prediction error. However, attention depends on the predictability of the stimulus: there should be no strong expectation that an unpredicted stimulus is going to be precise. So there should be less attention-induced enhancement of the prediction error for unpredicted stimuli than for better predicted stimuli. Using fMRI, Kok et al. very elegantly provides evidence for this interaction in early visual cortex (V1).

The contrast to endogenous attention is exogenous attention, where attention is not directed but instead grabbed by something. This is what happens when your attention is drawn to a loud noise or to sudden movement, or in general, a stimulus that is abrupt in some feature space. This can happen even as your endogenous attention is engaged somewhere else. The simplest way of conceiving abruptness is in terms of signal strength. A relatively strong signal will stand out and attract attention. If we compare a weak and a strong signal both on a somewhat noisy background, then the stronger signal will have a higher signal-to-noise ratio, that is, higher precision. This is again a regularity in nature, namely the regularity that *stronger signals are more precise* (see Feldman and Friston 2010: 9; Appendix). When the sensory system is exposed to a high strength signal it should thus (i) expect high precision, (ii) increase the gain on the prediction error associated with that signal, and (iii) preferentially explain away this sensory input: the system then has its attention grabbed by the signal. This gives a way for the precision optimization account to deal with exogenous attention as well.

That is how expected precisions factor in to the overall prediction error minimization efforts, and how different types of learned regularities of precisions map on to the conceptual roles for endogenous and exogenous attention one finds in paradigmatic examples like the Posner paradigm. This is not a story about bandwidth limits, or some kind of intrinsic salience, or about some kind of mental searchlight taking possession of things. Instead it is a story about an essential part of perceptual inference: in a world with state-dependent noise, the system could not engage efficiently in prediction error minimization without attention, understood in this manner. This is part of what makes this an attractive proposal. We do not have to add attention to the story, attention falls out if it naturally: we have attention because otherwise state-dependent noise would undermine perceptual inference.

## VOLITIONAL ATTENTION AS ACTIVE INFERENCE

Perhaps the story does not yet capture the active element in James' idea that "it is the taking possession by the mind". Endogenous attention often seems to come with a volitional element that is not quite captured by the relatively mindless cue directing in the Posner paradigm. We decide to attend to some feature, and then act on that decision. In prediction error parlance, this aligns volitional attention with active inference. The question is, can we conceive of active inference such that it accommodates expectations for precisions?

I think we can. Volitional attention to a spatial region (for example, trying to spot if there is something moving in the tree top) may be a situation where the world is selectively sampled to fit with a hypothesis about it. The hypothesis would be that something with high precision will occur in that region. This turns up the gain for prediction error for that region and makes it more likely that, if something actually occurs there, it is quickly detected. As we did in the Posner case before, we can add that if there is a prior belief about what exactly may be spotted (for example, it was probably a galah in the tree top), then that facilitates spotting just those things.

The relevant precision regularity in this case is not that different from the endogenous Posner case. There is a cue, which in this case is a decision to sample from that region, and there is a target, in this case a moving animal in the tree top. There is also a learned association between the two such that more often than not when we do decide to sample from a region there is a high precision target there. This is a learned regularity rather than wholly a case of self-fulfilling prophesying as can be seen by the fact that attention is very hard to sustain if nothing after all happens in the attended region within a reasonable time—attention in the shape of active inference then fails to minimize prediction and cannot be sustained.

All this seems no different in principle from the active inference we have come across before: a counterfactual hypothesis induces a prediction error causing us to change our relation to the world. It is a slightly unusual instance of action because the way we change our relation to the world is to increase the sensory gain in one region of space. The difference is then that the active inference is driven not by *which* prediction error we expect, but by the *precision* of the expected prediction error—just as we can sample prediction error selectively, we can sample their precisions selectively.

For some cases of volitional attention, this may be a story of self-fulfilling prophecies (see also Phillips 2012). To decide to attend is to expect precision, the expectation turns up the prediction error gain, and this makes it more likely that something will be perceived in that region. So my expectation to see something can make it the case that I do. But there is nothing untoward about this: of course my desire for ice cream makes it more likely I'll end up with ice cream. That doesn't make it a self-fulfilling prophecy in any damaging sense. The world needs to cooperate to make the prophecy be fulfilled. Similarly, if the world does not cooperate and deliver the expected high precision signal, then I will not perceive much from that region after all.

There is a kind of case that may seem to be a more problematic self-fulfilling prophesying. This is found in Carrasco's intriguing finding of covert attention that increases the perceived strength of weak gratings being viewed at the periphery (see Chapter 6; Figure 19). Here something is perceived because it is expected, not because it is true (namely high precision content). But as we argued back then, the system self-corrects when fixation is allowed to be directed squarely at the weak grating. Similarly, the effect drops away after a few seconds, presumably as the system is allowed to sample more from the attended region and discovers the true stimulus strength. There may be a transient period where the prophecy is self-fulfilling, but there are enough resources for reality testing in the system in the long run for that to be a negligible problem. In this dynamic process, the regularity governing cued expectations for precisions (i.e., high precision cue at one location predicts high precision target at another) is overruled as more evidence comes in.

## INATTENTIONAL BLINDNESS AS LOW GAIN AND PRIOR

If the gain on one signal is turned up, then the gain on other signals must be turned down. Otherwise the notion of gain is meaningless: weights must sum to one. So, as expectations for precision turn up the gain on one prediction error, the gain for others will turn down. In addition, it may be that cues increase the prior probability of a validly cued target, as we saw in the discussion of the Posner paradigm. If a weaker, low precision stimulus is nevertheless shown in the non-cued region then it will struggle against both low gain and low prior probability. As a result this stimulus may never be perceived. The causal regularities governing precision and perceptual inference in an attentional episode can thus conspire against perception of other things. This maps very nicely on to the phenomenon known as inattentional blindness.

In inattentional blindness paradigms, attention directed at some task causes blindness to other otherwise salient stimuli. For example, if the participant is asked to track some black discs moving around amongst other moving discs on a changing background, then they will be blind to a briefly appearing natural scene occurring for 70ms milliseconds in the background; without the attentional task such changes in background are easy to spot (Cohen, Alvarez et al. 2011).

Similarly, in a famous study, Simons and colleagues demonstrated inattentional blindness to a very salient person in a gorilla-costume appearing during an attention-demanding task of counting passes in a basketball drill (Simons and Chabris 1999). A realistic version of this effect is a new study from this group of researchers, where they demonstrate blindness to a fist-fight taking place while the participant is chasing someone else (Chabris, Weinberger et al. 2011).

Full engagement in the attentional task, for example of tracking the moving discs, comes with an expectation of high precision for the attended regions and features, and so entails turning up the gain on prediction error related to that particular task, as well as increased priors for the task events. This raises the threshold for perceiving other events and could explain such instances of inattentional blindness. Hence changes in the series of background images go unnoticed. Likewise, when attending to one's chase of somebody the gain on prediction error associated with input from the chased person is turned up, leaving little expected precision and thus little gain from other events happening on the way, even when this is an otherwise highly salient bashing of someone.

## ENDOGENOUS AND EXOGENOUS ATTENTION

Appealing to down-weighting and to differences in priors seems to be the most direct way of accommodating inattentional blindness within the prediction error minimization framework. It is however not entirely obvious why gain and prior probability would be so low as to render things like natural scenes, gorillas, and fights entirely invisible, which is a very dramatic weakening. I think there is a further way to employ the prediction error mechanism, which can make actual blindness more likely.

This additional account of inattentional blindness appeals to the idea discussed above, that attention is a moment in active inference: one is selectively sampling the world under expectations of high precision. This sampling occurs on the basis of perceptual inference that has delivered a sufficiently tight bound on surprise. Recall from the end of Chapter 7 that a proper balance must be found between minimizing the bound on surprise in perceptual inference and minimizing prediction error by selectively sampling the world. Maintaining this balance includes being able to switch from active to perceptual inference as appropriate. In order to determine how to selectively sample the world, the hypothesis about the world should be held reasonably fixed; I cannot know how to move around in the world if my hypothesis about the world constantly changes. But, then, if the hypothesis of the world is not updated regularly enough it may miss important changes in the world that were not encompassed in the original model. Switching to perceptual inference too early will impede active inference; and sticking with active inference too long may lead to blindness to some things. Endogenous attention could then have the functional role of prolonging active inference to enable engagement in a task for which high precision is expected, even though it thereby increases the risk of inattentional blindness. Treating endogenous attention as active inference would serve as an additional contributor to inattentional blindness. This is attractive because blindness is predicted during prolonged active inference, when the model must fail to be updated.

Behind this is a pleasing account of the opposing functional roles of endogenous and exogenous attention, both fleshed out in terms of expected precisions. Endogenous attention is selective sampling of expected high precision stimuli, which entails that the system will be less sensitive to change in the environment. This facilitates very efficient prediction error minimization essentially because the model of the world is kept constant so selective sampling will tend to succeed. The function of endogenous attention is then to maintain a given hypothesis for so long that this kind of efficient error minimization is maximized—it ensures one does not jump back to passive, perceptual inference too soon. Exogenous attention on the other hand has the function of ensuring that non-predicted high precision stimuli are not missed—its function is to ensure one is not lost in active inference, at least not for too long.

Attention then has a dual role to play in maintaining the above balance between perceptual and active inference. Endogenous attention prolongs active inference on the basis of predicted precisions and it makes sure we do not stick too much with perceptual inference; exogenous attention prolongs perceptual inference on the basis of predicted precisions and it makes sure we do not stick too much with active inference.

Cases of inattentional blindness then exploit more extreme cases of our attempt to use attention to maintain this balance. Given a certain level of engagement of active inference (that is, a very demanding, sustained attentional task of the sort often used in a laboratory setting), even stimuli that are very abrupt in some feature space can fail to generate enough gain (that is, exogenous attention) to force the system to revert to perceptual inference and update the original model. I claim these are more extreme cases and this seems reasonable since as soon as the experimental task has decent ecological validity, such as the studies by Simons and Chabris, the proportion of people experiencing inattentional blindness begins to drop.

## ATTENTION AND CONSCIOUS PERCEPTION

So far I have made an attempt to unpack and further develop the idea that attention is optimization of expected precisions. As suggested at the beginning, the relation between attention and consciousness is not obvious. Therefore, it is worth asking whether this account of attention might help elucidating its relation to conscious experience.

To attempt such an answer we first need some kind of grip on how conscious perception might fit into the prediction error minimization framework. This is easy, though needs a disclaimer. Conscious perception is the upshot of unconscious perceptual inference. We are not consciously engaging in Bayesian updating of our priors in the light of new evidence, nor of the way sensory input is predicted and then attenuated. What is conscious is the result of the inference—the conclusion. That is, conscious perception is determined by the hypotheses about the world that best predicts input and thereby gets the highest posterior probability. More specifically, since the inversion of the generative model is implicit, what is conscious is the interconnected set of currently best performing predictions down throughout the perceptual hierarchy (down to some level of expected fineness of perceptual grain).

This idea tracks characteristics of conscious perception nicely: binding, penetrability, reality testing, illusions, inextricably rich experience, and first-person perspective are all aspects of conscious perception and have been explained within the purview of prediction error minimization in the previous chapters of this book.

The mentioned disclaimer is that this is not intended as a proposal that can explain *why* perceptual states are phenomenally conscious rather than not. It is merely a proposal that describes the states that *are* conscious: they are those representations of the world that currently best predict sensory input. I am not here intending to touch upon the *metaphysical* mind-body problem—the "hard problem" of consciousness (Chalmers 1996).

From the perspective of prediction error minimization, it is *in principle* possible to have conscious perception without attention. This is because the fundamental need for attention comes from the fact that noise and uncertainty is state-dependent. In the distant possible world where the noise and uncertainty is always the same, there would be no need to optimize precision expectations, because precisions would always be the same. A creature could minimize prediction error, and be conscious, without attention. All that would matter would be the size of the prediction error, not the variance about them. That is, in such a possible world the more the predictions given an internal model manage to suppress prediction error, the more accurate the model will be. This shows, at least in principle, that attention and consciousness are dissociable and that we should not expect them to be related necessarily.

Of course, in the noisy world in which we actually live, second order statistics are needed for perceptual inference, with the result that perception is determined not only by the amplitude of prediction error but also by their precisions. This suggests the system needs some kind of association between them. The idea would be that perceptual inference moves around in a space determined by both prediction error accuracy and prediction error precisions. This can be depicted in a simplified way, if we conceive of prediction error accuracy as increasing with the inverse amplitude of the prediction error itself, and prediction error precision as increasing with the inverse amplitude of random fluctuations around or uncertainty about predictions; see Figure 27.

This points to a unified account of the relation between conscious perception and attention. They stand to each other as first order and second order statistical inference. In our world of state-dependent noise, both are in fact needed to minimize prediction error, and they determine conscious perception together. This picture immediately raises the possibility of interactions between the two aspects of prediction error minimization and how they together determine conscious perception.

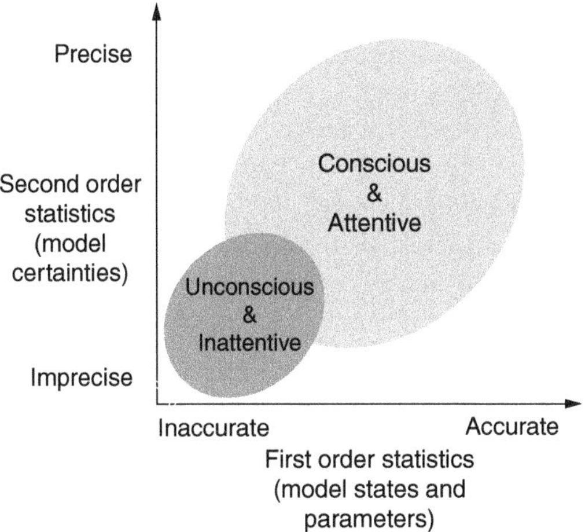


**Figure 27.** Schematic of statistical dimensions of conscious perception. The accuracy afforded by first order statistics refers to the inverse amplitude of prediction errors *per se*, while the precision afforded by second order statistics refers to the inverse amplitude of random fluctuations around, or uncertainty about, predictions. This allows for a variety of different types of states such that in general, and depending on context, inattentive but conscious states would cluster in the lower right corner and attentive but unconscious states would cluster in the upper left; see main text for further discussion (figure from Hohwy 2012).

It is not given that it is always the most accurate *and* the most precise perceptual inference that determine conscious perception. Instead we have to think of prediction error minimization as a landscape of hills and valleys where perception is determined by the deepest valley, but where valley depth can come about from excellent accuracy together with high precision, or from excellent accuracy and so-so precision, or from so-so accuracy with high precision. We may thus have a complex constellation of valleys at the same time. In other words, there may be situations of one valley being created by high accuracy together with so-so precision, and another valley being created by lower accuracy together with high precision. These two valleys may compete for determination of conscious perception, and small fluctuations in the landscape could decide how things end up. For example, cranking up precisions or prior probabilities could determine perception in different ways.

This could then be what gives rise to the dissociations between conscious perception and attention that Van Boxtel, Tsuchiya and Koch anticipated in the quote above (and have demonstrated too). It is reasonable to say that if high precision prediction error creates one valley but a deeper valley is created by high accuracy but low precision, then the shallower valley is a case of attention without consciousness and the deeper valley a case of consciousness without attention. The key here is however that this dissociation is not the upshot of two wholly distinct mechanisms: there is still a measure of attention for the conscious perception because precision will be part of the inference at that deeper valley, and there is a measure of perception, albeit unconscious perception, for the attended state because there is some accuracy to the inference at that more shallow valley.

This is illustrated by a study that combined a version of binocular rivalry with a version of the Posner paradigm (described earlier) using cues that attract exogenous attention. If one eye is shown a static image of something like a face but the other eye is shown a rapidly changing image of overlapping geometrical figures, then the static image can be suppressed from consciousness for a very long time. This is known as continuous flash suppression (Tsuchiya and Koch 2004). Jiang and colleagues (Jiang, Costello et al. 2006) used this effect to suppress the attention-grabbing Posner-style cues presented at the target location. The valid suppressed cue was an image of a nude; the invalid suppressed cue was a scrambled image. Even though people were not conscious of the cues, due to the suppression, the nudes but not the scrambled images facilitated detection of the subsequent target stimulus (Figure 28).

This shows that a paradigmatic attentional mechanism, namely that identified in the Posner paradigm, works in the absence of conscious perception—

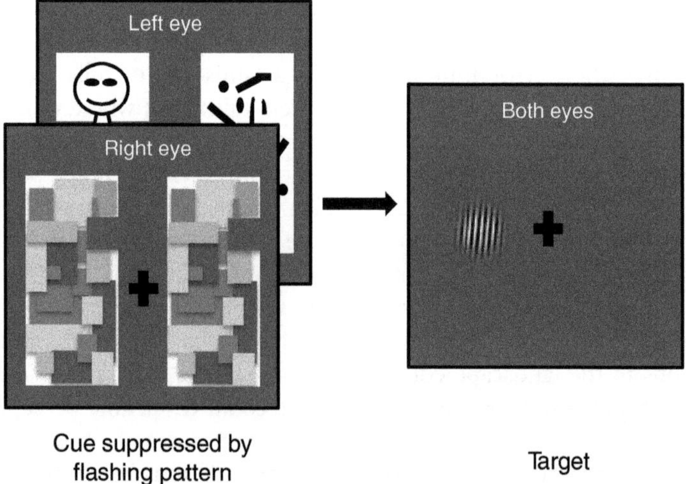


**Figure 28.** Exogenous attention grabbed by perceptually suppressed cues. The nude presented to one eye for 800 ms attracts attention and facilitates subsequent target detection even though the cue is suppressed from consciousness by the flashing patterns shown to the other eye (adapted from Jiang, Costello *et al.* 2006).

we don't have to be conscious of the thing we attend to. When there are competing models (stemming from the rivalrous conditions of continuous flash suppression) conscious perception is determined by the hypotheses that are best overall at suppression of prediction error. Here this would be the model predicting the highly dynamic stimulus of shifting and flashing patterns. Though the model predicting the nude image cannot compete in this regard it may still induce precision-related gain for a particular region. Even though a high-precision expectation could thus be present for the region of the suppressed stimulus, it is possible for the overall prediction error landscape to not favour the hypothesis for that stimulus over the hypothesis for the abruptly flashing Mondrian pattern in the other eye. The result is that the nude image is not selected for conscious perception but that there nevertheless is an expectation of high precision for its region of the visual field, explaining the effect.

## SUMMARY: STATISTICAL ASPECTS OF ATTENTION AND CONSCIOUSNESS

We have pursued the idea that attention is optimization of expected precisions in hierarchical perceptual inference. The work of Friston and colleagues suggests that this is a plausible candidate for explaining key findings in the study of attention. Moreover it fits nicely with a range of further findings and considerations about attention, including inattentional blindness, the functional roles of exogenous and endogenous attention, as well as the volitional aspects of attention. Finally it encompasses in a natural way the relation between attention and conscious perception within the same one framework: we can see them as different ways of maintaining the overall statistical process of perceptual inference. Again we see that the prediction error scheme has considerable unifying explanatory promise.

The account of attention is interesting because it reduces attention to a simple matter of learning regularities of precision in nature. This means it can be treated on the same footing as the very problem of perception with which we began, albeit one at the level of second order statistical inference about the variances of prediction errors. Interestingly, it may also be, as I argued, that attention plays a key role in maintaining the crucial balance between perceptual and active inference.

In this way, the prediction error account of attention helps us understand the perceptual fluctuations that we experience as our minds take possession of the world, and as the world takes possession of the mind.

## NOTES

*Page 193.* ["There is reason to think our..."] My translation of Helmholtz, the original is "Der natürliche ungezwängte Zustand unserer Aufmerksamkeit ist herumzuschweifen zu immer neuen Dingen, und so wie das Interesse eines Objectes erschöpft ist, so wie wir nichts Neues mehr daran wahrzunehmen wissen, so geht sie wider unseren Willen auf anderes über. Wollen wir sie an ein Object fesseln, so müssen wir eben an diesem selbst immer Neues zu finden suchen, besonders wenn andere kräftige Sinneseindrücke sie abzulenken streben."

*Page 202.* ["The mentioned disclaimer..."] Here I explain how my account is not intended as a solution to the mind-body problem. This is the point that, in spite of telling the full prediction error story, there seems however to be no *contradiction* involved in conceiving a creature with all the machinery for prediction error minimization who engages in the same perceptual inference as we do—to whatever degree of natural, neuronal detail we care to specify—and yet who is not phenomenally conscious. We would expect the creature to be conscious, of course, but nothing in the total physical story entails that it will be. This means it is left an open question whether consciousness is something over and above the physical or not. This limitation on the proposal is essentially a metaphysical concern, which matters greatly for our understanding of the place of consciousness in nature. It does not matter so much for our understanding of the relation between conscious perception and attention. Exploration of that issue can proceed under the assumption that the creatures in question are conscious, and that the mechanism in question explains what it is for them to have this rather than that conscious perception (a rich one rather than a phenomenally poor one, for example). A very large discussion lies buried in these remarks about the metaphysics of consciousness, see the key work by Nagel (1974), Levine (2001), and Chalmers (1996) and ensuing debate for more.

*Page 204.* ["This shows that a paradigmatic..."] In general, in the processing of emotional stimuli, there is clear empirical evidence to suggest that fast salient processing, which could mediate optimization of precision expectations, can be separated from slower perceptual classification (Vuilleumier, Armony et al. 2003). Evidence for this separation rests on the differences in visual pathways, in terms of processing speeds and spatial frequencies that may enable the salience of stimuli to be processed before their content.

# 10

# Perceptual unity in action

This chapter explores the link between prediction error minimization and conscious perception that the previous chapter put on the table. It draws out the reasons why there might be such a link and why it might be interesting. Then I discuss a special property of conscious perception, namely its unity. This is an important but evasive part of our phenomenology. To explain it one needs to deal with at least two aspects: (1) why the elements of conscious unity are *united*, that is how they hang together; this is an issue that harks back to the binding problem of Chapter 5, but which here is given a more general treatment; (2) why conscious unity is *unitary*, that is why there is only one overall perceptual state which subsumes all other states, and not more. By appealing to prediction error minimization, and in particular the notion of active inference, an interesting explanation of these two aspects of perceptual unity becomes available.

## FROM CAUSAL INFERENCE TO CONSCIOUSNESS?

Perception is the business of inferring the causes of our sensory input. This feat is performed by a prediction error minimization mechanism that is replicated hierarchically up through the brain. Prediction error minimization in hierarchical inference is able to capture much of our first-person perspective; it makes room for perceptual binding of sensory attributes, as well as the ways in which prior beliefs can penetrate perceptual experience, and the ways in which perception can be disrupted. It provides a framework for understanding attention and how attention relates to conscious experience. At least these are the things I have been arguing in the foregoing chapters. I have also made the observation, in Chapter 8, that these aspects of perception, which the prediction error mechanism can accommodate, feature high on the list of canonical aspects of *conscious* perception. It is tempting then to pursue further the idea that whereas perceptual inference itself is unconscious, the upshot of it is conscious experience.

I find this a good position to be in, for someone interested in the nature of consciousness. Rather than setting out with the intention to reveal the nature of consciousness we are looking at a mechanism that solves the problem of perception by appeal to internal generative models, and we are discovering that this mechanism may harbour just the aspects we consider characteristic of consciousness. This type of idea is captured nicely by Thomas Metzinger:

> [A] fruitful way of looking at the human brain [ . . . ] is as a system which, even in ordinary waking states, constantly hallucinates at the world, as a system that constantly lets its internal autonomous simulational dynamics collide with the ongoing flow of sensory input, vigorously dreaming at the world and thereby generating the content of phenomenal [i.e., conscious] experience. (Metzinger 2004: 52)

This kind of explanatory potential is part of the reason why the prediction error minimization idea is so attractive. But care is needed in how the question of consciousness is handled. If the question is the straightforward one whether prediction error minimization is the mechanism in the brain that explains why some perceptual content is conscious rather than not conscious, then the answer is 'no'. To explain this answer we need to recall the disclaimer from the previous chapter that there is little reason to think that we can solve the hard problem of consciousness in its most thorny version (Chalmers 1996; Levine 2001).

But there is something else we can do to answer the question whether prediction error minimization is the mechanism in the brain that explains why some perceptual content is conscious rather than not conscious. We will not explain why there is *something it is like* for the creature, but we can answer it by focusing on *properties* of conscious perception. The use of 'conscious' in expressions like " . . . why some perceptual content is conscious rather than not conscious . . . " should be taken to mean 'conscious, that is, perceptual inference that is characterized by first-person perspective, inextricable richness, sensory binding, is cognitively penetrable, is subject to illusions and reality testing, relates in an intimate way with attention etc.'.

This conception of conscious perception thus consists of a core cluster of descriptors arising from conceptual analysis of our common-sense concept of conscious perception, and this is combined with relatively broad empirical information about enduring projects in cognitive psychology (finding the binding mechanism), psychophysics (explaining illusions), and psychopathology (mental illness). The idea is that we should explore the underlying mechanism that brings about these characteristics because it is close enough to capturing many of the things we care about in conscious experience. If we could find a mechanism that explains all of these characteristics, then we will have made inroads on the nature of consciousness.

There is one characteristic of conscious experience that I have not discussed in any of the preceding chapters. This is the unity of conscious perception. There is also one aspect of prediction error minimization that I have not yet brought to bear much on the characteristics of conscious perception. This is active inference. This chapter will attempt to remedy this, because I think active inference is the key to understanding the unity of conscious perception.

## PERCEPTUAL UNITY

When you introspect you find that your mind is populated by conscious experiences. There is a constant flow of sensations, perceptions, moods, thoughts. One striking feature is that at any one time all these conscious aspects are bound together in one unified conscious field. We never seem to find two or more completely distinct conscious streams when we introspect. This is phenomenal unity ('phenomenal' means 'conscious' but picks out a characteristic that pertains specifically to the qualitative aspect of consciousness rather than other notions of unity relating to personal identity, or mere representational unity; I shall focus on the subset of these states that are perceptual).

Tim Bayne argues convincingly that consciousness is always phenomenally unified. Here is how he explains the notion:

> Let us say that a subject has a unified consciousness if, and only if, every one of their conscious states at the time in question is phenomenally unified with every other conscious state. We can think of such subjects as fully unified. Where a subject is fully unified, we can say that they enjoy a single total conscious state. A total conscious state is a state that is subsumed by nothing but itself, where one conscious state subsumes another if the former includes the latter as a 'part' or 'component'. This total state will capture what it is like to be the subject at the time in question. In specifying the subject's total conscious state one thereby provides a full specification of the subject's specific conscious states. By contrast, if we are dealing with a creature whose consciousness is disunified, then there will be no single conscious state that 'subsumes' each of their specific conscious states. (Bayne 2010: 15)

Bayne argues that consciousness is unified in that sense:

> How common is it for human beings to have a unified consciousness in this sense of the term? Quite common, it seems to me. Take any set of conscious states that you are currently enjoying—visual experiences, auditory experiences, emotional experiences, bodily sensations, conscious thoughts, or whatever. Irrespective of the degree to which these states might be representationally unified with each other, they will—I wager—be mutually phenomenally unified with each other. You might not have been aware of this unity until I drew your attention to it, but

> having drawn your attention to it I trust that you recognize it in your own experience. (ibid.)

And he uses this to propose that unity is essential to consciousness:

> Generalizing somewhat, we might hazard the guess that unity in this sense is a deep feature of normal waking experience. Indeed, we might even go further, and suggest that this kind of unity is not just a feature of normal waking experience but also characterizes other kinds of background states of consciousness, such as those that are present in REM dreaming, hypnosis, and various pathologies of consciousness. One might even hazard the thought that this kind of unity is an essential feature of consciousness—one that it cannot lose (at least when it comes to creatures like us). (ibid.)

This is the *unity thesis*, that "the conscious states that any subject of experience enjoys at any one point in time will occur as the components of a single total phenomenal state—a unitary 'phenomenal field' (Bayne 2010: 75). Bayne's strategy is to present the thesis, appeal to introspection to defend it (and defend this against objections), and then show how purported cases of disunity fail to be persuasive or to target efficiently the unity thesis.

I think the unity thesis as stated and defended by Bayne is true and captures an essential characteristic of our consciousness. I will consider how and to what extent the prediction error minimization mechanism can help us understand phenomenal unity. That is, why should a prediction error minimizing system like us have unified rather than disunified conscious states?

Before starting on this task, some preliminaries. First a limitation. Bayne discusses unity for all conscious experience; I will only consider conscious *perception*. This is because we have so far mainly considered perceptual inference and been silent on the extent to which other conscious experiences (moods, emotions, thoughts) can be explained by prediction error (for an attempt at emotion, see Hohwy 2011; Seth, Suzuki et al. 2012; and Chapter 12). For this reason, I will discuss a more limited notion of what I call *perceptual unity*. Transposed to Bayne's idiom this is the idea that the conscious perceptual states that any subject of experience enjoys at any one time will occur as the components of a single subsuming total phenomenal perceptual state.

The second preliminary is that the unity thesis, even though it is offered as something essential about consciousness, is instead a contingent truth about our consciousness. There is no conceptual pressure towards unity—mere a priori, conceptual analysis of the concept of consciousness does not lead to the unity thesis. It might be difficult to positively conceive what it would be like to have a genuinely disunified conscious state but it doesn't seem impossible in the sense square circles are impossible. For this reason, the mechanism that guarantees unity for us can be quite specific to our neuronal machinery and allow that creatures in a relatively close possible world to us can fail to have unified consciousness.

This is an important facet, when trying to locate unity. It means that we can look for a genuinely causal property that we happen to possess, rather than something any conscious creature must have irrespective of which logically possible world it inhabits. It also means that we can attribute perceptual unity to ourselves but can withhold it to other creatures even if we allow the possibility that they are conscious. Finally, contingency rather than necessity comes with more of a risk of fragility. Even though Bayne is right and we are all in fact always enjoying perceptually unified experience it might still be that, at least in principle, it wouldn't take much to upset the phenomenal applecart and produce disunified perception. The trick would be to explain why this doesn't in fact ever seem to happen to us.

## UNITY, AND IGNITION OF THE GLOBAL NEURONAL WORKSPACE

It would count strongly in favour of a theory of consciousness if it could explain perceptual unity. Theorizing on consciousness is still somewhat in its infancy but among the more developed theories Bayne singles out Tononi and Edelman's dynamic core theory as the one most likely to accommodate unity (Edelman and Tononi 2000). As Bayne points out, this is no surprise since this theory is one of the few that begins with unity as a constraint on the theory (Bayne 2010: Ch. 10). According to this intriguing theory, thalamocortical loops (i.e., looping neuronal pathways between the cortex and the deeper thalamic structures in the brain) sustain the conscious field in which perceptual content is unified.

I want to make one further move with respect to theories of consciousness. The basic idea motivating the dynamic core theory is included in the kind of *global neuronal workspace theory*, which Stanislas Dehaene, Jean-Pierre Changeux, and Lionel Naccache and their colleagues are developing. Dynamic core theory builds on the notion of informational re-entry, which is the bidirectional exchange of signals across parallel cortical maps coding for different aspects of the same object. This is what helps build up a unified percept, according to this theory. Dehaene and colleagues sought to integrate this idea with a wider range of characteristics of consciousness such as executive supervision and limited capacity, and to that end introduced the global neuronal workspace theory:

> We [propose] the Global Neuronal Workspace (GNW) model as an alternative cortical mechanism capable of integrating the supervision, limited-capacity, and re-entry properties. [...] Global broadcasting allows information to be more efficiently processed (because it is no longer confined to a subset of nonconscious

> circuits but can be flexibly shared by many cortical processors) and to be verbally reported (because these processors include those involved in formulating verbal messages). Nonconscious stimuli can be quickly and efficiently processed along automatized or preinstructed processing routes before quickly decaying within a few seconds. By contrast, conscious stimuli would be distinguished by their lack of "encapsulation" in specialized processes and their flexible circulation to various processes of verbal report, evaluation, memory, planning, and intentional action, many seconds after their disappearance. [We] postulate that this global availability of information is what we subjectively experience as a conscious state. (Dehaene and Changeux 2011: 210)

This idea develops Baars' (1989) earlier global workspace theory of consciousness according to which content is conscious once it enters the global workspace because there it gains the capacity to be broadcast to a host of higher-level cognitive consumer systems for executive control, motor control, report, and so on.

The global neuronal workspace theory is attractive because it follows the strategy of trying to pinpoint the mechanism in the brain that endows perceptual content with a set of properties considered central to consciousness, including perceptual unity. It is also attractive because in an extremely impressive series of studies, these researchers are delivering empirical evidence about what governs the entry of perceptual content to the global neuronal workspace. What they find is that

> human neuroimaging methods and electrophysiological recordings during conscious access, under a broad variety of paradigms, consistently reveal a late amplification of relevant sensory activity, long-distance cortico-cortical synchronization at beta and gamma frequencies, and "ignition" of a large-scale prefronto-parietal network. (Dehaene and Changeux 2011: 209)

For example, in a study using intracranial electroencephalogram (which measures electrical activity directly from the surface of the cortex), Gaillard and colleagues compared conscious and nonconscious processing of masked visual stimuli and observed a pattern of neuronal activity that "fits with the global workspace model, which postulates that once a representation is consciously accessed, a broad distributed network, involving in particular prefrontal cortex, ignites and broadcasts its content" (Gaillard, Dehaene et al. 2009: 486).

The crucial question here is what "ignition" is and why some contents ignite and others do not. A good answer to this question should also help us understand why perceptual experience is unified rather than not. As far as I can see, the proponents of the global neuronal workspace theory primarily use "ignition" in a descriptive sense, to capture the rapid spread of activity in prefrontal and parietal cortex that is a signature of conscious perception. It is then noted, as in the quote above, that this is just the kind of pattern of activation we should expect if something like the workspace theory is correct. Notice though that this descriptive approach does not yet explain what ignition *is* or *why* it should sustain perceptual unity.

Dehaene has offered a more substantial explanation of ignition, in terms of evidence accumulation:

> [C]onscious access would correspond to the crossing of a threshold in evidence accumulation within a distributed global workspace, a set of recurrently connected neurons with long axons that is able to integrate and broadcast back evidence from multiple brain processors. During nonconscious processing, evidence would be accumulated locally within specialized subcircuits, but would fail to reach the threshold needed for global ignition and, therefore, conscious reportability. (Dehaene 2008: 89)

A threshold is set for when one out of two or more competing interpretations of the sensory input has accumulated enough evidence in its favour, and when this happens it enters the global workspace. This is a proposal that is kindred in spirit to the idea of using Bayesian, probabilistic tools to account for perception (though strictly speaking it generates different predictions than the prediction error approach, see Hesselmann, Sadaghiani et al. 2010).

Let us attempt to transpose this into the prediction error minimization framework. Global ignition is achieved when a hypothesis about the world is better able to explain away input than its competitor, and therefore achieves higher posterior probability. What counts as being better able to explain away input is modulated by the expected levels of noise and uncertainty. All up, this is what sets the threshold for ignition. Upon ignition, the perceptual content is made available to consumer systems throughout the brain, and can guide action and decision-making, and be introspectively reported. As such it is close to the way conscious perception was discussed in the previous chapter on attention and its relation to consciousness.

This proposal is attractive. Not only does it fit nicely with the global neuronal workspace theory, the focus on disambiguation and uncertainty-reducing inference repeats themes from our discussion of binding and cognitive penetrability. However, this does not yet seem to quite explain perceptual unity in satisfactory terms. Of course, in so far as global ignition is associated with something like re-entrance (cf. the dynamical core theory), it could be claimed to account for perceptual unity. In his wide-ranging work on the self, Metzinger considers a line of reasoning congenial to this:

> The principle is that the almost continuous feedback-loops from higher to lower areas create an ongoing cycle, a circular nested flow of information, in which what happened a few milliseconds ago is dynamically mapped back to what is coming in right now. In this way, the immediate past continuously creates a context for the present—it filters what can be experienced right now, [ . . . ] if we apply this idea to the brain's unified portrait of the world as a whole, then the

> dynamic flow of conscious experience appears as the result of a continuous large-scale application of the brain's prior knowledge of the current situation. (Metzinger 2009: 30)

This is appealing but sidelines the probabilistic aspect of the explanation, which is crucial to make sense of ignition in the first place. It seems to me that what is needed is a more substantial link between the unity and the probabilistic explanation of ignition. We need to know *why*, from the point of view of perceptual inference, unity would arise. That would provide a deeper, more satisfactory proposal concerning conscious perception, and perceptual unity specifically. The next section will attempt this explanatory task.

## IGNITION, ACTIVE INFERENCE, AND UNITY

The idea of ignition is important because global dominance suggests unity, and it is this idea we must put into the context of the prediction error minimization mechanism. The first question to ask is why ignition should occur when the hypothesis that best explains away sensory input is selected?

The picture we have painted of prediction error minimization in previous chapters focuses on two facets of error minimization. On the one hand there is perceptual inference and on the other hand there is active inference. At various points, I have appealed to the alternation between these two processes. It is important to do both, and to get the balance between them right. I think ignition reflects what happens in the switch from perceptual to active inference, and that conscious perception therefore is tied specifically to active inference. I hope to show that this provides a reasonable candidate for perceptual unity in prediction error terms.

Creatures like us maintain a perceptual hierarchy that models a deeply causally structured world. Having hit on a good hypothesis whose predictions efficiently minimize the prediction error bound on surprise, it is a non-trivial matter to then go on to figure out how to engage active inference. That is, there are many ways that changes to the world or one's position in it could interact with a favoured hypothesis about the world to minimize prediction error. The trajectory of the agent is itself a hidden cause of its own sensory input, which can evolve in a non-linear way as the agent engages the environment. Prediction of the flow of sensory input, conditional on agency, is therefore going to involve many assumptions and thus parameters on many levels of the perceptual hierarchy.

Described like this, going from perceptual to active inference is a situation that calls for something like a global workspace. Here is an everyday illustration of the point: you perceive a café in front of you and experience thirst.

Now prediction error can be minimized by getting something to drink from the café, but it can also be minimized by waiting until you get home and having a glass of water there. A whole range of considerations can make this a difficult decision (for those of us who are slightly neurotic, perhaps): is it worth the money, would you end up getting too much caffeine for the day if you go to the café, what is the chance of genial social interactions in the café, what will happen if you're delayed etc.? If you are with a companion you might need to report some of these deliberations verbally, or you might need to call someone if you anticipate being late. For each of these considerations there is a complicated calculation of fictive actions and counterfactual prediction error cost across multiple spatiotemporal scales. Such wide-ranging generation of scenarios thus matters to active inference. That is, it seems that active inference requires something like ignition of a selected hypothesis into a global space where the predictions can be assessed by subordinate (consumer) systems, conditional on some action. If we had no agency at all—if we had no way of changing the way we sample the world in response to prediction error—then it seems there would be no need for ignition into such a global space. Put simply, we can only do one thing at a time and this thing is prescribed by our singular hypothesis about what we are doing. This necessarily entails predictions that are internally unified throughout the hierarchy—in a global sense.

The proposal is then that anointing one hypothesis about the world as the best prediction error minimizer leads to ignition because the system will be using this hypothesis to inform predictions of the flow of sensory input as it acts on the world. Ignition would be the point at which the system, given a specific context, is satisfied with the posterior probability for a hypothesis (or, in Dehaene's terms, when enough evidence has been accumulated) to warrant a shift to active inference and the production of descending proprioceptive predictions that mediate action.

This gives a rationale for the idea of a threshold—ignition—being central to conscious presentation. A threshold is needed to ensure there is a switch from perceptual to active inference, a point at which a model is held fixed and prediction error minimized given the way the world is assumed to be. It makes sense that ignition goes with global broadcasting because it is a complicated task to figure out how to minimize prediction error given action—a task that requires generation of expected flows of sensory consequences along many dimensions. Of course, how the threshold is set will be highly context-dependent: the planned action and its salience will matter, as will the expected precisions of the prediction error and the confidences in the hypothesis and its competitors.

We might even speculate that the reason this global, multimodal hypothesis is *conscious* is that being conscious serves as a reminder of which hypothesis is currently held fixed for active inference. This would resonate with an early idea from Gregory that consciousness (or qualia) "flags the present" (see also

Metzinger 2004: 127; 188). The point here would be that there is a need to flag the present not only because, as Gregory speculates, hypotheses are essentially timeless, or because the present is potentially dangerous, but rather because the system needs to know which hypothesis is currently prescribing action.

With this I have suggested a way to tie together prediction error minimization with the ignition characteristic of conscious experience. They can be related under considerations of active inference. Now to the question that began it all: why is there perceptual unity? Specifically, why would fixing on a model and beginning to generate policies for active inference invariably go with unity?

The unity thesis is that perceptual experience is never split up between distinct phenomenal fields: there is always just one overall phenomenal field that subsumes any conscious perceptual state you have. Now 'phenomenal field' is not an easy notion to make precise and explicit, even though the intuitive idea extracted from introspection is appealing enough. Nevertheless, as I will suggest next, there are reasons to expect that active inference comes with some kind of unity.

The first point to make in this regard is that active inference ties together represented states in a causal manner. This is because active inference relies on the sensory consequences of *intervention* on the states of affairs in the world, and intervention is crucial to extract causal rather than mere associative information. This is one of the central tenets in contemporary accounts of causation (see Pearl 2000: Ch. 1). If there were no active inference at all, then our hypotheses would be much more loosely tied together; they would be conjectured but never verified. As such they would not need to present the states of affairs of the world as being related in anything but a statistical sense (at best causal inference would be serendipitous). This brings us some way towards expecting unity since a deeper causal structure generalizes across events and will in that sense do more to unify. It seems more likely that when we introspect perception that is based on a hypothesis with a deep causal structure it will appear more unified, than when we introspect perception based on a merely associative hypothesis with no causal information.

However, this notion of unity by causal generalization does not yet explain the key notion that there is *just one* overarching causally structured hypothesis. To explain this, we need to appeal to our possibilities of minimizing prediction error in active inference. The idea here is simple: you cannot simultaneously use two or more different, competing causal hypotheses as a basis for sampling the world to minimize prediction error. In active inference you have to rely on just one hypothesis. *Two* people can rely on two competing hypotheses because they can selectively sample each their own hypothesis of the world in the different ways mandated by their respective hypotheses. But *one* person is tied to modelling intervention in the world in terms of one bodily trajectory giving rise to one flow of input. This restriction tallies well with the notion of the Bayesian brain we rehearsed in Chapter 1–2, you can only select one hypothesis among competing hypotheses—you cannot accept both the null and alternative hypotheses at the same time, on the basis of the same evidence.

This can be illustrated by appeal to binocular rivalry scenarios. If we have *two* individuals and present one with an image of a face and the other with an image of a house, then there is, in a trivial way, disunified perception. One person experiences a face and the other a house. Even though this is a trivial sounding case, we can explain the "disunity" like this: one person can selectively sample the world (via eye movement) on the basis of the hypothesis that it is a face, the other can sample on the basis of the hypothesis that it is a house. Now present the images, one to each of two eyes of the *same* individual, as done in binocular rivalry. Here there is one unified phenomenal field in which the face and the house perception neatly alternate. The proposed explanation for this is that this single individual cannot selectively sample on the basis of the hypothesis that it is a face and, *simultaneously*, sample on the basis of the hypothesis that it is a house. There is only one set of eyes to move around in active inference and so only one causal hypothesis (either "sensory input is caused by a face" or "sensory input is caused by a house") can be fixed on for active inference at any time.

This then is how we can explain perceptual unity within a prediction error minimization scheme. Perception is *unified* because it is based on hypotheses in a causally structured hierarchical model, and there is perceptual *unity* (that is, one hypothesis only) because the nature of active inference in creatures like us prevents more than one hypothesis from being used as a basis for selective sampling at any time.

If this account of perceptual unity is correct, then we should expect unity to diminish gradually as active inference loosens its grip. Now this is not an easy prediction to test experimentally. I don't think we, in any realistic laboratory situation, can extricate ourselves entirely from active inference so we should probably not expect any introspection of real disunity (as Bayne also insists). Indeed, it may be that as we descend deeply into more inactive inference it is not just unity but consciousness itself that deserts us—if there is no action then there is no reason for ignition. But perhaps there can be conditions under which our confidence in unity should begin to waver as active inference is beginning to be curbed. There seems to be some evidence for this, again from studies of binocular rivalry.

Binocular rivalry can be modulated but not extinguished by endogenous attention to one of the two stimuli. The more one attentively explores one stimulus, the more it tends to dominate in perception. We have construed endogenous attention as a type of active inference so, if decreasing active inference predicts more disunity, we should expect less attention to bring less rivalry. This seems to happen. In a study of binocular rivalry, Zhang and colleagues directed participants' attention elsewhere and found that alternation seems to stop (Zhang, Jamison et al. 2011; see also Brascamp and Blake 2012). They conclude that attention is necessary for rivalry, which is reasonable enough. The way I prefer to interpret this within the prediction error framework is that as attention is withdrawn there is less active exploration of the stimuli so there is less imperative to subscribe to just one of two competing causal hypotheses and both stimuli are then beginning to be accommodated. Now this is not clearly a case of disunity since it is hard to know whether instead of having a *dis*unified perceptual field the participants in this study just adopt *one* fused hypothesis of the stimuli—that is, a unified hypothesis that ignores the causal structure of the two stimuli. The problem is of course that getting a firm fix on whether there is perceptual disunity would require getting participants in the study to attend to the stimuli, to report them better, and this would reinstate active inference. It is suggestive however that the strong urge towards a unified hypothesis with temporal alternation between causally distinct percepts weakens as active inference (here, in the shape of endogenous attention) is withheld.

One hallmark of the global workspace is that perceptual content in the workspace becomes available for introspective report. Such reporting of conscious experience is a moment in active inference in the sense that engaging in that kind of verbal or button-pressing behaviour is just engaging in prediction error minimization. This means that when an individual is requested to introspectively report on something, then there will automatically be a bias towards perceptual unity. Therefore, if we wanted to discover instances of disunity by curbing active inference, then it would be better to not acquire introspective reports—but of course then it is very hard to know what participants in a study experience. This appears to be a bind.

Another rivalry study is relevant for this apparent bind. Naber and colleagues exposed participants to rivalry between stimuli that moved in opposite directions, asked them to report what they experienced, and meanwhile recorded eye movements (Naber, Frässle et al. 2011). One of their dependent measures was optokinetic nystagmus, which is the rapid back-and-forth movement of the eyes when they are following a moving object (such as when a person looks out a car window). They observed that optokinetic nystagmus follows the reported percepts well. When subjects report seeing a leftward motion then the optokinetic nystagmus would be that characteristic of observed leftward motion. This is of course itself an exemplification of active inference: the hypothesis predicts a leftward motion and the eyes move accordingly in a selective sampling of the world, constrained by knowledge of head-movement. Next the participants were *not* asked to report their experience with button-presses and instead only the eye movement was recorded during rivalry. The reasoning here was that the eye movement had been shown to be a reliable indicator of the experienced percept, so the rivalry could be studied without muddying measurement with requirements to introspectively report what was experienced. It turned out that the alternation between optokinetic nystagmus in the two different directions slowed down under these more passive conditions. Hence, when there is less pressure to engage active inference and actively report our experiences there seems to be less need to maintain distinct hypotheses of the world. As before, it is hard to establish unequivocally that there is disunity in this case, but it is suggestive that when report is not required the requirement for unity, where one or the other hypothesis is chosen, seems to drop off.

These studies of binocular rivalry are consistent with the idea that perceptual unity is fuelled by the need for unequivocal selective sampling in active inference. As the requirement for sampling goes down so does the inclination to work with only one model of the world.

## ACTION-BASED UNITY AND INDIRECTNESS

Though progress has been made in our understanding of the unity of consciousness (see Bayne 2010), it is still a notion that is difficult to understand and make clear. Much of our grasp of it is sourced in relatively murky introspection. My account attempts to offer fairly concrete mechanisms for what *unites* perceptual experience, namely hierarchical causal structure, and what makes perceptual unity *unitary*, namely the requirements of active inference. To me, this is attractive because it not only describes unity but because it explains why we should expect there to be unity.

When looking at consciousness science more broadly, this proposal fits nicely with the global neuronal workspace theory, proposed by Dehaene and others. It comes with the twist that the contents making it to the global workspace are the ones necessary for active inference. These are representations of the world modelled up against our agency in the world, generating prediction error and thereby initiating action. This means there is a deep connection between conscious perception and unity and action.

This relates to work by Susan Hurley, which does much to connect the unity of consciousness with action. She points out that a dichotomous conception of perception as input to the system and action as the output of the system is not fruitful. A more dynamic concept of perception and action is proposed instead:

> [T]he unity of consciousness has both normative, personal-level and subpersonal aspects. The relations between these levels can be approached via the closely related but more general idea of a perspective: the interdependence of perception and action that perspective involves can be explained in terms of their

> co-dependence on a subpersonal dynamic singularity. This subpersonal aspect of unity does not support sharp causal boundaries either between mind and world or between perception and action. Moreover, it can provide an antidote to the inward retreat of the mind in modern philosophy. At the personal level, the self does not lurk hidden somewhere between perceptual input and behavioral output, but reappears out in the open, embodied and embedded in the world. (Hurley 1998: 3)

Much in this sentiment sits reasonably well with much of what the prediction error minimization account can offer. It seems to me Hurley is right that we cannot understand unity unless we factor in the way action and perception work in tandem. In particular, as I have been emphasizing above too, there would be no need for unity if there were no agency. The prediction error account gives a principled explanation of why something like a singularity (that is to say, I take it, a unity) should arise when perception and action works in tandem, namely in order to minimize prediction error.

The embodied and externalist aspects of Hurley's approach (and by extension that of others in the embodied cognition camp) are much less attractive, from the point of view of prediction error minimization. The prediction of the generative model of the world maintained in the brain is an internal mirror of nature, it recapitulates the causal structure of the world and prediction error is minimized relative to the model's expected states. Similarly, the starting point for the prediction error account of unity is one of indirectness: from inside the skull the brain has to infer the hidden causes of its sensory input, which crucially depends on interaction with the creatures' body. It turns out that such inference requires close tandem work by perception and action, but this is because the inferential task is essentially indirect. As such it is difficult to free it from suspicions of being what Hurley calls a "traditional view of content [that] generates skeptical worries about how knowledge of the world is possible: why couldn't our beliefs about the external world be rampant delusions produced by mad scientists manipulating our brains?" (Hurley 1998: 8).

This suspicion is inevitable for the prediction error account (and was acknowledged and set aside in Chapter 8). Selecting and shaping parameters certainly happen in close causal commerce with the world, but it is nevertheless an inferential process of explaining away the ever changing but oftentimes predictable patterns of sensory input. What are behind the barrier of sensory input are *hidden* causes in the sense that they must be revealed in causal inference. An appeal to action, on the prediction error scheme, reduces to an appeal to inferences about different kinds of patterns of sensory input. If a mad scientist was a hidden common cause of all that sensory input we would have no way of knowing unless she made an independent causal contribution to sensory input. The mad scientist would have a difficult job at keeping up with our selective sampling of the world in active inference but in principle it is just about projecting sensory data that are close enough to what we expect on our sensory "screens".

It seems to me that it is better to accept the indirectness implications of the prediction error minimization framework than trying to force it into an embodied and externalist shape. It is better, that is, to live with the risk of radical scepticism than to belie the core idea that perception and action are both inferences on the statistical properties of the sensory input.

The final picture is then that our grasp of the world—the way we mirror its causal structure—is at the mercy of the inferential tools we have internally in the brain. This lends a certain kind of fragility to its representations and to the self, which will be the focus of the next chapter.

## SUMMARY: UNITY AND CAUSAL SECLUSION

We were after an explanation of perceptual unity from the perspective of prediction error minimization. The explanation begins by noting that conscious perception belongs in the global neuronal workspace, which houses the perceptual content (or hypothesis under an internal model) deemed good enough for active inference. Active inference requires prioritizing just one hypothesis of the world, and this delivers unity in the sense of ensuring there is never more than one subsuming perceptual field. The sense of unity of the conscious field itself was explained in terms of the causal rather than merely associative nature of internal models.

Even though this account relies on the individual's actions in the world to account for facts about perceptual structure, it in fact cements the indirect, inferentialist view of mind and action. This is a theme I will explore in the next chapter.

## NOTES

*Page 208.* ["This conception of conscious perception . . . "] I propose a way to address the problem of consciousness without stumbling into the hard problem. The view I propose essentially is a kind of empirically enhanced commonsense functionalism; it adds empirical information to Jackson's list of core properties, discussed in Chapter 8.

*Page 211.* ["It would count strongly in . . . "] The development of the dynamic core theory of consciousness by Tononi in terms of an information theoretical quantity called information integration is also attractive and not entirely alien to probabilistic accounts of perception (Tononi 2005).

*Page 211.* ["I want to make one further . . . "] This global neuronal workspace is described in terms of neural activity and connectivity: "Our proposal is that a subset of cortical pyramidal cells with long-range excitatory axons, particularly dense in prefrontal, cingulate, and parietal regions, together with the relevant thalamocortical loops, form a horizontal 'neuronal workspace' interconnecting the multiple specialized, automatic, and nonconscious processors [ . . . ]. A conscious content is assumed to be encoded by the sustained activity of a fraction of GNW neurons, the rest being inhibited. Through their numerous reciprocal connections, GNW neurons amplify and maintain a specific neural representation. The long-distance axons of GNW neurons then broadcast it to many other processors brain-wide" (Dehaene and Changeux 2011: 210).

*Page 214.* ["The picture we have painted . . . "] The claim is that active inference requires something like ignition because active inference requires promoting one hypothesis as the best prediction error minimizer, and as the hypothesis on the basis of which input in the longer run is predicted. This view seems to me consistent with very recent work by Friston, Breakspear and Deco (2012), who explains the perceptual switching associated with ignition in terms of how the system visits states with good prediction error minimization but then (because such states by definition have flat prediction error landscapes) vitiates those states, which enables (re-)ignition and visiting of new states. This relates to the imperative to shift between perceptual and active inference I have discussed in Chapter 4 and 7.

*Page 219.* ["These studies of binocular rivalry . . . "] The prediction error framework is flexible, and unity may be explained in other ways within it. Wanja Wiese and Thomas Metzinger (Wiese and Metzinger 2013) propose that unification of perceptual content happens because not only must individual perceptual processes predict what happens in the world, they must also predict what other perceptual processes know. If all of them are doing this, then part of what they will be representing is how they are themselves being represented. This creates a nested series of representations. This aims at explaining a phenomenological account of unity of consciousness in terms of global self-embedding (or self-representation). The question is of course why such mutual representation should be required on a predictive coding story. Wiese and Metzinger propose that there is such nested mutual emulation because it facilitates the quality, or reliability, of individual representations, and because it could facilitate examinations of how well individual representations fit together, of how coherent they are. I think care must be taken in how these ideas are fleshed out. First, the question of reliability is just the question of precision optimization, and we have seen that that is a matter of second order statistical inference, which does not require knowledge of what the means represent. So ensuring reliability, in this sense at least, does not mandate nested representation of the content itself. Second, the coherence of individual representations is related to the question of sensory integration, and we have seen how this is a matter of precision optimization under top-down causal expectations; this is a story that does not obviously lend itself to the notion of nested emulations. However, perhaps these ideas can be worked out in different ways, to avoid these initial objections. There is something very appealing about the suggestion because it implies that the brain benefits from common knowledge: not only must the individual representations have mutual knowledge of the same things in the environment, they must also have *common knowledge*—that is know of each other what they know about what they each know, and so on. There are well-described epistemic, agential, and practical reasoning benefits to such common knowledge between independent individuals (Chwe 1999; Chwe 2000). It is therefore not inconceivable, and a rather beautiful idea, that similar processes could be at play within the human brain as are in play among human brains. I briefly explore this theme in the final chapter of the book.

# 11

# The fragile mirror of nature

In this third part of the book, the prediction error minimization scheme is explored in the context of difficult themes concerning the nature and structure of the mind. Chapter 9 considered the nature of attention and its connection with conscious perception. Chapter 10 continued the theme of consciousness and developed an account of perceptual unity. That chapter ended on a note of indirectness in the sense of how hypotheses under internal models of the world are fundamentally constrained by our ability to probabilistically infer hidden causes of sensory input.

This basic kind of inferentialist predicament is put nicely by Marius Usher: "noisy messages are the rule in the perceptual life of animals and humans who need to make the best of it." (Usher 2001: 325). We are good at 'making the best of it' but this is because the world is a uniform kind of place that kindly affords reliable statistical inference. This reliability belies an underlying fragility borne by the fact we are trapped inside our skulls with only sensory data to go by.

This chapter pursues these more subtle aspects of indirectness and fragility. In particular I look at challenges to our seemingly robust background beliefs about the nature of our own body. Having established this very general outlook on us as fundamentally fragile prediction error minimizing machines, the chapter then explores some challenging notions about how we relate to the world in perception. The final picture of the human mind is both disconcerting and comforting.

## TRUTH TRACKERS OR JUST A PENCHANT FOR ERROR MINIMIZATION?

Here is a very robust idea of perception. It is the once canonical idea that perception arises in a bottom-up fashion with sensory signals being analysed, bound, and presented. On this picture we are passive receivers of sensory input and not actively trying to predict input, and even less trying to change input in self-fulfilling ways by changing the world. On this picture we simply perceive what the world "tells" us to perceive. In order to perceive the world we do not have to try to use prior beliefs to interpret what it "tells" us. This of course is a caricature of the substantial body of research driven by the bottom-up, feature-detection idea. But it is fundamentally in stark contrast to the prediction error minimization idea.

This contrast is captured in the reversal of the functional roles of top-down and bottom-up processing, captured in Figure 7 in Chapter 3. The bottom-up signal is merely *feedback* to the queries generated on the basis of the brain's internal model. The top-down, backwards messages in the brain are not feedback on the sensory processing, somehow modulating it, instead they are predictive signals, which when successful embody perceptual experience. With this, the robustness of the world "telling" us how it is begins to disappear. The world only tells us things in the sense that it provides answers to the questions we pose of it—it does not impress itself upon us. Perception depends on what we ask, and moreover, our ability to ask is constrained by the fact that the world has statistical regularities we can trust.

This less direct engagement with the world appears to be a more fragile process than the more straightforward (but probably unworkable) bottom-up conception of perception. Of course, it feels like we go through life with the world robustly telling us what it is like. We see things, bump into them, and talk about them with each other, and so on. But all this arises in a constant, dynamic process of hypothesis generation and revising, and predicting and manoeuvring around in the world. As shown in Chapter 7, this dynamic process relies on getting a number of different epistemic checks and balances right all at the same time. It does not take much disruption or suboptimal prediction error minimization for the overall model of the world to take a wrong or even pathological path.

This is nicely illustrated by a computational study of out-of-body experiences by Lars Schwabe and Olaf Blanke (Schwabe and Blanke 2008). They hypothesize that vestibular processing contributes to out of body experiences. The idea is that a mismatch between top-down expectations of movement/position and bottom-up signals from the vestibular otoliths can lead to illusions of movement (otoliths are little hairs in the inner ear that are sensitive to dynamics of movement). The signal from the otoliths can be ambiguous between, for example, being stationary with the head in a particular position and accelerating forwards with the head in a different position (see Figure 29). If other modalities that could be used to reality test on the perceived movement are rendered non-informative (which may happen during sleep or in a laboratory setting), then one could end up experiencing acceleration even though one's body is in fact stationary. Thus, "'wrong' inputs to otherwise optimal [Bayesian] processing could lead to illusions such as out-of-body

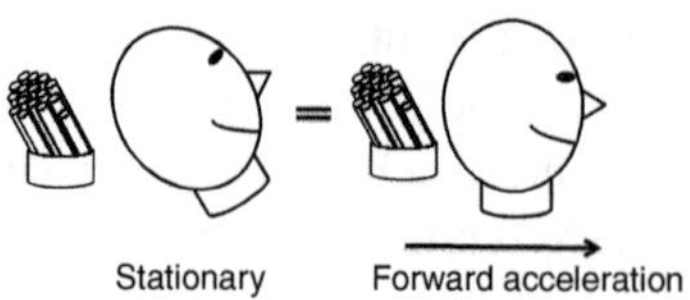


**Figure 29.** The otoliths of the vestibular system deliver the same signal under different bodily situations. This ambiguity can contribute to out-of-body experiences (see Schwabe and Blanke 2008).

experiences" (Schwabe and Blanke 2008: 7). The awareness that one is lying still and yet accelerating could be part of what triggers some out of body experiences ("I must be leaving my body behind").

The key point here is that very little coincidence in the right circumstances—for example, a particular head position when going to sleep—is sufficient to initiate a radical change in perceptual inference. The fragility of the situation is captured succinctly by Schwabe and Blanke:

> Hence, online processing of body-related multisensory information in the brain is more like ongoing puzzle solving of which the normally experienced embodied self-location is just a fragile and only temporarily stable solution, which is a setting that is naturally suited for the Bayesian approach to sensory information processing. (2008: 8)

It is this kind of fragility, for the perceptual system overall, I will seek to describe in this chapter. Even though the experience of being in our own body is something that accompanies most of us all the time, there is a sense in which it is "a fragile and only temporarily stable solution".

In addition to the way prediction error minimization seems to be led seriously astray by the "wrong" kinds of input, it also seems to have a penchant for efficiently minimizing a lot of prediction error rather than for minimizing it in a way that directly facilitates truth-seeking. This comes out very dramatically in the rubber hand illusion and full body versions of the rubber hand illusion.

In these illusions, the individual is presented with a barrage of low-level proprioceptive, tactile, and visual sensory input. It needs to adjust its hypothesis' parameters accordingly and predict how the input will evolve, partly on the basis of prior beliefs about the nature of the body and the statistical regularities in the world. Instead of sticking with the known truth ("that rubber item is not my hand and so touch cannot be felt there") the system goes with whatever alternative hypothesis about the world can most efficiently reduce prediction error down through the perceptual hierarchy. In fact, as we saw earlier (Ch. 7), this happens even if sensory input must be explained away under blatantly untrue causal hypotheses about invisible extensions of fingers, opposed magnets under the skin, and so on. Should such perverted sensory input become more chronic and inescapable, then it seems reasonable to think that our prior beliefs will follow suit and we become delusional.

We thus appear to weigh actual suppression of sensory input higher than we weigh sticking with what we know. This makes sense if we briefly return to the reading of prediction error minimization in statistical physics terms as the organism's attempt to maintain its integrity against the onslaught of entropy (cf. Chapters 2–4; 8). Sticking with a veridical long-term prior belief may be useless if doing so means the organismic integrity is breached at a much faster time scale by a barrage of unexplained, high precision sensory input. We can consider ourselves lucky that by and large, for most of us, the world cooperates and delivers reliable statistical regularities most of the time. I stress that this is for "most of us" because the world does in fact shatter for the surprisingly large minority of us afflicted by mental illness.

What makes perception fragile is then both the imperative to stem prediction error at as many levels as possible and the fact we are restricted to using only the internal resources of the brain in doing this. The fragility can be difficult to acknowledge both because, to most of us, perception seems remarkably robust throughout life, and because, on the prediction error minimization scheme itself perceptual inference is supervised by the reliable statistical regularities offered up by the world. But we fail to understand the nature of perception if we gloss over its fundamental fragility. This is not so very difficult from failing to understand the true nature of a teacup if we gloss over its fragility, even if it never in fact breaks.

In the next section I will seek to place this notion of fragility within an understanding of the perceptual mind-world relation.

## IS PERCEPTION INDIRECT?

The prediction error minimization mechanism suggests perception is fundamentally fragile. It is not directly determined in a bottom-up fashion by the sensory input from the world. Instead it is in some sense indirectly determined. As Metzinger puts it concerning his own theory, which shares the indirectness with the view we are considering here "Of course, an external world does exist, and knowledge and action do causally connect us to it—but the conscious experience of knowing, acting, and being connected is an exclusively internal affair" (Metzinger 2009: 23).

On our account, this is captured in the idea that perceptual content is maintained in internal models that always seek to be ahead of events, and which are under an imperative to rid themselves expediently of prediction error. However, the notions of 'direct' and 'indirect' are not very clear and unambiguous when applied to the way the mind relates to the world. The danger of deeming perception 'indirect' is that it suggests a return to an old-fashioned and unsustainable picture where we are internal, homuncular spectators of sense data (Hohwy 2007a; Clark 2013). This picture would sit poorly with prediction error minimization since this framework does not posit or invite the extra step of having both sense-data and internal observers.

It is thus not satisfactory just to claim the perceptual relation is direct, nor to claim it is indirect. The right response to this situation is not to force a choice between them but to try to reconceive the perceptual relation to the world such that we do not have to choose between perception being "direct" or "indirect" in the first place. Instead we should be able to retain the grain of truth in both sides of the debate.

The prediction error minimization scheme seems biased in favour of indirectness because it is based on internal models generating predictions. But at the same time, prediction error minimization anchors us in the causal order of things, as captured in the way perceptual inference is supervised by the prediction error given through the senses. It is this causal conception of the perceptual relation I want to seize on.

Here is how I think of it: the implicit inversion of the generative model, which happens in the overall process of suppressing prediction error, means the brain becomes like a *mirror* of the causal structure of the world. This is one way to illustrate the idea that a prediction error minimization mechanism must come to recapitulate the causal structure of the world (this was the upshot of the Friston-inspired mechanism described in Part I of this book). For the states of a mirror themselves, as opposed to the states of one of us looking *at* a mirror image, it doesn't make clear sense to say these states either directly or indirectly represent the world. The relation of the states of the mirror to the states of the world is as direct as a causal relation is direct, namely in the sense that the states of the mirror exist in virtue of causal input from the states of affairs on the world, and are carrying information about those states. But the relation is also as indirect as a causal relation is indirect, namely in the sense that the causal relata are distinct existences that could in principle exist without being related to each other. If this simple description of an actual mirror is transferred to the case of prediction error minimization, the relation of perceptual states to the states of the world is as direct as a causal relation is direct and, also, as indirect as a causal relation is indirect.

Viewed like this, it is a mistake to take on the challenge of choosing between the perceptual mind–world relation being either direct or indirect. Instead, the intuition that perception is indirect is captured by its reliance on priors and generative models to infer the hidden states of the world, and the intuition that perception is direct is captured by the way perceptual inference queries and is subsequently guided by the sensory input causally impinging upon it. Understanding the perceptual relation then lies in working out the relation between these two aspects. In large part, this is what the chapters in Part II focused on. I find this plea for a causal conception of the mind–world relation compelling because it places us squarely as just elements in the overall natural, causal nexus of states and events in the world.

It might be objected that the mirror analogy is unattractive because it suggests perception is a passive, receptive process far removed from the active hypothesis-testing mechanism we have been at pains to portray. There is some truth in this complaint: perception is highly active and mirroring is not. However, the passivity conveyed by the mirror analogy is important. There is a very fundamental sense in which we find ourselves ending up in unsurprising states: given who we are, as defined by what states we expect to occupy (the model), we are continually nudged by surprise (unexpected states) to end up closer to just those expected states. In this process, the models are shaped to recapitulate the world as received through the senses. This is essentially a passive and conservative process where prediction error pushes and pulls our perception of the world. In the long run, all the inferential activity integrates out uncertainty, leaving us as more passively conceived models. It is in that sense that we are mere pawns in the causal nexus.

None of this is to deny that human interaction in culture and technology plays an enormous and deeply integrated role in aiding prediction error minimization (see Roepstorff, Niewöhner et al. 2010; Clark 2013), nor does it deny that it can be beneficial for us to engage in local itinerant, exploratory behaviour at transient prediction error cost (Friston, Daunizeau et al. 2010). Underlying these active, non-conservative elements is the idea that we do all that to stay clear of surprising sensory input and thereby maintain the integrity of the organism. This process is optimized to the kind of input and low-surprise conditions that define us and therefore it seems plausible to say that it does not take much disruption to the input or to the way the input is processed for perception to alter dramatically.

The causal conception of the mind-world relation, under this passive mirroring, captures well the notion of fragility. The directness of the causal relation means the hypotheses generated on the basis of our internal model are reliably guided by the states of affairs in the world, through the prediction error signal. The indirectness of a causal relation however makes us expect that this reliable guidance relation is not going to be robust across changes in conditions. There is nothing in the notion of a causal relation that dictates that the mechanism in question will continue to work close to normally under various permutations of its normal conditions of operation (as defined by the expected states). Some causal mechanisms are very fragile, even if they do work reliably within a circumscribed set of conditions. It doesn't take much to upset them. I have been arguing that the mind is fragile in this sense. In terms of hypothesis-testing, the idea is that even though we through evolution and neurodevelopment are saddled with one model ($m$, our brain), there is a surprisingly wide range of hypotheses ($h$) to select from under that model. When put in challenging situations, the hypotheses chosen can give rise to radically altered perception. I suspect that the reason this fragility can be hard to acknowledge is that we are just so used to trusting the senses we don't realize their underlying fragility.

In other words, the mind is a truth-tracker in the sense that it is a mechanism that is optimized such that it reliably recapitulates the structure of the world. However, the nature of the mechanism is such that when its normal conditions are tampered with, for example in the shape of input that is surprising relative to the states the organism is expected to be found in, then it stops reliably recapitulating the world. The mechanism is not very good at sticking to its learned truths when it moves outside its narrow zone of comfort. In this light, the truth-tracking nature of the mind comes across as rather serendipitous—a function of how we must self-organize rather than an aim in itself.

Next, I will substantiate the notion of fragility through studies of our body-perception. At the end of the chapter I then turn to related issues of situatedness and embodiment.

## THE BAYESIAN BODY

Here is something that comes across as very robust: the way we perceive our body and its interaction with the world. Perception is anchored in the body, and the body is, obviously, a key ingredient in agency. There is very little doubt that the body shapes the perspective-dependent way we perceive and interact with the world and each other (Gallagher 2005). Ovid-like metamorphosis is a very improbable state for us. It is difficult to see how perceptual fragility could infect this stable body sense and its central role for perceptual inference. And yet, recent research suggests very strongly that it is disconcertingly easy to disturb our body perception.

This research takes off in extensions of the rubber hand illusion, which strongly emphasize the fragility of our body sense. Recall that in the rubber hand illusion, synchronous touch on the rubber hand you can see and on your own, hidden hand induces the illusion that this touch is delivered by the experimenter's visible hand on what is clearly a rubber hand. What is striking about this illusion is that it flies in the face of what must be a very strong, deeply embedded prior belief about your body, namely that when you can feel a touch it is delivered to your own body and not to what ought to be an inanimate object.

There is an amazingly swift sell-out of this prior belief about the body image in the rubber hand illusion. I have been suggesting that what drives this sell-out is our penchant for getting rid of high precision prediction error. It is as if we just cannot believe that visuotactile synchrony is anything but bound in one location. The true hypothesis, that the experimenter is a more deeply hidden common cause of the differently located visual and tactile touch, is set aside as too complex and not good enough for minimizing prediction error here and now.

These comments revisit rubber hand related themes from previous chapters, concerning binding, penetrability and reality-testing. But does it really show a deep fragility of our body perception? It is possible to argue that this is just a transient, localized, and understandable misperception but that underlying this is an immutable body image. After all, the mislocated touch is felt on a hand-looking object and the illusion seems strongest when the rubber hand and the real hand are close to each other, or overlapping in visual space (Lloyd 2007; Paton, Hohwy et al. 2011).

However it didn't take long for the rubber hand illusion to be extended in various ways that pertain to this question. There are two parts to the prior beliefs about the body, which are being challenged by these illusions. Most basically there is the (true) belief that this rubber hand is not part of my body. This belief is ignored in every version of the rubber hand illusion: the illusion cannot be penetrated by this belief. This is really the strongest indication that our body image is fragile. But most research has focused on a second aspect of prior belief, namely that touch felt on one's hand should be seen to occur on a hand-like object. The thought is this: for us to overrule the knowledge that this object doesn't belong to our body, the object at least needs to be hand-shaped.

Initial studies suggested that this prior played no role: the illusion could arise for any kind of object, it seemed. For example, when a simple table top was tapped in synchrony with tapping on one's real hand, the illusion still seemed to occur (Armel and Ramachandran 2003): people seemed to experience the sensation of touch on a bare table top! But, as often happens, later research complicated things. It seemed that for touch on objects that didn't look hand-like, the illusion was in fact absent or at least very weak (Tsakiris and Haggard 2005; Tsakiris, Carpenter et al. 2010). This research suggests that our prior conception of the body plays a very strong and robust role in perceptual inference, consistent with its role as a fairly immutable anchor for perception.

But if we transpose some of this discussion into a Bayesian vernacular, then a different position becomes available. It should not surprise that the illusion is more evasive when the touched object is not hand-like. There is more prediction error to explain away for a non-hand-like object than a more hand-like object. In the former case, perceptual inference needs to also overcome the surprise associated with the fact that the touched object is not hand-like. However, the Bayesian story should also make us expect that if that prediction error is diminished first, then the illusion should solidify, even for non-hand-like objects. This is just a way of saying that if the set-up has already successfully challenged some of our prior beliefs about the body ("touch is not felt on rubber hands located where I proprioceptively do not feel my own hand"), then it will be easier to explain away even far-fetched scenarios like touch on non-hand-like objects and thereby come to experience dramatic changes in body image.

This then provides a way to adjudicate between the different results of studies seen in the rubber hand illusion. Both sets of findings can be explained in terms of Bayesian inference because on the one hand it takes a dynamic, probabilistic journey to leave behind the prior belief that touch is always felt on hand-like objects, but on the other hand, given the right sequence of evidence, this prior belief can in fact be left behind. I suspect what will count as the right sequence of events will be highly dependent on the specific context, expected levels of noise, and so on. (The Armel and Ramachandran result can then be explained in terms of their experimental set-up, where participants in many instances had already experienced the standard rubber-hand illusion before trying the table-top illusion).

There is evidence for this line of reasoning concerning the fragility of body perception. In one of our own studies, we tried to induce the rubber hand illusion on a little cardboard box instead of on a rubber hand (so we can think of the illusion as the cardboard box illusion). As expected from previous studies, this failed. Then we tried first to induce the normal rubber hand illusion, and then quickly swap to a view of the cardboard box being tapped. Now the illusion persisted even though it happened on a non-hand-like cardboard box. This suggests that, given the right context, the prior belief that touch is felt on body-like objects can be left behind in favour of a belief that touch is felt on such inanimate objects. Our body sense is thus rather promiscuous, at least when coaxed in the right Bayesian way. As long as we can efficiently explain away the current sensory input we will locate feelings of touch on cardboard boxes (Hohwy and Paton 2010).

Could we push this even further? We presented people with a virtual version of the rubber hand illusion, where the rubber hand is held up in front of them rather than put on a table, and the illusion was induced with the normal kind of tapping. Then we removed the hand from view so that all they see is the index finger from the experimenter's hand moving up and down in thin air in front of them. Surely this should destroy the illusion because to feel it would be to accept that one's body has immaterialized or become invisible. But it didn't. Instead some participants felt, at least for a short while, that the touch they could feel was located in thin air, at the tip of the experimenter's finger. The experience is truly magic (unpublished data).

There have been a number of further extensions of the rubber hand illusion, which seem to underscore this Bayesian story. A main contributor is Henrik Ehrsson and colleagues who, for example, tried having two rubber hands placed before the participant and finding that people can multiply the sense of touch: they only actually received one touch in one location but feel two in two locations, when there were two rubber hands before them. The illusion was weakened somewhat by doing this, as if there is a limited quantity of touch to distribute (Ehrsson 2009; Guterstam, Petkova et al. 2011; see also Folegatti, Farnè et al. 2012).

Hands are part of the body, but what about the whole body itself? Could it be that the whole body sense is more solid than mere flailing parts of the body? Is there such a thing as a rubber *body* illusion, and if there is, how fragile is the body sense? Even this seemingly outlandish question has been investigated in the lab.

To approach this body of research, let us briefly step back. Thomas Metzinger has proposed a view of the self that is congenial to the Bayesian story. The reason we experience having a self is that we entertain a model of the world, which also represents our bodies and our location in the world. This appeals to the idea that a model without a centre that says "I am here, now" is pretty useless for action planning and decision. This view is clearly congenial to the prediction error minimization framework.

Thus to the extent we have a self it is founded in a perceptual, centred model of the world. If it is just a model then it should be possible to challenge its predictions. For this reason, Metzinger focused research on the tricky topic of out-of-body experiences (Metzinger 2004; Metzinger 2009). Though some impressive research began to show that by manipulating the brain, something like out-of-body experiences could be induced (Blanke, Landis et al. 2004), it was still hard to study in the lab. Metzinger teamed up with Bigna Lenggenhager, Tej Tadi, and Oluf Blanke, and did a full-body version of the rubber hand illusion (Lenggenhager, Tadi et al. 2007). Whereas this did not create a strong out of body illusion, it did create the illusion that a touch really delivered to one's back was felt outside of one's body on a virtual body standing with its back to one. The illusion occurred when subjects saw their own virtual body (Figure 30), or a virtual fake body being touched in synchrony with the touch they felt on their back. As in the rubber hand illusion, the illusion failed to occur when the touch was delivered on a non-body object (though based on our rubber hand illusion experiment mentioned above, I predict it would occur if the illusion was first induced on a body-like object and then swiftly transferred to a non-body object).

This again suggests a certain fragility of the body image, which is compatible with the Bayesian story proposed here. Ehrsson's lab provided a different version of this type of illusion (Ehrsson 2007), also using virtual reality goggles, and have since expanded it in dramatic ways. For example, by making the participant and the experimenter shake hands, but through the goggles giving the participant the visual perspective of the experimenter, it is possible to achieve a very real experience of inhabiting another person's body while observing oneself as if from the outside (Petkova and Ehrsson 2008), see Figure 31.

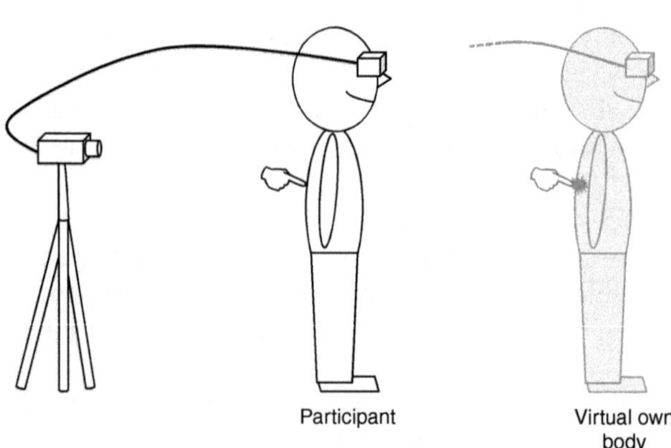


**Figure 30.** The Full Body Illusion. The participant is stroked on the back; a camera records this from behind and transmits to head-mounted video goggles, making it appear the participant is standing in front of him or herself. Touch delivered on the back is then felt as being located on that virtual body in front of the participant (touch can also be seen as delivered on a fake body or as delivered on a non-body object (Lenggenhager, Tadi et al. 2007).

**Figure 31.** Body swap by swapping visual perspective; the participant is standing left, through the goggles experiencing the visual perspective of the experimenter, standing on the right; the experience is as of occupying the experimenter's body, shaking hands with oneself (Petkova and Ehrsson 2008).

I have replicated this many times in the lab and in class, and part of the experience is that if a tactile element (such as tapping the participant's arm) is subsequently introduced then it really feels as if it is delivered to the other person's body, which the participant is experiencing as inhabiting. This to such an extent that if one is touched on one's real arm in this condition, but no touch is visibly delivered on the experimenter's arm, which appears to be one's own, then it eerily feels as if an invisible finger is touching one's newly acquired, strange-looking arm.

Are there limits to this kind of full body illusion? It certainly facilitates the illusion when the object is body-like but it can be highly unusual. Ehrsson's group has induced a full body illusion for a doll much smaller than the participant; the illusion is so persuasive that there are subsequent movement effects (van der Hoort, Guterstam et al. 2011). In our lab we have been able to generate the experience that participants have a tiny articulated, wooden body. By strapping a little camera on the head of an articulated doll we could give people the perspective of looking down the doll's front. Synchronous tapping on the belly of the doll and of the person induces the illusion of being touched on a wooden stomach. The illusion is so persuasive that when a toy spider is placed on the doll people are startled to experience a giant spider crawling over their chest (unpublished data, see Figure 32).

There are many more versions of the rubber hand illusion and the full body illusion. There is still debate about the limits of the illusion, in terms of how wild the violations of prior beliefs of body image can be. But the emerging picture is that with careful and sometimes gradual manipulation, there are few limits to the kinds of objects that we can accept as being the recipient of the touch we can feel and the ways we can be influenced by objects in the world. It seems that our penchant for simple hypotheses that efficiently suppress sensory prediction error easily overrides the otherwise incredibly familiar body image. We are just lucky that this kind of thing rarely happens in everyday life. This is the kind of fragility that the prediction error minimization scheme brings in its wake, and in this case it goes to the core of even our bodily self-awareness.

Now let us return to the objection that this fragility is relatively inconsequential. Not only do most of us seemingly go through life without having our fragile perceptual worlds shatter, there is also some evidence that these distorted body images fail to carry over into movement, that is, that the way prediction error is minimized in perceptual inference during the illusions fails to influence active inference (Kammers, de Vignemont et al. 2009). This follows on from the point noted in Chapter 7 that many illusions seem to be sequestered in this way (for example the Ebbinghaus illusion doesn't seem to strongly influence grasping tasks). Three things can however be said in response, all of which suggest that the fragility is not inconsequential. Firstly, a surprisingly large

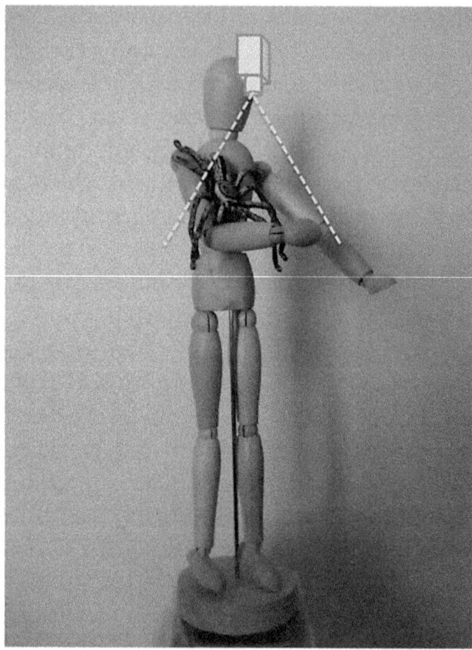

**Figure 32.** A sinister way to test the full body illusion that people inhabit the body of the little wooden doll. A camera is attached to the head of the doll, relaying its perspective to the participant's goggles; synchronous tapping on the chest makes them experience that they embody the doll's body, and the spider then seem gigantic.

proportion of us will in fact have severe disturbances that seem related to the body image and self-awareness that is modulated in the illusions, namely in various mental disorders such as schizophrenia, anorexia, body dysmorphic disorder, and so on. Secondly, as noted in Chapter 7, there are likely different learned constraints on perceptual and active inference, meaning that not all perceptual information will be carried over to movement control. Thirdly, there are in fact situations under which illusions, such as the rubber hand, do influence movement (Kammers, Kootker et al. 2010; Paton, Hohwy et al. 2011; Palmer, Paton et al. 2013; see p164).

The overall impression one gets from the research on the rubber hand illusion and the full body illusion is that the perceptual body image is highly malleable. In order to explain away sensory input we will accept very weird metamorphoses of our customary way of experiencing our body. The fragility of perception applies even to our own body perception and underscores the idea that our bodily self-awareness is itself entertained as an internal model, which is sensitive to the way we minimize prediction error of its hypotheses.

## FRAGILITY, INTERNALITY, AND SITUATEDNESS

I have been stressing the fragility of perceptual inference, and have given a characterization of the perceptual relation that weights its indirectness strongly. There is an influential and important current in contemporary thought that strongly resists such an indirectness story. This is the idea that our perceptual efforts seem best explained in terms of a close interaction between our brains and how we organize and exploit our environment, giving a crucial role to the body. Andy Clark notices the initial tension between the prediction error scheme and situatedness but rightly sees the potential for a deeper connection:

> At least on the face of it, the predictive processing story seem to pursue a rather narrowly neurocentric focus, albeit one that reveals [. . .] some truly intimate links between perception and action. But dig a little deeper and what we discover is a model of key aspects of neural functioning that makes structuring our worlds genuinely continuous with structuring our brains and sculpting our actions. (Clark 2013: 194)

Here is how Clark characterizes the connection:

> At multiple time-scales, and using a wide variety of means (including words, equations, graphs, other agents, pictures, and all the tools of modern consumer electronics) we thus stack the dice so that we can more easily minimize costly prediction errors in an endlessly empowering cascade of contexts from shopping and socializing, to astronomy, philosophy, and logic. (op.cit. 195)

There is much that is right in this: we organize our environment to facilitate prediction error minimization. But, it seems to me, it is possible to capture all this in a way that serves to emphasize the indirectness.

If we think back to the many ways prediction can be disrupted (Chapter 7), the common theme is that the perceptual "game" is riddled with uncertainty and the core task of the different facets of the prediction error mechanism is to navigate the uncertainty and make sure perception does not shatter. Much of the uncertainty is caused by noise in the organic tissue that is the brain, but at least prediction error minimization can begin when sensory data enters the brain, even if hampered by sensory noise. This is because it is only when the system gains access to the two key quantities, its own predictions and the actual input, that it can begin to deal with the problem of perception. But there is one main source of uncertainty that lies beyond this process—namely the causal link between the states of the world itself and the sensory input.

This can be illustrated in terms of the simplified scheme used to explain prediction error minimization in Chapter 2. Prediction error is minimized between the hypotheses generated on the basis of the internal model, maintained in the brain, and sensory input (how the world impinges on the senses).

This yields causal inference on the hidden environmental (or bodily) causes of the sensory input, that is, inference on the states of affairs in the world. Though the brain can optimize precisions on its internal prediction errors, it is hostage to the signal strength in the causal link from the world's states of affairs to the sensory input that impinges upon it. If the signal strength from the world to the senses is poor then the brain cannot do much about it there and then.

Because the brain is isolated behind the veil of sensory input, it is then advantageous for it to devise ways of optimizing the information channel from the world to the senses. This is a very simple point: through active inference the brain can minimize prediction error, not only by changing the sensory input in the ways we have described so far (that is selecting predicted sensory input), but also by increasing the precision of the sensory input; for example, illuminating a dark room to increase visual signal-to-noise. This can generally be done by removing sources of noise in the environment and by magnifying signal strength. To give an analogy, voltage in traditional computer chips is kept surprisingly high (about 5v) precisely in an attempt to make the chip reliable by minimizing the possibility that noise might perturb signalling (the voltage example is from Eliasmith 2000).

It seems to me that many of the ways we interact with the world in technical and cultural aspects can be characterized by attempts to make the link between the sensory input and the causes more precise (or less uncertain). This ranges from the benefits of the built environment (letting us engage in active inference unperturbed by wind and weather), to technical and electronic devices (e.g., radio lets us hear things directly rather than through many causal, unreliable testimonial links) and perhaps even to language (as I am reminded when I tell the kids to "use their words").

Conceived like this, our interaction with the environment should be described in terms of first and second order statistics, somewhat like we did for perception and attention. Second order active inference is optimizing sensory input so we can go about our activities and perceptual inference in confidence. The key point I am aiming at here is that this is a picture that accentuates the indirect, skull-bound nature of the prediction error minimization mechanism. To me then, the main truth in the notion of situated cognition is that the situated mind is drawn closer to the world through culture and technology, in the basic sense of improving the mutual information between events in the world and the sensory input. Culture and technology facilitates inference in this way. But this happens, always, with the mind solidly set over against the rest of the world. Indeed, our preoccupation with organizing our environment in this way makes sense precisely on the background of fragility. It is because the mind–world relation is fragile that we need to do everything we can to optimize signalling within the narrow set of states we can occupy without perception breaking down.

I would thus agree with Clark that situatedness makes environment and brains "genuinely continuous" but only in the sense that it makes the causal link from the senses to the world more reliable. That is, it is genuinely continuous only in the sense causal factors can be genuinely continuous. Since this causal relation is also indirect in the sense described above, the mind remains secluded from the hidden causes of the world, even though we are ingenious in using culture and technology to allow us to bring these causes into sharper focus and thus facilitate how we infer to them.

In some respects this debate reflects opinions about where to put the stress in interpretations of the prediction error minimizing brain—on the way the brain is nicely attuned to the world or on the inferential aspects of the story. But behind this debate lies a principled, deeper epistemological point, which I believe forces us to make the secluded nature of the mind's position in the world explanatorily prior.

Consider the following, everyday example, taken from Peter Lipton's discussion of inference to the best explanation (Lipton 2004). You come home one day and observe some unexpected footprints in the snow outside the window. The hypothesis that a burglar has been around best explains the occurrence of the footprint evidence, so you come to believe a burglar has been around. At the same time, the footprint becomes evidence for the burglar hypothesis. By minimizing (explaining away) the surprising evidence one maximizes the evidence for the hypothesis doing the explaining. I believe Lipton's example can then, in simplified form, capture a machine learning insight at the very heart of prediction error minimization, expressed by Friston like this "[S]urprise is called the (negative) model evidence. This means that minimizing surprise is the same as maximizing the sensory evidence for an agent's existence, if we regard the agent as a model of its world." (Friston 2010: 128–9).

That is, the hypotheses maintained in the internal generative model stand in just this explanatory-evidentiary relation to the sensory input: the hypotheses explain away the sensory input and thereby the sensory input becomes evidence for the hypotheses and the model generating them. This becomes a rather profound point, given the close relation between the existence of the model and the existence of the agent in question. It tells us that as a matter of principle, the sensory input accounts for the existence of the agent, and that causes extraneous to the sensory input must all of them enter the explanation as external entities inferred by the model. From this perspective it becomes hard to blur the line between the inner and the outer.

The explanatory-evidentiary relation looks dangerously circular, but the circle is benign unless used to counter a certain kind of doubt, namely about the occurrence of the evidence. If someone objects that the footprints might be part of an elaborate hoax perpetrated against you, then you cannot rationally respond by appealing to your belief in the burglar hypothesis. That would be viciously circular. In other words, there are certain possibilities that you can only distinguish amongst if you have additional, conditionally independent evidence (for example, about the presence of hoaxers). Without access to conditionally independent evidence, the doubt is epistemically insurmountable. Applied to the brain's situation, this means that should doubts arise about the occurrence of the totality of the sensory evidence—as it might in solipsistic or evil demon-style skeptical worries—then there is no way to respond. This tells us that the sensory boundary between the brain and the world is not arbitrary, but rather a principled, indispensable, and epistemically critical element for identifying what is inferring what in perceptual and active inference.

## SUMMARY: A DISCONCERTING AND COMFORTING PERCEPTUAL RELATION?

In this chapter, I have tried to convey the sense in which perceptual inference is fragile, even though it seems robust to most of us most of the time. This fragility leads to a causal understanding of the perceptual mind–world relation. This is both disconcerting and comforting.

It is disconcerting because it depicts us as being mere causal pawns at the mercy of the ways we make the best of our sensory predicaments. Sometimes, this can lead us badly astray, when we opt for very unlikely hypotheses in our quest to explain away input; as we saw this may even afflict our very bodily self-awareness. But it is also a comforting picture of our perceptual hypotheses only being able to get away with predictions that actually fit the incoming input well.

These dual aspects capture the sense in which the causal perceptual relation is both indirect and direct. The overall picture is that we more often than not (and setting aside sceptical scenarios with evil scientists deceiving us) represent the world close to the way it truly is. However, this comes about not because we are seeking truth for truth's sake. Rather we seek prediction error minimization, and mostly gain truth in the process. One consequence of this kind of picture is that many cases of situated and extended cognition begin to make sense as merely cases of the brain attempting to optimize its sensory input so it, as positioned over against the world, can better minimize error.

In the next, last, chapter, I broaden the perspective to deep aspects of our mental lives: emotion, introspection, sense of self, and privacy of mind. All of these aspects of mind are constrained by the fragility of perception.

## NOTES

*Page 227.* ["We thus appear to weigh actual . . . "] Here I am claiming a high number of us are afflicted by mental disorder. Here is some evidence for this claim. Lifetime prevalence of major depressive disorder, where one's affective world shatters, is 5–12 per cent for men and 10–25 per cent for women; lifetime morbid risk of schizophrenia is about 7–8/1,000, and autism incidence in the Western world is about 60–70/10 000 and seemingly rising (American Psychiatric Association, 2000; McGrath, Saha et al. 2008; Zaroff and Uhm 2012).

*Page 239.* ["I would thus agree with Clark . . . "] To make the mind wholly situated or extended, prediction error minimization in all its facets would need to occur relative to a distributed system taking input from hidden causes extraneous to it. This is not inconceivable. There could be distributed prediction error minimization mechanisms and perhaps some existing systems can be described as such. I am told that when miners use remote control robots they sometimes run themselves over when reversing the robot. Perhaps this happens because their generative model of the world is distributed so as to include the active robot. They might minimize prediction error relative to the system including themselves and the robot and forgetting to model themselves as autonomous agents. I am not sure this is a strong example of extended prediction error minimization however, due to the way the model shatters when the miner runs himself over. In general, I suspect the best explanation of the kinds of example Clark and others highlight is that they are cases where prediction error is optimized (in both first and second order statistical senses) relative to just the nervous system.

# 12

# Into the predictive mind

In this last chapter, the prediction error mechanism is extended deep into matters of the mind. I will consider what to say about emotions, introspection, privacy of mind, and the self. These are certainly aspects where the application of prediction error minimization becomes more tenuous. However, the prediction error minimization idea, especially in its generalized, free energy formulation and related to statistical physics (Friston 2010), has extreme explanatory scope. As the prominent neuroscientist Stanislas Dehaene, whose work was discussed in Chapter 9, puts it "It is the first time that we have had a theory of this strength, breadth and depth in cognitive neuroscience... Most other models, including mine, are just models of one small aspect of the brain, very limited in their scope. This one falls much closer to a grand theory" (quoted in *New Scientist* 2658: 30–33, 2008).

Given this maximal explanatory scope, it seems reasonable to anticipate, even if only briefly, what it will have to say about further, deep aspects of mentality. As it turns out, by applying the prediction error scheme, new, interesting and seemingly explanatorily fecund perspectives arise.

## EMOTIONS AND BODILY SENSATIONS

A famous theory of emotion originates in William James and Carl Lange, according to whom feeling states arise as responses to states of bodily arousal including rise in heart rate, perspiration, and so on. On this account we "feel sorry because we cry, angry because we strike, afraid because we tremble" so that it is "not that we cry, strike, or tremble, because we are sorry, angry, or fearful, as the case may be" (James 1890: Vol. 2, pp. 449–50). This broad kind of account of the emotions has been developed and discussed in influential ways in psychology (Schacter and Singer 1962; Scherer 1999), neuroscience (Damasio 1996), and philosophy (Griffiths 1997; Prinz 2004).

The idea is that the type of interoceptive input and the context in which it occurs serves as cues as to its causes, and that the process of inferring this is what determines our specific emotional experience. It is a provocative theory because not only does it reverse a commonsense causal role of emotion, as the quote from James makes clear, but also because it reduces all emotion to basic interoceptive states and explains emotional differentiation in terms of our cognitive response to them. The upshot is that, in some sense, emotion arises as a kind of perceptual inference on our own internal states (cf. Prinz 2004). It is hard not to think of this in terms of prediction error minimization (Hohwy 2011; Seth, Suzuki et al. 2012).

The key is to view interoceptive signals as internally generated and highly ambiguous prediction error, which is explained away by interoceptive expectations in a hierarchical manner that can draw on all sorts of statistical regularities in the overall prediction error landscape. That is, interoceptive states, such as levels of arousal, are highly ambiguous between a large number of hypotheses of the states of the world and the body (some of which hypotheses are good for me and others bad). This is similar to the way the state of the otoliths can be ambiguous between states of the world (namely between whether you are reclining or accelerating forward, as described in the previous chapter). Emotions then arise as interoceptive prediction error is actually explained away. Emotional differentiation occurs just as other kinds of perceptual differentiation of ambiguous cues occur, by appeal to prior belief and context. For example, your arousal goes up and the context of being shouted at by your boss disambiguates that signal between anger and happiness. Analogously, when given the information that the duck is eating the rabbit in the double duck-rabbit (Figure 16) you may disambiguate accordingly. In the case of emotions, this can then lead to *emotional illusions*. In a famous study, when participants met with an attractive confederate of the experimenter they experienced their state of high arousal as sexual attraction, when in reality the arousal was caused by a prior anxiety-inducing condition associated with running over a dangerous bridge (Dutton and Aron 1974).

In general, heightened arousal is considered prediction error because we expect to occupy states defined by many different exogenous inputs but a uniform, relatively stable level of heart rate, perspiration, etc. It seems then that prediction error minimization in the interoceptive domain is a natural conceptual home for the broadly James–Lange way of looking at emotion.

There is a sense in which contemporary developments of the James–Lange view are conceptualist (e.g., Scherer 1999). Emotions become the upshot of having a conceptual response to bodily states. This is somewhat unattractive because it also seems emotions are in some sense very basic states, which can be had by non-conceptual creatures and those with disorders of consciousness, whose conceptual apparatus is compromised (Panksepp, Normansell et al. 1994; Griffiths 2003; Panksepp 2005; Merker 2007). Luckily the sharp distinction between percepts and concepts begins to wash out in the perceptual hierarchy. Concepts are just fairly invariant, long term expectations, percepts fairly variant, perspective dependent, shorter term expectations (as discussed in Chapter 3). Both can be used in top-down attempts to explain away affective prediction error. It doesn't seem to me creatures need to have a language to be considered conceptual in this washed-out sense. This means that individuals with little orthodox conceptual apparatus can have emotions too, even on this view of the emotions. It does follow that the character of emotional experience should change depending on which top-down prediction a given creature is able to employ to explain away arousal.

This general prediction error take on emotion can be developed in different ways. A recent intriguing proposal ties it in with the burgeoning research on interoception in general, and argues that the phenomenological *sense of presence* is associated with the precision of interoceptive prediction error minimization. Roughly, the less surprised you are by your bodily state, the less removed you will feel from the world. When prediction error imprecision sneaks in, the sense of presence in the world is diminished, as might happen in feelings of strangeness and unreality in depersonalization disorder (Seth, Suzuki et al. 2012).

By appealing to the prediction error mechanism for emotional inference new opportunities for understanding emotional processing begin to open up. Recall from Chapter 3, 7, and 9 that we have created an important role for precision optimization, and in particular expected precisions and learning. The notion of precision was related directly to attention, such that attention is nothing but precision optimization in hierarchical inference (Feldman and Friston 2010). These aspects of the machinery should apply to the internal inferential process too. So we are invited to think about our expectations for the precisions of arousal-related prediction error, that is, about the role of *emotional attention*.

This adds a new layer of processing to the classic James–Lange picture of top-down conceptual emotion appraisals. We should expect that sometimes it is our expectations for arousal or interoceptive precision that determine where we end up emotionally—different contexts differentially modulate the gain of interoceptive signals and thus makes different demands on top-down explanations. In particular, within this framework, I think there would be good reason to expect emotional analogues of various attentional phenomena (some of which were discussed in Chapter 9). Perhaps we can begin to view some cases of emotional processing as inattentional emotion blindness (for a study in this vein, see Wayand, Levin et al. 2005), as emotion change blindness, or as bringing out a difference between endogenous emotion attention and emotion grabbing, and between emotional Troxler fading and emotional contrast enhancing. It would be especially interesting to look at these attention-related emotion constructs in the context of mental illness, such as mood disorders and other afflictions such as alexithymia.

## INTROSPECTION IS INFERENCE ON MENTAL CAUSES

Sometimes we go about our business and perceive the world in the process. Sometimes we direct attention inwards and engage in thought and imagery about ourselves, our memories, emotions, and plans. Sometimes, however, we direct attention at our mental states themselves. This is introspection. For example, you might direct attention at the pain you feel in your toe, wondering whether it has shifted from a sharp, piercing pain to a more dull pain, or you might delight in your experience of brilliant colours when seeing some artwork.

Here I consider how the prediction error minimization scheme could apply to introspection. This turns out to give a somewhat unorthodox take on the function played by introspection in our mental economy. This matters because the function of introspection is not well-described—it is unclear why we need to be able to introspect our own experience on top of just having it. This approach also unifies introspection well with other aspects of perception. This matters because introspection is sometimes seen as fundamentally different from perception; for example in terms of the special and private privilege that some believe goes with introspection.

If introspection is unconscious probabilistic inference then introspection must be construed such that there are some hidden causes, some hidden sensory effects, and a generative model under which prediction error can occur. To many, this would make inference a non-starter as an account of introspection since it seems unlikely that conscious experiences are themselves hidden causes impinging on an introspective sensory organ. In spite of this immediate reaction, there is a reasonable way of letting introspection into the prediction error minimization fold.

The starting point would have to be a consideration of how experiential prediction error might arise. Do our experiences ever defy our expectations about them? I think there are such cases across all domains of experience. An individual might be surprised at the sharpness of a pain experienced when stumping the toe lightly against the leg of a chair, introspect that experience itself, and arrive at the judgement, based on the introspection, that the toe is broken and needs medical attention. An individual might be surprised that a normal active inference relative to an experience does not have the usual effect (for example, scratching an itch causes a painful sensation so the individual introspects to ascertain whether it is an itch or perhaps really a pain; or, walking around something to get the sun from behind doesn't have the expected effect of making colours more discernible so the colour experience is revisited in introspection). Or, an individual might be surprised about the precision of an experience (this espresso is supposed to taste like coffee but the individual begins having trouble recognizing the coffee taste—something that might happen as a sign of pancreatic cancer—and therefore introspects the taste sensation). Introspective surprise also seems to occur in mental illness, for example in prodromal phases of psychosis where patients say things like "my eyes became markedly oversensitive to light. Ordinary colours appeared to be much too bright, and sunlight appeared dazzling in intensity" (Freedman 1974).

Perhaps these are all cases where there is prediction error in the system, but where attention to and revisiting worldly matters does not immediately help in explaining away this prediction error. In those cases, it makes sense to consider the experience itself as the cause presenting itself for probabilistic inference. In terms of the mirror analogy mooted in the last chapter, sometimes it may pay to consider the possibility that there is a fault or a change in the mirror itself, rather than in the world.

If it is accepted that there can be violations of experiential expectation, then there is experiential prediction error, and then it will make sense to operate with generative models of experience and with predictions of experience based on these models. When these elements are put together, prediction error minimization for experience itself emerges: aligning expectations with experiences to prevent their future violation. There is nothing untoward about this idea of introspective inference. It is just an inferential process that treats the deliverances of perceptual inference as causes of the input to a model. And of course the deliverances of perceptual inference itself are themselves causes in the world in any case. For example, in binocular rivalry, the current deliverance of the system may be that there is a face out there, and this experience, we may assume, partly causes the participant to push the 'face'-button rather than the 'house'-button. In introspection, experiences are also treated as causes but this time of input to the experiential model—the model that monitors experience rather than the world.

A first objection against allowing this kind of introspective inference is that it entails an unreasonable degree of double bookkeeping. It seems a waste of energy to experience things twice over, both in our perceptual inference and again in our model of perceptual inference. And it seems to tally poorly with our phenomenology: it does not appear to be the case that perception is somehow chronically shadowed by introspection.

There are three things to say in response. First, once we accept there can be violations of experiential expectations, then there must be internal representation of experience; and from there the step to introspective inference seems inevitable. Second, phenomenological awareness of the internal model of experience need only occur in case of experiential prediction error. That is, we become aware of the workings of the model only when it deviates from standard experience. This might not happen very often because mostly our prediction error can be put down to issues with perceptual inference on environmental causes themselves, and introspection is then only called upon when we suspect that the prediction error arises not in virtue of what the world is like but in virtue of some issue with perceptual inference itself. Third, there is some reason to think that introspective awareness of experiential states is a crucial element of the way minds interact with each other, and in the way a mind interacts with itself over time. This role would be accommodated by just the kind of introspective inference argued for here—I will expand on this social aspect of private introspective inference in the next section.

There is a more fundamental reason to believe that creatures like us introspect. This relates to active inference and our ability to control the environment through action. In particular, any agent who represents its own actions must in some sense introspect. Representation of action or control of the environment is a subtle point and may only be a faculty of higher organisms; representing one's own action is not necessary for simple reflexes or homoeostasis—and yet it becomes imperative for creatures like us who engage in planning and entertaining fictive outcomes (see Hohwy 2011 for further reasons for this idea). Note that in active inference, action per se is a real state of the physical world, not just a hidden state that is represented by the brain. This means that there is a fundamental distinction between representations of action in the mind and the actual motor trajectories in the physical world. As soon as we make inferences about our own behaviour our inferences become tied to our self and we become quintessentially meta-representational. I will return to this central aspect of agency and self-made acts in the last section of the chapter, which focuses on the nature of the self.

I want next to consider how this proposal of introspection as a type of prediction error minimization fares against what I call *introspective dissonance*. Introspective dissonance is my label for our torn attitude towards introspection, which fuels much of the philosophical debate. When we introspect, the introspected state seems easily accessible, for example, the pain or colour experience is as it were *right there*; and introspection seems certain and sometimes beyond doubt (if it hurts or I experience a blue colour there is no genuine doubt about this state of affairs). But equally, when we introspect, it doesn't take much for the introspection to be elusive, fleeting, and uncertain: we are stumped for words when trying to describe precisely whether the experience was like this or like that; we find it hard to sustain an experience stably in introspection for any length of time and the experience often seems to slip out of grasp when we focus on its individual aspects. When we introspect it seems we harbour both attitudes: introspection seems both accessible and certain, and inaccessible and uncertain. This is a kind of dissonance in introspection.

When one looks back at much of the classic and contemporary debate about introspection, signs of dissonance abound. The dissonance also seems to me palpable and almost irritating in my own actual attempts at introspection:

at a coarse-grained level of analysis it is easy to categorize what I experience but hard to pin down what the more fine-grained character of the introspected state actually is.

If introspective dissonance is so pervasive, then it appears to be something to explain. An account of introspection that can make room for both sides of our introspective efforts will therefore be desirable. The prediction error approach to introspection can accomplish this.

The 'voice of certainty' in introspection arises because the perceptual inference that is first and foremost the target of introspective inference is the current probabilistic winner—it is based in the hypothesis that enjoys the highest posterior probability. As such it will engage higher levels of the perceptual hierarchy and is therefore marked by some degree of invariance and perspective independence: it will be represented under longer-term temporal regularities and thus with less noise and less detail. Being high in the hierarchy also means its different sensory attributes will be well-integrated, and treated like a unified cause in the world. All this sits well with easy and certain access to introspection. No wonder introspection delivers easy and certain access to experience if the experience accessed is processed as a probabilistic winner, as relatively invariant and noise-free.

The 'voice of uncertainty' in introspection is however also catered for. A challenge to analyse in detail what one's introspection delivers is a challenge to go deeper down the perceptual hierarchy, to decompose the winning inference. But this means visiting parts of the inference marked with more variance, more noise, and more disintegration. No wonder then that introspection delivers messier and more uncertain verdicts when trying to deconstruct perceptual inference. This is even more so because this type of "backwards" perceptual inference violates the idea that evaluation of different sources of evidence should be conditionally independent to be maximally informative. For example, in introspecting my experience of the auditory component of the ventriloquist illusion my judgement is influenced by the initial, integrated audiovisual percept.

Both the voices in introspective dissonance can then be allowed within the notion of introspective predictive inference. One way of presenting a unified account is by focusing on introspection as an attentional phenomenon, in our favoured sense of attention as precision optimization. There is initial certainty because we are pretty certain what we experience, and we then attend to the experience in order to optimize the parameters for the experience to get a more fine-grained, perspective-dependent take on what the experience is like. But this process induces mounting uncertainty because decomposition of the experience is challenging. Introspective attention is doomed to failure because the very existence of high-level representations that are not bound to concurrent sensory evidence depends upon a suppression of precision at sensory levels (as for example in dreaming). In other words, introspective attention quickly meets a lower bound on precise sensory details that would otherwise subvert the introspective nature of inference.

Overall, the picture of introspection that comes with the prediction error minimization scheme appears unattractive initially. But once we accept that there can be violations of experiential expectation, the picture seems inescapable and there are then ways to make it more attractive. Moreover, this picture has some promise as an account of what I called introspective dissonance.

## THE PRIVATE MIND IN INTERACTION

When we introspect there is a further phenomenological aspect: conscious experience seems inherently private to the experiencing individual. This is a defining characteristic of consciousness, which remains unexplained. I want to explore this from the epistemic perspective of the mind as a courtroom, which I proposed in Chapter 7. Specifically, I will suggest that the privacy plays an epistemic role when minds interact with each other. The conclusion is that consciousness is private so that it can be social.

In Western intellectual history there is wide agreement that conscious experience is private, subjective, first person perspectival, shielded from the view of others. There are philosophers, beginning mainly with Wittgenstein (1953), and other researchers who for various reasons disagree with this. I think they are wrong and thus side with the historical majority view. Here, for example, is Descartes "[T]here is no occasion on which we know anything whatever when we are not at the same time led with much greater certainty to the knowledge of our own mind" (Descartes 1644 [1983], I.XI). Locke concurs:

> Man, though he have great variety of thoughts, and such from which others as well as himself might receive profit and delight; yet they are all within his own breast, invisible and hidden from others (Locke 1690, III, ii, 1). [O]ne man's mind could not pass into another man's body, to perceive what appearances were produced by those organs. (op.cit., II, xxxii, 15)

Kant pre-empts behaviourism by pointing out that privacy threatens to undermine any proper science of mind:

> Another thinking subject [does not] submit to our investigations in such a way as to be conformable to our purposes . . . [The study of the mind] can therefore never become anything more than a historical natural doctrine of the internal sense, *i.e.*, a natural description of the soul, but not a science of the soul, nor even a psychological experimental doctrine. (Kant 1983 [1977]; Ak. IV; preface)

J. S. Mill points to the inherent skeptical challenge posed by the privacy of mind

> By what evidence do I know [ . . . ] that there exist other sentient creatures; that the walking and speaking figures which I see and hear, have sensations and thoughts, or in other words, possess Minds? (Mill 1865: Ch XII).

As we saw in Chapter 7, he suggests a solution, the argument from analogy, where one infers the conscious life of others from their behaviour by analogy with the private knowledge of one's own experience when one has the same behaviour: "I conclude it from certain things, which my experience of my own states of feeling proves to me to be marks of it" (ibid.).

It is difficult to define precisely wherein this privacy of consciousness consists, save to say that other people have a more indirect and restricted access to your own conscious states than you do yourself when you introspect.

But privacy itself is a puzzle. If conscious experience is so private—so hidden from anyone but the experiencing subject itself—then it is difficult to see what it could be *for*. This sentiment is expressed eloquently by Nietzsche:

> The problem of consciousness [ . . . ] first confronts us when we begin to realize how much we can do without it; and now we are brought to this initial realization by physiology and natural science. For we could think, feel, will, remember and also 'act' in every sense of the terms and yet none of all this would have to 'enter our consciousness' (as one says figuratively). All of life would be possible without, as it were, seeing itself in the mirror; and still today, the predominant part of our lives actually unfolds without this mirroring—of course also our thinking, feeling and willing lives, insulting as it may sound to an older philosopher. *To what end* does consciousness exist at all when it is basically superfluous? (Nietzsche 1882/1887: 354)

This is the puzzle of privacy: what function does it play? The answer I will offer is that consciousness is private so that it can be social. I will appeal to a basic element of probability theory to substantiate this claim. First, however, I will set the scene by pointing to the less often told story of the social function of consciousness.

The idea that conscious experience plays a social function is not new. In the quotes above, both Descartes and Locke lament the privacy of consciousness in the context of discussing our ability to communicate our ideas. Writing in the same century, Hobbes acknowledged the privacy but went further by foregrounding the social aspect of the notion of consciousness:

> When two, or more men, know of one and the same fact, they are said to be *conscious* of it one to another; which is as much as to know it together.
>
> And because such are fittest witnesses of the facts of one another [ . . . ] it was, and ever will be reputed a very evil act, for any man to speak against his conscience. Afterwards, men made use of the same word metaphorically, for the knowledge of their own secret facts, and secret thoughts. (Hobbes 1651 [1994]: I, Ch VII, p36)

Nietzsche, much later, offered a social function as the solution to the problem he set out in the quote above:

> If one is willing to hear my answer and its possibly extravagant conjecture, it seems to me that the subtlety and strength of consciousness is always related to a person's (or animal's) *ability to communicate. [C]onsciousness in general has developed only under the pressure of the need to communicate*; that at the outset, consciousness was necessary, was useful, only between persons. Consciousness is really only a net connecting one person with another—only in this capacity did it have to develop; the solitary and predatory person would not have needed it. (op.cit.)

I want to bring the Nietzschean sentiment into contact with the contemporary idea that "consciousness is for other people" as argued by Chris Frith, who is specifically interested in the *function* of consciousness. He explains:

> Shareable knowledge ([that is,] the contents of consciousness) is the necessary basis for the development of language and communication. [ . . . ] [T]he major mistake of most theories of consciousness is to try to develop an explanation in terms of an isolated organism. (Frith 1995: 682-3)

And with Uta Frith this view is developed to closely cohere with social cognition: "Meta-cognition plays a crucial role in human social interactions and provides a basis for human consciousness" (Frith and Frith 2012).

I will assume here that this kind of view is correct: the function of consciousness is in some sense social. However, this makes the privacy of consciousness even more puzzling. If the function of consciousness is essentially social, then why is it inherently private? My proposal, as advertised already above, is that consciousness is private so that it can be social.

Within the brain, representation happens via perceptual inference using the multiple sources of evidence provided by the senses. Inference can be given a social dimension, such that between individuals, inference happens by using the multiple sources of evidence provided by each individual in communication. This element of relying on multiple sources of evidence in different contexts allows us to invoke very basic Bayesian considerations.

As we saw in Chapters 6–7, there is now very substantial evidence that within the brain the evidence delivered by different senses is integrated in an optimal Bayesian manner which depends on precision optimization. Very recently, this kind of picture has been extended to interacting minds. When two people have to discuss and agree on the location of a faint visual stimulus they have both seen, they communicate their confidences in their estimates and on that basis they integrate their perceptual estimates in a confidence-weighted, optimal fashion (Bahrami, Olsen et al. 2010).

In both cases the integrated estimate is more reliable than either individual estimate. That is, under a model where the sensory estimates arise from one common cause in the world, it is best to rely on multiple sources of reasonably reliable sensory evidence from within the brain, and on multiple sources of evidence from different brains.

The key question is then what is required for such optimal Bayesian integration between neural processing streams, or between interacting minds? To answer this question we can consider the Bayesian courtroom analogy again.

A fundamental requirement for a Bayes optimal courtroom is that the witness reports are probabilistically *independent* conditional on the case in question. If witness *A* says that the robber was Mr Naughty but only says so because he has heard witness *B* say so, then we should not treat his testimony as strengthening the case against Mr Naughty. That is, conditional on the issue of Mr Naughty being the robber, the probability of obtaining witness *A*'s report should not be affected by obtaining any other report (Report *B*) or on any other state of affairs (*B*), conditional on the facts (*A*) in question (e.g., Bovens and Olsson 2000: 690).

I argued in Chapter 7 that this conditional independence requirement also holds for what happens within the brain, and that this motivates the informational encapsulation associated with Fodorian modularity (Fodor 1983). The key point is that this independence requirement then also applies to what happens between interacting minds. The processes leading to each individual's estimate should be conditionally independent of each other. If not then their Bayes optimal integration will be compromised.

Conditional independence within the brain is made possible by the brain's organic structure preventing information flow across processing streams in lower parts of the cortical hierarchy—in neuroscience, this is known as functional segregation. This is not too dissimilar from the courtroom where witnesses might be kept in separate rooms, and be prevented from phoning each other.

But whereas this kind of segregation can be had within a genetically controlled bodily organ like the brain, and within the orderly world of the legal system, it is much harder to establish for the fluid interactions between individuals on a day to day basis. Our lines of communication are very flexible and unruly (think for example of rapidly shifting conversational flows at a lively cocktail party, or the intrusive and impulsive nature of email, mobile phones, and social media).

Nature needs to remedy this situation with some other tool, in order to make conditional independence between interacting minds possible. The privacy of consciousness could be this tool. Nature evolved the private, subjective character of experience to enable each of us to report how the world seems to us independently of the reports of others.

When we introspect our current conscious experience we get access to the brain's best estimate about the world in such a way that we get a sense of the confidence in that inference about the world. What is introspected is not seen by others, and, being first-person perspectival, it is not influenced by others' reports about the events in question. That is, consciousness is private, and thereby it can play its social role in optimal inference between interacting minds. Conversely, if we wore our conscious experiences on our sleeves—if they were public and not private—then they could unduly influence other individuals' reports and we would not then benefit from integrating our reports with theirs.

We could imagine the counterfactual situation, where perceptual estimates are not accessible to report, that is, where it is "dark inside". In that scenario, there would have to be a different method for facilitating conditional independence. Perhaps in such a scenario our means of communicating with each other would be as regimented as the sensory processing streams are in the brain. If not, creatures in this counterfactual scenario would not gain Bayesian benefit from interacting.

What we report to each other in communication is not the conscious experience itself, which is private. Instead we rely on introspection to report on the parameter of interest ("the Gabor patch occurred in the top left corner"; "I saw Mr Naughty enter the bank with a gun"), and we report on the confidence in our estimate ("I'm sure . . . ", "I think . . . ", etc.). That is, we communicate the posterior precision of our estimate.

Of course, part of our communicative efforts also goes towards establishing common ground, that is ensuring we have the same model about the world in mind ("where were you on the night of the alleged robbery?"). This corresponds to the courtroom's "establishing the facts of the case". It also corresponds to selection of common cause models for multisensory integration (Körding, Beierholm et al. 2007). This helps exclude cases where we have seen different things and thus should not begin to integrate our estimates.

The probabilistic independence afforded by the privacy of consciousness is not total and timeless. Over time, there may be influences from other people and events even on the unconscious perceptual inferences that generate the contents of conscious perception. In this sense what I see now may be conditionally dependent on what others have seen previously (for classification of some degrees of influence, see Clark and Yuille 1990: 72–83).

The key point is that there is a good chance that my report of my current conscious experience is independent of what others experience now, with respect specifically to the particular event in question. This is what is needed to reap the Bayesian benefits of interacting minds: that my estimate is independent of others' estimates, conditional only on the state of affairs currently in question (for example, if a junior and a senior radiologist optimally integrate their estimates of an x-ray image before them, their estimates are not independent conditional on past x-ray images they have seen together, but are independent conditional on the current image).

If consciousness is private so that it can play this social role, then we should expect introspective reports to work best for estimating experienced parameters and our confidences, and to be less reliable for reporting the flavour of the actual experience itself. Perhaps this partly explains the introspective dissonance discussed in the previous section. In the same vein, it is striking that many synaesthetes appear to live much of their lives without being aware their conscious experience is so different from the majority of people: they can communicate perfectly well but since they only need to inform others of experienced parameters and their confidence level, the unique flavour of their synaesthetic experiences can remain hidden for years.

I began this section with the question what consciousness is for, if it is so private? Privacy is especially puzzling given the idea that the function of consciousness is in some sense social. The puzzle is resolved when we acknowledge that the social function of consciousness is to integrate perceptual estimates of the world in an optimal Bayesian fashion. The key point is that the privacy of consciousness can facilitate the conditional independence of the estimates required by this kind of integration. The motto is then that consciousness is private so that it can play its social role.

## THE SELF AS A SENSORY TRAJECTORY

We are creatures with a first-person perspective on the world, we respond emotionally to what happens, and we are able to introspect and report on our own but not other's mental states. We can remember the past, experience the present, and project our mental lives in to the future. We decide what to do and sometimes learn from our mistakes. All these core aspects of us suggest we are selves—entities with a first-person perspective, who respond, introspect, and experience, and who are the subjects of remembered events and are projected into the future and who make the decisions. But the nature of this self is deeply puzzling and has been the subject of intense philosophical and psychological speculating at least since Hume famously failed to spot the self in introspection:

> For my part, when I enter most intimately into what I call myself, I always stumble on some particular perception or other, of heat or cold, light or shade, love or hatred, pain or pleasure. I never can catch myself at any time without a perception, and never can observe any thing but the perception. (Hume 1739–40: Pt 4; Sect 6)

This is puzzling because on the one hand we all have a thick sense of having, or being, selves and yet we cannot easily pin it down in inner perception. Some have suggested this is a function of what kind of entity—or rather non-entity—the self is:

> [W]e are all virtuoso novelists, who find ourselves engaged in all sorts of behaviour, more or less unified, but sometimes disunified, and we always put the best "faces" on it we can. We try to make all of our material cohere into a single good story. And that story is our autobiography. The chief fictional character at the centre of that autobiography is one's self. (Dennett 1992)

This is an intriguing but metaphorical suggestion. A much more worked out proposal comes from Thomas Metzinger, who suggests that the self is a mere representation: it is the part of the internal model that represents itself. The reason Hume cannot capture himself in perception is that the self-model is transparent, we "look" through it to the world itself. Though Metzinger does not subscribe to Dennett's metaphor, an internal model of the subject's trajectory through the world is a good way to flesh out the idea of a narrative and the result is again that there is no entity that is the self: there is no self, there is a phenomenal self-model the content of which is the Ego (Metzinger 2004; Metzinger 2009).

I think this is a reasonable way to go with the notion of the self. This is because many aspects of it fit with the prediction error minimization view. Specifically, as we saw in Chapter 4, for active inference to be possible we need models of ourselves as causal trajectories in the world, which elicit non-linear effects on our own sensory input. Action arises when prediction error minimization happens by acting on the world while sticking with one's counterfactual about the world. For this kind of strategy to be feasible we need an ordering of policies for how to go about minimizing error in this way. Such policies are expectations about how flows of error are minimized as we move through the world. These expectations must rely on hypotheses under a hierarchical model of ourselves including our own mental states as coherent and unitary causal trajectories. This harks back to the treatment in Chapter 10 of perceptual unity and now we can see how this unity in a wider time-perspective can connect to the self. Moreover, this causal self is inextricably linked to agency, which makes sense of the idea that the self is deeply involved in decision-making. Who we end up being—what trajectory we end up describing—is then in part shaped by the way we manage the balance between perceptual and active inference: we get different trajectories if we tend to act on a loose bound on surprise than if we tend to act on a tighter bound on surprise (cf. Chapter 7). In short, I am a model of the world that I inhabit that, by definition, cannot be a model of your world.

So the existence of a self-model makes sense from the perspective of the prediction error story. It is a fairly deflationary idea because it reduces the self to a hierarchically described hidden cause of one's sensory input. Though it is not immediately obvious, this also satisfies the Humean predicament that we cannot capture the self in introspection (as well as perhaps Metzinger's notion of transparence). The reason we need a causal self-model is that we need to predict how acting on the world forces new sensory input on us. This means that the main processing task for the self-model is to predict changes in experiences (how a scene will change as we move around it, or how an emotion will change when we enter a new peer group, for example). It is then no wonder that this is exactly what Hume sees when he enters most intimately into himself: just more experiences—because that is what the self is primarily concerned with. The key point is that these experiences should be seen as the upshot of Hume's own causal commerce with the world and thus part of the self-model he must maintain to be an agent (some of these themes are developed further in Hohwy 2007b).

There is one further bit we can add to this account of the self. Part of the job we normally give to the self is that of being an *agent*—the entity that makes things happen via the body's movement. Not even this can Hume capture when he looks inward. From the prediction error minimization perspective, this is no wonder. As we saw in Chapter 4 (p83), agency is triggered not by some neuronal first-mover but instead by optimizing expected precisions of proprioceptive input. What makes a creature an agent rather than a passive, barnacle-like perceiver is nothing more than learning a regularity in nature: that in the long run expecting actual proprioceptive input to be imprecise leads to average prediction error minimization in the long run.

Though this proposal can no doubt be developed more it seems able to begin to explain puzzling aspects of the self. The self may fit nicely with the overall prediction error minimization mechanism.

## SUMMARY: THE PROBABILISTIC AND CAUSAL MIND

The challenge in this chapter was to really extend the explanatory engine in the idea that the mind is fundamentally nothing but a prediction error minimization mechanism. If this is true it ought to deliver at least reasonable and somewhat interesting accounts of mental phenomena beyond perception and action. Brief discussions of emotion, introspection, privacy, agency, and self suggest that there is such explanatory promise.

The emerging picture is that even these deep aspects of the mind derive from our causal commerce with the world and from the brain's attempt to stem prediction error. Emotion is just predictive inference on interoceptive states, introspection is linked to what happens when experience expectations are violated, the privacy of mind is needed to secure social Bayesian inference, and the self is an agent-bound sensory trajectory.

## NOTES

*Page 243.* ["There is a sense in which contemporary..."] Here I make the point that emotional engagement alters emotional experience. For empirical evidence in favour of this see, for example, (Hariri, Bookheimer et al. 2000) who say that "higher [cortical] regions attenuate emotional responses at the most fundamental levels in the brain and suggest a neural basis for modulating emotional experience through interpretation and labelling".

*Page 244.* ["This general prediction error take..."] Another way to expand on the role of prediction error in emotion is to use it in explorations of emotion *introspection*. This begins with acknowledging the variability and evasiveness of introspection of our emotions (Schwitzgebel 2008). The project is to explain this introspective variability via the dynamic nature of perceptual inference. Introspection of emotions is itself a moment in active inference where the mental state is explored under some hypothesis about what it is. In that active process the input must change, and therefore the prediction error landscape changes in introspection. This means that sustained attention to an emotion in introspection should be expected to reveal an evolving, variable emotional state (Hohwy 2011).

*Page 245.* ["Sometimes we go about our business..."] Introspection has been a focus of philosophers for a long time. It has been dealt with in terms of judgement about mental states, or inner perception of mental states (an "inner eye" directed at experience). Other approaches have been more deflationary, dealing with introspection as really just increased attention to what the mental states represent in the world (introspection of my experience of a tree is just attending more closely to the tree itself). There is also debate about whether introspection of conscious perceptual states is reliable or unreliable, with some arguing it is deeply unreliable and others that it is reliable (for en overview, see Schwitzgebel 2010).

*Page 247.* ["I want next to consider..."] The best way to appreciate introspective dissonance is in the work of Eric Schwitzgebel, who brings it out very forcefully and uses it to argue against the reliability of introspection (Schwitzgebel 2011). I think it is possible to accept the presence of dissonance without going along with Schwitzgebel's introspective skepticism (Hohwy 2011).

*Page 250.* ["Nietzsche, much later, offered..."] Nietzsche concluded his proposal on the social use of consciousness with characteristic aplomb: "everything which enters consciousness thereby becomes shallow, thin, relatively stupid, general, a sign, a herd-mark" (1882/1887: 354). Though this provocative conclusion hasn't found widespread support, the general idea of a social function of consciousness is beginning to find its way into contemporary approaches to consciousness. Humphrey (2007), for example, appeals directly to Nietzsche and points to deception as a socially motivated function of privacy. Gopnik (1993), on the other hand, analyses privacy as an illusion of expertise and thereby obviates the distinction between private and public access to mental states. There is much of interest in these views but they do not seem to capture a truly social function for consciousness.

*Page 252.* ["I argued in Chapter 7 that this..."] It is interesting to note that Fodor supports modularity in epistemic terms too. For example, informational encapsulation helps ensure the objectivity of scientific inquiry through a reasonably robust theory–observation distinction (Fodor 1983; Fodor 1984).

# Concluding remarks: The mind in prediction

The mind exists in prediction. Our perceptual experience of the world arises in our attempts at predicting our own current sensory input. This notion spreads to attention and agency. Perception, attention, and agency are three different ways of doing the same thing: accounting for sensory input as well as we can from inside the confines of the skull. We are good at this, mostly, but it is a precarious and fragile process because we are hostages to our prior beliefs, our noisy brains, the uncertain sensory deliverances from the world, and to the brain's urge to rid itself efficiently of prediction error.

The mind is shaped by how we manage these predictive efforts. We continually need to adjust, regulate, and revisit the balances and checks on prediction. The way we do this determines how we bind sensory attributes and how much our preconceptions can penetrate experience; more chronic, systematic failures to manage prediction can tip us into mental illness.

The predictive mind has extreme explanatory reach. Conscious unity, emotion, self, and introspection can all seemingly be brought under the prediction error minimization mechanism that maintains and shapes the mind. With this mechanism we can see ourselves as mere cogs in nature's causal machinery and also as mental islands set over against the world, which is hidden behind the veil of sensory input.

This is the picture of the mind brought out in this book. First I relied on an emerging research literature to help myself to the key elements of the mechanism—perceptual inference, expected precisions, active inference, and complexity reduction—and how these are harnessed in the message passing in the brain's cortical hierarchy. Then I used just those elements to explain and unify a suite of characteristics of mind and conscious experience, both narrowly focused on perceptual experience of the world and more broadly focused on deep, puzzling aspects of mind.

In the course of applying the prediction error minimization mechanism many new and interesting approaches to the mind have appeared. This is striking because all that is needed is an appeal to the core mechanism for prediction error minimization. This strategy supports the framework in virtue of being a move in an inference to the best explanation. We marshal a suite of core phenomena to explain, and find that there is a good explanation of them all. Specifically, the prediction error minimization account explains them. What makes the prediction error explanation best is that it has some of the traditional best-makers: it unifies, it is theoretically and experimentally fecund, it explains mechanistically and across levels, in detail and in more broad terms—and it is beautiful.

# *Acknowledgements*

Figure 3 is adapted from *Vision Research*, 47(21), Ngo, T.T., G. B. Liu, et al., "Caloric vestibular stimulation reveals discrete neural mechanisms for coherence rivalry and eye rivalry: A meta-rivalry model," 2685–2699. Copyright (2007), with permission from Elsevier.

Figure 4 is adapted from *Cognition*, 108(3), Hohwy, J., A. Roepstorff, et al., "Predictive coding explains binocular rivalry: An epistemological review," 687–701. Copyright (2008), with permission from Elsevier.

Figure 6 is adapted from Springer, *Pattern Recognition and Machine* Learning, 2006, Christopher Bishop, Figure 1.4, page 7, with kind permission from Springer Science and Business Media B.V.

Figure 11 is adapted from *Trends in Cognitive Sciences*, 12(10), Ross, J. and D. Burr, "The knowing visual self," 363–364. Copyright (2008), with permission from Elsevier.

Figure 12 is adapted with kind permission from Manuel Cazzaniga (flickr.com/ezioman).

Figure 16 is reprinted from Jensen, M. S. and K. E. Mathewson (2011) "Simultaneous perception of both interpretations of ambiguous figures," *Perception* 40(8): 1009–1011 with permission from Pion Ltd, London, <www.pion.co.uk> and <www.envplan.com>.

Figure 18 is from Whitson, J. A. and A. D. Galinsky (2008) "Lacking control increases illusory pattern perception," *Science* 322(5898): 115–117. Reprinted with permission from AAAS.

Figure 19 is adapted by permission from Macmillan Publishers Ltd: Nature Neuroscience 7(3), Carrasco, M., S. Ling, et al., "Attention alters appearance," 308–313, Copyright (2004).

Figures 22 and 23 are reprinted from Frith, C. D. and R. J. Dolan (1997). "Brain mechanisms associated with top-down processes in perception." *Philosophical Transactions of the Royal Society London B* 352: 1221–1230, by permission of the Royal Society.

Figure 24 is reprinted from Hohwy, J. and B. Paton (2010) under the Creative Commons Attribution Licence.

Figure 28 is adapted from Jiang, Y., P. Costello, et al. "A gender- and sexual orientation-dependent spatial attentional effect of invisible images," *Proceedings of the National Academy of Sciences* 103(45): 17048–17052. Copyright (2006) National Academy of Sciences, U.S.A.

Figure 29 is adapted from Schwabe, L. and O. Blanke (2008) under the Creative Commons Attribution Licence.

# *References*


Adams, R. A., L. U. Perrinet and K. Friston (2012). "Smooth pursuit and visual occlusion: active inference and oculomotor control in schizophrenia." *PloS One 7* (10): e47502.

Adams, W. J., E. W. Graf and M. O. Ernst (2004). "Experience can change the 'light-from-above' prior." *Nature Neuroscience 7*(10): 1057–8.

Aglioti, S., J. F. X. DeSouza and M. A. Goodale (1995). "Size-contrast illusions deceive the eye but not the hand." *Current Biology 5*(6): 679–85.

Aimola Davies, A. M., R. C. White and M. Davies (2013). "Spatial Limits on the non-visual self-touch illusion and the visual rubber hand illusion: subjective experience of the illusion and proprioceptive drift." *Consciousness and Cognition* 22: 613–36.

al-Haytham, I. A. (ca. 1030; 1989). *The Optics of Ibn al-Haytham*. Translated by A. I. Sabra. London: Warburg Institute.

Alais, D. and D. Burr (2004). "The ventriloquist effect results from near-optimal bimodal integration." *Current Biology. 14*: 257.

Alink, A., C. M. Schwiedrzik, A. Kohler, W. Singer and L. Muckli (2010). "Stimulus predictability reduces responses in primary visual cortex." *J. Neurosci. 30*(8): 2960–6.

American Psychiatric Association (2000). *Diagnostic and Statistical Manual of Mental Disorders* (4th edn., Text Revision). Arlington, VA: American Psychiatric Association.

Armel, K. C. and V. S. Ramachandran (2003). "Projecting sensations to external objects: evidence from skin conductance response." *Proceedings of the Royal Society of London. Series B: Biological Sciences 270*(1523): 1499–506.

Armstrong, D. (1973). *Belief, Truth and Knowledge*. Cambridge: Cambridge University Press.

Arnold, D. H. (2011). "Why is binocular rivalry uncommon? Discrepant monocular images in the real world." *Frontiers in Human Neuroscience 5*: 116.

Ashby, W. R. (1947). "Principles of the self-organizing dynamic system." *The Journal of General Psychology 37*(2): 125–8.

Baars, B. J. (1989). *A Cognitive Theory of Consciousness*. Cambridge: Cambridge University Press.

Badcock, P. B. (2012). "Evolutionary systems theory: a unifying meta-theory of psychological science." *Review of General Psychology 16*(1): 10–23.

Bahrami, B., K. Olsen, P. E. Latham, A. Roepstorff, G. Rees and C. D. Frith (2010). "Optimally interacting minds." *Science 329*(5995): 1081–5.

Bar, M. (2011). *Predictions in the Brain: Using Our Past to Generate a Future*. Oxford: Oxford University Press.

Barlow, H. (1961). "Possible principles underlying the transformation of sensory messages." In *Sensory Communication*, ed. W. A. Rosenblith. Cambridge, MA: MIT Press: 217–34.

Barlow, H. (1990). "Conditions for versatile learning, Helmholtz's unconscious inference, and the task of perception." *Vision Research. 30*: 1561–71.

Barlow, H. B. (1958). "Sensory mechanisms, the reduction of redundancy, and intelligence." *National Physical Laboratory 4*(1): 1–25.

Bayne, T. (2010). *The Unity of Consciousness*. Oxford: Oxford University Press.

Bell, V., V. Reddy, P. Halligan, G. Kirov and H. Ellis (2007). "Relative suppression of magical thinking: a transcranial magnetic stimulation study." *Cortex 43*(4): 551–7.

Bishop, C. M. (2007). *Pattern Recognition and Machine Learning*. Dordrecht: Springer.

Blake, R. and H. Wilson (2011). "Binocular vision." *Vision Research 51*(7): 754–70.

Blanke, O., T. Landis, L. Spinelli and M. Seeck (2004). "Out-of-body experience and autoscopy of neurological origin." *Brain 127*(2): 243–58.

Block, N. (1995). "The mind as the software of the brain." In *An Invitation to Cognitive Science*, D. Osherson, L. Gleitman, S. Kosslyn, E. Smith, and S. Sternberg (eds.). Cambridge, Mass.: MIT Press.

Block, N. (2005). "Review of Alva Noë, *Action in Perception.*" *The Journal of Philosophy CII*(5): 259–72.

Block, N. (2010). "Attention and mental paint." *Philosophical Issues 20*(1): 23–63.

Bortolotti, L. (2009). *Delusions and Other Irrational Beliefs*. Oxford: Oxford University Press.

Botvinick, M. and J. Cohen (1998). "Rubber hands 'feel' touch that eyes see." *Nature 391*(6669): 756–756.

Bovens, L. and S. Hartmann (2003). *Bayesian Epistemology*. Oxford: Oxford University Press.

Bovens, L. and E. Olsson (2000). "Coherentism, reliability and Bayesian networks." *Mind 109*(436): 685–719.

Braddon-Mitchell, D. and F. Jackson (2006). *The Philosophy of Mind and Cognition: An Introduction*. Oxford: Wiley-Blackwell.

Brascamp, J. W. and R. Blake (2012). "Inattention abolishes binocular rivalry: perceptual evidence." *Psychological Science 23*: 1159–67.

Brock, J. (2012). "Alternative Bayesian accounts of autistic perception: comment on Pellicano and Burr." *Trends in Cognitive Sciences 16*(12): 573–4.

Brown, H., R. Adams, I. Parees, M. Edwards, K. Friston. (2013). "Active inference, sensory attenuation, and illusions." *Cognitive Processing* 14(4): 411–427.

Brown, H. and K. J. Friston (2012). "Free-Energy and illusions: the Cornsweet effect." *Frontiers in Psychology 3*: 43.

Brugger, P., M. Regard, T. Landis, N. Cook, D. Krebs and J. Niederberger (1993). "'Meaningful' patterns in visual noise: Effects of lateral stimulation and the observer's belief in ESP." *Psychopathology 26*(5–6): 261–5.

Bruner, J. S., J. J. Goodnow and A. George (1956). *A Study of Thinking*. New York: John Wiley & Sons.

Bruno, N. and V. H. Franz (2009). "When is grasping affected by the Müller-Lyer illusion?: A quantitative review." *Neuropsychologia 47*(6): 1421–33.

Bubic, A., D. Y. Von Cramon and R. I. Schubotz (2010). "Prediction, cognition and the brain." *Frontiers in Human Neuroscience 4*: 25. doi: 10.3389/fnhum.2010.00025

Carrasco, M., S. Ling and S. Read (2004). "Attention alters appearance." *Nature Neuroscience 7*(3): 308–13.

Cascio, C. J., J. H. Foss-Feig, C. P. Burnette, J. L. Heacock and A. A. Cosby (2012). "The rubber hand illusion in children with autism spectrum disorders: delayed influence of combined tactile and visual input on proprioception." *Autism 16*(4): 406–19.

Chabris, C. F., A. Weinberger, M. Fontainc and D. J. Simons (2011). "You do not talk about Fight Club if you do not notice Fight Club: Inattentional blindness for a simulated real-world assault." *iPerception 2*(2): 150–3.

Chadha, M. (2009). "An independent, empirical route to nonconceptual content." *Consciousness and Cognition 18*(2): 439–48.

Chalmers, D. (1996). *The Conscious Mind.* Harvard: Oxford University Press.

Chater, N., J. B. Tenenbaum and A. Yuille (2006). "Probabilistic models of cognition: Conceptual foundations." *Trends in Cognitive Sciences 10*(7): 287.

Churchland, P. M. (1979). *Scientific Realism and The Plasticity of Mind.* Cambridge: Cambridge University Press.

Churchland, P. M. (1988). "Perceptual plasticity and theoretical neutrality: a reply to Jerry Fodor." *Philosophy of Science 55*(2): 167–87.

Churchland, P. M. (1998). "Conceptual similarity across sensory and neural diversity: the Fodor/Lepore challenge answered." *The Journal of Philosophy 95*(1): 5–32.

Chwe, M. S.-Y. (2000). "Communication and coordination in social networks." *The Review of Economic Studies 67*(1): 1–16.

Chwe, M. S. Y. (1999). "Structure and strategy in collective action." *The American Journal of Sociology 105*(1): 128–56.

Clark, A. (2012). "Dreaming the whole cat: generative models, predictive processing, and the enactivist conception of perceptual experience." *Mind 121*: 753–71.

Clark, A. (2013). "Whatever next? Predictive brains, situated agents, and the future of cognitive science." *Behavioral & Brain Sciences 36*(3): 181–204.

Clark, J. J. and A. L. Yuille (1990). *Data Fusion for Sensory Information Processing Systems.* Dordrecht: Kluwer Academic Publishers.

Cohen, M. A., G. A. Alvarez, et al. (2011). "Natural-scene perception requires attention." *Psychological Science 22*(9): 1165–72.

Colombo, M. and P. Seriés (2012). "Bayes in the brain—On Bayesian modelling in neuroscience." *The British Journal for the Philosophy of Science 63*: 697–723.

Coltheart, M., R. Langdon and R. Mckay (2011). "Delusional belief." *Annual Review of Psychology 62*(1): 271–98.

Coltheart, M., P. Menzies and J. Sutton (2009). "Abductive inference and delusional belief." *Cognitive Neuropsychiatry 15*(1–3): 261–87.

Conant, R. C. and W. R. Ashby (1970). "Every good regulator of a system must be a model of that system." *International Journal of Systems Science 1*(2): 89–97.

Corlett, P. R., J. R. Taylor, X. J. Wang, P. C. Fletcher and J. H. Krystal (2010). "Toward a neurobiology of delusions." *American College of Neuropsychopharmacology 92*: 345–69.

Cover, T. M. and J. A. Thomas (2006). *Elements of Information Theory.* New Jersey: John Wiley & Sons.

Cox, R. T. (1946). "Probability, frequency and reasonable expectaion." *American Journal of Physics 14*: 1–13.

Craver, C. (2007). *Explaining the Brain: Mechanisms and the Mosaic Unity of Neuroscience.* Harvard: Oxford University Press.

Cummins, R. (1991). *Meaning and Mental Representation.* Cambridge, Mass.: MIT Press.

Damasio, A. R. (1994). *Descartes' Error: Emotion, Reason and the Human Brain.* New York: Putnam.

Davies, M. (2000). "Interaction without reduction: The relationship between personal and subpersonal levels of description." *Mind and Society 1*: 87–105.

Davies, M. and M. Coltheart (2000). "Introduction: pathologies of belief." *Mind and Language 15*(1): 1–46.

Dawkins, R. (2009). *The Greatest Show on Earth: The Evidence for Evolution*. New York: Free Press.

Dayan, P. and L. F. Abbott (2001). *Theoretical Neuroscience*. Cambridge, Mass.: MIT Press.

Dayan, P., G. E. Hinton, R. M. Neal and R. S. Zemel (1995). "The Helmholtz machine." *Neural Computation 7*: 889–904.

de Gardelle, V. and C. Summerfield (2011). "Robust averaging during perceptual judgment." *Proceedings of the National Academy of Sciences 108*(32): 13341–6.

de Witt, L. H., J. Kubilius, J. Wagemans and H. P. Op de Beeck (2012). "Bistable Gestalts reduce activity in the whole of V1, not just the retinotopically predicted parts." *Journal of Vision 12*(11). doi: 10.1167/12.11.12

Dehaene, S. (2008). "Conscious and nonconscious processes: distinct forms of evidence accumulation?", Séminaire Poincaré XII: 89–114.

Dehaene, S. and J.-P. Changeux (2011). "Experimental and theoretical approaches to conscious processing." *Neuron 70*(2): 200–27.

DeLoache, J. S., D. H. Uttal and K. S. Rosengren (2004). "Scale errors offer evidence for a perception-action dissociation early in life." *Science 304*(5673): 1027–9.

den Ouden, H. E., J. Daunizeau, J. Roiser, K. J. Friston and K. E. Stephan (2010). "Striatal prediction error modulates cortical coupling." *Journal of Science 30*: 3210–19.

den Ouden, H. E., K. J. Friston, N. D. Daw, A. R. McIntosh and K. E. Stephan (2009). "A dual role for prediction error in associative learning." *Cerebral Cortex 19*: 1175–85.

den Ouden, H. E., P. Kok and F. P. De Lange (2012). "How prediction errors shape perception, attention and motivation." *Frontiers in Psychology 3*: 548.

Denison, R. N., E. A. Piazza and M. A. Silver (2011). "Predictive context influences perceptual selection during binocular rivalry." *Frontiers in Human Neuroscience 5*: 166.

Dennett, D. (1992). "The self as a center of narrative gravity." In *Self and Consciousness: Multiple Perspectives*, F. Kessel, P. Cole, and D. Johnson (eds.). Hillsdale, NJ: Erlbaum.

Descartes, R. (1644 [1983]). *Principles of Philosophy*. Dordrecht: Riedel.

Desimone, R. and J. Duncan (1995). "Neural mechanisms of selective visual attention." *Annual Review of Neuroscience. 18*: 193.

Diaz-Caneja, E. (1928). "Sur l'alternance binoculaire." *Annales d'Oculistique 165*: 721–31.

Doorn, G., J. Hohwy, and M. Symmons (ms). "Can you tickle yourself if you swap bodies with someone else?"

Doya, K. (2007). *Bayesian Brain: Probabilistic Approaches to Neural Coding*. Cambridge, Mass.: MIT Press.

Dretske, F. (1983). *Knowledge and the Flow of Information*. Cambridge, Mass.: MIT Press.

Dutton, D. G. and A. P. Aron (1974). "Some evidence for heightened sexual attraction under conditions of high anxiety." *Journal of Personality and Social Psychology 30*(4): 510–17.

Edelman, G. M. and G. Tononi (2000). *A Universe of Consciousness: How Matter Becomes Imagination*. London, Allen Lane.

Ehrsson, H. H. (2007). "The Experimental Induction of Out-of-Body Experiences." *Science 317*(5841): 1048.

Ehrsson, H. H. (2009). "How many arms make a pair? Perceptual illusion of having an additional limb." *Perception 38*(2): 310.

Eliasmith, C. (2000). *How Neurons Mean: A Neurocomputational Theory of Representational Content.* Ph.D., Washington University in St. Louis.

Eliasmith, C. (2003). "Moving beyond metaphors: Understanding the mind for what it is." *Journal of Philosophy C*(10): 493–520.

Eliasmith, C. (2005). "A New Perspective on Representational Problems." *Journal of Cognitive Science 6*: 97–123.

Eliasmith, C. (2007). "How to build a brain: from function to implementation." *Synthese 159*(3): 373–88.

Fang, F., D. Kersten and S. O. Murray (2008). "Perceptual grouping and inverse fMRI activity patterns in human visual cortex." *Journal of Vision 8*(7): 1–9.

Feldman, H. and K. Friston (2010). "Attention, uncertainty and free-energy." *Frontiers in Human Neuroscience 4*: 215.

Fenton, N., M. Neil and D. A. Lagnado (2013). "A general structure for legal arguments about evidence using Bayesian networks." *Cognitive Science 37*(1): 61–102.

Fletcher, P. C. and C. D. Frith (2009). "Perceiving is believing: a Bayesian approach to explaining the positive symptoms of schizophrenia." *Nature Reviews Neuroscience 10*(1): 48–58.

Fodor, J. A. (1983). *The Modularity of Mind.* Cambridge, Mass.: MIT Press.

Fodor, J. A. (1984). "Observation reconsidered." *Philosophy of Science 51*(1): 23–43.

Fodor, J. A. (1988). "A reply to Churchland's 'Perceptual Plasticity and Theoretical Neutrality'." *Philosophy of Science 55*(2): 188–98.

Fodor, J. A. (1990). *A Theory of Content and Other Essays.* Cambridge, Mass.: MIT Press.

Folegatti, A., A. Farnè, R. Salemme and F. de Vignemont (2012). "The Rubber Hand Illusion: two's a company, but three's a crowd." *Consciousness and Cognition 21*(2): 799–812.

Freedman, B. J. (1974). "The subjective experience of perceptual and cognitive disturbances in schizophrenia. A review of autobiographical accounts." *Archives of General Psychiatry 30*: 333–40.

Frege, G. (1892). "Über Sinn und Bedeutung." *Zeitschrift für Philosophie und philosophische Kritik. 100*: 25–50.

Friston, K. (2002a). "Beyond phrenology: What can neuroimaging tell us about distributed circuitry?" *Annual Review of Neuroscience 25*(1): 221–50.

Friston, K. (2002b). "Functional integration and inference in the brain." *Progress in Neurobiology 68*: 113–43.

Friston, K. (2003). "Learning and inference in the brain." *Neural Networks 16*(9): 1325–52.

Friston, K. (2005a). "A theory of cortical responses." *Philosophical Transactions of the Royal Society of London. Series B: Biological Sciences 360*: 815–36.

Friston, K. (2005b). "A theory of cortical responses." *Philosophical Transactions of the Royal Soceity B: Biological Sciences 369*(1456): 815–36.

Friston, K. (2008). "Hierarchical models in the brain." *PLoS Computational Biology 4*(11): e1000211.

Friston, K. (2009). "The free-energy principle: a rough guide to the brain?" *Trends in Cognitive Sciences 13*(7): 293–301.

Friston, K. (2010). "The free-energy principle: a unified brain theory?" *Nature Reviews Neuroscience 11*(2): 127–38.

Friston, K. (2012). "Embodied inference and spatial cognition." *Cognitive Processing 13*(0): 171–7.

Friston, K., R. Adams, L. Perrinet and M. Breakspear (2012). "Perceptions as hypotheses: saccades as experiments." *Frontiers in Psychology 3*: 151.

Friston, K., M. Breakspear and G. Deco (2012). "Perception and self-organised instability." *Frontiers in Computational Neuroscience 6*: 44.

Friston, K., J. Daunizeau, J. Kilner and S. Kiebel (2010). "Action and behavior: a free-energy formulation." *Biological Cybernetics 102*(3): 227–60.

Friston, K., and S. Kiebel (2009). "Predictive coding under the free-energy principle." *Philosophical Transactions of the Royal Society B: Biological Sciences 364*(1521): 1211–21.

Friston, K., R. Lawson and C. Frith (2013). "On hyperpriors and hypopriors: comment on Pellicano and Burr." *Trends in Cognitive Science 17*(1): 1.

Friston, K., S. Samothrakis and R. Montague (2012). "Active inference and agency: optimal control without cost functions." *Biological Cybernetics 106*(8): 523–41.

Friston, K. and K. Stephan (2007). "Free energy and the brain." *Synthese 159*(3): 417–58.

Friston, K., C. Thornton and A. Clark (2012). "Free-energy minimization and The Dark Room Problem." *Frontiers in Psychology 3*:130.

Friston, K. J., J. Daunizeau and S. J. Kiebel (2009). "Reinforcement Learning or Active Inference?" *PLoS ONE 4*(7): e6421.

Frith, C. D. (1992). *The Cognitive Neuropsychology of Schizophrenia*. Hillsdale, NJ: Lawrence Erlbaum Ass.

Frith, C. D. (1995). "Consciousness is for other people." *Behavioral and Brain Sciences 18*(4): 682–3.

Frith, C. D. (2007). *Making Up the Mind: How the Brain Creates Our Mental World*. Oxford: Blackwell.

Frith, C. D. and R. J. Dolan (1997). "Brain mechanisms associated with top-down processes in perception." *Philosophical Transactions of the Royal Society B: Biological Sciences 352*: 1221–30.

Frith, C. D. and U. Frith (2012). "Mechanisms of Social Cognition." *Annual Review of Psychology 63*(1): 287–313.

Frith, U. (2003). *Autism: Explaining the Enigma*. Oxford: Blackwell.

Frith, C. D. and Wentzer, T. S. (in press) "Neural hermeneutics." In B. Kaldis (ed.), *Encyclopedia of Philosophy and the Social Sciences*, vol. 1. London: Sage.

Fuentes, C., S. Mostofsky and A. Bastian (2010). "No Proprioceptive Deficits in Autism Despite Movement-Related Sensory and Execution Impairments." *Journal of Autism and Developmental Disorders 41*(10): 1352–61.

Fuster, J. M. (2001). "The prefrontal cortex—an update: time is of the essence." *Neuron 30*(2): 319–33.

Gaillard, R. l., S. Dehaene, C. Adam, S. p. Clémenceau, D. Hasboun, M. Baulac, L. Cohen and L. Naccache (2009). "Converging intracranial markers of conscious access." *PLoS Biol 7*(3): e1000061.

Gallagher, S. (2005). *How the Body Shapes the Mind*. Oxford: Oxford University Press.

Garrido, M. I., K. J. Friston, S. J. Kiebel, K. E. Stephan, T. Baldeweg and J. M. Kilner (2008). "The functional anatomy of the MMN: A DCM study of the roving paradigm." *NeuroImage 42*(2): 936–44.

Garrido, M. I., J. M. Kilner, S. J. Kiebel, K. E. Stephan, T. Baldeweg and K. J. Friston (2009). "Repetition suppression and plasticity in the human brain." *NeuroImage 48* (1): 269–79.

George, D. and J. Hawkins (2009). "Towards a mathematical theory of cortical micro-circuits." *PLoS Computational Biology 5*(10): e1000532.

Gigerenzer, G. and R. Selten, Eds. (2001). *Bounded Rationality: The Adaptive Toolbox.* Cambridge, Mass.: MIT Press.

Gilovich, T. (1993). *How We Know What Isn't So: The Fallibility of Human Reason in Everyday Life.* New York: Free Press.

Gold, I. and J. Hohwy (2000). "Rationality and schizophrenic delusion." *Mind and Language 15*: 146–67.

Goodale, M. A. and A. D. Milner (1992). "Separate visual pathways for perception and action." *Trends in Neurosciences 15*(1): 20–5.

Gopnik, A. (1993). "How we know our minds: The illusion of first-person knowledge of intentionality." *Behavioral and Brain Sciences 16*(1): 1–14.

Gregory, R. L. (1980). "Perceptions as hypotheses." *Philosophical Transactions of the Royal Society B: Biological Sciences 290*(1038): 181–97.

Gregory, R. L. (1997). "Knowledge in perception and illusion." *Philosophical Transactions of the Royal Society B: Biological Sciences 352*(1358): 1121–7.

Gregory, R. L. (1998). *Eye and Brain.* Oxford: Oxford University Press.

Griffiths, P. E. (1997). *What Emotions Really Are: The Problem of Psychological Categories.* Chicago: University of Chicago Press.

Griffiths, P. E. (2003). "Basic emotions, complex emotions, Machiavellian emotions." *Royal Institute of Philosophy Supplement 52*(1): 39–67.

Griffiths, T. L., N. Chater, C. Kemp, A. Perfors and J. B. Tenenbaum (2010). "Probabilistic models of cognition: exploring representations and inductive biases." *Trends in Cognitive Sciences 14*(8): 357–64.

Grush, R. (2004). "The emulation theory of representation: motor control, imagery, and perception." *Behavioral and Brain Sciences 27*: 377–442.

Grush, R. (2006). "How to, and how not to, bridge computational cognitive neuroscience and Husserlian phenomenology of time consciousness." *Synthese 153*(3): 417–50.

Guterstam, A., V. I. Petkova and H. H. Ehrsson (2011). "The Illusion of Owning a Third Arm." *PloS One 6*(2): e17208.

Hammeke, T. A., M. P. McQuillen and B. A. Cohen (1983). "Musical hallucinations associated with acquired deafness." *Journal of Neurology, Neurosurgery & Psychiatry 46* (6): 570–2.

Happé, F. and U. Frith (2006). "The weak coherence account: Detail-focused cognitive style in autism spectrum disorders." *Journal of Autism and Developmental Disorders 36*(1): 5–25.

Hariri, A. R., S. Y. Bookheimer and J. C. Mazziotta (2000). "Modulating emotional responses: effects of a neocortical network on the limbic system." *Neuroreport 11*(1): 43–8.

Harrison, L., S. Bestmann, M. J. Rosa, W. Penny and G. G. R. Green (2011). "Time scales of representation in the human brain: weighing past information to predict future events." *Frontiers in Human Neuroscience 5*: 37.

Hatfield, G. (2002). "Perception as unconscious inference". In *Perception and the physical world.* D. Heyer and R. Mausfeld (eds.). New Jersey: John Wiley & Sons, Ltd: 113–43.

Hawkins, J. and S. Blakeslee (2005). *On Intelligence.* New York: Owl Books.

Helmholtz, H. (1855; 1903). "Über das Sehen des Menschen (1855)." In *Vorträge und Reden von Hermann Helmholtz.* 5th ed. Vol.1. Braunschweig: F. Vieweg: 85–117.

Helmholtz, H. v. (1867). *Handbuch der Physiologishen Optik.* Leipzig: Leopold Voss.

Hesselmann, G., S. Sadaghiani, K. J. Friston and A. Kleinschmidt (2010). "Predictive coding or evidence accumulation? False inference and neuronal fluctuations." *PloS One 5*(3): e9926.

Hillis, J., M. Ernst, M. Banks and M. Landy (2002). "Combining sensory information: mandatory fusion within, but not between senses." *Science 298*: 1627ff.

Hinton, G. E. (2007). "Learning multiple layers of representation." *Trends in Cognitive Sciences 11*(10): 428–34.

Hinton, G. E. and T. J. Sejnowski (1983). "Optimal perceptual inference." *Proceedings of the IEEE Conference on Computer Vision and Pattern Recognition.* Washington 1983: 448–453.

Hobbes, T. (1651 [1994]). *Leviathan.* Indianapolis: Hackett Publishing Company.

Hobson, J. A. and K. J. Friston (2012). "Waking and dreaming consciousness: Neurobiological and functional considerations." *Progress in Neurobiology 98*(1): 82–98.

Hohwy, J. (2004). "Top-down and bottom-up in delusion formation." *Philosophy, Psychiatry and Psychology 11*(1): 65–70.

Hohwy, J. (2007a). "Functional integration and the mind." *Synthese 159*(3): 315–28.

Hohwy, J. (2007b). "The sense of self in the phenomenology of agency and perception." *Psyche 13*(1): 1-20.

Hohwy, J. (2009). *The hypothesis testing brain: some philosophical implications.* 9th Conference of the Australasian Society for Cognitive Science, Sydney: Macquarie Centre for Cognitive Science.

Hohwy, J. (2011). "Phenomenal variability and introspective reliability." *Mind & Language 26*(3): 261–86.

Hohwy, J. (2012). "Attention and conscious perception in the hypothesis testing brain." *Frontiers in Psychology 3*: 96.

Hohwy, J. (2013). "Delusions, illusions, and inference under uncertainty." *Mind & Language 28*(1): 57–71.

Hohwy, J. and C. Frith (2004). "Can neuroscience explain consciousness?" *Journal of Consciousness Studies 11*: 180–98.

Hohwy, J. and B. Paton (2010). "Explaining away the body: experiences of supernaturally caused touch and touch on non-hand objects within the rubber hand illusion" *PLoS ONE 5*(2): e9416.

Hohwy, J., A. Roepstorff and K. Friston (2008). "Predictive coding explains binocular rivalry: An epistemological review." *Cognition 108*(3): 687–701.

Hohwy, J. and R. Rosenberg (2005). "Unusual experiences, reality testing, and delusions of control." *Mind & Language 20*(2): 141–62.

Howson, C. and P. Urbach (1993). *Scientific Reasoning: The Baysian Approach.* Open Court: LaSalle.

Huang, Y. and R. P. N. Rao (2011). "Predictive coding." *Wiley Interdisciplinary Reviews: Cognitive Science 2*(5): 580–93.

Hume, D. (1739–40). *A Treatise of Human Nature*. Oxford: Clarendon Press.

Humphrey, N. (2007). "The society of selves." *Philosophical Transactions of the Royal Society B: Biological Sciences 362*(1480): 745–54.

Hurley, S. L. (1998). *Consciousness in Action*. Cambridge, Mass.: Harvard University Press.

Jackendoff, R. (1987). *Consciousness and the Computational Mind*. Cambridge, Mass.: MIT Press.

Jackson, F. (2003). "Mind and Illusion." *Royal Institute of Philosophy Supplements 53*: 251–71.

Jackson, F. (2007). "Reference and description from the descriptivists' corner." *Philosophical Books 48*: 17–26.

Jagnow, R. (2012). "Representationalism and the perspectival character of perceptual experience." *Philosophical Studies 157*(2): 227–49.

James, W. (1890). *The Principles of Psychology*. New York: Holt.

Jensen, M. S. and K. E. Mathewson (2011). "Simultaneous perception of both interpretations of ambiguous figures." *Perception 40*(8): 1009–11.

Jiang, Y., P. Costello, F. Fang, M. Huang and S. He (2006). "A gender- and sexual orientation-dependent spatial attentional effect of invisible images." *Proceedings of the National Academy of Sciences 103*(45): 17048–52.

Kahneman, D., P. Slovic and A. Tversky (1982). *Judgment under Uncertainty: Heuristics and Biases*. Cambridge: Cambridge University Press.

Kammers, M., J. Kootker, H. Hogendoorn and H. Dijkerman (2010). "How many motoric body representations can we grasp?" *Experimental Brain Research 202*(1): 203–12.

Kammers, M. P. M., F. de Vignemont, L. Verhagen and H. C. Dijkerman (2009). "The rubber hand illusion in action." *Neuropsychologia 47*(1): 204–11.

Kant, I. (1781). *Kritik der reinen Vernunft*. Hamburg: Felix Meiner.

Kant, I. (1983 [1977]). *Prolegomena to Any Future Metaphysics*. Indianapolis: Hackett Publishers.

Kaplan, D. M. (2011). "Explanation and description in computational neuroscience." *Synthese 183*: 339–73.

Kawato, M., H. Hayakawa and T. Inui (1993). "A forward-inverse optics model of reciprocal connections between visual cortical areas." *Network: Computation in Neural Systems 4*: 415–22.

Kersten, D., P. Mamassian and A. Yuille (2004). "Object perception as Bayesian inference." *Annual Review of Psychology 55*(1): 271–304.

Kiebel, S. J., J. Daunizeau and K. J. Friston (2008). "A Hierarchy of time-scales and the brain." *PLoS Computational Biology 4*(11): e1000209.

Kilner, J. M., K. J. Friston and C. D. Frith (2007). "The mirror-neuron system: a Bayesian perspective." *NeuroReport 18*(6): 619–23.

Kim, J. (2008). "Reduction and reductive explanation: is one possible without the other?" In *Being Reduced*. J. Hohwy and J. Kallestrup (eds.). Oxford: Oxford University Press.

Knill, D. C. and W. Richards (1996). *Perception as Bayesian Inference*. Cambridge: Cambridge University Press.

Koch, C. (2004). *The Quest for Consciousness: A Neurobiological Approach*. Englewood, Col.: Robert and Company Publishers.

Koch, C. (2013). "The end of the beginning for the brain." *Science 339*(6121): 759–60.

Kok, P., Janneke F. M. Jehee and Floris P. de Lange (2012). "Less is more: expectation sharpens representations in the primary visual cortex." *Neuron 75*(2): 265–70.

Kok, P., D. Rahnev, J. F. M. Jehee, H. C. Lau and F. P. de Lange (2011). "Attention reverses the effect of prediction in silencing sensory signals." *Cerebral Cortex 22*(9): 2197–206.

Körding, K. P., U. Beierholm, W. J. Ma, S. Quartz, J. B. Tenenbaum and L. Shams (2007). "Causal inference in multisensory perception." *Plos One 2*(9): e943.

Kouider, S., V. de Gardelle, J. Sackur and E. Dupoux (2010). "How rich is consciousness? The partial awareness hypothesis." *Trends in Cognitive Sciences 14*(7): 301–7.

Kripke, S. (1972/1980). *Naming and Necessity*. Cambridge, Mass.: Harvard University Press.

Kripke, S. (1982). *Wittgenstein on Rules and Private Language*. Oxford: Oxford University Press.

Kusch, M. (2006). *A Sceptical Guide to Meaning and Rules: Defending Kripke's Wittgenstein*. Chesham: Acumen.

Lagnado, D. A., N. Fenton and M. Neil (2012). "Legal idioms: a framework for evidential reasoning." *Argument & Computation 4*(1): 1–18.

Lee, T. S. and D. Mumford (2003). "Hierarchical Bayesian inference in the visual cortex." *Journal of the Optical Society of America, A 20*: 1434–48.

Lenggenhager, B., T. Tadi, T. Metzinger and O. Blanke (2007). "Video ergo sum: manipulating bodily self-consciousness." *Science 317*(5841): 1096.

Lenoir, T. (2006). "Operationalizing Kant: Manifolds, models, and mathematics in Helmholtz's theories of perception." In *The Kantian legacy in nineteenth-century science*. M. Friedman and A. Nordmann (eds.). Cambridge, Mass.: MIT Press, 141–210.

Leopold, D. A. and N. K. Logothetis (1999). "Multistable phenomena: changing views in perception." *Trends in Cognitive Science. 3*: 254–64.

Levine, J. (2001). *Purple Haze: The Puzzle of Consciousness*. Oxford: Oxford University Press.

Lewis, D. (1970) "How to define theoretical terms." *The Journal of Philosophy 67*(13): 427–46.

Lewis, D. (1973). "Causation." *The Journal of Philosophy 70*(17): 556–67.

Lindberg, D. C. (1976). *Theories of Vision: From Al Kindi to Kepler*. Chicago: Chicago University Press.

Linsker, R. (1988). "Self-organisation in a perceptual network." *Computer 21*: 105–17.

Lipton, P. (2004). *Inference to the Best Explanation*. London: Routledge.

Lloyd, D., E. Lewis, J. Payne and L. Wilson (2012). "A qualitative analysis of sensory phenomena induced by perceptual deprivation." *Phenomenology and the Cognitive Sciences 11*(1): 95–112.

Lloyd, D. M. (2007). "Spatial limits on referred touch to an alien limb may reflect boundaries of visuo-tactile peripersonal space surrounding the hand." *Brain and Cognition 64*(1): 104–9.

Locke, J. (1690). *Essay concerning Human Understanding*. London: Everyman.

Logothetis, N. K., D. A. Leopold and D. L. Sheinberg (1996). "What is rivalling during binocular rivalry?" *Nature 380*: 621–4.

MacKay, D. M. (1956). "The epistemological problem for automata." In *Automata studies*. C. E. Shannon and J. McCarthy (eds.). Princeton: Princeton University Press: 235–51.

Macpherson, F. (2012). "Cognitive penetration of colour experience: rethinking the issue in light of an indirect mechanism." *Philosophy and Phenomenological Research 84*(1): 24–62.

Maher, B. A. (1974). "Delusional thinking and perceptual disorder." *Journal of Individual Psychology 30*: 98–113.

Maier, A. (2008). "Divergence of fMRI and neural signals in V1 during perceptual suppression in the awake monkey." *Nature Neuroscience. 11*: 1193–200.

McCauley, R. N. and J. Henrich (2006). "Susceptibility to the Müller-Lyer Illusion, theory-neutral observation, and the diachronic penetrability of the visual input system." *Philosophical Psychology 19*(1): 79–101.

McClelland, J. L., M. M. Botvinick, D. C. Noelle, D. C. Plaut, T. T. Rogers, M. S. Seidenberg and L. B. Smith (2010). "Letting structure emerge: connectionist and dynamical systems approaches to cognition." *Trends in Cognitive Sciences 14*(8): 348–56.

McDowell, J. H. (1994). *Mind and World*. Harvard: Harvard University Press.

McGrath, J., S. Saha, D. Chant and J. Welham (2008). "Schizophrenia: a concise overview of incidence, prevalence, and mortality." *Epidemiological Reviews 30*: 67–76.

McKay, R. (2012). "Delusional Inference." *Mind & Language 27*(3): 330–55.

Melnyk, A. (2003). *A Physicalist Manifesto*. Cambridge: Cambridge University Press.

Merker, B. (2007). "Consciousness without a cerebral cortex: A challenge for neuroscience and medicine." *Behavioral and Brain Sciences 30*(1): 63–81.

Metzinger, T. (2004). *Being No One: The Self-Model Theory of Subjectivity*. Cambridge, Mass.: MIT Press.

Metzinger, T. (2009). *The Ego Tunnel*. New York: Basic Books.

Mill, J. S. (1865). *An Examination of Sir William Hamilton's Philosophy*. London: Longmans.

Morgan, M., C. Chubb and J. A. Solomon (2008). "A 'dipper' function for texture discrimination based on orientation variance." *Journal of Vision 8*(11): Article 9.

Morgenstern, Y., R. F. Murray and L. R. Harris (2011). "The human visual system's assumption that light comes from above is weak." *Proceedings of the National Academy of Sciences 108*(30): 12551–3.

Muckli, L., A. Kohler, N. Kriegeskorte and W. Singer (2005). "Primary visual cortex activity along the apparent-motion trace reflects illusory perception." *PLoS Biology 3*(8): e265.

Mumford, D. (1992). "On the computational architecture of the neocortex. II. The role of cortico-cortical loops." *Biological Cybernetics 66*: 241–51.

Murray, S. O., D. Kersten, B. A. Olshausen, P. Schrater and D. L. Woods (2002). "Shape perception reduces activity in human primary visual cortex." *Proceedings of the National Academy of Science 99*(23): 15164–9.

Naber, M., S. Frässle and W. Einhäuser (2011). "Perceptual rivalry: reflexes reveal the gradual nature of visual awareness." *PloS One 6*(6): e20910.

Nagel, T. (1974). "What is it like to be a bat?" *Philosophical Review 83*: 435–50.

Nardini, M., R. Bedford and D. Mareschal (2010). "Fusion of visual cues is not mandatory in children." *Proceedings of the National Academy of Sciences 107*(39): 17041–6.

Neander, K. (2006). "Naturalistic theories of reference." In *The Blackwell Guide to the Philosophy of Language*, M. Devitt and M. Hanley (eds.). Oxford: Blackwell, 374–91.

Neisser, U. (1967). *Cognitive psychology*. New York: Appleton-Century-Crofts.

Nietzsche, F. (1882/1887). *The Gay Science, with a Prelude of Rhymes and an Appendix of Songs*. New York: Random House.

Noë, A. (2004). *Action in Perception*. Cambridge, Mass.: MIT Press.

Norwich, K. H. (1993). *Information, Sensation, and Perception*. San Diego: Academic Press.

O'Regan, J. K. and A. Noë (2001). "A sensorimotor account of vision and visual consciousness." *Behavioral and Brain Sciences 24*(5): 939–73.

O'Shea, R. P. (2011). "Binocular rivalry stimuli are common but rivalry is not." *Frontiers in Human Neuroscience 5*.

Oddie, G. (2008). "Truthlikeness." *Stanford Encyklopedia of Philosophy*. E. N. Zalta (ed.).

Palmer, C., B. Paton, J. Hohwy and P. Enticott (2013). "Jerk differences on the autism spectrum as a sign of precision expectations." Under review.

Panksepp, J. (2005). "Affective consciousness: Core emotional feelings in animals and humans." *Consciousness and Cognition 14*: 30–80.

Panksepp, J., L. Normansell, J. F. Cox and S. M. Siviy (1994). "Effects of neonatal decortication on the social play of juvenile rats." *Physiology & Behavior 56*(3): 429–43.

Paton, B., J. Hohwy and P. Enticott (2011). "The Rubber Hand Illusion reveals proprioceptive and sensorimotor differences in autism spectrum disorders." *Journal of Autism and Developmental Disorders 42*(9): 1–14.

Pearl, J. (1988). *Probabilistic Reasoning in Intelligent Systems: Networks of Plausible Inference*. San Fransisco: Morgan Kaufmann Publishers.

Pearl, J. (2000). *Causality*. Cambridge: Cambridge University Press.

Peled, A., A. Pressman, A. B. Geva and I. Modai (2003). "Somatosensory evoked potentials during a rubber-hand illusion in schizophrenia." *Schizophrenia Research 64*(2–3): 157–63.

Peled, A., M. Ritsner, S. Hirschmann, A. B. Geva and I. Modai (2000). "Touch feel illusion in schizophrenic patients." *Biological Psychiatry 48*(11): 1105–8.

Pellicano, E. and D. Burr (2012). "When the world becomes too real: a Bayesian explanation of autistic perception." *Trends in Cognitive Sciences 16*(10): 504–10.

Petkova, V. I. and H. H. Ehrsson (2008). "If I were you: perceptual illusion of body swapping." *PLoS ONE 3*(12): e3832.

Phillips, W. A. (2012). "Self-organized complexity and coherent infomax from the viewpoint of Jaynes's Probability Theory." *Information 3*(1): 1–15.

Piccinini, G. and A. Scarantino (2011). "Information processing, computation, and cognition." *Journal of Biological Physics 37*(1): 1–38.

Plewan, T., R. Weidner, S. B. Eickhoff and G. R. Fink (2012). "Ventral and dorsal stream interactions during the perception of the Müller-Lyer Illusion: evidence derived from fMRI and dynamic causal modeling." *Journal of Cognitive Neuroscience 24*(10): 2015–29.

Porta, J.B. (1593). *De Refractione. Optices Parte. Libri Novem*. Naples: Salviani.

Posner, M. I. (1980). "Orienting of attention." *Quarterly Journal of Experimental Psychology. 32*: 3.

Prinz, J. J. (2004). *Gut Reactions: A Perceptual Theory of Emotions.* Harvard: Oxford University Press.

Prinz, J. J. (2012). *The Conscious Brain: How Attention Engenders Experience.* Oxford: Oxford University Press.

Pylyshyn, Z. (1999). "Is vision continuous with cognition?: The case for cognitive impenetrability of visual perception." *Behavioral and Brain Sciences 22*(03): 341–65.

Qian, N. and R. M. Lipkin (2011). "A learning-style theory for understanding autistic behaviors." *Frontiers in Human Neuroscience 5*: 77.

Quiroga, R. Q., L. Reddy, G. Kreiman, C. Koch and I. Fried (2005). "Invariant visual representation by single neurons in the human brain." *Nature 435*(7045): 1102–7.

Rao, R. and D. Ballard (1999). "Predictive coding in the visual cortex: a functional interpretation of some extra-classical receptive-field effects." *Nature Neuroscience 2*: 79–87.

Rao, R. P. N. and D. H. Ballard (1999). "Predictive coding in the visual cortex: a functional interpretation of some extra-classical receptive field effects." *Nature Neuroscience 2*(1): 79–87.

Rao, R. P. N., B. A. Olshausen and M. S. Lewicki (2002). *Probabilistic Models of the Brain.* Cambridge, Mass.: MIT Press.

Rescorla, M. (in press). "Bayesian Perceptual Psychology". In *Oxford Handbook of the Philosophy of Perception.* M. Matthen (ed.). Oxford: Oxford University Press.

Riesenhuber, M. and T. Poggio (1999). "Hierarchical models of object recognition in cortex." *Nature Neuroscience 2*(11): 1019.

Rock, I. (1983). *The Logic of Perception.* Cambridge, Mass.: MIT Press.

Roepstorff, A., J. Niewöhner and S. Beck (2010). "Enculturing brains through patterned practices." *Neural Networks 23*(8–9): 1051–9.

Rogers, S. J. and S. Ozonoff (2005). "What do we know about sensory dysfunction in autism? A critical review of the empirical evidence." *Journal of Child Psychology and Psychiatry 46*(12): 1255–68.

Rohde, M., M. Di Luca and M. O. Ernst (2011). "The Rubber Hand Illusion: feeling of ownership and proprioceptive drift do not go hand in hand." *PloS One 6*(6): e21659.

Rolls, E. T. (2012). "Invariant visual object and face recognition: neural and computational bases, and a model, VisNet." *Frontiers in Computational Neuroscience 6*: 35.

Rolls, E. T. and G. Deco (2010). *The Noisy Brain.* Oxford: Oxford University Press.

Roskies, A. L. (1999). "The binding problem." *Neuron 24*: 7.

Ross, J. and D. Burr (2008). "The knowing visual self." *Trends in Cognitive Sciences 12*(10): 363–4.

Rumelhart, D. E., G. E. Hinton and R. J. Williams (1986). "Learning representations by back-propagating errors." *Nature 323*(6088): 533–6.

Russell, B. (1905). "On denoting." *Mind 14*(4): 479–93.

Schacter, S. and J. E. Singer (1962). "Cognitive, social and physiological determinants of emotional state." *Psychological Review 69*: 379–99.

Schellenberg, S. (2008). "The situation-dependency of perception." *The Journal of Philosophy 105*(2): 55–84.

Schellenberg, S. (2010). "Perceptual content defended." *Nous 45*(4): 714–50.

Scherer, K. R. (1999). "Appraisal theory." In *Handbook of Cognition and Emotion.* T. Dalgliesh and M. J. Power (eds.). Sussex: John Wiley & Sons: 637–63.

Schroeter, L. and J. Bigelow (2009). "Jackson's classical model of meaning." In *Mind, Ethics, and Conditionals: Themes from the Philosophy of Frank Jackson*. I. Ravenscroft (ed.). Oxford: Oxford University Press. 85–109.

Schwabe, L. and O. Blanke (2008). "The vestibular component in out-of-body experiences: a computational approach." *Frontiers in Human Neuroscience 2 (Article 17)*: 1–10.

Schwitzgebel, E. (2008). "The unreliability of naive introspection." *The Philosophical Review 117*(2): 245–73.

Schwitzgebel, E. (2010) "Introspection." *The Stanford Encyclopedia of Philosophy* (Winter 2012 Edition), Edward N. Zalta (ed.), <http://plato.stanford.edu/archives/win2012/entries/introspection/>.

Schwitzgebel, E. (2011). *Perplexities of Consciousness*. Cambridge, MA: MIT Press.

Searle, J. R. (1980). "Minds, brains, and programs." *Behavioral and Brain Sciences 3*(03): 417–24.

Seth, A. K., K. Suzuki and H. D. Critchley (2012). "An interoceptive predictive coding model of conscious presence." *Frontiers in Psychology 2*: 395.

Simmons, D. R., A. E. Robertson, L. S. McKay, E. Toal, P. McAleer and F. E. Pollick (2009). "Vision in autism spectrum disorders." *Vision Research 49*(22): 2705–39.

Simons, D. J. and C. F. Chabris (1999). "Gorillas in our midst: sustained inattentional blindness for dynamic events." *Perception 28*(9): 1059–74.

Skewes, J., A. Roepstorff and C. Frith (2011). "How do illusions constrain goal-directed movement: perceptual and visuomotor influences on speed/accuracy trade-off." *Experimental Brain Research 209*(2): 247–55.

Smart, J. J. C. (1959). "Sensations and brain processes." *Philosophical Review 68*: 141–756.

Smith, F. W. and L. Muckli (2010). "Nonstimulated early visual areas carry information about surrounding context." *Proceedings of the National Academy of Sciences 107*(46): 20099–103.

Sotiropoulos, G., A. R. Seitz and P. Seriés (2011). "Changing expectations about speed alters perceived motion direction." *Current Biology: CB 21*(21): R883–4.

Spratling, M. W. (2008). "Predictive coding as a model of biased competition in visual attention." *Vision Research 48*(12): 1391–408.

Stephan, K. E., K. J. Friston and C. D. Frith (2009). "Dysconnection in schizophrenia: from abnormal synaptic plasticity to failures of self-monitoring." *Schizophrenia Bulletin 35*(3): 509–27.

Stokes, D. (in press). "Cognitive penetrability of perception." *Philosophy Compass*.

Summerfield, C. and T. Egner (2009). "Expectation (and attention) in visual cognition." *Trends in Cognitive Sciences 13*(9): 403–9.

Summerfield, C. and T. Egner (2014). "Attention and decision-making." In A.C. Nobre and S. Kastner (Eds), *The Oxford Handbook of Attention*. Oxford University Press, pp. 837–864.

Summerfield, C. and E. Koechlin (2008). "A neural representation of prior information during perceptual inference." *Neuron 59*(2): 336–47.

Synofzik, M., P. Thier, D. T. Leube, P. Schlotterbeck and A. Lindner (2010). "Misattributions of agency in schizophrenia are based on imprecise predictions about the sensory consequences of one's actions." *Brain 133*(1): 262–71.

Tenenbaum, J. B. and T. L. Griffiths (2001). "Generalization, similarity, and Bayesian inference." *Behavioral and Brain Sciences 24*(04): 629–40.

Tenenbaum, J. B., C. Kemp, T. L. Griffiths and N. D. Goodman (2011). "How to grow a mind: statistics, structure, and abstraction." *Science 331*(6022): 1279–85.

Todorovic, A., F. van Ede, E. Maris and F. P. de Lange (2011). "Prior expectation mediates neural adaptation to repeated sounds in the auditory cortex: an MEG study." *The Journal of Neuroscience 31*(25): 9118–23.

Tononi, G. (2005). "Consciousness, information integration, and the brain." *Progress in Brain Research 150*: 109–26.

Tononi, G. (2010). "Information integration: its relevance to brain function and consciousness." *Archives italiennes de biologie 148*(3): 299–22.

Trappenberg, T. (2010). *Fundamentals of Computational Neuroscience*. Oxford: Oxford University Press.

Treisman, A. (1996). "The binding problem." *Current Opinion in Neurobiology* 6(2): 171–8.

Treisman, A. and H. Schmidt (1982). "Illusory conjunctions in the perception of objects." *Cognitive Psychology 14*(1): 107–41.

Treisman, A. M. and G. Gelade (1980). "A feature-integration theory of attention." *Cogn. Psychol. 12*: 97–136.

Tribus, M. (1961). *Thermostatistics and Thermodynamics*. Princeton NJ: D. van Nostrand Company, Inc.

Tsakiris, M., L. Carpenter, D. James and A. Fotopoulou (2010). "Hands only illusion: multisensory integration elicits sense of ownership for body parts but not for non-corporeal objects." *Experimental Brain Research 204*(3): 343–52.

Tsakiris, M. and P. Haggard (2005). "The rubber hand illusion revisited: visuotactile integration and self-attribution." *Journal of Experimental Psychology. Human Perception and Performance 31*(1): 80.

Tsuchiya, N. and C. Koch (2004). "Continuous flash suppression." *Journal of Vision 4* (8): 61.

Usher, M. (2001). "A Statistical Referential Theory of Content: Using Information Theory to Account for Misrepresentation." *Mind & Language 16*(3): 311–34.

van Boxtel, J. J., N. Tsuchiya and C. Koch (2010). "Consciousness and attention: on sufficiency and necessity." *Frontiers in Psychology 1*: 217.

van der Hoort, B., A. Guterstam and H. H. Ehrsson (2011). "Being Barbie: The Size of One's Own Body Determines the Perceived Size of the World." *PloS One 6*(5): e20195.

von der Malsburg, C. (1981). "The correlation theory of brain function." *Internal Report, Dept Neurobiology, MPI for Biophysical Chemistry.*

van Doorn, G., J. Hohwy, M. Symmons (2014). "Can you tickle yourself if you swap bodies with someone else?" *Consciousness & Cognition* 23: 1–11.

Vuilleumier, P., J. L. Armony, J. Driver and R. J. Dolan (2003). "Distinct spatial frequency sensitivities for processing faces and emotional expressions." *Nature Neuroscience. 6*: 624–31.

Wacongne, C., E. Labyt, V. van Wassenhove, T. Bekinschtein, L. Naccache and S. Dehaene (2011). "Evidence for a hierarchy of predictions and prediction errors in human cortex." *Proceedings of the National Academy of Sciences 108*(51): 20754–9.

Wade, N. J. (1998). *A Natural History of Vision*. Cambridge, Mass.: MIT Press.

Wade, N. J. (2005). "Ambiguities and rivalries in the history of binocular vision." In *Binocular Rivalry*. D. Alais and R. Blake (eds.). Cambridge, Mass.: MIT Press: 29–46.

Ware, E. A., D. H. Uttal and J. S. DeLoache (2010). "Everyday scale errors." *Developmental Science 13*(1): 28–36.

Wayand, J. F., D. T. Levin and D. A. Varakin (2005). "Inattentional blindness for a noxious multimodal stimulus." *The American Journal of Psychology 118*(3): 339–52.

Wheatstone, C. (1838). "Contributions to the physiology of vision. Part I. On some remarkable, and hitherto unobserved, phenomena of binocular vision." *Philosophical Transactions of the Royal Society B: Biological Sciences 128*: 371–94.

Whitson, J. A. and A. D. Galinsky (2008). "Lacking control increases illusory pattern perception." *Science 322*(5898): 115–17.

Wiese, W. and T. Metzinger (2013). "Desiderata for a mereotopological theory of consciousness: First steps towards a formal model for the unity of consciousness." In *Being in Time*, S. Elderman, T. Fekete, and N. Zach (eds.). Amsterdam: John Benjamins B. V., pp. 185–210.

Winterer, G. and D. R. Weinberger (2004). "Genes, dopamine and cortical signal-to-noise ratio in schizophrenia." *Trends in Neurosciences 27*(11): 683–90.

Wittgenstein, L. (1953). *Philosophical Investigations*. Oxford: Basil Blackwell.

Wolpert, D. M., Z. Ghahramani and J. R. Flanagan (2001). "Perspectives and problems in motor learning." *Trends in Cognitive Sciences 5*(11): 487.

Woodward, J. (2003). *Making Things Happen*. New York: Oxford University Press.

Yu, A. J. and P. Dayan (2005). "Uncertainty, Neuromodulation, and Attention." *Neuron 46*(4): 681.

Zaroff, C. and S. Uhm (2012). "Prevalence of autism spectrum disorders and influence of country of measurement and ethnicity." *Social Psychiatry and Psychiatric Epidemiology 47*(3): 395–8.

Zhang, P., K. Jamison, S. Engel, B. He and S. He (2011). "Binocular rivalry requires visual attention." *Neuron 71*(2): 362–9.

Zhou, W., Y. Jiang, S. He and D. Chen (2010). "Olfaction modulates visual perception in binocular rivalry." *Current Biology 20*(15): 1356–8.

# *Index*